Anecdotes from the History of Modern Computing

V. RAJARAMAN
Emeritus Professor
Supercomputer Education and Research Centre
Indian Institute of Science, Bangalore

PHI Learning Private Limited
Delhi-110092
2024

₹ 850.00

ANECDOTES FROM THE HISTORY OF MODERN COMPUTING
V. Rajaraman

ISBN-978-81-19364-43-5 (Print Book)
ISBN-978-81-19364-96-1 (e-Book)

Published by Asoke K. Ghosh, PHI Learning Private Limited, Rimjhim House, 111, Patparganj Industrial Estate, Delhi-110092 and Printed by Sanjay Printers, 12/31, Site-4, Sahibabad Industrial Area, UP-201010..

In the Memory of

Sri ASOKE KUMAR GHOSH

My publisher and friend for over five decades

— V. Rajaraman

Contents

Preface

The advent of the modern computer in 1945 and its rapid development have changed how we live. Almost all gadgets we use today have built-in computers. The history of the evolution of computers and their applications is fascinating. In eight decades, a mere blink in the history of humankind, computers have transformed how we live.

Several books on the history of computers have been published in the last few years. Most of them are scholarly tomes written by professional historians and begin with Charles Babbage's difference engine, a mechanical computer built in 1832, and end with modern computers and their applications. My intention is not to write yet another traditional history book. Instead, I look at the history of computers as a sequence of essential milestones in the evolution of modern computers and narrate them as a sequence of anecdotes.

There are seventy-two anecdotes in this book. Each account is short (between 1500 and 2500 words) and recounts one or more milestones and the key persons involved in their development. I have written the anecdotes in simple English and have not used unnecessary jargon. This style will allow anyone with a high school education to understand and appreciate the history of modern computing. I begin the book with an anecdote that recounts the building of ENIAC (Electronic Numerical Integrator and Calculator), the first modern stored-program electronic computer in 1946 by John Mauchly, J. Presper Eckert, Jr., and their team. I end the book with an anecdote that describes ChatGPT and Gemini the generative large language model chatbots that give natural language answers to any arbitrary natural language questions, writes poetry, and computer programs!

The genesis of this book was my desire to recount historical events to the Communications of the Computer Society of India (CSI) readers as short, readable articles and the subsequent invitation by the magazine editors to me to write the articles. I titled them "Titbits from the History of Computing". CSI Communications started publishing them in August 2019. After the 18th Titbit appeared, the magazine ceased publication. The Titbits I wrote were in random order. Many readers liked these articles. I decided to expand and rewrite these Titbits as anecdotes and cover the history of computing, beginning with the story of ENIAC. I thank the editors of CSI Communications for inviting me to write the Titbits.

Many important historical events occurred after I started writing the anecdotes to publish them as a book. The most notable event was the release of ChatGPT, the generative large language model chatbot, in November 2022 followed by Google's chatbot Gemini and Microsoft's AI assistant Copilot. I immediately wrote an anecdote about them. Another historical event was breaking the ExaFLOPS (10^{18} Floating Point Operations per Second) barrier by the Cray-HPE Frontier supercomputer in May 2022, about which I wrote an anecdote.

I expanded some of the anecdotes, including the one on ChatGPT, and published them in RESONANCE, a science education magazine published by the Indian Academy of Sciences, Bengaluru. I thank the academy for permission to include them in this collection of anecdotes.

I thank Professor P.C.P. Bhatt, Dr. N. Dayasindhu, Professor R. Govindarajan, and Professor S. Ramani for reading most of the anecdotes and their perceptive comments that improved them. Besides them, I sent the anecdotes relevant to their area of interest to the following persons (in alphabetical order) for their review. I thank them for their suggestions. Dr. Siddharth Aravindan, Professor Venkat Arun, Professor Radha Balakrishnan, Dr. S. Balakrishnan, Professor Jayant Haritsa, Mr. H. Krishnamurthy, Mr. R. Krishnamurthy, Professor M. N. Murthy, Dr. A. Neeharika, and Professor T. V. Prabhakar.

Without my wife Dharma's enthusiasm and wholehearted support, I could not have written this book. She read the entire manuscript, suggested improvements, and assisted me in numerous ways. I thank her sincerely.

When I wrote to Mr. Asoke Ghosh about my plan to write a book on the history of modern computing comprising anecdotes, he immediately agreed to publish it. I was shocked and grieved when he passed away on 1 February 2024. I dedicate this book to his memory. We were friends for over five decades and he published over twenty books I wrote. I thank Mrs. Sagarika Ghosh and Ms. Pushpita Ghosh, who have encouraged me over the last five decades. The PHI Learning team has always done an excellent job of copy editing and production. Their enthusiasm has encouraged me to continue writing.

Despite my best efforts, there may be some errors and some aspects of the book I could improve. I would be grateful to receive suggestions at my email id rajaraman.v37@gmail.com.

V. Rajaraman

Introduction

"If history were taught in the form of stories, it would never be forgotten"

—Rudyard Kipling

John Mauchly, J. Presper Eckert, Jr., and their team built ENIAC (Electronic Numerical Integrator and Computer) in 1946, the first modern stored-program electronic computer. They built it primarily to design weapons during the Second World War. Since then, computers have entered every facet of our daily life. Nowadays, we use computers extensively to process data in banks, government offices, and commercial establishments. We use them to book train tickets, airline tickets, and hotel rooms. They control systems such as satellites and moon landers in real time. They create complex graphics and animation. They synthesize speech and music. They write essays and draw pictures. They control Robots. Publishers use them as tools. They are used to play video games. Many devices, such as audio and video tape recorders and film cameras, have died and been replaced by digital devices. They have eliminated many jobs, such as type-setters, and created new jobs, such as programmers, requiring better skills. It is fascinating to trace this history. Many professional historians have written books on the history of computing. Most of them begin with an account of Charles Babbage's difference engine, a mechanical computer built in 1832, and end with modern computers and their applications.

This book is not yet another exhaustive history of computers in the same scholarly style, starting with Babbage's difference engine.

Instead, I trace the history of modern computing as a sequence of seventy-two *anecdotes*, beginning with how engineers at the University of Pennsylvania built the modern stored program computer ENIAC in 1946. I end with the story of the evolution of ChatGPT, Gemini, and Copilot, the generative large language model neural networks, released between 2022 and 2024. These give natural language answers to natural language questions, write essays, compose poems, and write computer programs and are our AI assistants.

The Oxford English dictionary meaning of anecdote is: "*a short amusing or interesting story about a real incident or person*". The anecdotes in this book are short. Each anecdote is between 1500 and 2500 words and recounts the story of an important invention in the evolution of modern computing and the people who innovated. Though not all amusing, these stories are, I believe, interesting.

I have arranged the anecdotes in a loose chronological order. Arranging in a strict chronological order is impossible as many inventions evolved over decades. For example, Joseph Weizenbaum wrote the first natural language chatbot program, ELIZA, in 1966. The latest, almost human-like chatbot, ChatGPT, was released in 2022. The Internet started as the ARPANET, connecting four computers across the United States in 1971. The Internet as we know it was released to the public in 1989 and became usable with the advent of the World Wide Web in 1993. I have based the chronology on the first significant historical development of the subject of the anecdote.

ANECDOTES IN THE BOOK

There are seventy-two anecdotes in this book. The anecdotes cover the history of computer hardware, software, applications, computer communications, and artificial intelligence. The set of anecdotes on hardware systems describes, among others, the history of the evolution of computers such as the IBM 701, CDC 6600, IBM 360 family, Digital Equipment Corporation's PDP series, Apple—the early personal computer, and Atlas – a pioneering British computer, IBM PC, Connection Machine, Cray series supercomputers, computing cluster Beowulf, IBM Roadrunner – the fastest and the most expensive ($ 600 million) computer in the World in 2022, Raspberry Pi—the cheapest ($35) computer. The group of anecdotes on software describes the evolution of Fortran, COBOL, BASIC, Compatible

Time-shared systems, Unix, CP/M OS, MS-DOS, Project MAC, and open-source software movement, among others. Some anecdotes are on computer applications such as Data Base Management Systems (DBMS), spreadsheets, cryptography, and Global Positioning Systems (GPS). The anecdotes on computer communications recount the evolution of computer communication networks such as ALOHAnet, Ethernet, ARPA net, and the Internet, among others. The anecdotes on Artificial Intelligence (AI) start with "Who coined the word Artificial Intelligence?" and recounts early chess-playing programs, the evolution of neural networks, Expert Systems, the history of chatbots, AI assistants, and Robots.

These anecdotes are similar to a short story collection. You may read them in any order. Each anecdote is self-contained, and you may read the one that interests you. Happy reading!

1
The ENIAC Story

PROLOGUE

The United States of America was neutral when the Second World War began in 1939. It was, however, helping the United Kingdom and its allies with armaments and logistics. The United States entered the war when Japan attacked it in 1941. One of the important wartime efforts was to calculate artillery firing tables using the trajectories of shells and bombs. Tables for artillery were prepared at the US Army's Ballistics Research Laboratory (BRL) located in Aberdeen, Maryland. A mechanical differential analyser designed by Vannevar Bush of the Massachusetts Institute of Technology was used to prepare the tables. The Moore School of Electrical Engineering at the University of Pennsylvania at Philadelphia owned a similar, more powerful, differential analyser. The University was a few hours' train ride from Aberdeen. The army decided to contract out the preparation of some artillery firing tables to the university. It appointed Lieutenant Herman Goldstine, who had a doctorate in mathematics and had been inducted into the army, to liaise with Moore School and oversee the progress of the project. As there were a lot of calculations, the university also employed around 200 ladies who were trained to use mechanical desk calculators to prepare the tables. Adele Goldstine, Herman's wife was a qualified mathematician and assisted in selecting and training the ladies. These ladies were called "computers"! The calculation of the tables was laborious. It took 20 hours of manual calculation to tabulate a 60-second shell trajectory. The differential analyser was faster and took 15 minutes for the same task. As the number of tables required was huge the project was behind schedule. A faster device for calculation was required.

Moore School of Electrical Engineering had a group of engineers who were teaching electronics. Among them was John Mauchly, who was interested in developing electronic computers. He had earlier visited John Atanasoff in June 1941 when Atanasoff was building a digital computer with vacuum tubes at the University of Iowa to solve simultaneous algebraic equations. Atanasoff and his student Clifford Berry used binary numbers and Boolean logic in designing their machine. The computer called Atanasoff-Berry Computer (ABC) was not fully functional as war intervened and the navy drafted Atanasoff. Mauchly saw how vacuum tubes were used to perform arithmetic operations and took copious notes about the design of the machine [1]. He teamed up with J. Presper Eckert, an excellent designer of electronic systems, and proposed to John Brainerd, the head of Moore School, that an electronic computer be built to calculate the artillery tables. Brainerd agreed. Eckert and Mauchly wrote a proposal in early 1943 requesting funding of $ 61,700 from the US Army to build an Electronic Numerical Integrator and Computer (ENIAC). Goldstine who was liaising with the group at Moore School supported the proposal. The US Army agreed to fund the project and released the funds in June 1943 and classified the project as top secret.

DESIGN OF ENIAC

Eckert and Mauchly started constructing ENIAC as soon as the money was released. Mauchly designed the logic of the system. Eckert, an excellent electronics engineer, designed the electronic circuits with a

J. Presper Eckert
(Photo courtesy nationalmedals.org)

John Mauchly
(Photo courtesy ethw.org)

team of talented engineers and built the computer. The computer stored decimal digits in accumulators. Each accumulator was 10 digits long and there were 20 accumulators. Counters were used for arithmetic operations and accumulators stored the results. ENIAC could add, subtract, multiply, divide, and find the square root of a number. It had three function tables to store values of arbitrary functions. The circuits were driven by a clock that gave a pulse once in 10 microseconds. It could add 5000 ten-digit numbers in one second. Data were input to the computer using an IBM card reader and the results of the computation were punched on an IBM card punching machine. The punched results were printed by an offline printer. ENIAC was programmed by interconnecting its units by plugging wires on a large 1 square metre plugboard. It was tedious and required a good knowledge of the logical structure of the computer. It took weeks to set up a program to solve a problem and debugging was difficult. It could be programmed to perform looping, conditional branches, and subroutine calls. Six mathematically savvy ladies were selected from among the ladies operating the desk calculators and trained to program the computer. Their contribution was invaluable in using ENIAC to solve problems. Unfortunately, at that time, their importance was not recognized. They were not even invited to the dinner that was given to celebrate the successful completion of ENIAC [2]. Belatedly, in 1997 they were inducted into the Women in Technology International Hall of Fame.

ENIAC was constructed one unit at a time. As the construction progressed, the project was frequently running out of funds. On the

A view of ENIAC (Photo courtesy Wikipedia.org)

recommendation of Goldstine, the project was periodically renewed and funds were released. When it was completed, it cost a little over $ 485,000. It used around 18,000 vacuum tubes, 7200 diodes, 1500 relays, 70,000 resistors, and 10,000 capacitors. It weighed 27 tons, occupied an 1800 sq. ft. room, and consumed 150 kW. It required a massive air circulation system to cool it.

One of the major problems encountered during ENIAC's use was the failure of vacuum tubes. The average time between failures of a vacuum tube was 3000 hours. With 18,000 tubes the probability of failure of one of the tubes and consequently the computer was around 10 minutes. Eckert reduced the failure of tubes by operating the tubes at two-third the rated voltage which increased the average time between failures a hundred-fold. The filaments of the tubes fail if they are turned on and off frequently. Eckert decided to keep the computer always on. With these changes, the computer stabilized and used to fail only once a day. Procedures were found to quickly locate the bad vacuum tube and replace it. ENIAC could tabulate the 60-second trajectory of an artillery shell in 30 seconds, 30 times faster than the differential analyser.

The machine was fully functional in early 1946 and was unveiled on February 15, 1946.

VON NEUMANN'S INVOLVEMENT WITH ENIAC

John Von Neumann was a famous mathematician and a professor at the Institute for Advanced Studies at Princeton. He was a consultant to the US Army and was a frequent visitor to BRL at Aberdeen. He was interested in computing and had visited the computing laboratory at Harvard University and the Bell Telephone Laboratories. Computers there used electro-mechanical relays and were slow. Goldstine met Von Neumann at the Aberdeen railway station in August 1944. During a conversation, he mentioned ENIAC and that it was using vacuum tubes and could perform 333 multiplications of ten-digit numbers per second. Von Neumann evinced keen interest in this computer and he was

Herman Goldstine
(Photo courtesy Wikipedia.org)

invited to see ENIAC. He went to Moore school later in August and became a consultant to the ENIAC group. In 1944, Eckert and Mauchly were exploring how to design a memory for ENIAC and use it to ease programming. When Von Neumann joined the group, the discussion was steered towards programming ENIAC. During several brainstorming sessions, the idea of storing programs and data to be processed by the programs in the main memory of a computer emerged. The construction of ENIAC had progressed far and it was too late to incorporate in it a memory to store programs. Even though Eckert had an idea of designing a memory it would have taken too long to build it. It was decided to build a memory and use it in a successor computer EDVAC (Electronic Discrete Variable Automatic Computer).

Extensive notes of these discussions were kept. Von Neumann sent a hand-written document describing the logical structure of the proposed computer titled "First draft of a report on EDVAC" to Goldstine. Goldstine got it typed and attributed the document solely to Von Neumann, even though it was the result of a group effort. Several copies were made and distributed in June 1945 to all the participants of the brainstorming sessions.

ENIAC—SECOND AVATAR

Due to a patent dispute between Eckert-Mauchly, and the University of Pennsylvania, regarding ENIAC, Eckert and Mauchly left the university in March 1946. They started a company named Electronic Control Company to manufacture computers in late 1946. It was renamed Eckert-Mauchly Corporation in December 1947. They took along with them many engineers and programmers from the ENIAC team. Those who were left continued to use ENIAC. In December 1946, ENIAC was disassembled, packed, and shipped to BRL at Aberdeen. A group of engineers at BRL reassembled it. It was a tedious job and it was quite a challenge to get it back to a working state. In late July 1947 ENIAC was switched on and started working. Between December 1946 and July 1947, Von Neumann and Adele Goldstine started exploring methods of simplifying programming ENIAC as plug board wiring was inflexible and tedious. ENIAC had three function tables each storing 1200 digits. They realised that these function tables could be used as a read-only memory in which programs can be stored. Pulses generated from these tables could be used to control the sequence of calculations.

A group of scientists that included Richard Clippinger of BRL designed a set of around 80 instructions (called order code) each 2 digits long. Von Neumann suggested how some accumulators could be used as a program counter and ENIAC converted to a single address computer. ENIAC was modified and a unit was added to facilitate the use of function tables as program memory. The modified ENIAC initially failed to execute programs. The engineers slowed down the computer by reducing the clock speed and it worked [3]. ENIAC started working almost like a stored program computer in March 1948. It was used to successfully run simulation programs (using what is known as the Monte Carlo method) to aid in the development of hydrogen bombs. With this success, ENIAC was used for solving numerous problems such as weather prediction and wind tunnel design. Programming a new problem took days rather than weeks. ENIAC was the fastest and most easily programmable computer in the world between 1948 and 1950.

EPILOGUE

ENIAC was the workhorse for the US defence department during the late 1940s. It was improved with additional hardware, including a high-speed shift register in 1952 and a 100-word random-access magnetic core memory (see Anecdote 4 on the invention of magnetic core memory) built by Burroughs Corporation in 1953. Meanwhile, faster and more versatile commercial computers were entering the market. ENIAC was closed down on October 2, 1955. It is now in the Smithsonian Museum in Washington D.C. The US post office released a stamp with the picture of ENIAC in 1996 on its golden jubilee.

REFERENCES

[1] Walter Isaacson, The Innovators, Simon & Schuster, 2014.

[2] ENIAC, http//en.wikipedia.org

[3] Thomas Haigh, Mark Priestly, and Crispin Rope, Engineering "The Miracle of the ENIAC": Implementing the Modern Code Paradigm, IEEE Annals of the History of Computing, April–June 2014.

2

The First British Stored-Program Computer

PROLOGUE

The idea of storing programs and data in the main memory of a computer originated during the brainstorming sessions held at the Moore School of Electrical Engineering at the University of Pennsylvania in early 1945. J. Presper Eckert, John Mauchly, John von Neumann, Herman Goldstine, and several ENIAC (Electronic Numerical Integrator and Computer) design team members attended these sessions. EDVAC (Electronic Discrete Variable Automatic Computer) was to succeed ENIAC and use the stored program idea. Von Neumann wrote: "First Draft of a Report on EDVAC", which was distributed by Goldstine in June 1945. The US Army's Ballistics Research Laboratory (BRL) in Aberdeen funded the design and development of EDVAC. Construction of EDVAC began in April 1946 and it was delivered to BRL in 1949. It became operational only in 1951 due to numerous hardware problems [1].

Another historical event was an eight-week course titled: "Theory and Techniques for Design of Electronic Digital Computers" held at the Moore School in July-August 1946 [2]. J. Presper Eckert, John Mauchly, Herman Goldstine, John von Neumann, the faculty of Moore School, and many invitees gave these lectures. Most lectures were on EDVAC, numerical methods to use digital computers, and the stored-program idea. The course also included some talks on and a demonstration of ENIAC. Around 30 participants attended. The attendees included several US Army engineers, a few MIT scientists, Howard Aiken of Harvard, Claude Shannon of Bell Labs, Maurice Wilkes and Douglas Hartree of Cambridge University, and David Rees of Manchester University. These lecture notes were widely distributed. These lectures were important as the ideas presented in them led to the design of several early stored-program computers.

THE BRITISH TAKE THE LEAD

The Moore School lectures convinced computer designers Wilkes of Cambridge University and Rees of Manchester University of the importance of the stored-program idea. They returned to England with a plan to build stored-program electronic computers. The main problem was to design and build an electronic memory. The groups at Manchester and Cambridge solved the problem using different approaches. The group at Manchester built the first working stored-program computer: Manchester Small-Scale Experimental Machine (also called Manchester Baby), albeit a toy. It demonstrated the feasibility of stored-program computers and ran very simple programs in June 1948. Wilkes and his group at Cambridge University built the second more usable stored-program computer called EDSAC (Electronic Delay Storage Automatic Computer). It ran successfully in May 1949.

The success of the British teams in designing the "first" stored-program computers in the world was perhaps because Britain was short of funds after the Second World War and the British projects were modest with clear goals.

MANCHESTER SSEM (SMALL-SCALE EXPERIMENTAL MACHINE)

Frederic Williams was a British electronics engineer who worked during the Second World War on radars that used Cathode Ray Tubes (CRT) for display. After the war ended he started exploring whether CRT could be used to store digital data. In December 1946, he succeeded in storing a bit as a charge on the screen of a CRT and patented his invention. He joined Manchester University as a professor in Electro-Technics soon after. He invited two of his earlier associates, Tom Kilburn and Geoff Tootill, to join him in Manchester. By the end of 1947, they improved the memory and could store 2048 bits on a single CRT.

Max Newman was a professor of mathematics at Manchester who was earlier in the team that built the top-secret codebreaking computer Colossus. He had deputed David Rees, a member of his group, to the Moore School Lectures on EDVAC and knew about the stored-program idea and the need for a good memory unit for computers. He encouraged Williams and his team to use their memory (now known as Williams tube memory) to build a computer and obtained funding from the Royal Society to build it. Williams and his group decided to build a small-scale experimental computer (christened Manchester Baby) primarily to test Williams tube memory. An important feature of Williams tube memory was that it was a random access memory, that is, the time taken to read a word from the memory was independent of where it was stored.

Alan Turing joined the faculty of mathematics at Manchester University after he left the National Physical Laboratory where he had tried unsuccessfully to build a computer named ACE. Turing and Neumann assisted with the logical design of the computer built by Kilburn and Tootill.

Frederic Williams

Tom Kilburn

(Photos courtesy curation.cs.manchester.ac.uk)

Kilburn and Tootill began building the computer in early 1948 and it was ready in six months [3]. It used the stored-program idea and Williams tube memory was used to store both data and programs. Each Williams tube memory was organized as an array of 32 bits per row (each row called a word) and 32 rows. Two Williams tubes were used as the main memory storing 64 words. Two more Williams tubes were used for the accumulator register, an instruction register, and a program counter. A CRT was used to display the results of the computation. The arithmetic and control units were built with vacuum tubes. Data was input using switches; one switch per bit. The Manchester Baby was designed with a set of 7 instructions. The set consisted of subtract, change the sign of a number, jump, relative jump, jump on negative, store, and stop. Observe the absence of add, multiply, and divide instructions. Addition could be done by changing the sign and subtracting. Multiplication is successive addition and division is successive subtraction. The computer could carry out one instruction in 1.2 milliseconds. The first program was written by Kilburn to find the greatest common factor of a number. The program was tested with small numbers and it worked. Finally, a large number, 2^{18} was given as input to Manchester Baby. It ran successfully on 21 June 1948, giving 2^{17} as the answer in 52 minutes.

ELECTRONIC DELAY STORAGE AUTOMATIC COMPUTER (EDSAC)

Maurice Wilkes was a British academic who obtained a Ph.D. in physics from Cambridge University in 1936. After a stint at the University, he was drafted for war service during the Second World War. He was assigned to the Telecommunications Research Centre (TRC) and worked on Radar and operations research. After the war, he was appointed as Director of the mathematical computation laboratory of Cambridge University in 1945. The laboratory was primarily meant to aid the faculty of Cambridge University in their mathematical calculations. The laboratory had a mechanical differential analyser and several mechanical calculators. In May 1946, J.C. Comrie, a colleague who had visited the University of Pennsylvania, brought the First Draft Report on EDVAC and gave it to Wilkes. Wilkes eagerly read it overnight and was convinced that the logical design of all future digital computers would be similar to EDVAC [4]. Soon after, he received an invitation to attend Moore School lectures on computers to be held during July and August 1946. Due to post-war constraints, he could not immediately get funding and approval to travel to the USA. He, however, got a delayed approval and reached Moore School two weeks after the course began. As the lectures in the earlier part of the course were on numerical analysis that he knew, he did not miss much. Wilkes learnt a lot from the latter part of the course, particularly the stored-program idea for designing computers. He also attended the demonstration of ENIAC. During his return voyage to England which lasted five days, he sketched the logical design of a computer modelled after EDVAC. Wilkes' primary goal was to design and build a workable computer that would be easy to program. His emphasis was hardware simplicity as he had limited funding. On his return to Cambridge, he recruited a gifted electronic engineer William Renwick as the chief engineer and assembled a small team to build the computer. Fortunately, the laboratory was given a grant of £3000 by J. Lyons & Co. which enabled him to start the project. Wilkes also got a gift of around 3000 vacuum tubes he needed from the office of surplus war disposals. His first major task was to design and build the main memory of the computer. During his stint at TRC, he had seen the use of mercury delay lines in Radar. He decided to design similar delay lines as storage. EDVAC design also proposed a delay line memory. He consulted a colleague who had built acoustic delay lines, followed his suggestions, and built a memory. This memory consisted of a set of sixteen 5 feet 4 inches long steel tubes filled with mercury. At one end of each steel tube, a quartz crystal was mounted. Electrical pulses fed to it were converted to mechanical vibrations and were transmitted by the column of mercury in the tube as sound waves. After a delay, these waves reached the other end of the tube and a quartz crystal mounted there sensed them and converted them back to electrical pulses. The pulses were fed back to the input crystal so that the bits circulated indefinitely in the tube (delay line). The time taken by a pulse to travel from one end of the tube to the other was around 1.12 milliseconds. 576 pulses equivalent to 576 bits were travelling in the tube during this time and were effectively "stored" in it. The computer had 16 tubes giving a total memory of 512, 18-bit words. A word was retrieved from the memory by waiting for an appropriate period and electronically reading the pulses. A major problem with the delay line was the variation of delay with ambient temperature due to the thermal expansion of mercury. This problem was solved by enclosing the tubes in a thermostat-controlled tank.

The computer called Electronic Delay Storage Automatic Computer (EDSAC) had an instruction set with 14 instructions each 17 bits long. Even though 18 bits were available in a word, only 17 bits were used due to timing problems in the delay line memory. The arithmetic and control units were built using vacuum tubes. The Input unit was a paper tape reader used by telegraph offices. The output unit was a punched paper tape printer.

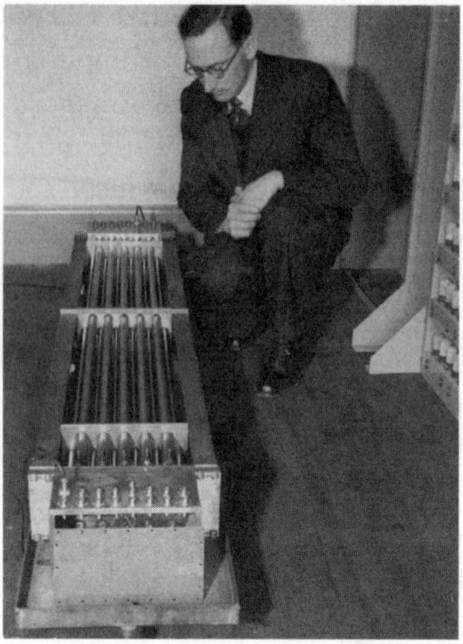

Maurice Wilkes inspecting the mercury delay line of the EDSAC during construction (Photo courtesy of Department of Computer Science and Technology, University of Cambridge. Reproduced by permission)

The vacuum tubes were operated at lower voltages just as in ENIAC to increase the reliability of the computer. The time to execute one instruction was 1.5 milliseconds. Its power consumption was 11 kW.

The team wrote two programs; one to list the squares of integers and the other to list the prime numbers. These successfully ran on 6 May 1949. Several programming innovations were made by Wilkes' group including an assembly language and subroutine libraries. Scientists and engineers at Cambridge University regularly used EDSAC until 1958 [5]. It was the world's first working stored-program computer that solved non-trivial problems. Three Nobel Prize winners at Cambridge University acknowledged their use of EDSAC in their calculations.

EPILOGUE

The computer groups at Manchester University and Cambridge University were encouraged by their initial success, improved their computers, and later commercialised them.

At Manchester University the computer group was expanded and a more powerful computer was built based on the experience in building the Manchester Baby computer. It was ready in 1949 and was called the Manchester Mark 1 computer. It had a main memory that stored

512–20-bit words and had an instruction set with 30 instructions. Its cycle time was 1.2 milliseconds and its multiplication time was 2.16 milliseconds. The British government requested Ferranti, an electronics manufacturer, to build a machine based on Manchester Mark 1 specifications. This resulted in a Ferranti Mark 1 computer with the same specifications as Manchester Mark 1 [6]. Ferranti Mark 1 was sold in February 1951, the world's first commercially marketed general-purpose electronic computer.

At Cambridge University, EDSAC 2 succeeded EDSAC in 1958 [8]. In EDSAC 2, a magnetic core random-access 1024 words, 20 bits per word memory replaced the delay line memory. It was faster than EDSAC and could multiply two floating-point numbers in 0.3 milliseconds. It was the first computer in the world to use a microprogram control unit.

Cambridge University also commercialised EDSAC. J. Lyons & Co which had partially funded EDSAC development decided to build LEO (Lyons Electronic Office) to aid in their bakery operations. (Lyons was one of the largest bakeries in Britain). Lyons had sent one of their engineers to Cambridge and hired others based on the recommendation of Wilkes. Lyons built LEO which had 2K, 35-bit word acoustic delay line memory (4 times larger than EDSAC), 500 kHz clock speed, and carried out most instructions in 1.5 milliseconds. It had better Input/output devices with a card punch whose output was printed with a 100 lines per minute tabulator. It was the first computer in the world specifically designed for use by businesses. It ran its first program on 5 September 1951 [7]. LEO Computers Ltd. merged with English Electric Company in 1963.

REFERENCES

[1] Electronic Discrete Variable Automatic Computer (EDVAC), en.m.wikipedia.org

[2] Moore School Lectures, en.m.wikipedia.org

[3] Manchester Baby or Small-Scale Experimental Machine, en.m.wikipedia.org

[4] M. Campbell-Kelly et al., Computer—A History of the Information Machine, Routledge, New York, 2014.

[5] Electronic Delay Storage Automatic Computer (EDSAC), en.m.wikipedia.org

[6] Ferranti Mark 1 computer, en.m.wikipedia.org

[7] LEO Computer, en.m.wikipedia.org

[8] Maurice V. Wilkes, EDSAC 2, IEEE Annals of the History of Computing, Vol. 14, No. 4, 1992, pp. 49–56.

3

The First American Commercial Computer

PROLOGUE

J. Presper Eckert and John W. Mauchly resigned from their jobs at the University of Pennsylvania on 31 March 1946, when the university introduced new rules that required all employees to assign patent rights to any inventions to the university. They had already started designing EDVAC (Electronic Discrete Variable Automatic Computer) in 1944, and the new rules would have prevented them from patenting it in their names. Mauchly was entrepreneurial and had foreseen the possibility of selling EDVAC to customers, mainly from the government [1]. He discussed with the US Census Bureau in the mid-1940s using computers in their census tabulation in 1950, and they were interested. Mauchly proposed to Eckert that they start a company to manufacture and market EDVAC primarily to government agencies. As Eckert already had a job offer from von Neumann, who was planning to build a computer at the Institute of Advanced Studies at Princeton, he was reluctant to venture into a project with no capital. His wife and father convinced him to join Mauchly and start a company. There was no venture capital concept in those days, and neither was independently wealthy. Despite this, they decided to create Electronic Control Company (ECC).

In April 1946, the US government sanctioned $300,000 to the US Census Bureau to buy a computer. Eckert and Mauchly offered to build a computer similar to EDVAC, which they called UNIVAC (UNIVersal Automatic Computer), to the Census Bureau for $300,000.

They estimated the cost of building the computer to be $400,000 and decided to compensate for the loss from future sales. The Census Bureau sought the opinion of the National Bureau of Standards (NBS), which had expertise in electronics, about this offer. NBS appointed, in the usual bureaucratic way, a committee with George Stiblitz as the Chairman to examine ECC's proposal. The committee was lukewarm in its recommendations. In June 1946, NBS recommended granting ECC an advance of $75,000 to study how to design a mercury delay line memory and an eight-channel metallic magnetic tape unit. This amount was start-up capital, and ECC hired some members of the ENIAC team and started operations in Philadelphia.

BUILDING BINARY AUTOMATIC COMPUTER (BINAC)

Eckert and Mauchly underestimated the difficulty of designing a delay line memory and tape drives. The study took one year. Meanwhile, ECC changed its name to Eckert Mauchly Computer Corporation (EMCC). NBS took nine months to study the design and finally gave, in June 1948, a contract of $169,000 to EMCC to build these units. EMCC had a hand-to-mouth existence with very little working capital. In April 1947, Northrop Aircraft Company in California hired Mauchly as a consultant to study the navigational control of a long-range guided missile. Mauchly suggested using a digital computer for navigational control in a report and gave them a rough design.

Mauchly's report convinced Northrop Aircraft Company of the usefulness of a digital computer. As a private company, Northrop did not delay decisions and gave a contract to Eckert and Mauchly in October 1947 to build a small digital computer and deliver it in May 1948. The contract amount was $100,000 with an advance payment of $80,000 and $20,000 on completion [2]. This advance was a life-saver to EMCC, and it immediately started building a computer they named BINAC (BINary Automatic Computer). The design of BINAC was unique. It had two identical processors, each with its own memory. The system compared the results from the two processors after executing an instruction. If they were equal, it was accepted. Otherwise, the instruction was executed again. This comparison ensured the reliability of computation and was essential as the computer was to control a missile. As the primary component used in those days was a vacuum tube prone to failure, and the delay line memory was new, this precaution was essential.

There were two memory units, each with 512 words—31 bits per word. The memory unit used 16 mercury delay lines, each storing 32 words. It was enclosed in a thermostat-controlled chamber. Each processing unit used 700 vacuum tubes. It performed 3500 add/subtract per second and 1000 multiplications/divisions per second. BINAC was a binary computer. All arithmetic was binary, and the results were displayed as octal digits. Input/output units were teletypewriters or magnetic tape. It was a general-purpose computer and could be programmed to solve numerical problems relevant to science and engineering.

BINAC was ready for the acceptance test by Northrop in April 1949—a year later than the date promised to Northrop [2]. After resolving numerous glitches, the acceptance tests were completed in August 1949, and BINAC was ready for delivery. EMCC wanted to transport BINAC by air after disassembling, packing, and reassemble it at Northrop's factory. Northrop decided to reassemble BINAC themselves due to security issues.

BINAC arrived at Northrop in September 1949, and their engineers reassembled it. BINAC did not work as it was fragile with numerous vacuum tubes and an unreliable mercury delay line memory. Besides, inexperienced Northrop engineers assembled it. EMCC's engineers were not allowed to fix the problems as they were not security-cleared. Northrop, however, paid $20,000 as it had accepted the machine in EMCC's factory.

The actual cost of BINAC was $278,000, well above the contracted price. EMCC requested the reimbursement of the cost, but Northrop refused. Eckert and Mauchly were excellent engineers but poor businessmen. As the technology was new, cost estimates were way off the mark. BINAC was the first stored-program computer commercially sold in the world in August 1949. EDSAC (Electronic Delay Storage Automatic Computer), the first functional stored-program computer, was operational in May 1949, three months before BINAC. However, it was for use in-house by Cambridge University in England.

UNIVAC DEVELOPMENT

Mauchly wanted to build more BINACs, but Eckert vetoed it as he was keen on building UNIVAC. No BINACs were made after that.

However, the design and development of BINAC greatly aided the design of UNIVAC.

UNIVAC was intended for commercial use, processing decimal numbers, and print alphanumeric text. The contract with NBS for UNIVAC required it to achieve specific milestones for releasing funds. The development of the mercury delay line store and tape drives of BINAC were shown to NBS as completed milestones. BINAC was also demonstrated to the prospective buyers of UNIVAC. In December 1948, Prudential Life Insurance Company signed a contract to buy UNIVAC for $150,000, with the delivery of the computer scheduled for September 1950 and paid in advance. A.C. Nielson Co., an advertising company, also signed a contract to buy UNIVAC for a similar amount. The loss incurred in building BINAC almost bankrupted EMCC. In 1948, EMCC started negotiations with the American Totalisator Company (ATC), which specialised in building calculating machines related to betting in horse races, to buy UNIVAC. Henry L. Strauss, a Vice President of ATC, was technically savvy and a good business executive. The work done at EMCC impressed him. He also foresaw the promise of the computer business. He saved EMCC from bankruptcy by buying a 40% share in EMCC for $500,000 and became the Chairman of the Board of EMCC in August 1948. He wisely left the responsibility of day-to-day operations of EMCC to Eckert and Mauchly. ATC also gave loans to EMCC whenever it ran out of funds. By September 1949, EMCC obtained four more contracts to sell UNIVAC to the US Air Force, US Map Service, and Atomic Energy Commission. Their order book was healthy, with $1.2 million in prospective sales.

REMINGTON RAND BUYS EMCC

In October 1949, misfortune struck EMCC. Strauss, the primary supporter of EMCC, died in an air crash. The new management of ATC was lukewarm in its support of EMCC. In January 1950, ATC asked EMCC to repay its loans, bankrupting EMCC. EMCC had no alternative but to look for prospective buyers of their corporation. Mauchly started negotiations with several companies, including IBM, National Cash Register Company, Burroughs Corporation, and Remington Rand. In February 1950, Remington Rand agreed to buy EMCC and make it a wholly owned subsidiary of their company. It cleared outstanding loans and paid $438,000 to ATC for their shares and $100,000 to other shareholders, including Eckert and Mauchly. Eckert and Mauchly became employees of Remington Rand and devoted their energy to building UNIVAC.

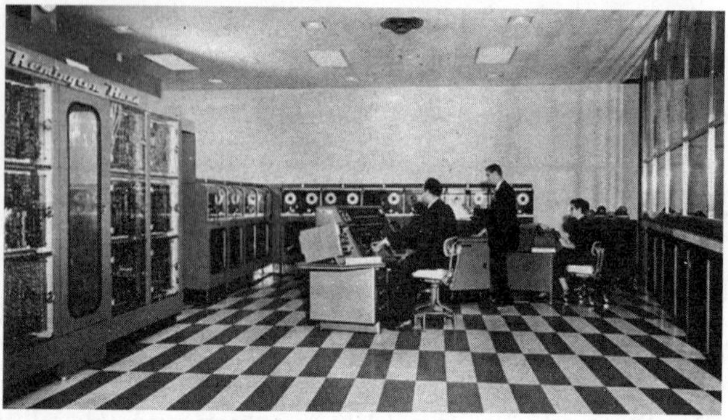

UNIVAC I—See the tape drives (Photo courtesy Wikipedia.org)

Remington Rand reviewed the order book and saw that many quotations needed to be higher. Remington Rand cancelled the contracts with Prudential Insurance Company and A.C. Neilson as they were unwilling to renegotiate them. The Census Bureau accepted the first UNIVAC on 31 March 1951. The Census Bureau agreed to use the computer at the EMCC factory without moving it. EMCC engineers maintained UNIVAC, saving Census Bureau maintenance costs. This arrangement allowed Remington Rand to show the working UNIVAC to prospective customers. Foreseeing improved models, UNIVAC was renamed UNIVAC I.

UNIVAC I HARDWARE SPECIFICATIONS

UNIVAC I had a central processing unit that used a 2.25 MHz clock. It was a decimal computer whose operand size was 11 binary-coded decimal digits with a one-bit sign. It had two arithmetic units whose results were compared by the CPU and only accepted if they were equal, ensuring reliability. The main memory was a mercury delay line that stored 1000 words. The word length was 12 alphanumeric characters. The characters used 7-bit code. The 1000 words of the main memory consisted of 100 mercury delay lines with ten words per line. All the delay lines were enclosed in a thermostat-controlled tank.

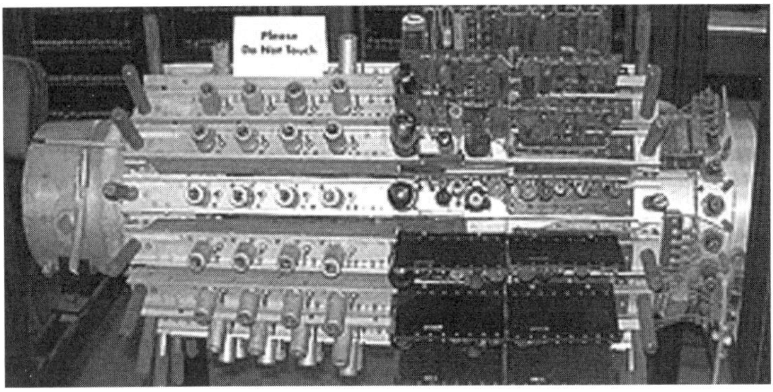

Mercury delay line memory of UNIVAC I (Picture Courtesy Wikipedia.org)

As UNIVAC I was designed to process large volumes of data, such as census data processing, input and output units were paid special attention. The input/output unit of UNIVAC I used specially designed servo-controlled magnetic tape drives. The tape employed in the tape drive was ½ inch wide magnetically plated phosphor bronze. It was 1500 feet long and stored approximately 1.5 million characters. The storage density was 100 characters per inch, and the reading speed was 7200 characters per second [3]. These tape drives were called UNISERVOS. UNIVAC I supported up to 8 drives. There were two 60-word buffers to hold data to be written on and read from the tapes. An offline punched card-to-tape unit recorded data on the tapes. An offline printer read the computed results from the tape and printed them.

Numeric data were input as decimal digits. UNIVAC I used decimal arithmetic as it was essential in processing business applications such as payroll and accounting. The arithmetic speed was around 2000 adds and 500 multiplications per second of 11-digit operands. Two instructions, each six digits long, were packed in a word. There were 45 types of instructions.

Grace Murray Hopper led UNIVAC's programming group. This group invented high-level programming languages for business data processing.

UNIVAC I used 5000 tubes, consumed 125 kW, and occupied around 400 sq. ft. of floor space. It required chilled-air cooling. The filaments of the tubes were turned on gradually to increase their life. Due to the careful selection of tubes and redundant arithmetic units, UNIVAC I was very reliable, with an average time between failures of many days and often weeks. The primary source of failure was the tapes and mechanical units such as typewriters.

UNIVAC I AFTER REMINGTON RAND TAKEOVER

Early sales of UNIVAC I were primarily to government organizations. They were to the US Army, Navy, and Air Force, and two units to the Atomic Energy Commission. Remington Rand had a brilliant idea of demonstrating the power of UNIVAC I to the public by arranging with CBS Television Network to use it to forecast the result of the 1952 US Presidential election. UNIVAC I programmers wrote a program to forecast the election outcome from early voting data with the help of a statistician. Based on 3.4 million early votes, the program predicted, at 8.30 PM EST, a landslide victory for Eisenhower. Gallup polls had forecasted a close race between Eisenhower and Stevenson, and the news anchor was reluctant to announce UNIVAC I's prediction. However, as more results came in, it became evident that Eisenhower would win by a huge margin. CBS then announced UNIVAC I's prediction and praised its performance. The network flashed a picture of UNIVAC I with its whirring tapes. This image made UNIVAC I synonymous with the computer (christened electronic brain) in the public's mind. The use of computers to forecast election results became standard from then on. This publicity also convinced some commercial organizations to order UNIVAC I computers. The first big commercial sale was to General Electric (GE) in 1953. GE used UNIVAC for payroll processing and inventory control. GE reported saving $1 million in inventory costs using UNIVAC I [3]. Following this, many manufacturing companies and insurance companies ordered UNIVAC I. Ultimately, Remington Rand sold 46 UNIVAC I computers at an average price of around $1 million. Customers used many UNIVAC I computers for over ten years.

EPILOGUE

UNIVAC I was the first computer sold in the USA for business data processing. Remington Rand's takeover of EMCC infused capital and better management, leading to its success. Its early sales were to the government, and its first sale to a private company was in 1953. Remington Rand did not profit from its "first mover" advantage. With its aggressive management, financial clout, and mass manufacturing experience, IBM rapidly overtook it. Remington Rand was taken over by Sperry Gyroscope Company in 1955 and renamed Sperry Rand. Sperry Rand built the last UNIVAC brand computer in 1986. Eckert continued working with UNIVAC computers until 1989. Mauchly left Remington Rand in 1952 to start a consultancy.

REFERENCES

[1] Martin Campbell-Kelly et al., Computer, A History of the Information Machine, Routledge, New York, 2018.

[2] Nancy Stern, The BINAC: A Case Study in the History of Technology, Annals of the History of Computing, Vol. 1, No. 1, July 1979, pp. 9–20.

[3] George Gray, UNIVAC I: The First Mass-Produced Computer, Unisys History Newsletter, Vol. 5, No. 1, January 2001.

4

The First Real-Time Computer—Whirlwind

PROLOGUE

The U.S. Bureau of Aeronautics of the Office of Naval Research (ONR) wanted a real-time aircraft flight simulator to train pilots to fly several aircraft types. The simulator was to have a cockpit with all the controls available in an aircraft and give feedback on the aerodynamic forces encountered during flight to the cockpit controls, providing a realistic flying experience to a pilot. It was a real-time simulator because it mimicked events while an aircraft flew.

The servomechanisms laboratory at the Massachusetts Institute of Technology (MIT) was famous and had designed many control systems to aim guns at moving targets during the Second World War. ONR requested MIT to build the simulator. Jay Forrester, who was a member of the servomechanisms laboratory, was given the task. In May 1945, he agreed to build a simulator in 18 months for $875,000 [1] and began making it using an analog computer. After working for a year to assemble it, he found that it needed to be faster, and its accuracy needed to be improved to meet the specifications of the simulator. Perry Crawford, a colleague, mentioned to him that ENIAC (Electronic Numerical Integrator and Computer) was being built at the University of Pennsylvania. Forrester realised immediately that only a digital computer would be fast and flexible to meet the design goals of the simulator and decided to design one. He found that the computer had to be much faster than ENIAC to fulfill the real-time requirement. He gave a revised proposal to ONR to build a digital computer-based simulator in March 1946. This proposal requested funding of $1.9 million and two years for completion. ONR accepted this proposal.

WHIRLWIND COMPUTER

The proposed computer would be much faster and highly reliable than existing computers to meet the simulator's real-time specifications. ONR named the computer *Whirlwind.* MIT rented a building and set up a digital computer laboratory, and the project moved to it from the servomechanisms laboratory. Forrester requested Robert Everett, a servomechanisms laboratory colleague, to join him as associate director to design and build the computer.

The Whirlwind team spent a year designing the architecture of Whirlwind. The essential aspects of the architecture were the number of operation types, the size and type of the main memory, the number of bits in the operands (namely, the numbers used in computation), the method to do arithmetic, the operations performed, how to control the operations, and the type of input and output units.

The simulator inputs were from instruments whose range was not large and whose accuracy was around 1%. Sixteen bits were adequate to represent these inputs. The design team used a 16-bit word length with 5 bits to represent 32 operation types and 11 bits to address 2048 word memory.

Whirlwind was to be at least a hundred times faster than existing computers to meet the real-time requirement. All existing computers performed arithmetic operations serially by taking bits of the numbers to be added one by one, starting from the least significant bit. This method, called bit-serial arithmetic, was too slow. To speed up arithmetic, the designers added all the bits of the two operands simultaneously, in parallel. Adding 16 bits in parallel required more than 16 times the number of components used to add the bits serially, and the circuits were more challenging to design.

The computer had to be highly reliable. Making Whirlwind reliable was a big challenge as Whirlwind used thousands of vacuum tubes. They were unreliable due to the burning out of cathodes that emitted electrons. The Whirlwind team conducted extensive research and found that the main reason for the failure of cathodes was that they used nickel contaminated by silicon. The Whirlwind team got a batch of tubes manufactured with pure nickel cathodes, and the tubes' life increased 1000 times from 500 to 500,000 hours! [2]. Further research on the optimal operation of tubes increased their life tenfold.

The other tricky problem was designing the main memory of Whirlwind. The speed and reliability of the main memory governed the speed and reliability of Whirlwind. Contemporary computers such as EDSAC (Electronic Delay Storage Automatic Computer) at Cambridge University used acoustic delay line memory, which was serial access and very slow. Williams cathode ray tube memory, used in Manchester Mark I computer, was faster and was a random-access memory. The technology, however, was unstable. Forrester decided to modify the Williams cathode ray tube memory and make it more reliable. His group spent over a year developing this memory, which could store 1024 16-bit words. The time to retrieve a word from this memory was 25 microseconds, which was too slow compared to the speed of arithmetic. The life of the Williams tubes was also short. Better memory technology was required.

Even though Forrester had estimated two years to build the simulator, designing Whirlwind took more than two years, and the fabrication could start only in 1948. The project employed around 100 people, including research students, design engineers, and technicians. Expenses were ballooning to about a million dollars a year. The original estimate of time and cost to build a simulator Forrester gave had already been exceeded. Whirlwind was to be the means to an end, namely, part of an aircraft simulator, but it now became the end! ONR decided to drop the simulator project and instead use Whirlwind for a naval air-defence system. Meanwhile, the U.S. government cut ONR's budget, and ONR wanted to terminate the Whirlwind project in 1950.

Fortunately, when ONR wanted to withdraw, the U.S. Air Force came to Whirlwind's rescue. The Cold War between the USSR and the USA was heating up. The air defence system built during the Second World War was protecting attacks from the east of the U.S. As USSR's bombers may attack the U.S. across the North Pole, an air defence system was required in the north, in Canada, and the U.S. The system called SAGE (Semi-Automatic Ground Environment) was to gather data from an array of Radars on enemy aircraft positions, process them in real-time, and give commands to fighter aircraft to intercept them. A real-time computer was essential to process the data. The only real-time computer that was almost ready in 1950 was Whirlwind. The U.S. Air Force agreed to fund the Whirlwind project with adequate funds to expedite its completion. Whirlwind was up and running reliably by early 1951 with modified Williams Tube memory [3].

Jay Forrester
(Photo courtesy IIM/L)

Robert Everett
(Photo courtesy computerhope.com)

MAGNETIC CORE MEMORY

As mentioned earlier, the modified Williams tube memory was slow and temperamental. Forrester started exploring other memory technologies. He came across an advertisement in early 1949 for a magnetic material named Deltamax with a rectangular hysteresis loop. This characteristic allowed it to be placed in one of two stable states representing 0 or 1. Forrester persuaded the manufacturers of ferrite material with properties similar to Deltamax to provide him with doughnut-shaped cores. He preferred a doughnut-shaped core, which could be magnetized in a clockwise or anti-clockwise direction to represent two states, a 0 or 1. Forrester went to a corner of the laboratory and started experimenting with these cores to build a memory. He had always thought of a three-dimensional memory. His idea was to string magnetic cores through wires in the horizontal and vertical directions, with one core at each intersection. He threaded a third wire through all cores. Half the current needed to change the magnetic state of the core was passed through the horizontal (x) wire and half through the vertical (y) wire (See Figure). Only the core at the intersection changed state writing a bit. Stacking 16 planes as a cube and sending currents through the corresponding x and y wires in each plane, wrote 16 bits. The third wire read the contents of a core in a plane when it changed its state. Sixteen sense wires, one wire in each plane, read 16 bits. By June 1949, he could build a prototype memory using magnetic cores that worked. He then assigned the task of constructing a core memory for Whirlwind to William Papian, one of his post-graduate students. Papian started his experiments with many core samples and built a magnetic core memory with an access time of 9 microseconds by early 1952. The core memory was a computing breakthrough as a reliable random-access memory with fast access time was available for the first time. Magnetic core memory was the primary memory in all computers built during the next two decades. MIT patented it in 1951, and after years of legal wrangling, it sold the patent to IBM for 13 million dollars in 1964.

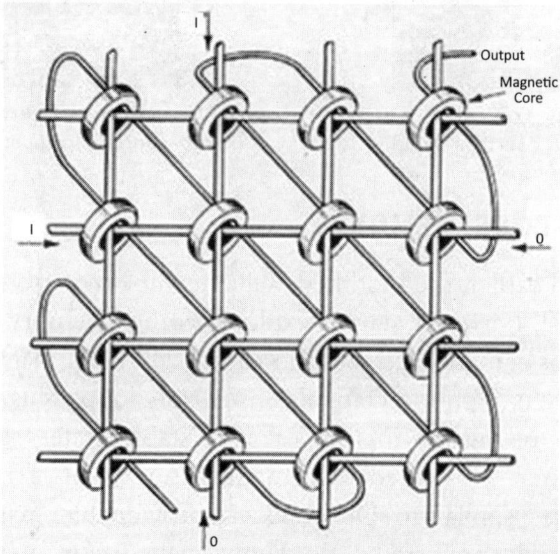

One plane of a magnetic core memory (Picture courtesy https://ub.fnwi.uva.nl)

WHIRLWIND WITH CORE MEMORY

A light pen (Photo courtesy history-computer.com)

In August 1953, a core memory replaced Whirlwind's CRT memory. Apart from a memory and a processing unit, Whirlwind pioneered designing input and output units. Besides paper tape input/output, the Whirlwind team built a large CRT display as an output. CRT display was necessary to use Whirlwind in the SAGE system. Another innovation was a light pen invented by Everett that could sense dots on the CRT screen and give their coordinates. This unit was also necessary for the SAGE system. Besides these, drum and tape memories were also incorporated into the system. A Whirlwind with a core memory of 2048 words (16 bits per word) with an access time of 9 microseconds was running in 1953. It performed 330,000 additions and 62,500 multiplications per second, 500 times faster than contemporary computers. It used around 5000 tubes, weighed 10,000 kg, and occupied 20,000 sq. ft.

A view of the Whirlwind Computer. Forrester is standing next to the chair, and Everett is behind him. See the CRT display.
(Photo courtesy history-computer.com)

EPILOGUE

A project that began in 1945 to design an aircraft simulator at an estimated cost of $875,000 ended in 1953 as a real-time computer to process data received from multiple Radars in an air defence system costing $5 million. During Whirlwind's design and development, it employed over 100 engineers and numerous post-graduate students. Many of these students became pioneers in computer development, including Kenneth Olsen, who founded Digital Equipment Corporation. Whirlwind was the first real-time computer in the world. Besides this, it achieved many other firsts, including the invention of random-access magnetic core memory—a memory used by all computers for the next two decades. The other significant achievements were increasing the life of vacuum tubes by a thousand times, self-checking circuits, parallel arithmetic, CRT digital display, light pen, software for directing interceptor aircraft towards targets based on signals picked up by Radar, and sending digital data on telephone lines [3].

The U.S. Air Force decided to replicate Whirlwind for use in the SAGE air defence system. IBM received a contract to produce fifty-six IBM AN/FSQ-7 computers based on Whirlwind design, costing $30 million each between 1953 and 1963 [4]. MIT sent Ken Olsen to IBM to transfer the Whirlwind technology. IBM got both technology and capital from this project, making it the foremost computer manufacturer in the world from the 1950s to the 1980s.

Whirlwind continued to work at MIT until 1959. After Whirlwind shut down, William Wolf, an alumnus of the Whirlwind project, leased it from the U.S. Navy (which was deemed its owner) for $1 per year, dis-assembled it, moved it to his company in Boston, and kept it operational till 1970 [3]. Most of Whirlwind is now in the Smithsonian Museum in Washington, D.C.

Jay Forrester left the digital computer laboratory and became a professor at the Sloan School of Management at MIT. He applied control theory ideas to soft systems and did seminal work in system dynamics. Robert Everett joined Lincoln Laboratory, an offshoot of the Whirlwind project. In 1958, he co-founded MITRE Corporation, a contractor that built high-technology equipment for the U.S. Department of Defence, and was president of MITRE from 1969 to 1986.

REFERENCES

[1] Martin Campbell-Kelly et al., Computer—A History of the Information Machine, Routledge, New York, 2018.

[2] Jay Forrester, Whirlwind Computer, https://www.youtube.com/watch?v=JZLpbhsE72I

See too: https://history-computer.com/inventions/whirlwind-complete-history-of-the-whirlwind-computer/#page-content

[3] Kent C. Redmond, Thomas M. Smith, Lessons from 'Project Whirlwind', IEEE Spectrum, October 1977.

[4] IBM-100 SAGE, See too: https://en.wikipedia.org/wiki/History_of_IBM

5

IBM's First Stored-Program Computer—IBM 701

PROLOGUE

International Business Machines Corporation (IBM) was a successful manufacturer of electro-mechanical equipment (known as unit record equipment) for business data processing. These included card punches, card readers, printers, sorters, and accounting machines. Under the leadership of Thomas J. Watson Sr., IBM expanded and overtook competitors Remington Rand, Burroughs, National Cash Register Company, Bull, and International Computers and Tabulators. IBM had an excellent marketing team, IBM's machines were reliable, and maintenance services were superb. In 1944, IBM funded and collaborated with Howard Aiken of Harvard University to build the electro-mechanical relay-based Automatic Sequence Controlled Calculator, also known as the Harvard Mark I calculator. IBM felt slighted when Aiken did not acknowledge the credit due to it for funding and building Mark I. In response, Watson Sr. hired engineers in 1944 to build a large calculator named the Selective Sequence Electronic Calculator (SSEC) that used vacuum tubes and relays. Even though it was a computer, it was called a calculator by Watson Sr. because, in the 1940s, the word computer meant a person who used a calculator. He did not want people to feel that machines were eliminating their jobs. SSEC was ready in January 1948. IBM placed it on the ground floor of a building next to its headquarters in New York. The building had large windows, and SSEC was visible to people walking on the footpath. The clicking sound of its relays, the whirring of its tapes, and the blinking of hundreds of neon lamps attracted them. It was a gigantic machine that used approximately 12,500 vacuum tubes and 22,000 relays. The primary purpose of SSEC was publicity and to inform the World about the prowess of IBM in manufacturing complex electronic calculators. Watson Sr. also emphasised that SSEC was to aid advancement in science and engineering by providing a fast calculating device. It cost around a million dollars and was unmarketable. IBM built only one machine, and its customers used it to solve complex mathematical problems. The EDVAC report was published when SSEC was ready, making SSEC obsolete.

IBM began using vacuum tubes in 1946 in their accounting machines to increase their speed. In 1947, it developed a Card Programmed Calculator (CPC) in collaboration with Northrop Aircraft. CPC used an IBM accounting machine connected by a flexible cable to an electronic calculating punch. It executed a sequence of arithmetic operations coded on an 80-column punched card. It branched to different sequences of operations based on the results of computation. It was not a stored-program computer but was fast and reliable and could perform 2000 add/subtract and 86 multiply operations per second. IBM started delivering CPC in late 1949; by the mid-1950s, IBM delivered approximately 700 units. The success of CPC demonstrated the pent-up demand for a high-speed calculator for use by scientists and engineers.

THE GENESIS OF THE HIGH-SPEED DEFENCE CALCULATOR

The conservative marketing team of IBM was reluctant to foray into the field of stored-program electronic computers because it had a suite of well-established unit record equipment and CPC. Thomas Watson Sr., in his mid-seventies, was also not inclined to jump into this new technology. In 1951, Remington Rand began delivering UNIVAC and was capturing the market for stored-program computers. Thomas J Watson Jr., next in command to his father at IBM, wanted to avoid ceding the market for electronic computers to Remington Rand. In late 1950, he asked his executive assistant, James Birkenstock [1], to explore the need for high-speed electronic computers for government research laboratories and large companies such as Boeing and Monsanto. Birkenstock requested that Cuthbert Hurd, the Director of the Applied Sciences Division of IBM, accompany him on a tour of these laboratories. They visited twenty-two laboratories in August 1950, including the Ballistic Research Laboratories at Aberdeen, the Los Alamos scientific laboratory, the Rand Corporation, and aircraft companies on the West Coast of the U.S. The team was convinced that the computer specifications for these organizations were similar and that designing a general-purpose scientific computer would be appropriate. They then consulted Ralph Palmer, the head of the Poughkeepsie Research Laboratory of IBM, and finalised the computer's specifications. It was envisaged as a stored-program computer with 2000 words of random access memory, an arithmetic speed of approximately 5000 additions and 1000 multiplications per second, tape drives, a magnetic drum, punch-card input, and printer output. They estimated it would cost $3 million to design and build a prototype and could be rented for $8000 monthly. (IBM usually rented all their machines as most commercial customers preferred it rather than spend a considerable amount to own a machine. As a thumb rule, the cost of a machine was equal to 60 months' rental). They went again to several laboratories, showed the specifications, and returned in November 1950 with letters of intent to rent the machine from around 20 prospective customers. These letters of intent convinced Watson Jr. to proceed with designing and manufacturing a high-speed stored-program scientific computer. He had to sell his decision to Watson Sr. and his marketing staff. In late June 1950, the Korean War began. Watson Sr. sent a telegram to the U.S. President offering IBM's assistance in the war effort. Watson Jr. told his father about building a high-speed defence calculator. Using the term defence calculator rather than a general-purpose computer was an astute political move to convince Watson Sr. and the marketing department to approve the project. In February 1951, IBM decided to design and build the defence calculator at its Poughkeepsie laboratory and deliver the first machine by March 1952—an extremely tight schedule for a new computer. IBM also decided to fully fund it from its internal resources to ensure it owned all the patents filed for inventions during its design.

DESIGN OF THE DEFENCE CALCULATOR

Ralph Palmer assigned two engineers, Nathaniel Rochester and Jerrier Haddad, to the project. Rochester's task was to design the machine's architecture, and Haddad's task was to manage engineering design, build a prototype, and plan manufacturing and servicing. Rochester obtained a B.S. in Electrical Engineering from MIT in 1941 and continued working in the MIT radiation laboratory. He later joined the Whirlwind computer group and designed its arithmetic unit. He joined IBM in 1948. Haddad was of Syrian Lebanese origin, born in New York. He obtained a B.S. in Electrical Engineering from Cornell University in 1945 and immediately joined IBM. The Institute of Advanced Study (IAS) Computer, which was being built at Princeton University by von Neumann and his group, served as the model for the architectural design of the defence calculator. Von Neumann became a consultant. The proposed machine was a binary computer with a word length of 36 bits and a parallel arithmetic unit. Rochester chose a 36-bit word length because the tape drives used six parallel tracks for recording, and 36 was a multiple of six. The computer used a floating-point representation of decimal numbers with eight significant digit precision. A 36-bit word was divided into two 18-bit parts. Each 18-bit part was utilized to code an instruction. The machine performed 32 different operations and addressed 4096 half-words or 2048 full-words. The processor used quality-assured vacuum tubes and germanium diodes. The processor's arithmetic speed was 16,000 floating-point add/subtract and 2000 multiply/divide per second.

Nathaniel Rochester
(Photo courtesy ibm.com)

Jerrier Haddad
(Photo courtesy Wikipedia.com)

The computer used Williams cathode ray tube memory as the main memory. Special cathode ray tubes were ordered and tested. Seventy-two Williams tubes, each storing 1024 bits, were assembled to make up a 2048-word memory with an access time of 12 microseconds. (Later, magnetic core memory replaced William tube memory).

The peripheral units received special attention. IBM already had designed reliable tape drives and magnetic drums. The tape drives used plastic tapes coated with magnetic material, unlike UNIVAC, which used metal tapes. A 1200-foot tape stored 2 million characters, and the reading speed was 12,500 digits per second. The drum was designed with 36 tracks to store words. Its capacity was 8192 words, and its average access time was 50 ms. The IBM 407 accounting machine was modified as a printer that printed 150 lines per minute. A card reader and punch were used as input/output units. IBM had the advantage that customers were already using these peripheral units and these units were very reliable.

IBM was happy that it had many prospective customers for the defence calculator. At the same time, IBM was anxious about its inexperience in mass-producing stored-program computers. All computers in the early 1950s, such as BINAC and Whirlwind, were built in a laboratory environment. The transition from a laboratory prototype to production in a factory was a big step. The marketing team demanded a fault-free operation for at least eight hours. Customer engineers were trained to maintain the computers. Manuals were prepared to isolate faults and repair them quickly.

The Central Processing Unit (CPU) was constructed modularly with pluggable logic modules to ease maintenance. The computer consisted of a set of units. Each unit was compact and enabled IBM to move the computer from the factory to customer sites and through standard doors at the sites. Cables concealed below a false floor connected the units at customers' locations. It was the first computer to transition from a laboratory to a manufacturing environment. IBM designed it as a mass-market computer. IBM brought future products and marketing groups into the loop. Their suggestions were valuable in developing the final product, ensuring its usability and maintainability.

A pluggable unit used to construct the CPU of the IBM 701 computer
(Photo courtesy Wikipedia)

An IBM 701 installation (Photo courtesy ibm.com)

IBM announced the availability of the defence calculator (renamed IBM 701) on 29 April 1952. After manufacturing the first unit, IBM had a better estimate of the monthly rental. From the earlier estimate of $8000 per month, it was revised upwards to $11900 for the minimum configuration and $17600 for the largest configuration. By May 1952, the marketing group had firm orders for ten machines. This revised price did not seriously affect the market because the customers were primarily government-funded research laboratories keen to install reliable high-speed computers. The first 701 was shipped for installation at IBM Headquarters on 31 December 1952. It replaced SSEC and was ready for use on 27 March 1953. J. Robert Oppenheimer, director of the Institute of Advanced Study, presided over the unveiling of IBM 701 at a function on 7 April 1953. Hurd successfully demonstrated a program on neutron scattering. He informed the gathering that the second 701 was shipped to Los Alamos Scientific Laboratory on 31 March 1953, installed by 3 April 1953, and was already running application programs [2]. Los Alamos Laboratory accepted IBM 701 on 17 April 1953 and began paying IBM rent.

When 701 was shipped, it had an assembly language developed by Rochester. Later, John Backus developed Speedcode, a high-level language that speeded up computations requiring calculations with floating-point numbers. Arthur Samuel wrote the first artificial intelligence program to play checkers with 701 in 1956.

EPILOGUE

IBM 701 development was remarkable as it took only two years from conceptualisation in January 1951 to the delivery of the first machine on 31 December 1952. IBM's Poughkeepsie plant started producing one 701 computer per month beginning in January 1953. IBM built nineteen 701s. The last 701 was shipped to Lockheed Aircraft Company in June 1954. Magnetic core memory replaced the Williams tube memory in all the rented machines in October 1954.

The design and manufacture of 701 was a significant turning point in IBM's history as it transitioned from a unit record manufacturer to a computer manufacturer. The success of 701 convinced IBM's conservative marketing group of the importance of stored-program computers. IBM 702, a computer designed for business data processing, followed IBM 701. A higher-speed scientific computer, 704, was announced in 1954. The 7000 series of IBM scientific computers followed. IBM soon dominated the stored-program computer market.

REFERENCES

[1] Special Issue of IEEE Annals of the History of Computing Commemorating the 30th anniversary of the release of IBM 701, Vol. 5, Issue 2, 1983.

[2] Charles J. Bashe et al., IBM's Early Computers, The MIT Press, Cambridge, MA., 1986.

6

The First Mass Produced Computer—IBM 650

PROLOGUE

IBM introduced Card Programmed Calculator (CPC) in May 1949, primarily for use by scientists and engineers. It consisted of three units. An electronic calculating punch that took data punched on cards, performed a sequence of predetermined calculations based on a program punched on cards. It also performed a different sequence of calculations based on the results of previous calculations. The results were printed using IBM 407, an accounting machine with a built-in printer. IBM did not manufacture an independent printer in the 50s. The monthly rental for CPC was about $1000. IBM rented around 700 units in the first two years. CPC was a combination of existing machines with some modifications. It was not a stored-program computer. IBM researchers felt it was time to design a successor to CPC that would use the stored-program idea that had emerged during the design of ENIAC in 1946.

HAMILTON'S DESIGN OF A MAGNETIC DRUM CALCULATOR

Frank Hamilton, born in 1898, was a veteran IBM engineer. He joined CTR (the predecessor of IBM) in 1923 as a draftsman. He teamed up with Claire Lake and A.W. Mills, gifted engineers of IBM, to develop many early IBM products. In 1939, along with Claire Lake, he was assigned to design and construct the Automatic Sequence Controlled Calculator (ASCC), also called Harvard Mark 1, for Howard Aiken of Harvard University. It was built at the Endicott Laboratory of IBM, shipped to Harvard, and installed there in 1944 by Hamilton and his team. Thomas Watson Sr. was invited to attend the formal inauguration of Harvard Mark 1. He was shocked when he saw the press release by Harvard on this occasion that did not mention IBM's role in the design and construction of the calculator and its financial contribution of $10,000 for its maintenance. Thomas Watson Sr. felt slighted and ordered Hamilton and his team to build a calculator 250 times faster than Harvard Mark 1. Hamilton took up the challenge and built the IBM Selective Sequence Electronic Calculator (SSEC) between 1944 and 1948. SSEC was a gigantic machine that used 12,500 vacuum tubes and 21,400 relays. It had a small memory but was not a stored-program computer. It was showcased at the IBM Headquarters in New York.

After the successful installation of SSEC, Hamilton was transferred to the Endicott Laboratory of IBM to design and build a smaller version of SSEC for "ordinary businesses," the core customer base of IBM. A survey revealed that CPC was a popular machine serving scientific and business users, and the sales team wanted a more powerful successor.

In 1949, Frank Hamilton, Ernest Hughes Jr., and James Troy started designing a stored-program computer called Magnetic Drum Calculator (MDC) as a successor to CPC. A magnetic drum was its main memory. The drum recorded bits as magnetic spots (which could be in one of two states) on tracks around its circumference. There were several parallel tracks, and one read/write head per track. The drum rotated at a high speed, and the data stored in a buffer store was recorded on the drum by the recording heads. Read heads read the data stored on the drum when it rotated and stored them in a buffer. Drums at that time rotated at around 3400 revolutions per minute. A complete revolution took 17 milliseconds. The average time to access data was thus 8.5 milliseconds.

A Magnetic Drum memory
(Photo Courtesy edubilla.com)

In comparison, the average access time of a delay line memory used at that time was 0.5 milliseconds, and that of Williams Tube memory was 10 microseconds. The main advantage of the magnetic drum was that it was more reliable compared to delay lines and Williams Tube. The cost of storing a bit on drums was also much lower. However, the technology was immature, and the drum's storage capacity was low. The future products division of IBM was pessimistic about the use of drums and rejected Hamilton's proposal. The management also felt that the Poughkeepsie Laboratory of IBM had better expertise in building electronic systems, and Endicott Laboratory was unnecessarily duplicating the effort. The sales group wanted a low-cost machine with a monthly rental of about $1000. Hamilton persevered with his experiments with drum memory. He designed a drum with two heads per track separated by half a revolution [1] to reduce the data access time from the drum. IBM's patents department examined and rejected this idea as Remington Rand had patented a similar idea. Hamilton continued his experiments with the drum memory. He doggedly pursued his quest to design a drum that could store 20,000 digits with an access time of a few milliseconds.

Frank Hamilton
(Photo courtesy invent.org)

Meanwhile, Bill Woodbury, Greg Toben, and Truman Wheelock at the Poughkeepsie laboratory designed a computer that used an electronic arithmetic unit based on CPC design augmented with a small Williams tube memory. This computer code named Wooden Wheel (arrived at by combining the names of the three members of the team) was slightly faster than the Magnetic Drum Calculator (MDC) designed by Hamilton's team. However, it was less reliable and more difficult to program. The Future Machines department and the sales group of IBM were squabbling, and no decision was taken on the next machine. An eight-member evaluation committee was appointed in late 1952 to compare the MDC with the Wooden Wheel. The committee favoured the Wooden Wheel as it was faster but made no decision. Meanwhile, UNIVAC came into the limelight in November 1952 with its forecast of the US presidential election on national television. Thomas Watson Jr. called a meeting and asked the managers to stop "fiddling around" and announce a new IBM machine [2]. The committee responded; it selected the MDC. IBM announced it as a Type 650 Magnetic Drum

Calculator on 2 July 1953. The primary factor that led to the selection of MDC was the ease of programming.

DRUM MEMORY OF IBM 650

The drum memory finally designed by Hamilton and his group after three years of experimentation [3] was a cobalt-nickel plated drum. It was 4 inches in diameter and 14 inches long, was mounted on high-precision ball bearings, and rotated at 12,500 revolutions per minute. It was a very high-speed drum compared to existing drums. The drum could store up to 20,000 digits using 200 read/write heads. An instruction word of IBM 650 was ten digits long. Thus, the maximum storage of a drum was 2000 words. IBM sold a standard configuration with a 1000-word store.

One revolution of the drum took 4.8 milliseconds, and the average time to access a word was 2.4 milliseconds. A decimal digit was coded using 7 bits to enable error detection. The drum could operate for many hours without an error.

INSTRUCTION STRUCTURE OF IBM 650

The primary goal of Hamilton in designing the IBM 650 was the ease of programming. IBM 650 was a decimal machine. Using decimals eased programming and debugging as the early models were programmed using machine language. Each IBM 650 instruction had an operation code and two addresses. As the maximum memory was 2000 words, the addresses used four digits. IBM 650 performed 44 different operations coded using two digits. Each instruction had two addresses. Figure 6.1 shows the structure of an instruction. Address 1 was the address of the operand (i.e., the data on which the operation was to be performed), and Address 2 was the address of the next instruction to be carried out. The use of the second address in the instruction was clever. If instructions were stored in successive addresses, one would have to wait for a complete drum revolution, which would take 4.8 milliseconds to access the instruction.

Operation Code	Address 1	Address 2
2 Digits	4 Digits	4 Digits

Figure 6.1 Instruction Word of IBM 650.

The average instruction execution time was 3 milliseconds, meaning the computer would unnecessarily wait 1.8 milliseconds to access the next instruction. The second address reduced this time. The manual for programming IBM 650 gave the time to carry out each instruction. Using this time, a programmer calculated the rotational distance that the drum would have travelled in carrying out an instruction and calculated the address where the head of the drum would be. This address was entered as Address 2 in the instruction. The next instruction was placed in that address. This optimization often worked but put an onerous burden on a machine language programmer. It was done automatically by an assembly language called SOAP (Symbolic Optimal Assembly Program) written for IBM 650 in 1955.

CODING OF DECIMAL DIGITS IN IBM 650

Internally, all computers use binary digits. The decimal numbers used in IBM 650 were coded internally as binary using a Bi-quinary coding system. The term *Bi-quinary* is a combination of *Bi*–two states and *quinary* – five states. Figure 6.2 illustrates the coding of 0 to 9 in *Bi-quinary*. Observe that 7 bits are used to code a decimal digit. The *Bi* part uses 2 bits to represent 0 and 5, and the *quinary* part uses 5 bits to represent 0, 1, 2, 3, and 4.

	Binary Part of Code		Quinary Part of Code				
Digit	0	5	0	1	2	3	4
0	1		1				
1	1			1			
2	1				1		
3	1					1	
4	1						1
5		1	1				
6		1		1			
7		1			1		
8		1				1	
9		1					1

Figure 6.2 Bi-quinary representation of decimal numbers.

Numbers from 0 to 4 have a 1 coding a 0 in the *bi* part and another 1 in the *quinary* part. Numbers 5 to 9 have a 1 coding a 5 in the *bi* part and another 1 in the *quinary* part. Thus, the binary code of each decimal digit, including 0, has precisely two 1s. There were two reasons for using this coding. The first was the ease of error detection. The binary code of every digit has exactly two 1's. During computing, the circuits checked if a digit had two 1 bits — one 1 in the *bi* part and another 1 in the *quinary* part. If not, it was an error. As circuits using vacuum tubes in IBM 650 were prone to errors, this coding of decimal digits facilitated error detection during computing. The second was the ease of interpreting the digits displayed on the IBM 650 console. Neon lights displayed Biquinary decimal instructions and data on the IBM 650 console. It was easy for programmers to interpret these. Whenever there was an error during the computation, the computer displayed the erroneous instruction and stopped. After correcting the error, the programmer resumed computation.

SPECIFICATIONS OF IBM 650

IBM 650 used approximately 3000 tubes and around 4000 germanium diodes. It performed around 36800 additions/subtractions, 4600 multiplication, and 3500 divisions per minute with 10-digit operands. A unique feature of the computer was a table look-up instruction that was very useful in applications such as calculating utility billing and insurance premia. It was a general-purpose machine used for scientific and business applications.

IBM 650 (Power Supply at the back, Main processor, and Card Read/Punch)
(Photo Courtesy ibm.com)

The computer was announced with an IBM 533 card reader/punch as the Input/Output unit. The reader could read 200 cards per minute, and the punch could punch 100 cards per minute. The monthly rental was $3250 for an IBM 650 with 1000 word memory and $3750 for one with 2000 word memory [2]. The price of IBM 650 was $195,000, one-fifth of the price of IBM 701.

IBM 650 SOFTWARE

Machine language programming requires a programmer to understand the logical organization of IBM 650 and use the table giving the execution time of instructions to find the second address to place the next instruction. Often, a programmer sat at the console to debug programs. The first attempt to reduce programming time was to develop an assembly language that used mnemonics for operation codes and meaningful alphanumeric symbols for addresses. The first assembly language named SOAP (Symbolic Optimizing Assembly Program) was developed in 1955 by Stan Poley, who worked at the IBM Thomas J. Watson Sr. Research Centre. As and when new features were added to IBM 650, SOAP was enhanced. SOAP II was designed in 1957, SOAP IIA in 1958, and SOAP 4L in 1961. Besides this, users of IBM 650 wrote assemblers. Donald Knuth was a student at the Case Institute of Technology (now part of Case Western Reserve University) in the mid-50s and wrote SOAP III in 1958 and Super SOAP in 1959.

FOR TRANSIST, a subset of FORTRAN, was developed in 1959. It was a multi-pass compiler. Besides these, many application programs were written and shared by users for both businesses and scientific applications. IBM facilitated sharing by requesting developers to submit their programs to SHARE. SHARE programs were publicized and distributed by IBM free of cost to those ordering them. IBM 650's large user community led to a vast library of applications.

EPILOGUE

Initially, IBM's marketing team estimated 250 as the sales of IBM 650. Soon after the announcement, orders started pouring in from "ordinary businesses," the traditional customers of IBM, for commercial applications. In late August 1953, IBM increased the estimate of sales to 550. As it turned out, by 1962, over 2000 IBM 650s were sold. IBM installed the first 650 at John Hancock Mutual Life Insurance Company on 8 December 1954. Commercial companies found the table look-up instruction of IBM 650 particularly useful.

When IBM announced 650, it did not have floating-point arithmetic and no peripherals other than a card reader/punch. It only had machine language. Gradually, IBM improved 650 with floating-point instructions, a printer, tape drives, disks, and a small 60-word magnetic core memory. The core memory was a buffer between the drum and the tape and disk memories. From 1956, IBM's factory at Endicott produced one 650 a day. It was the largest-selling computer in the mid-50s, and IBM made a tidy profit. It was popular both for scientific and business applications.

In an astute move, IBM gave a 60% discount to colleges that ordered a 650 and introduced a course in programming using it. This discount made IBM 650 affordable to educational institutions, and several colleges installed it. Many pioneers in computer science learnt to program using 650. Interestingly, a famous computer science teacher, Donald Knuth, used IBM 650 as a student, enjoyed the experience, and dedicated his book "Art of Computer Programming" to IBM 650!

REFERENCES

[1] George R. Trimble, The IBM 650 Magnetic Drum Calculator, IEEE Annals of the History of Computing, Vol. 8, No. 1, January 1986, pp. 20–29. (This is a special issue featuring the history of IBM 650).

[2] Charles J. Bashe et al., IBM's Early Computers, The MIT Press, Cambridge, MA., 1986.

[3] F.E. Hamilton and E.C. Kubie, The IBM Magnetic Drum Calculator Type 650, IEEE Annals of the History of Computing, Vol. 8, No. 1, January 1986, pp. 14–19.

7

Who Coined the Term Artificial Intelligence?

PROLOGUE

Speculation about designing a machine simulating a human brain is as old as humanity. In each era of history, scientists and philosophers tried to use the then-prevalent mechanisms to mimic a brain and its functions. In the twentieth century, Warren McCullough, a neurophysiologist, and Walter Pitts, a mathematical prodigy, collaborated to model the operation of a brain using a neural net in 1943. They formally established that the neural net could be employed for computation. When the first analog computers and feedback systems appeared, Norbert Weiner, a mathematics professor at the Massachusetts Institute of Technology, defined Cybernetics in 1948 as "the scientific study of control and communication in the animal and the machine." He primarily used analog communications in his studies. Alan Turing, working in England, wrote a paper, Computing Machinery and Intelligence, in 1950, which starts with the question "Can machines think?" and argues that trying to answer such a question may lead to absurd conclusions. Instead, he designed an imitation game between a woman, a man, and an interrogator in which the interrogator has to decide who the man is and who the woman is based on the answers to questions posed by the interrogator. The imitation game has been modified as the Turing Test [1], in which a computer replaces the woman. The interrogator asks the man or the computer a series of questions. At the end of the interrogation, if the interrogator cannot decide which answers the computer gave and which the man, then one may conclude that the machine exhibits intelligent behaviour. Passing the Turing Test involves the computer understanding language and having a vast knowledge repository, including cultural nuances.

Alan Turing
(Photo courtesy Wikipedia.org)

Norbert Weiner
(Photo courtesy bri.ee.wasington.edu)

Another stream of work was related to the fundamental limitation on what is computable by machines based again on the seminal work of Turing in 1936–37 in which he described an abstract machine called the Turing machine that, in principle, can compute anything that a computer can compute and showed that there exist some problems that are not computable.

AUTOMATA STUDIES

John McCarthy entered this scenario in 1952. He obtained a Ph.D. in mathematics from Princeton University in 1951 and was an instructor there during 1951–52. McCarthy spent the summer of 1952 at the Bell Telephone Laboratories, where he worked with Claude Shannon, the father of Information Theory and one of the early pioneers in computing who wrote a computer program to play chess. McCarthy convinced Shannon of the need to publish a volume of invited papers on the emerging area of cybernetics and automata. Shannon and McCarthy invited active researchers in cybernetics and automata to contribute articles that peers would referee. They received thirteen articles and categorised them into three broad areas: Finite Automata, Turing Machines, and Synthesis of Automata. The first set of five articles were related to neural network models treated mathematically; the second set of four were on extensions of Turing machine models; and the third set of four were on cybernetic models of machines. Shannon and McCarthy debated on the title of the volume [2]. McCarthy suggested "Towards Intelligent Automata," which was overruled by Shannon, and the final title was "Automata Studies" [3].

The experience of editing this volume convinced McCarthy of the need for a broader discussion. He was disappointed that no paper described the possibilities of computers exhibiting intelligence. McCarthy was inclined towards using digital symbolic processing in future research on automata and away from analog cybernetic models of Wiener. In 1952, he joined Stanford University as an assistant professor of mathematics. McCarthy was busy editing Automata Studies till late 1954. Princeton University Press published the book in 1956.

John McCarthy
(Photo courtesy engadget.com)

Claude E. Shannon
(Photo courtesy ias.edu)

GENESIS OF THE DARTMOUTH WORKSHOP ON ARTIFICIAL INTELLIGENCE

Stanford University denied McCarthy tenure, and he moved to Dartmouth College in Hanover, New Hampshire, as an assistant professor of mathematics in February 1955. He talked to Shannon about organizing a workshop on automata and brain modelling. He met with Warren Weaver of the Rockefeller Foundation in early April 1955 about the possibility of the foundation funding a workshop at Dartmouth College in the summer of 1956 on automata and brain modelling that would have around ten researchers working together for six weeks. Weaver felt that it would be more appropriate for

McCarthy to discuss the proposal with his colleague Robert Morison, who was in the area of funding biological and medical research [2]. McCarthy, Marvin Minsky of MIT, Nathaniel Rochester of IBM, and Claude Shannon of Bell Labs wrote a proposal titled: "A proposal for the Dartmouth Research Project on Artificial Intelligence" and sent it to the Rockefeller Foundation. After discussions among Shannon, McCarthy, and Morison, the Rockefeller Foundation agreed it would fund the workshop. The Rockefeller Foundation reduced the grant from US$13,500 to US$7,500 [2]. The formal proposal to the Rockefeller Foundation was sent in September 1955 by McCarthy and stated in its introduction – I quote.

"We propose that a 2-month, 10-man study of artificial intelligence be carried out during the summer of 1956 at Dartmouth College in Hanover, New Hampshire. The study is to proceed based on the conjecture that every aspect of learning or any other feature of intelligence can in principle be so precisely described that a machine can be made to simulate it. An attempt will be made to find how to make machines use language, form abstractions and concepts, solve kinds of problems now reserved for humans, and improve themselves. We think that a significant advance can be made in one or more of these problems if a carefully selected group of scientists work on it together for a summer."

This proposal was the first time the term Artificial Intelligence was used, and John McCarthy, the main proposer, coined it. The term Artificial Intelligence (AI) was used to describe a set of diverse topics stated in the proposal, including natural language understanding by computers, neural networks, computational complexity, self-improvement or learning by computers, abstraction, randomness, and creativity.

As it transpired, many of the invitees attended for two weeks scattered over the eight weeks of the workshop. Only a few, including McCarthy, Minsky, and Ray Solomonoff, were present throughout the eight weeks from mid-June to mid-August 1956. Notable participants included Allen Newell and Herbert Simon, who later did seminal research on programming computers to prove theorems in elementary symbolic logic and machine learning. The group did not write a report giving the conclusions of the workshop. However, many papers based on the research done during those eight weeks were presented at conferences [2].

EPILOGUE

The Dartmouth College Artificial Intelligence conference is considered a turning point in the history of computing. The term Artificial Intelligence (AI) came into general use after this conference. Cybernetics with analog processing waned, and symbolic processing using digital computers thrived in AI research. In July 2006, Dartmouth College hosted a conference titled "The Dartmouth College Artificial Intelligence Conference: The next 50 years (AI@50)" [4], and five of the original participants, including McCarthy, attended along with around 50 active researchers in AI. The participants discussed the status of AI since the first Dartmouth workshop. At the conclusion of the conference, the participants generally agreed that AI is thriving. It is interesting to observe that the topics discussed in the Dartmouth workshop are now active research areas.

REFERENCES

[1] V. Rajaraman, "Turing test and after", Resonance, Indian Academy of Sciences, Volume 2, No. 8, August 1997, pp. 50–59.

[2] Ronald R. Kline, "Cybernetics, Automata Studies, and the Dartmouth Conference on Artificial Intelligence", IEEE Annals of History of Computing, Volume 33, Number 4, October-December 2011, pp. 5–16.

[3] C. E. Shannon and J. McCarthy (Editors), "Automata Studies", Princeton University Press, Princeton, New Jersey, USA, 1956.

[4] James Moor, "The Dartmouth College Artificial Intelligence Conference: The Next Fifty Years", AI Magazine, Volume 27, Number 4, 2006.

8

The First Commercial High-level Programming Language

PROLOGUE

The earliest high-level programming language, Plankalkül, was designed by Konrad Zuse in 1948. It was a binary-oriented non-von Neumann language that was not implemented. It was unknown outside Germany as it was developed in Germany during the Second World War [1]. The first persons to design and implement a high-level programming language for a stored program electronic digital computer were Halcombe Laning and Niel Zierlar in 1953 at MIT, USA. The language used single letters for variable names, could translate statements such as A = B + C, had built-in routines for trigonometric functions, and allowed simple loops. They wrote an assembly language program for translating programs written in their high-level language to machine instructions of the Whirlwind I computer [2]. This computer had a magnetic core RAM with 1024, 16-bit words. This small size of RAM was a severe limitation for writing a translator for the language, and it is to their credit that they wrote one that worked. The machine language compiled by their translator was about ten times longer than a hand-coded assembly language program to solve a problem. It was not widely used as it was inefficient. Research projects to design high-level computer languages were conducted in Germany and England in the mid-1950s. They, however, did not aim to obtain efficient object codes on commercial computers.

Programmers used assembly language during the 1950s to write all programs. Writing programs was time-consuming as one had to understand the architecture of the computer in addition to the algorithm to write an assembly language program. As one programmer said, "Programming was a hand-to-hand combat with the computer."

DEVELOPMENT OF FORTRAN

John Backus, a programmer at IBM's New York office, calculated that the cost of developing programs for IBM computers using assembly language was nearly the same as that of the computer hardware, which was relatively high in the 1950s. Besides this, the difficulty of programming in assembly language inhibited many engineers and scientists from using computers to solve their problems. He decided to develop a better language to simplify programming. In 1954, IBM released the Model 704 computer to solve numerical problems arising in science and engineering. It was the first computer with a hardware floating point arithmetic unit and three index registers. It used vacuum tubes and had 4K words (36 bits/word) RAM built using magnetic cores, magnetic tapes as secondary memory, a card reader, and a printer as I/O. It cost US$2 million. In December 1953, John Backus wrote a memo to his manager explaining that programming costs using assembly language were becoming very high and there was a need to develop a higher level language that was easy to learn by non-programmers such as engineers and scientists and a translator to translate it to machine code. His proposal was quickly approved, and he was allowed to hire programmers to develop a high-level language and its translator. Backus was convinced that users would only accept such a language if the translator of the language produced machine code as efficient as that written by professional assembly language programmers to solve problems. Thus, from the outset, his aim was not only to design a high-level language appropriate to solve problems arising in science and engineering but also to make its translator produce machine code approaching the efficiency of a human coder [3].

Backus assembled a team to develop the system gradually, with new employees joining the team as the project progressed. The first person employed by Backus was Irving Ziller in January 1954, and Harlan Herrick joined in May. The third employee was Robert Nelson, a cryptographer, who was hired as a technical typist but soon became a programmer. Backus, Ziller, Herrick, and Nelson formed the core team that started designing the language.

John Backus **Harlan Herrick** **Irving Ziller** **Robert Nelson**

The initial IBM FORTRAN development team (Photos courtesy IBM archives)

The team did not consider language design as important as the design of a translator to produce an efficient code. By November 1954, the group prepared a 30-page report: "Preliminary Report, Specifications for the IBM Mathematical FORmulaTRANslating System FORTRAN." In this report, they proposed variable names of one or two characters, recursively defined arithmetic expressions that could have constants, floating point and integer variables, arithmetic statements, conditional branch and loop statements, subscripted variables with up to three subscripts, and functions. It also had sections on input and output written by Roy Nutt, loaned to IBM by the United Aircraft Corporation. The team did not pay much attention to debugging programs in the preliminary version, called FORTRAN I. Backus mentions that their approach to language design in the early days was quite casual. The team added features to the language they thought would be useful as they went along [3].

After releasing the preliminary report, Backus and his team gave five to six talks to prospective users who had ordered IBM 704, expecting feedback to improve the language. They were disappointed as they hardly got any suggestions. Most customers wondered whether the translator could produce efficient code.

The team could compile FORTRAN I programs for IBM 704 and were very happy and somewhat surprised by the translator's efficiency in producing object code as good as that of an assembly language programmer. However, FORTRAN I had many shortcomings, particularly poor error checking of the source language and short length of variable names. The team improved it and developed FORTRAN II, which had six-character variable names (possibly because IBM 704 had 36-bit words and each word could store six 6-bit characters), better handling of subscripted variables, FORMAT statements, computed GO TO, CONTINUE, and EQUIVALENCE statement and function definitions.

COMPILER DESIGN

Backus and his team should have considered the difficulty of writing an efficient translator for FORTRAN II. They thought it would take six months to write a translator after designing the language, but it took two years. The four-member team that developed the language was too small, and nine more members were added as and when there was a need. Backus, with twelve co-authors, presented a research paper describing the first version of FORTRAN II and its compiler at the Western Joint Computer Conference in Los Angeles in February 1957 [4]. In this paper, they mention that after attending a one-day course on FORTRAN II, and with the help of a manual, a novice programmer could write a FORTRAN II program to solve a scientific problem in 4 hours, which he estimated would have taken him three days plus an unknown amount of time to debug it if he had used assembly language. The FORTRAN II program written by the novice had 47 statements, and the compiled program had 1000 machine instructions. The compiled program was almost as efficient as the manually written assembly program.

The FORTRAN compiler had 24,000 assembly language instructions and took 18 person years of effort to develop. FORTRAN was officially released in April 1957 and distributed free to all IBM 704 installations. By November 1958, a survey of 26 IBM 704 users revealed that more than half used FORTRAN for more than 50% of their programs and some for 80%. By 1962, FORTRAN was the primary language used by scientists and engineers to write programs.

EPILOGUE

FORTRAN was the first high-level language to be released commercially and became highly successful due to its simplicity and the efficiency of the code it produced. Programmers wrote FORTRAN compilers for many computer models. It made computers accessible to scientists and engineers who did not use computers earlier as they found assembly language programming tedious and error-prone. Improved versions of FORTRAN appeared regularly, starting with FORTRAN IV in 1962. The latest version is Fortran 2023. Over 200 high-level programming languages have appeared after FORTRAN, but Fortran is still widely used by scientists and engineers to program high-performance computers 67 years after its invention! Fortran 2023 is very modern and has incorporated many features that simplify parallel programming. Tony Hoare, Turing award winner, said in 1982, "I don't know what the language of the year 2000 will look like, but I know it will be called Fortran"—how prophetic!

REFERENCES

[1] Wolfgang K. Giloi, Konrad Zuse's Plankalkül: The First High-Level, "non-von Neumann" Programming Language, IEEE Annals of the History of Computing, Vol. 19, No. 2, 1997.

[2] J. H. Laning and N. Zierler, A Program for Translating Mathematical Equations for Whirlwind I, January 1954. http://www.softwarepreservation.org/projects/FORTRAN/paper/Laning%20and%20Zierler%201954.pdf/view

[3] John Backus, The History of FORTRAN I, II, and III, ACM SIGPLAN Notices, Vol. 13, No. 8, August 1978.

[4] John Backus and 12 others, The FORTRAN Automatic Coding System, Proceedings of the Western Joint Computer Conference, February 1957.

9

Programs that Play Board Games

PROLOGUE

Ever since the advent of modern electronic computers, scientists started wondering whether they could be programmed to exhibit intelligence similar to that of humans. John McCarthy, when he was an Assistant Professor of Mathematics at Dartmouth College in Hanover, New Hampshire, in 1955, proposed along with Marvin Minsky of MIT, Nathaniel Rochester of IBM, and Claude Shannon of Bell Laboratories to the Rockefeller Foundation to sponsor a workshop on "Artificial Intelligence" a word coined by McCarthy. (See Anecdote 7). Many Artificial Intelligence (AI) pioneers attended this workshop, and it catalyzed research on natural language processing, machine learning, game playing with computers, and neural networks.

McCarthy moved to MIT in 1957 and started a thriving AI group with Minsky. McCarthy was dissatisfied with Fortran and wanted a theoretically sound language for manipulating non-numeric data appropriate to solve problems in AI. He led a group that designed a list processing language, LISP, to manipulate strings easily. LISP pioneered many novel ideas in programming languages, including automatic storage management, dynamic typing, and recursion. Several dialects of LISP have appeared over the years. Besides Fortran, it is one of the programming languages still used sixty-seven years after its invention!

Playing board games is challenging. It requires strategic thinking, memory, decision-making, and learning from mistakes made in earlier plays, traits we associate with intelligence. Early researchers in AI wrote programs for computers to play board games with humans and attempted to endow these programs with abilities as good as those of humans. It was the beginning of serious research in AI.

TWO SCHOOLS OF AI

Two different approaches to solving AI problems evolved in the mid-1950s. One was to write programs that simulate how humans solve problems using their knowledge and logical reasoning. The other was to mimic a human brain, which consists of a complex interconnected network of neurons, on a computer and train it to solve problems. Mimicking the human brain and training it requires enormous computing power and massive data for training. These became available only around 2010, and a field of AI called *Deep Learning* evolved and is currently (2024) dominant.

COMPUTER PROGRAMS TO PLAY BOARD GAMES

Board games such as chess provide a very complex environment, and the rules are clear; a winning position is well-defined, requires strategic thinking ahead of several moves, and appeals to the general public, challenging AI researchers to write computer programs that could play as well as humans and even beat them, thereby exhibiting intelligence. Researchers chose two board games: Checkers and Chess. Of these, Checkers is relatively simple. A.L. Samuel wrote a Checkers playing program during 1958–59 for an IBM 704 using assembly language. It was a clever program that learnt from its mistakes and improved its game. It beat Robert Nealy, one of the foremost Checkers players in the US [2]. A group at the University of Alberta wrote a Checkers-playing program called *Chinook*. It consisted of a book of openings, a library of opening moves played by grandmasters, a deep search algorithm, an optimized move evaluation function, and an endgame database. It beat the world champion Checkers player in 1994.

Chess is several orders of magnitude more complex than Checkers and is a favourite of AI researchers. Even before computers were built, developing algorithms to play chess was a challenge. Claude Shannon took up this challenge [3]. He estimated that there are around 10^{120} chess games, and it is impossible to find the best move in a game analytically. In 1949, he presented a paper at a conference of the Institute of Radio Engineers (USA) in which he described two types of heuristic tree-search algorithms to play chess, called Type A and Type B. Type A is a brute force search that evaluates all legal moves by a player up to a reasonable depth (around 4). Type B drastically reduces the number of moves by eliminating many unpromising moves using a heuristic. Since then, most chess-playing programs have used Shannon's idea, and their variations are based on "better" heuristics and examining patterns of pieces on a chess board to make an appropriate move.

In 1948, Turing and Champernowne wrote a program to play chess called Turbo Champ, which was not executed on a computer. Dietrich Prinz wrote one of the first chess programs in 1951 and ran it on the Ferranti Mark I computer at Manchester University.

Several computer scientists, beginning with A. Newell, J.C. Shaw, and H.A. Simon, in 1957, wrote chess-playing programs using Shannon's Type B search. These programs primarily differed in the heuristics used to prune the search tree. Computers were slow, and computer chess programs could not beat a good player. In 1968, David Levy, a chess grandmaster, and John McCarthy were at a party hosted by Donald Michie (an AI researcher), and they played a friendly game of chess in which Levy easily beat McCarthy. McCarthy told him not to be cocky and that a computer program will beat him in 10 years. Levy placed a bet that no computer program would beat him till 1978. He placed his bet based on his assessment of existing chess-playing programs. Others joined in the stake, and the kitty bulged to £ 1250. Levy played a match with Chess 4.7, a program Larry Atkin, Keith Gorlen, and David Slate of Northwestern University wrote on CDC Cyber 176 in 1978. By 1978, computers were relatively fast, and chess-playing programs had started using Shannon's Type A search, which explored many more moves than the Type B search. Chess 4.7 was considered one of the best chess-playing programs in the world at that time. Levy won the match 4.5 to 1.5 and his bet.

Meanwhile, computer scientists started building special-purpose computers to play chess. The earliest, *Belle*, was constructed at Bell Labs by Joe Condon (hardware) and Ken Thompson (software) in 1976, adding special hardware units to a PDP-11. The algorithm used Shannon's

Type A search. The Association for Computer Machinery (ACM), USA, started the United States Computer Chess Championship in 1970. With better hardware, Belle improved over the years and, in 1980, won the ACM computer chess championship. It reached a chess grandmaster-level capability in 1983. It was retired in 1986.

Claude Shannon giving the World Chess Championship Prize to Feng-Hsuing Hsu in 1989 (Photo courtesy Feng-Hsuing Hsu)

In 1987, Carnegie Mellon University students Feng-hsiung Hsu, Thomas Anantharaman, Murray Campbell, and Andreas Nowatzyk built a special-purpose chess-playing computer called ChipTest using spare chips and wrote an innovative search program. Hsu joined IBM, and a chess-playing computer named Deep Thought was built as a successor to ChipTest using two special-purpose chips and 200 commodity chips working in parallel. It became the fastest chess-playing computer and reached the grandmaster level of play. It beat Levy 4–0 in 1989.

Deep Blue vs Kasparov Chess match
(Photo courtesy of Wikipedia)

The final triumph of computer chess was the contest between Gary Kasparov, the world chess champion, and IBM Deep Blue. IBM Deep Blue was a parallel high-performance computer with hardware enhancements to play chess and could evaluate 200 million chess positions per second. A team led by Hsu wrote a chess-playing program and challenged Kasparov to play. Their program could recognize the positions of various pieces on a chess board, look 20 moves ahead, and learn from past games. Kasparov won the first match 4–2 in 1996. The software team tweaked the program, and Kasparov played a rematch in May 1997. Deep Blue won 3.5 to 2.5 and established AI's supremacy in chess. Kasparov was a poor loser and did not accept the defeat, claiming the IBM team cheated and that a grandmaster was helping it during the game!

Since Deep Blue's historic win, considerable progress in computer chess-playing programs has occurred. Today, programs on PCs can play at a grandmaster's level. Chess players, including those within the world's top 10, routinely play against computers to hone their skills.

PROGRAMMING TO PLAY GO

The next challenge for game-playing AI programs was the Chinese board game GO, popularised in Japan. Two players play the game on a 19 × 19 board. One player has white stones and the other black stones. Players place their stones in a square to surround the opponent's stones and capture maximum territory. The rules are simple, but the alternatives available to a player are enormous, making it a very complex game. It is estimated that GO has around 10^{170} board positions compared to about 10^{120} for chess. David Silver of DeepMind, a British AI company (since acquired by Google), and his research team took GO as a challenging game to be played by a computer. They started exploring methods of programming it to play at a championship level.

GO Board, 19 × 19 grid
(Photo courtesy Wikipedia)

David Silver
(Photo courtesy David Silver)

DeepMind used a combination of tree search and deep neural networks. It started by training the neural networks to play GO by playing against amateur players, and after learning the game, it made the neural nets play with themselves tens of thousands of times. It used a technique called reinforcement learning and improved the abilities of neural networks to learn from their mistakes. The final program, AlphaGo, played against 18-time world champion Lee Sedol in March 2016 and beat him 4 to 1. Since then, AlphaGo has always won against humans. AlphaGo has revealed many hitherto unknown and unimagined moves that have surprised champions. [4]

AlphaGo Zero succeeded AlphaGo in October 2017. It did not use human games for training but generated games it played with itself, improving its performance to the world champion level. Not using data from humans has profound implications. As stated by DeepMind's developers, "human data is expensive, often unreliable, and sometimes just not available" and self-training would lead to superhuman AI systems. AlphaGo Zero is estimated to have cost $25 million. Alpha Zero succeeded AlphaGo Zero in 2018, which was self-trained and played GO, chess, and Shogi (a Japanese board game similar to chess). Alpha Zero's chess-playing program beat the world champion chess-playing program Stockfish. The next version, called MuZero, was released in 2019. It could generate games and train by playing with itself without being given a database of rules. It could be trained to play GO, chess, Shogi, or each of a suite of 57 Atari games at a champion's level.

EPILOGUE

AI researchers call chess-playing programs the *Drosophila of AI*. Biologists use the common fruit fly drosophila in experiments because it is accessible, inexpensive, familiar, breeds fast, and yet generates valuable knowledge on more complex life forms. This choice had far-reaching implications in the development of genetics in the 20th century. In the same vein, the decision of AI researchers to choose chess-playing programs as a topic of research and development has led to many AI methods, such as search algorithms, the development of heuristics, the application of logic, machine learning, and the training of neural nets.

REFERENCES

[1] http://jmc.stanford.edu/articles/dartmouth/dartmouth.pdf

[2] Edward A. Feigenbaum and Julian Feldman (Editors), Computers and Thought, McGraw-Hill Book Company Inc., 1963 (Contains 20 seminal articles in AI).

[3] www.chessprogramming.org/Claude_Shannon chessprogramming.org has all the information one needs on the use of AI in chess.

[4] Adam Rogers, What Deep Blue and AlphaGo can teach us about Explainable AI.
https://www.forbes.com/sites/forbestechcouncil/2019/05/09/what-deep-blue-and-alphago-can-teach-us-about-explainable-ai/?sh=2da1717b52fd

10

Integrated Circuits

PROLOGUE

The advent of transistors was the first great technological revolution that led to more reliable computers. John Bardeen, Walter Brattain, and William Shockley demonstrated the prototype germanium point-contact transistor at the Bell Telephone Laboratories in 1947, followed by a more reliable junction transistor in 1948. Transistors did not have a filament, consumed a thousand times less power, and were highly reliable. They were commercially produced in 1951. The computer industry was tardy in adopting transistors. IBM released model 608, which used transistors only in 1955. A successful computer to be fully transistorised was IBM 7070 in 1958. IBM 1401, released in 1959, was the first widely used transistorised computer.

Computer circuits use many components such as resistors, diodes, and capacitors besides transistors. These components were mounted on a printed circuit board and interconnected by soldering the leads to copper strips printed on the other side. As circuits became more complex, the number of soldered connections increased, and the circuits became unreliable. The wires connecting the components became long, limiting the speed of the systems. These drawbacks led engineers to examine methods of fabricating transistors, resistors, and capacitors on a single semiconductor wafer called an Integrated Circuit (IC).

JACK KILBY'S INTEGRATED CIRCUITS

Jack St. Clair Kilby [1] and Robert Noyce independently invented ICs. Kilby invented an IC using germanium while at Texas Instruments

(TI) in 1958. Noyce invented a planar silicon IC in 1959 at Fairchild Semiconductors in Palo Alto, California.

Kilby obtained a B.S. degree from the University of Illinois, Urbana-Champaign, in 1947 and joined Centralab, an electronics company in Milwaukee that designed and manufactured radios, televisions, and hearing aids. He attended evening classes and obtained an M.S. degree from the University of Wisconsin, Milwaukee in 1950. Centralab sent Kilby to participate in workshops on transistors organized by Bell Laboratories, and he learnt how to design transistorised circuits. Returning to Centralab, he used transistors to design hearing aids. He realised that small companies could not invest enough to develop solid-state devices and circuits and explored opportunities in larger semiconductor companies. He was offered a job in Texas Instruments (TI) research laboratories and joined in the spring of 1958. As a new employee, he was ineligible for summer vacation and was left undisturbed in the research laboratories. He knew the difficulty of fabricating complex circuits with transistors on printed circuit boards. He wondered whether all components of an electronic circuit could be fabricated on a single germanium semiconductor. Resistors were easy to fabricate by varying the dimensions of the germanium strips. Capacitors could be fabricated by sandwiching an insulating layer between germanium conductors. Fabricating germanium transistors was the primary process. Most digital circuits do not require inductors. Thus, the main challenge in building an IC was interconnecting these components grown on a germanium base. Kilby solved this problem by using thin gold wires to interconnect them. This interconnection method was inelegant and difficult to automate. He fabricated an oscillator utilising this process on August 28, 1958. Nowadays, this process is called a hybrid IC. Kilby was honoured with the Nobel Prize for this invention in 2000. He passed away in 2005.

Jack Kilby

The first IC fabricated by Kilby

(Photos courtesy Wikipedia)

ROBERT NOYCE'S INTEGRATED CIRCUIT

Robert Noyce obtained a B.S. in physics from Grinnell College, Iowa, in 1949. He was an all-rounder, a champion swimmer and diver, an Oboe player, an actor, and a prankster. He played a prank and was almost thrown out of college. His physics professor, impressed by his brilliance, saved him. Noyce's classmates awarded him the Brown Derby Prize for being "the senior man who earned the best grades with the least work". Noyce obtained a Ph.D. in physics from MIT in 1953. Soon after graduation, he joined Philco Corporation, an electronics company in Philadelphia. Noyce was offered a position in Shockley Semiconductor Laboratory in 1956, which Shockley had started in 1955 in Palo Alto, California. Shockley chose Palo Alto because he grew up there, and it was near Stanford University. Shockley recruited many gifted scientists and engineers. He was a good scientist but a poor manager. In 1957, a core group of eight employees, which included Gordon Moore, William Noyce, and Jean Hoerni, named by Shockley as the *traitorous eight*, left his company because they did not like his management style. They started Fairchild Semiconductors, a Fairchild Camera and Instruments division, founded by Sherman Fairchild on the US East Coast. Noyce's passionate presentation on the future of semiconductor devices convinced Sherman Fairchild to invest in a division to manufacture them on the US West Coast. Noyce and his group advocated using silicon rather than germanium to build transistors. The first silicon transistor was designed and fabricated by Gordon Moore in 1958. In 1959, Hoerni developed a process to build transistors known as the planar process. This process reduced the cost of silicon transistors and improved their reliability. Soon after, Noyce invented a method of interconnecting semiconductor components, namely, transistors, resistors, and capacitors grown on a silicon substrate using the planar process by putting a layer of aluminium over them and etching away unwanted connections. His method of interconnecting the components was elegant compared to Kilby's and was suitable for mass production. All modern ICs use this technology. Noyce applied for a patent for his IC, which TI challenged in the courts. After approximately a decade of litigation, the two companies settled their dispute out-of-court by cross-licensing their patents.

Robert Noyce
(Photo courtesy Intel)

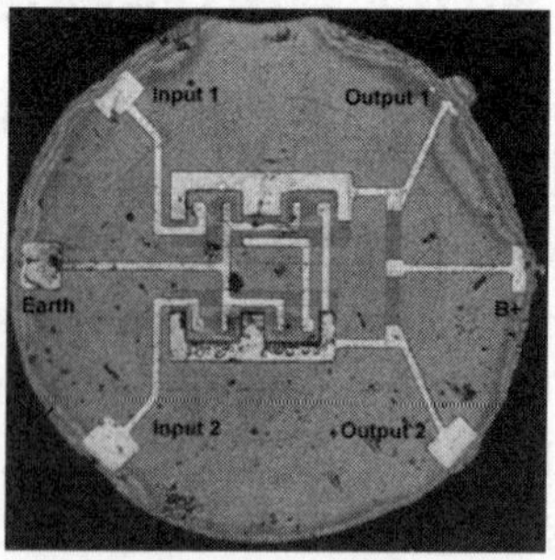

First IC chip of Noyce
(Photo courtesy Chip History)

Noyce suffered a heart attack in 1990 and passed away. He would have received the Nobel Prize along with Kilby for the invention of ICs but missed it as the Nobel prize is not awarded posthumously.

THE GROWTH OF IC MANUFACTURE

Early ICs were expensive to produce because the capital expense to set up mass-production assembly lines required large ultraclean rooms, photolithography units, precision cameras, and chemical etching units. The main advantages of ICs are their light weight and high reliability. The US aerospace industry, producing missiles with onboard computers for guidance, required lightweight, high-reliability components and was the major customer for ICs. Unlike consumer electronics and mainframe computer manufacturers, cost was not their primary consideration. About half a dozen Minuteman missiles were produced by the US aerospace industry every week in 1964. Each one of them used around 2000 ICs. Production systems for ICs required large volume sales to be economically sustainable. Orders from the manufacturers of Minuteman missiles in 1964 were crucial for sustaining early IC manufacturing companies. Another user of ICs was Apollo Guidance Computers. Approximately seventy-five were built starting in 1966 using around 5000 identical ICs each. This large order reduced the price of ICs from $1000 per chip to about $25 per chip.

The computer industry was not an early adopter of ICs because of their high cost. When prices came down, later models of PDP 8 by Digital Equipment Corporation began using them in 1968. IBM used ICs in IBM 360/85 in 1969. IBM System 370 computers, introduced in the 1970s, used ICs extensively. Since then, ICs have been the major components of all computers.

THE GROWTH OF THE IC INDUSTRY

Fairchild Semiconductor was a profitable company that pioneered many innovations. However, Noyce and his colleagues disliked the hierarchical structure of the company and the remote control by the parent company. Fairchild was not investing its profit in R&D and new technology. Noyce and Moore decided to start a new company, investing more in R&D and innovations in IC manufacturing. They left Fairchild and started Intel, a combination of the first two letters from Integrated Electronics in July 1968. When they found that a midwestern hotel chain was named Intelco, they bought the rights to use the name for $15,000. Intel got venture capitalist Arthur Rock to invest in the new company and invested their savings. Intel started in Mountain View, California, with a capital of $2.5 million in a building vacated by Union Carbide. It started with about a dozen employees. It promoted a non-hierarchical structure; all employees, including Noyce and Moore, sat in a hall with only small partitions separating them. It started operations by making memory chips that were easy to manufacture. Its first major success was the invention of the microprocessor in 1971(See Anecdote 31). Later, Intel dominated microprocessor manufacturing and designed path-breaking microprocessors, with its Pentium series dominating the market for several years. It has grown to a company employing around 130,000 persons and a market capitalisation of $135 billion in 2023.

The US government, which was a leading customer of ICs in its early days, wanted multiple suppliers as backups. It promoted new manufacturers by splitting orders. This policy of the US government led to the growth of the IC industry and competition. Several ex-employees of Fairchild Semiconductors (often called Fairchildren) started companies, including Advanced Micro Devices (AMD), National Semiconductor Corporation, and LSI Logic Corporation. The culture of venture capitalists, technical entrepreneurs with expertise in IC manufacture, and human resource availability from top-notch universities such as Stanford and the University of California, Berkeley promoted the growth of the IC industry in the San Francisco Bay area, which was soon known as Silicon Valley.

MOORE'S LAW

Gordon Moore, one of the founders of Fairchild Semiconductors, based on empirical data available to him since the time the first ICs were manufactured in 1960, predicted in an article he wrote in 1965 in the Electronics magazine [2] that the number of transistors in an IC would double every year. In 1975, he revised it and predicted doubling transistors on a chip every two years. This prediction was named "*Moore's Law*." Semiconductor manufacturers took Moore's prediction as a benchmark and a challenge to be met. Chip fabricators and suppliers of materials and components to the industry cooperated and provided better components, purer materials, and better fabrication techniques that doubled the number of transistors in a chip every two years, making Moore's law a self-fulfilling prophecy. As of 2023, no consensus exists on whether Moore's law is still valid. The number of transistors in Intel 4004, the first microprocessor, was 2300 in 1971. The latest microprocessor, Apple M2 Ultra, manufactured in 2023, has 134 billion transistors, an increase in transistor count by 5.8×10^7 in 52 years, closely following Moore's law. It is thus unclear whether Moore's law is dead! The number of transistors packed in an IC is the highest in flash memories. It is estimated to be 5.3 trillion in 2023 [3].

IC MANUFACTURE

The manufacturing of ICs primarily consists of three parts. They are design, fabrication, and testing. In the design phase, given the specifications of the IC, engineers draw the schematics of a transistor circuit showing how transistors, resistors, and capacitors are connected. This schematic is transformed into a layout design showing where the components are placed on a chip and connected. The design phase requires expert engineers who perform all these operations using an electronic design automation system (EDA). Companies only in the IC design space are called fabless companies. Until the early 1970s, most companies, such as Intel and TI, designed ICs and manufactured them in their silicon foundries, known as fabs. When ICs became more complex, establishing fabs became capital-intensive, costing around $150 million. Only large companies with deep pockets could set up fabs. Costly fabs led to the emergence of fabless companies in the mid-1970s, which primarily designed innovative ICs and outsourced manufacturing to fabs. Well-known fabless companies are Qualcomm, Nvidia, and Broadcom in the US and ARM in the UK, which are renowned for designing advanced microprocessors. China started many fabless companies designing low-end ICs when it opened its economy in the 1990s. TI established an IC design centre in Bangalore in 1985 to take advantage of the availability of well-educated and talented IC designers in India at a lower cost. Currently, there are over a dozen fabless IC design companies in India.

The second part is the chips' fabrication, assembly, and packaging, which are done in fabs. The IC production process consists of eight steps: silicon wafer processing, oxidation, photolithography, etching, film deposition, interconnecting, testing, and packaging. Fabs are classified based on the density of packing transistors in chips. The current terminology used is 65 nm, 7 nm, and 5 nm. This classification is more of a marketing term and is currently not directly proportional to transistor size, even though it was in the 1980s. Early fabs of the 1960s were in the range of a few μm (micro metre -10^{-6} metre), nominally proportional to gate width. Current fabs are in nm (nano metre – 10^{-9} metre) range. The most expensive unit in an IC fab is the photolithography unit. Nowadays, photolithography units use Extreme Ultraviolet (EUV) light. Manufacturing photolithography units for nm fabs requires high-precision engineering and the use of EUV. Currently (2023), ASML, a company in the Netherlands, is the only company with this capability [4].

Intel, TI, and several other companies established 10 μm fabs in the US in the 1960s. In the 1970s, it became 1 μm, down to 70 nm in the 2000s and 7 nm in the 2020s. In the late 1970s, Japan became a leader in designing and fabricating memories, followed by South Korea. Currently, the world's foremost fabs (5 nm, 3 nm) are built by TSMC in Taiwan, established in 1987, followed by Samsung in South Korea, Intel in the USA, and Kioxia in Japan. China, the UK, the Netherlands, Germany, Israel, and France also have several fabs of varying capabilities. Three companies are currently planning to establish 65 nm fabs in India. Setting up fabs requires capital expenditure to buy photolithography units, ultra-clean temperature and humidity-controlled rooms, ultra-clean water, chemicals, and well-trained human resources. A 65 nm fab will cost between \$2 and 3 billion. A 5 nm fab would cost between \$15 and 20 billion. 5 nm and 7 nm fabs manufacture high-end microprocessors such as A12 Bionic, used in high-end Apple smartphones and GPGPUs. 65 nm fabs are sufficient to manufacture low-end microprocessors such as Intel Pentium 4 and the ICs used by automobiles and consumer electronics.

The third phase is testing to ensure that the IC performs as per specifications, meets electrical specifications, and withstands the stresses of its intended environment. This phase is human resource intensive, and China is the current leader in testing.

EPILOGUE

ICs drive today's economy. It is a $500 billion industry and is growing. Each automobile has over 1200 ICs. Any gadget, such as a washing machine or a mobile phone, has several ICs. The IC production chain has become very complex and international. Automobile manufacturing during 2021 and 2022 was seriously affected due to a shortage of ICs manufactured in China, which shut down due to COVID-19. The US government realised in 2022 its over-dependence on other countries, particularly China, for its ICs and the strategic importance of ICs. It is currently (2023) investing $50 billion to build fabs in the US. It has plans to allocate $2 trillion over 15 years in R&D, fabs, and other infrastructure to become a leader in IC manufacturing. In a controversial move, the US government is also restricting (in 2023) the export of equipment and design know-how in advanced ICs to China.

REFERENCES

[1] N. Bhat, Jack St. Clair Kilby, Chip and Dare Saga, Resonance, Indian Academy of Sciences, Vol. 17, No. 11, November 2012, pp. 1035–1047. https://www.ias.ac.in/article/fulltext/reso/017/11/1035-1047

[2] Gordon E. Moore, Cramming more components onto Integrated Circuits, Electronics, Vol. 38, No. 8, April 19, 1965. https://hasler.ece.gatech.edu/Published_papers/Technology_overview/gordon_moore_1965_article.pdf

[3] Transistor Count, Wikipedia https://en.wikipedia.org/wiki/Transistor_count#Logic_functions

[4] Semiconductors-Fab Future, Insights, July 2021 https://www.synergiafoundation.org/sites/default/files/Insights%20July%20II.pdf

11

IBM 1401 Data Processing System—Darling of Small Businesses

PROLOGUE

Arthur K. Watson, the younger brother of Thomas J. Watson Jr., Executive Director of IBM, USA, became the general manager of IBM World Trade Corporation (IBM WTC), a wholly-owned subsidiary of IBM Corporation (USA), in 1952. This company looked after the sales and manufacture of IBM products outside the USA. Seventy-nine countries in the World had IBM installations, most of them called unit record equipment, namely, electro-mechanical machines that included accounting machines, card readers, card punches, sorters, and calculating punches. These machines were called unit records as they processed decks of 80-column cards, with each card punched with data about one entity, such as an item in stock or an employee. IBM WTC had manufacturing plants in Europe to meet the unique requirements of its European customers. There were IBM systems development laboratories in Paris, France, and Sindelfingen in Germany. The main competitors of IBM in Europe were International Computers and Tabulators of the UK and Compagnie Des Machines Bull in France. Bull introduced a machine named Bull Gamma 3 in 1952 that was a direct competitor of the IBM 407 accounting machine. Bull Gamma 3 had a small delay line memory, was more versatile than IBM 407, and cost less. Arthur Watson visited IBM headquarters and said he feared that Bull's machine might capture the IBM 407 market. This anxiety led to forming a committee of engineers, salespersons, and researchers to explore alternatives to IBM 407. This committee decided in early 1955 to design a Modular Accounting Calculator (MAC). However, even after several meetings, the committee did not finalise the specifications of MAC.

Meanwhile, the French and German engineers were restless and hosted a seven-week conference in Germany during June and July 1955 [1], inviting engineers from Endicott and Poughkeepsie. The conference's primary purpose was to choose the best design from the proposals of laboratories in the three countries for an accounting machine to compete with Bull Gamma 3. This machine was christened the Worldwide Accounting Machine (WWAM). French engineers' design used variable word lengths, an arithmetic unit using transistors, and magnetic core memory, and was accepted. The German engineers were designing a new printer for the WWAM with typefaces embossed on sticks. The French engineers spent a year at the Endicott and Poughkeepsie laboratories learning about transistor circuit design and manufacturing. On their return in 1956, they started designing WWAM. The main objective was to build a machine superior to and cheaper than Bull Gamma 3. The monthly rental was to be at most $2500. Soon, the group in France found that the projected cost was increasing. To reduce the price, they reverted to a machine with a manually wired plugboard—a backward step.

ENDICOTT LABORATORY ENTERS THE SCENE

The marketing head of IBM in New York was uncomfortable with the assignment of WWAM, which he considered an important future product, to an unknown group in France. In late 1956, the French group was still grappling with the problem of reducing the cost of WWAM. In February 1957, Ralph Palmer, the head of engineering at IBM headquarters, appointed Ralph G. Mork of the Endicott Laboratory to oversee the WWAM project. Mork examined the reason for the high cost of the French design. He found that it was due to electronics associated with the plugboard. He assigned the task of finding a solution to the problem to Francis Underwood, who had earlier participated in the meetings on WWAM. Underwood also found that the plugboard-based design was the culprit and decided to scrap it and use a stored-program design retaining the basic French design of variable length data and arithmetic using transistor circuits. He submitted a report with his design in August 1957. Meanwhile, Mork was transferred, and the management assigned his task to Charles Branscomb, a veteran IBM unit record equipment designer.

Branscomb reworked the cost of the French-designed machine and found that its rental would be equal to that of two IBM 407s and a calculating punch, making it unviable. Meanwhile, Underwood refined his design of WWAM and introduced the idea of variable length for data and instructions. The marketing staff of IBM was still not reconciled to the idea of giving the French group an important product design and manufacture. The project was in limbo as shifting it to IBM laboratories at Endicott would upset the French group. In late 1957, Thomas J. Watson Jr. was unhappy with the project's lack of progress. In March 1958, he moved the project to the Endicott laboratory. The head of the Endicott Laboratory appointed Branscomb as the manager and Underwood as the project's lead architect. The project was called Stored-Program Accounting and Calculating Equipment (SPACE) [1].

Francis Underwood **Charles Branscomb**
(Photo courtesy ibm.com)

The timing of the decision to proceed with the design of SPACE turned out to be fortuitous. Faster and more rugged card readers and card punches had been designed and were now available. A magnetic core memory had been designed for use in IBM 704 in early 1956 and standardised. IBM had set up an in-house junction transistor design and manufacturing line appropriate for digital circuits, as most existing transistor manufacturers were making them for radios and similar analog systems. IBM perfected standard modular system packaging for transistor-based switching systems using IBM-designed transistors. Printing was an essential requirement for business data processing systems. In its early machines, IBM used modified 407 accounting machines as printers. A chain printer that could print 132 characters per line and 600 lines per minute was designed in the Endicott Laboratory for use as a printer for future computers and was undergoing acceptance tests in 1958.

THE ARCHITECTURE OF IBM 1401

SPACE was renamed IBM 1401, and Underwood started the design in earnest. The main aim of Underwood was to provide the power of stored-program computers to a low-cost accounting machine with a rental of $2500 per month. It was to be a balanced system with a reliable processor and improved I/O. One of the most expensive parts of the machine was the main memory. Existing computers used fixed-length words for instructions and data. For example, IBM 650 used a fixed word length of 10 digits. This wasted memory space of around 40% as many instructions and data did not occupy the entire word. Underwood used variable-length words for data and instructions, requiring an end-of-word marker. Character code used 8 bits: 6 bits to code 64 symbols (decimal digits, upper case English letters, and special symbols such as +, $, and %), one parity bit for error detection, and an end-of-word mark bit. The parity bit was set to 1 or 0 to ensure that the number of 1s in the code of a character, including the parity bit, was odd.

The minimum memory size chosen for IBM 1401 was 1400 characters. Larger memory sizes of 2000, 4000, 8000, and 16000 digits were available. As memory was expensive, it was small to keep the rental low. The rental was $2500 for the basic machine. It was not much higher than the unit record machines it was to replace, making it competitive with Bull Gamma 3. Underwood picked an easy-to-remember one-character mnemonic for instructions as users of most of the early computers coded using machine language. Instruction codes were, for example, A to add, S to subtract, M to Move, and E to edit. Instruction length varied from 1 to 8 characters. Arithmetic instructions had two addresses. An instruction consisted of an instruction code and two operands' (data to be processed) addresses. Operands taken from the specified addresses were processed, based on the operation code, and stored in memory in one of the operand addresses. This "memory-to-memory" instruction did not use an accumulator, reduced program size, and the cost of the processor. Around 64 operations were available and were chosen carefully to aid business data processing.

IBM 1401 used an 87 kHz clock, and the time to read/write a character from memory was 11.5 microseconds. It used a serial arithmetic unit that performed arithmetic operations on pairs of digits one after the other, which was necessary as operand lengths were variable. It also reduced the cost of the processor. The processor performed 193,300 additions of 8-digit numbers and 25,000 multiplications of 6-digit by 4-digit numbers per minute [2].

IBM 1403 CHAIN PRINTER

One of the primary reasons for the success of IBM 1401 was the invention of the IBM 1403 chain printer by Fred Demer. Until its introduction, IBM 407's printer used many wheels, each embossed with the typefaces to print. IBM 1403 used a fast-moving horizontal chain with 240 engraved typefaces. The early model had five duplications of 48 typefaces to increase printing speed. The chain that looked like a bicycle chain rotated at a high speed. As the chain rotated, a character was selected by digital logic circuits and hit by an electronically timed hammer. The impact pressed the paper and an inked ribbon against the typeface, causing it to print. A perfectly aligned chain and nicely designed typefaces gave an excellent appearance to the printed reports.

The printer skipped blank spaces on forms, increasing the printing speed. The chain was interchangeable, allowing different character sets. The printer's speed was 600 lines per minute with 132 characters per line. If there were blank lines, the resultant speed would be higher.

IBM 1401 mainframe computer (Photo courtesy ibm.com)

IBM 1401 RELEASE

IBM announced several models of IBM 1401 Data Processing System with memory sizes of 1400, 2000, 4000, and 8000 characters, 1402 card reader/punch (800 cards/minute read and 250 cards/minute punch), 1403 printer (600 lines/minute print), and up to four IBM 729 Tape drives (2400-foot tape, 15,000 characters/minute transfer rate) in October 1959. IBM1401 was a computer for business data processing that would introduce unit record machine users to the new World of stored-program computers. It was also an I/O machine for the 7000 series scientific processors. The card reader input and printer output units of the expensive 7000 series machines were slow compared to their processing speed. IBM 1401, a cheaper computer, was used to read the input cards and store them on tape. The 7000 series machine would read the tape, process the data, and write the results on another tape, which IBM 1401 would read and print. The read/write operations of 1401 overlapped with processing by 7000, thereby optimally using the processing power of 7000.

The marketing group of IBM had forecast a sale of 5000 IBM 1401s during its lifetime. IBM was pleasantly shocked when it received 5200 orders within the first five weeks of its announcement. IBM 1401 was the most popular mainframe in the early 1960s and sold over 12,000 until IBM withdrew it in 1971. Half the mainframes installed in the World in the mid-1960s were IBM 1401.

IBM 1401 was gradually upgraded [2]. IBM added the IBM 1405 RAMAC disk drive (20 million character capacity) in 1961 and the IBM 1311 disk drive (up to 5) with removable 2 million character disk packs in 1962. IBM added a peripheral to read magnetic ink characters in cheques and another to optically recognise characters in 1961. IBM 1410, a faster machine, was announced in 1960 to allow users to upgrade 1401.

IBM 1401 SOFTWARE

IBM 1401 had an assembly language known as Symbolic Programming System (SPS) developed by Gary Mokotoff that ran on machines with 1400-character memory, a card reader/punch, and a printer in 1959. Tape drives and larger memories of 4000, 8000, 12000, and 16000 digits appeared later when the machine became popular. Autocoder, a more powerful assembly language, was developed for 1401s with a minimum of 4000-character memory and 4 Tape drives in 1961.

A vital software that led to the runaway success of IBM 1401 was the Report Program Generator (RPG). IBM 1401 was primarily designed to replace the IBM 407 accounting machine that produced stock registers and accounts receivable reports. IBM's marketing personnel were concerned about the lack of programming knowledge of accounting machine users. Bernie Silkowitz and Barbara Woods, two members of the applied programming department who were experienced accounting machine users, were assigned to design a report-writing program that would be easy for accounting machine users to learn. They designed a language that enabled users to specify the features of the required reports. It was called a Report Program Generator (RPG). In 1961, IBM released RPG for IBM 1401s with a card reader/punch, a printer, and a minimum of 4000-character memory. It became the most popular language for IBM 1401. RPG was continuously improved and made available also for machines with tapes and disks. RPG was copied by other computer manufacturers when they released competing computers.

IBM released a COBOL compiler for IBM 1401s with 4000-character memory and at least four tapes. It was, however, slow and unpopular. A FORTRAN II compiler was available for an 8000-character memory model, and FORTRAN IV was available for a 12000-character memory model with a disk drive.

IBM developed many application programs meant explicitly for businesses such as insurance companies, banks, and retailers and gave them free with IBM 1401. Many programs developed by users were available in the SHARE library that IBM managed.

IBM 1401 IN INDIA

One of the first computers installed in a business organization in India was an IBM 1401 in ESSO, an American oil marketing Company, in 1961. IBM-India, a subsidiary of IBM WTC, already had several customers of unit record machines in India. IBM sales group targeted them as potential customers of IBM 1401. In the 1960s, India had a huge balance-of-payments deficit, and the government restricted the import of non-essential items. Computers were considered not essential. There was also trepidation that computers would reduce the employment of white-collar workers. The government restricted importing computers.

To overcome the problem of import restrictions, IBM applied for licence to manufacture computers in India. In 1965, IBM proposed manufacturing IBM 029 keypunch machines in India with 80% locally sourced components, exporting them, and earning hard currency (US Dollars). With this earning, IBM would import used IBM 1401s, refurbish them, and rent/sell them to customers in India. After usual bureaucratic delays, this program started in 1968. IBM 360 was introduced in the USA in 1965 and replaced IBM 1401s in many organizations that returned their rented IBM 1401s. IBM sent these to the India plant set up in Mumbai. IBM steeply discounted the prices of these used machines and billed IBM-India a non-transparent, low inter-company billing price. Thus, the import price of an IBM 1401 was similar to that of the exported IBM 029 keypunches. By 1971, IBM 1401 was the most popular computer in India, with nearly 100 installations. The annual rental for a high-end 1401 (8000-character memory), 4 Tapes, 2 model 1311 disks) was around ₹850,000 (US$ 190,000 at the then prevailing exchange rate) [3]. It is interesting to note that IBM withdrew IBM 1401 from the US market in 1971. Customers accused IBM of profiteering by renting obsolete used machines. In its defence IBM maintained that it was not renting a machine but providing computing service. The rental included the services of maintenance engineers and systems engineers who assisted users with system design and even in developing programs. To its credit, IBM's services were excellent. IBM also trained a large number of system designers and programmers in India.

When I was heading the computer centre at the Indian Institute of Technology, Kanpur, an IBM 1401 was installed as an I/O machine for the IBM 7044—the only 7000 series computer in India.

EPILOGUE

IBM 1401 marked a breakpoint in the history of computing. Several features of IBM 1401 made it a darling of small businesses. It was low-cost, with a rent comparable with a set of unit record machines. It was highly reliable and worked for months without needing repair. It had an excellent high-speed printer. It was easy to program with RPG. Numerous application programs were available. Tape drives allowed users to store large master files and update them with card or tape-based transaction files.

Most IBM equipment in the early 1950s had a staid look—dark grey with rounded edges. Thomas Watson Jr. wanted to give a modern look to IBM machines and hired Eliot Noyes, a gifted industrial designer, to design the covers of the new machines [4]. It resulted in IBM 1401 having sharp corners and fancy blue paintwork. When IBM dominated the mainframe computer market with the introduction of IBM 1401, the media named IBM "The Big Blue".

REFERENCES

[1] Charles J. Bashe et al., *IBM's Early Computers*, The MIT Press, Cambridge, MA, 1986.

[2] Robert Garner and Fredrick Dill, *The Legendary IBM 1401 Data Processing System*, IEEE Solid-state Circuits Magazine, Winter 2010, pp. 28–39.

[3] V. Rajaraman, History of Computing in India (1955–2010), IEEE Computer Society, https://history.computer.org/pubs/2012-12-rajaraman-india-computing-history.pdf

[4] Martin Campbell-Kelly et al., *Computer—A History of the Information Machine*, Routledge, New York, NY, 2014.

12

Who Designed COBOL?

PROLOGUE

Professor H.V. Sahasrabuddhe, with whom I had written a book on COBOL Programming in 1980, sent me the URL: https://www.cnbc.com/2020/04/06/new-jersey-seeks-cobol-programmers-to-fix-unemployment-system.html in April 2020. My thoughts went down memory lane when COBOL was the reigning king.

During the Y2K problem, COBOL coders were in great demand, and I thought COBOL died after that. I was surprised when I read recently [1] that COBOL has over 220 billion lines of code *in use today*, mainly in financial institutions in the USA, which is 80% of code in daily use on mainframes! Although many attempts were made to rewrite old COBOL code, it is costly, and organizations using mainframes are afraid to touch "working code" on them. What was more surprising was that 1.5 billion lines of COBOL code *are still written* yearly!

Grace Murray Hopper is often called the designer of COBOL. It is incorrect, as we will see in this anecdote [2].

FLOW-MATIC: THE FIRST LANGUAGE FOR BUSINESS DATA PROCESSING

Grace Murray Hopper was a mathematics professor before she volunteered to join the US Navy when the Second World War started. The Navy sent her to program the Harvard Mark 1 relay computer in 1944. She did not know how to program, but learned quickly and became an expert programmer. She later joined the UNIVAC group at Remington Rand, where she was assigned to promote UNIVAC I for Business Data Processing (BDP). She soon found out that business managers were wary of mathematical formulae. Working with managers convinced her that using English keywords and a program written using English-like statements without any mathematical formulae would be more acceptable to them as they could read and understand how programs implement business rules. She proposed developing a high-level language for BDP in late 1953, designed one by 1955 and called it B-0. It impressed Remington Rand's management, and her group was encouraged to design a more robust language. Subsequently, her group designed FLOW-MATIC, ready for use in 1959. Its primary feature was separating the definition of data to be used by the program from the procedure, expressed using English-like sentences.

```
INPUT INVENTORY FILE A; PRICE FILE B;
OUTPUT PRICED INVENTORY FILE C.
COMPARE PRODUCT #A WITH PRODUCT
#B. IF GREATER, GO TO OPERATION 10; IF
EQUAL, GO TO OPERATION 5; OTHERWISE
GO TO OPERATION 2. TRANSFER A TO D;
WRITE ITEM D; JUMP TO OPERATION 8.
REWIND B; CLOSE OUT FILE C AND D;
STOP.                (FLOW-MATIC)
```

Flavour of FLOW-MATIC Code
(Image courtesy inf.fu-berlin.de)

Grace Murray Hopper
(Photo courtesy Wikipedia)

The availability of FLOW-MATIC to program UNIVAC I was considered a competitive advantage for Remington Rand, and other companies began developing language for BDP. IBM designed COMTRAN, Honeywell FACT, and the US Air Force AIMACO. These languages were incompatible.

GENESIS OF CODASYL

While companies were developing languages for BDP, IBM released FORTRAN in 1957. Scientists and engineers started using FORTRAN. A group of American and European Computer Scientists met in Zurich in 1958 and specified ALGOL 58 as a standard programming language for numeric intensive computing. Time was thus ripe to design a common language for business computing. Mary Hawes of Burroughs

Corporation met Saul Gorn, head of the University of Pennsylvania computer center, at the Western Joint Computer Conference in March 1959 and requested him to convene a meeting of academia, industry, and users to discuss the possibility of designing a machine-independent programming language for BDP. He convened a meeting in April 1959 at the University of Pennsylvania. Seven persons, including Grace Hopper, attended this meeting. The meeting resolved that it was a good idea to design a machine-independent language for BDP and to request Charles Phillips of the US Department of Defence to sponsor another meeting with more participants to discuss this. Phillips agreed, and a meeting was held on May 28-29,1959, at Washington D.C. that was attended by 15 representatives of government departments, one academic, 10 users' representatives, and 15 representatives of computer manufacturers: Burroughs, GE, Honeywell, IBM, NCR, Philco, RCA, Remington Rand, Sylvania, and ICT. Bob Bemer of Honeywell suggested that this group be named CODASYL (Conference on Data Systems Languages). The group at this meeting decided that BDP required a machine-independent language that should use simple English statements and be usable by business-oriented persons and that the language designers must not be concerned about how to compile it. The group also formed three groups to design the language with short, intermediate, and long-range objectives [3]. The executive committee supervised these groups. The goal of the short-range group was to study FLOW-MATIC, AIMACO, and COMTRAN and propose a short-range composite approach to design a machine-independent, business-oriented programming language (good at least for the next year or two) and report by September 1959 to CODASYL executive committee.

SHORT-RANGE GROUP'S WORK ON COBOL

Joseph Wegstein of the National Bureau of Standards (USA) chaired the short-range committee with eight more members. Two sub-committees were formed, one under the chairmanship of Mary Hawes (Burroughs) to design "data descriptions" and the other under the chairmanship of Jean Sammet (Sylvania) to design "procedural statements." These committees met regularly several times and submitted preliminary language specifications to CODASYL on 28 August 1959. The committee suggested dividing the language into three parts: an environment division to describe the machine in which the program will be compiled and the one where it will be executed; a data division to describe the data to be used; and a procedure division that defined the set of verbs to be used and the way they will operate on data. The group wanted more time—till December 1959 to finalise the language description. While this group was working, Honeywell released a language, FACT, in October 1959 that was superior to existing business languages. There was pressure from the intermediate-range committee to incorporate the features of FACT in the language proposed by the short-range committee. However, it was too late to rework the language the short-range committee designed. As a compromise, CODASYL formed a smaller six-member group of industry representatives that worked continuously for two weeks and presented a final language specification in November 1959. CODASYL discussed this and requested the group to draft a document. A document titled "COBOL—Specifications for a Common Business Oriented Language" was given to CODASYL in December 1959. CODASYL accepted this document in January 1960 and edited it. The US Government Printing Office published it in April 1960.

FLAVOUR OF COBOL

A COBOL program is divided into four parts called DIVISIONS. These are IDENTIFICATION DIVISION, which identifies the program and its author; ENVIRONMENT DIVISION, which specifies the computer and the peripherals used to compile the program and run it (indicating that computer X can compile it and any other computer Y can execute it); DATA DIVISION which defines the files and the description of records in the files and PROCEDURE DIVISION which describes the sequence of operations performed on the input files giving output files. Typical statements in the DATA DIVISION are:

Cover of COBOL Report
(Photo courtesy Wikipedia)

```
DATA DIVISION.
FILE SECTION.
FD OLD-STOCK-REGISTER
   VALUE OF ID IS 'STOCKDATA'
DATA RECORD IS OR-RECORD.
   01 OR-RECORD.
   02 OR-ITEM CODE PICTURE 9999.
   02 OR-ITEM-NAME PICTURE X(20.
   02 OR-QTY-IN-STOCK PICTURE 9999.
   02 FILLER PICTURE X(52).
```

Typical PROCEDURE DIVISION statements are:

```
MOVE STUDENT-ROLL-NO TO REP-NO.
READ STUDENT-FILE.
WRITE REPORT-RECORD.
GO TO READ-DATA.
ADD BASIC-PAY,DEARNESS-PAY GIVING GROSS-PAY.
SUBTRACT ISSUED-ITEMS FROM STOCK.
MULTIPLY RETAIL-PRICE BY DISCOUNT
                      GIVING NET-PRICE.
DIVIDE A BY B GIVING C ROUNDED
             ON SIZE ERROR GO TO XXX.
IF LOW-BIT = 0
   DISPLAY "THE NUMBER IS EVEN"
ELSE
   DISPLAY "THE NUMBER IS ODD"
STOP RUN.
```

These examples show that COBOL sentences are easy to read but verbose. COBOL uses over 300 reserved words that are not easy to remember. A well written COBOL program is self-documenting.

EPILOGUE

As soon as the official COBOL specifications were published, computer manufacturers were racing to write a COBOL compiler and show that it worked and was machine-independent. RCA and UNIVAC were the first to enter the race. On December 6-7, 1960, RCA and UNIVAC II computers ran the same COBOL program with minor changes in the ENVIRONMENT division. They gave the same results, showing that the language was genuinely machine-independent. CODASYL formed a Task Force that invited suggestions from users and manufacturers regarding their experience in compiling and using COBOL. Based on these suggestions, an improved version called COBOL-61 was published. The US Department of Defence forced program developers to use COBOL-61 in all defence contracts as it was portable. COBOL became the primary language for business programming. An ANSI standard COBOL appeared in 1968 with several desirable changes to COBOL-61. COBOL evolved and underwent four significant revisions to include structured programming ideas and object orientation. Microfocus, an American company, is currently a major vendor of COBOL. An open-source COBOL compiler is also available on the Web. COBOL is alive and kicking.

REFERENCES

[1] Jonathan Sayles, COBOL and the Enterprise Business Programming Paradigm, February 16, 2019, https://developer.ibm.com/mainframe/2019/02/26/cobol-and-the-enterprise-business-programming-paradigm/

[2] Jean E. Sammet, The Real Creators of COBOL, IEEE Software, March/April 2000, pp. 30–32.

[3] Jean E. Sammet, Brief Summary of the Early History of COBOL, Annals of the History of Computing, Vol. 7, No. 4, October 1985, pp. 288–303.

13

The Story of Digital Equipment Corporation

PROLOGUE

A team led by Jay Forrester built Whirlwind, the first real-time digital computer in the world, at the Massachusetts Institute of Technology (MIT) in 1953 (Anecdote 4). While building Whirlwind, Jay Forrester invented magnetic core memory in 1951 and used it as its main memory. Kenneth Olsen, a master's electrical engineering student at MIT, built a magnetic core memory test computer (MTC) for Whirlwind in a record time of nine months using functional modules that could be quickly built and tested [1]. MIT gave the Whirlwind computer's design to IBM to make it a product for use in the SAGE air-defence system. MIT sent Olsen to IBM in 1953 to transfer the technology of the Whirlwind. He worked with IBM engineers for 13 months until the first computer (IBM AN/FSQ-7) was ready for use in SAGE. He was appalled by the bureaucratic functioning of IBM and was happy to return to MIT [1].

Meanwhile, MIT disbanded the Whirlwind project, and its research and development team moved to MIT Lincoln Laboratory, a laboratory set up by the US Department of Defence, in Lexington, Massachusetts, a few kilometres from MIT's campus at Cambridge. On his return from IBM, Olsen joined his former colleagues at the Lincoln Laboratory. In 1955, Wesley Clerk designed a transistorised version of Whirlwind named TX-0 (Transistorised Experimental Computer Zero). It used 18-bit words, of which 2 bits were for operation code and 16 bits to address a 64 K word memory—huge by the then prevailing standards. Of the four operations available, the 2-bit operation code 00 stored data in memory, 01 added,10 was a conditional branch, and 11 was an operator that appended more bits from the address part of the word to code numerous extra operations. Olsen was the engineer in charge of building it. He used the newly announced Philco surface barrier transistors that were fast and suitable for building digital circuits. TX-0 used a teletype with paper tape as the input/output unit. It also had a video display device and a light pen input. Olsen designed a set of modular logic circuits with transistors and used them as building blocks of TX-0. TX-0 was ready in 1956. The engineers at Lincoln Laboratory used it as an interactive single-user computer. Some call it the first personal computer, although it cost over $100,000. In 1956, Lincoln Laboratory engineers started building TX-2, a 36-bit computer to follow TX-0. Olsen built many of the logic circuits of the TX-2 computer. Lincoln Laboratory kept part of the memory of TX-0 for use with TX-2 and moved TX-0 with 4K word memory to MIT in July 1958. TX-0 was thrown open to students at MIT [2], and the Artificial Intelligence Laboratory students used it extensively, which led to the "hacker" culture.

DIGITAL EQUIPMENT CORPORATION FOUNDED

Kenneth Olsen always wanted to be an entrepreneur. For funds, he approached a venture capital firm, American Research and Development (ARD), one of the earliest in the US, co-founded by General Georges Doriot. In 1957, ARD gave a $70,000 venture fund, and Ken Olsen founded Digital Equipment Corporation (DEC) with his brother Stan and MIT colleague Harlen Anderson. It occupied the premises of a defunct woolen mill in Maynard, Massachusetts. At first, the group planned to design and sell computers, but Doriot (an experienced manager) dissuaded them as it would be challenging to market computers with their small capital and compete with IBM. Instead, DEC started designing transistor-based digital logic modules using the designs Olsen had perfected at the Lincoln Laboratories. DEC found a ready market for

Kenneth Olsen
(Photo courtesy of wbur.org)

these modules with original equipment manufacturers, and sales grew fast. Olsen priced the modules with a good profit margin to accumulate funds to build computers, which was his passion [1]. Ken Olsen was the principal designer in DEC, Anderson was in charge of marketing, and Stan Olsen oversaw manufacturing.

DEC PDP-1 COMPUTER

With the funds accumulated from the sales of digital modules, DEC built PDP-1 (Programmed Data Processor-1) in 1959, using TX-0 design and the transistorised logic building blocks that DEC was mass-producing. DEC called it a data processor rather than a computer, as vendors sold computers in the late 1950s with numerous peripherals that cost nearly a million dollars. PDP-1 was an 18-bit computer with a 4 K word memory expandable to 64 K words. The memory access time was 5.35 microseconds, and the add time was 10.7 microseconds. It was built using four 19" relay racks and enclosed in a box [3]. Bolt, Beranek, and Neuman (BBN), a Boston R&D company, bought the first PDP-1 in November 1960 for $ 120,000. DEC gifted a PDP-1 to MIT in 1961, which MIT kept in a room adjoining the TX-0. PDP-1 had a large CRT display and a light pen. In addition, it had a teletype with punched paper tape input and a console typewriter. Steve Russel, a student at MIT, created the first interactive computer game, Starwars!, on PDP-1, which used a light pen and a large display. Among other notable programs developed by MIT students were a text editor, a word processor, an interactive debugger, and computer-generated music. The

DEC PDP-I computer. See the CRT display, teletype, and console.
(Photo courtesy of Wikipedia.org)

early sales of PDP-1 were not encouraging, but a large order for 15 machines from IT&T for use in message switching allowed DEC to proceed with further production [1]. Atomic Energy of Canada was another customer that used it as a control computer. BBN, with the assistance of John McCarthy, designed a time-sharing Operating System for PDP-1. Before its discontinuation in 1969, DEC sold Fifty-three PDP-1s.

DEC PDP-8 HERALDS THE ADVENT OF MINICOMPUTERS

DEC built several models of PDPs following PDP-1. The next in the series was PDP-4, identical to PDP-1 with a slower memory and different packaging. It was shipped in 1962, cost $65,000, and sold approximately 54 units.

Meanwhile, Wesley Clerk and Charles Molnar at the Lincoln Laboratory designed a Laboratory Instrument Computer (LINC), which the US National Institute of Health requested, with analog input and output to interface with medical devices. LINC was a 12-bit computer with 2K word memory built using DEC logic modules and delivered in March 1962. Lincoln Laboratories conducted a short course on LINC design and placed the design in the public domain—one of the first hardware designs that was "open source" [4]. DEC produced it as PDP-5 in 1963 and sold around a thousand at $27,000 each.

DEC subsequently designed and built PDP-6, a 36-bit machine with a time-sharing operating system (OS) in 1964. It entered a crowded 36-bit machine market and was unsuccessful, selling around 23 units. DEC went back to designing and selling PDP-7, an 18-bit computer that used cheaper building blocks called flip-chip modules, in 1965. It had 4K memory and sold 120 computers for $72,000 each. Ken Thompson at Bell Telephone Laboratories developed UNIX OS on a PDP-7 using assembly language in 1969.

PDP-6 was resurrected in 1966 with improved hardware and software and became the successful PDP-10 (also called DEC-10) time-shared system with TOPS-10 OS, whose sales touched 1500. PDP-10 was a popular computer with US universities, and many universities connected it to the ARPANET. DEC built several CPU models until 1983. (Three DEC-10s were installed in India at TIFR Mumbai, IIT/Kanpur, and IISc, Bangalore in the late 1970s).

DEC realised that there was a large market for small computers to be used in medical instruments and as parts of control systems. Gordon Bell and Edson de Castro resurrected PDP-5, improved it using smaller digital flip-chip modules, and named it PDP-8. PDP-8 was a turning point in the history of computing as it was the first computer sold at a relatively low price of $18,500 in 1965. DEC reduced the price to $10,000 with its Model S in 1966. DEC called PDP-8 a *minicomputer* as it was small and low-cost but did not have many peripherals that mainframe computers had. It was versatile and used for many applications, from controlling nuclear reactors to controlling lighting sequences in New York's Broadway theatres. Departments in universities could buy them and become "independent" from centralised mainframes. Students used them both as interactive computers and as controllers of laboratory instruments. DEC built ten models of PDP-8 between 1966 and 1974 for total sales of over 50,000, the most successful minicomputer in the mid-1960s. DEC went public in 1966 with a valuation of $77 million, more than 1000 times the original investment of $70,000!

ADVENT OF PDP-11

In 1967, Edson deCastro suggested that DEC should design a compatible series of computers just as IBM had done with its 360 series. He called it PDP-X and started designing it. DEC management did not support his efforts. He, along with two other engineers, Henry Burkhardt and Dick Sogge, quit DEC and started Data General (DG). The first machine DG designed was Nova, released in 1969. It was a 16-bit computer that used Medium-Scale Integrated circuits (MSI), was an instant hit with OEMs, and ate into DEC's market.

DEC decided in 1967 to launch a 16-bit machine to succeed PDP-8. DEC management asked a team of a dozen engineers led by Nick Masserese to design it. Progress was slow, and the team consulted Gordon Bell, who had left DEC and was teaching at Carnegie Mellon University (CMU). Bell, along with his colleague William Wolfe and graduate student Harold McFarland, brainstormed with the DEC team that went to CMU, and over a long weekend,

PDP-11/40 computer with DEC tapes
(Photo courtesy of Wikipedia)

the design of the 16-bit PDP-11 emerged [1]. A novel feature of PDP-11 was Unibus, a group of wires used to connect the computer's main memory with the CPU and peripherals. Unibus allowed addressing input/output devices as though they were memory locations. PDP-11 included general-purpose registers and an innovative instruction set that eased programming. Besides its use in OEM products, it also became a general-purpose minicomputer. DEC released PDP-11 in 1970 as model PDP-11/20, priced at $20,000. Dennis Ritchie wrote a C compiler for it in 1973. Thompson and Ritchie re-wrote the UNIX kernel the same year using C on PDP-11/20. PDP-11 had a long lifespan until 1997, with numerous models appearing regularly. DEC sold around 600,000 PDP-11s, making it one of the most popular minicomputers in the world. Many countries copied its design as it had a vast software library mainly developed by DECUS (DEC users' group).

VAX 11 SERIES COMPUTERS

In 1972, another minicomputer company, Prime Computers, was established in Massachusetts by several engineers who had worked on the Multics project at MIT. Prime manufactured and sold the Prime 200, the first 32-bit minicomputer, in 1972. DEC was then basking in the success of PDP-11. As Prime and DG started to eat into the minicomputer market, DEC realised it should leapfrog over the competition and started designing a very powerful 32-bit minicomputer called supermini. Bill Strecker, earlier a doctoral student of Gordon Bell at CMU, led the design team [5]. One of the aims was to make it compatible with PDP-11. In other words, programs written for PDP-11 were to run as is on VAX. The computer was named VAX-11 to emphasise this. VAX stands for Virtual Address eXtension. The first computer of the series, VAX-11/780, was released in 1977 and cost around $140,000, depending on the configuration. The operating system (OS) named VAX/VMS, a virtual memory system was a well-designed popular OS. On its 20th birthday in 1977, the total sales of DEC reached a billion dollars, second only to IBM, which dominated the mainframe market.

A large number of models at various price levels followed VAX-11/780. A successful model was VAX 8600, released in 1984, which was two times faster than VAX11/780 and ran VMS OS or Ultrix OS, DEC's version of UNIX OS. DEC sold the last VAX model in 1988.

During its lifetime, DEC sold around 400,000 VAXs. Micro VAX, which used Large-scale Integrated Circuits (LSI), succeeded the VAX series in 1984.

EPILOGUE

Observing the success of DEC, 92 companies entered the minicomputer market in the 1970s. Numerous entrepreneurs entered the minicomputer market for several reasons. Among them was the maturing of integrated circuits and cost reduction, all-round progress in OS, languages, and Database Management Systems, cheaper peripherals, availability of venture capital, market growth, particularly OEMs using minicomputers in control systems, and an increase in demand for computers from smaller companies that started using them when they became affordable [1]. The availability of well-educated human resources also helped as many universities started computer science courses in the early 1970s. Most of these 92 companies failed. The five big players who dominated the market were DEC, Data General, Prime, Hewlett-Packard, and IBM, which earlier ignored minis but joined in 1976 with the Series 1 computer. DEC was the market leader. DEC foresaw the networking of computers. DEC with Intel and Xerox standardised Ethernet.

The advent of 8- and 16-bit microprocessor chips and Personal Computers revolutionised computer technology. In 1982, DEC entered the PC market with Rainbow 100. It was a good product but expensive compared to IBM PC. However, it failed in the market. By 1988, DEC had become a very successful company, second only to IBM, with an annual revenue of $11 billion and 120,000 employees. While DEC was successfully marketing the VAX series machines, workstations were becoming very powerful using high-end RISC processors. They were becoming as fast as the minis at a fraction of the cost. DEC's products could not compete with the onslaught of PCs and workstations. In 1992, it reported a loss of $2.8 billion, and Kenneth Olsen retired. It failed in its attempt to enter the workstation market with its DEC Alpha 64-bit high-performance microprocessor in 1992.

DEC's story ended when Compaq, a successful manufacturer of PC clones, acquired it in 1998 for $ 9.6 billion.

REFERENCES

[1] History of computer communications, Chapter 2, Minicomputers (1959–79) https://historyofcomputercommunications.info/section/2.24/the-minicomputer-1959-1979/

[2] Jack Dennis, Oral History Interview https://conservancy.umn.edu/bitstream/handle/11299/107244/oh177jd.pdf?sequence=1&isAllowed=y

[3] PDP-1, https://en.wikipedia.org/wiki/PDP-1

[4] LINC, https://en.wikipedia.org/wiki/LINC

[5] PDP-11- Everything you need to know, https://history-computer.com/dec-pdp-11-computer/

14

Atlas—A Pioneering British Computer

PROLOGUE

Britain had an early lead in building computers. The Manchester Baby was the first stored-program computer built in the world in 1948. Ferranti Mark 1 followed it in 1951—the world's first stored-program computer sold commercially. It preceded UNIVAC by a month! Around the same time, Cambridge University built EDSAC. The first business data processing computer, LEO I (Lyon's Electronic Office), was built based on EDSAC's design in 1951. The British computer companies were not aggressive in marketing. They were satisfied building a few machines, mainly for the UK and the European markets, while the companies in the US were more ambitious. The US companies had a bigger market and received many orders from the US government-sponsored laboratories. The UK government's National Research and Development Corporation (NRDC) was concerned about the leadership in computers slipping away from the UK.

THE MUSE PROJECT

Meanwhile, Tom Kilburn of Manchester University, who led the development of Manchester's early computers, was aware of the need for a high-performance computer for researchers in the atomic energy establishments. He also learnt about IBM's plan to build 7030 for the US atomic energy laboratories, which was to be the fastest computer in the world. In 1957, he started a project with internally generated resources from Manchester University to build a computer called MUSE (Microsecond Engine), which would carry out one instruction every microsecond (1 million instructions per second computer)—a high-speed machine in the mid-1950s. All earlier computers used vacuum tubes and Williams Tube memory. Kilburn's team decided to build MUSE using transistors and magnetic core memory. As a university professor, Kilburn's primary goal was to train post-graduate students and do cutting-edge research on computers that would lead to publications in scholarly journals.

The Atomic Energy Authority of the UK government set up a group in early 1958 to advise it on the requirement of what it called a *supercomputer* for computations required to build nuclear reactors and weapons. The group recommended the design of a computer that could carry out one floating-point addition in a microsecond, would have a large main memory of around a million characters, a fast backup drum storage, and several tapes. The group tried to persuade Kilburn to build such a machine. Kilburn wanted a free hand in setting the design goals of a high-performance computer. The Atomic Energy Authority disagreed with this. Kilburn met with Sir Vincent de Ferranti, the chief executive of Ferranti Computers, during the summer of 1958 and persuaded him to collaborate with Manchester University to build a bigger MUSE version with the necessary peripherals. As was then the practice of Ferranti to name its computers after Greek mythological characters, MUSE was renamed Atlas (Earlier Ferranti machines had been named Pegasus and Mercury). NRDC loaned Ferranti £ 300,000 in May 1959 [1] to develop the Atlas computer.

Tom Kilburn
(Photo courtesy curation.cs.manchester.ac.uk)

THE ATLAS COMPUTER PROJECT BEGINS

MUSE group had around a dozen members (mostly post-graduate students of the Electrical Engineering Department of Manchester University) who had started designing electronic circuits using germanium transistors. Dave Aspinall, a doctoral student, had already designed a fast parallel adder by early 1959. Ferranti joined the MUSE group, now renamed Atlas Computer group, in January 1959 and deputed around a dozen engineers to join the group.

Kilburn led the group, and a broad architectural outline evolved in 1959. The word size was 48 bits and could store one floating-point number, two 24-bit integers, or eight 6-bit characters. The choice of 48 bits allowed 12-digit precision for floating-point numbers. An instruction was 48-bit long with a 10-bit instruction code, 24-bit memory address, and two 7-bit register addresses.

The processor had 128 high-speed 24-bit index registers (called B-lines). These were for multiple purposes, such as program counter, address modification, and interrupt control.

The processor was to have a high-speed arithmetic unit with an accumulator and other registers for floating-point arithmetic. The designers planned a separate fast integer arithmetic unit for both data and address calculations using data in B-Registers.

The design had two magnetic core memories. The larger one had a capacity of 16K words for user programs and data with a cycle time of 0.7 microseconds. The smaller memory was Read Only magnetic core memory (ROM) with 8K words and a cycle time of 0.3 microseconds. The introduction of a ROM was an architectural innovation. The ROM was to store invariant programs for often-used mathematical functions such as Sine, Logarithms, and Square root and complex non-hard-wired instructions. Instruction codes called *extra codes* invoked these routines. All extra codes had 1 as the most significant bit in the operation code part of an instruction. Routines stored in ROM were used when a program in the main memory was interrupted by calls for handling input/output or when unexpected events occurred during processing.

The designers incorporated a content-addressable or associative memory to implement one-level storage (virtual memory). Virtual memory was a seminal architectural innovation of the Atlas computer group. All computer architects now adopt it. I will explain virtual memory later.

The designers used transistors from Mullard—a British transistor manufacturer, to build arithmetic and logic circuits. They imported faster special transistors from the US. Researchers at Manchester University designed, breadboarded and tested all circuits. Ferranti factory subsequently manufactured them. The final production model of Atlas had 5172 printed circuit boards in the central processor. Plessey—a British company built the core memories [1].

The secondary memory consisted of 4 fast drums, each with a capacity of 24K words, which stored user programs. In addition, there was a slew of peripherals, including many tape drives, card readers, punches, line printers, and paper tape readers/punches.

The hardware design started in 1959 and was completed in September 1961. The arithmetic speed of Atlas was:

- Integer addition of 48-bit operands: 1.59 microseconds
- Floating-point addition of 48-bit operands: 1.61 microseconds
- Floating-point multiplication of 48-bit operands: 4.97 microseconds

VIRTUAL MEMORY

In the 1950s, the main memory size of computers was a few thousand digits. For example, the memory size of IBM 1401, one of the most popular computers in the mid-1950s, was 16 K digits. The size was small as the cost of storing a number in core memory was high (of the order of $0.25 per digit). Many users' programs were larger, around four times the main memory size. These programs were stored in a slower but larger secondary memory, usually a drum. Drums were around 100 times slower than core memory, but their cost was low (of the order of $0.0025 per digit). Programmers with programs larger than the capacity of the main storage stored their programs in the drum and moved a portion of the program that could fit into the main core store for execution. As soon as the processor executed this portion of the program, it was moved back to the drum, and another portion was moved from the drum to the core store for execution. This "program overlay" procedure was laborious and wasted programmers' time. The main contribution of Kilburn's group was to automate program overlay by a scheme they called a one-level store. It is now called virtual memory. I explain the idea of a one-level store below.

The capacity of the main RAM in Atlas was 16K words. Most users' programs were larger than 16K. Atlas had four drums with a total capacity of 96 K words to store these programs. The software system led programmers to believe that there were 50K words of main memory and that they could write programs as long as that.

The one-level storage scheme invented by Kilburn's group was a combined hardware-software solution [2]. The software called a supervisor, combined many programmers' programs and stored them in the drum. The supervisor divided each program into what were called pages of 512 words. The supervisor moved these pages of many users' programs to the main core memory for execution and assigned one page to use the CPU. If the program on this page required input data and held up the CPU while reading it from a slow input unit, the supervisor scheduled a page of a different user's program to use the CPU. The supervisor moved the page of a program on the completion of its execution from the core to the drum and replaced it with another page from the drum. Storing the pages of many users' programs in the main memory was brilliant as it minimised the CPU's idle time. The virtual address scheme included a relative addressing scheme that allowed pages of programs of different users to be stored anywhere in the main store and a locking facility to protect one user's program from interfering with another. Atlas was the first computer to have software that carried out the tasks of pagination of programs, transferring pages from the drum to the main memory, allocating storage to different programs, and scheduling CPU time to the programs. This software is presently called a "multiprogramming operating system". Atlas hardware design foresaw the development of a complex supervisor and provided hardware circuits to implement it efficiently. For instance, many extra codes implemented using the ROM met the supervisor's requirements. Atlas incorporated a special small content-addressable memory in the processor to store the identity of pages currently in the main memory for the supervisor's use.

The idea of virtual memory is relevant even today because, through generations of computers, the speed, cost, and size mismatch between the main and secondary memory has remained invariant.

SOFTWARE FOR ATLAS

While the hardware design and implementation were in progress, the software group of around a dozen engineers headed by David Howarth of Ferranti wrote the supervisor and developed a compiler-compiler [1]. Compiler-compiler was a programming tool that simplified the development of compilers of languages from formal descriptions of the language and the computer. A high-level language (a subset of

Algol) called Atlas Autocode, Algol 60, and Fortran were developed using it. The operating system (perhaps the first in the world for a computer) called supervisor by the Atlas group took longer to develop as it was written in assembly language and had 35,000 lines of machine instructions [1]. The supervisor took programs of multiple users, stored them on tapes and drums, and scheduled them to maximise CPU utilisation. It also handled Input and Output from slow peripherals and reduced CPU idle time.

The software development did not keep pace with the hardware development. Only the Atlas assembly language was ready when Atlas was formally inaugurated in 1962. High-level languages and the Atlas supervisor were ready in 1964. A remarkable aspect of the operating system development was that only seven programmers were employed in writing it [1].

Hugh Devonald, the head of Ferranti's software division, stated in 1962, "*The 'Supervisor' is the most ambitious attempt ever made to control automatically the flow of work through a computer. Its ability to handle the varied workload that a machine of this size tackles will influence the future design of all computers*"[1]. It was a prophetic statement as multiprogramming operating systems and virtual memory became the norm in later computers.

EPILOGUE

The prototype of the MUSE/Atlas computer was ready in September 1961. It was manufactured by Ferranti and installed with all peripherals at Manchester University. On 7 December 1962, Nobel Laureate Sir John Cockcroft formally switched on Atlas.

Atlas was the world's most powerful computer when it was released. In other words, if Atlas and its rivals executed a set of benchmark programs, Atlas would complete the set first. Atlas is often considered the world's first supercomputer.

International Computers and Tabulators (ICT), a leading computer manufacturer in the UK, bought Ferranti in October 1963. The commercial version of Atlas with the operating system and language compilers was ready in 1964. The sale price of Atlas was between £ 2 million and £ 4 million, depending on the configuration and the number of peripherals. At that price, there were very few customers for Atlas. Besides the Atlas of Manchester University, ICT sold two other Atlases:

one to a consortium of British Petroleum and London University in 1961 and the other to the National Institute for Research in Nuclear Sciences laboratory (taken over later by the Science and Engineering Research Council) in Chilton in 1961 for £ 3.5 million [3]. The Chilton Atlas was the largest configuration delivered in 1964. Universities and research laboratories used it extensively. The computer at Chilton was the last to be de-commissioned in 1973.

In 1961, Cambridge University found that its computer was saturated and planned to buy a faster computer. It did not have millions of pounds needed to buy Atlas. Ferranti suggested to Cambridge that it would sell the main processor of Atlas at a "cost price" and that Cambridge and Ferranti would design a simpler memory system with limited peripherals [1]. It was named Titan (The ICT marketing group renamed it Atlas 2, but Cambridge University used the name Titan). ICT installed Titan at Cambridge University in 1963. Cambridge University enhanced the system in 1965 and designed a Time-shared operating system. Titan retired in 1973.

ICT sold two more Atlas 2s, one to the Atomic Weapons Research Establishment in 1963 and the other to the Computer-Aided Research Centre of the Ministry of Technology in 1966.

The seminal contributions of Atlas to computer design are [4]:

- The idea of a virtual address larger than the physical address available in the main memory.
- Implementing one-level storage by combining a drum and core stores.
- The idea of pagination of user programs, storing pages of many user programs in the main memory, and scheduling pages to optimise CPU utilisation.
- An interrupt system that controls peripheral use and optimises CPU utilisation.
- Innovations in hardware design to assist a complex operating system implementation.

The Atlas computer design led to 15 patents and 20 scientific papers in renowned Journals [1].

REFERENCES

[1] Simon Lavington, The Atlas Story, Second Edition, 6th December 2012. http://ieeemilestones.ethw.org/images/0/07/Lavington_2012a.pdf

[2] T. Kilburn et al., One-level Storage System, IRE Transactions on Electronic Computers, Vol. 2, pp. 223–35, April 1962.

[3] Jack Howlett, The Atlas Computer Laboratory, IEEE Annals of the History of Computing, Vol. 21, No. 1, 1999.

[4] C. Gordon Bell and Allen Newell, Computer Structures: Readings and Examples, McGraw-Hill, New York, 1971.

15

CTSS—The First Time-sharing Operating System

PROLOGUE

In 1957, the Massachusetts Institute of Technology (MIT) installed a mainframe computer, IBM 704, one of the fastest IBM mainframes. It was programmed using SAP (Share Assembly Programming Language). FORTRAN was on the horizon but was not yet in everyday use. The input to the system used 80 column cards on which users punched their programs and data.

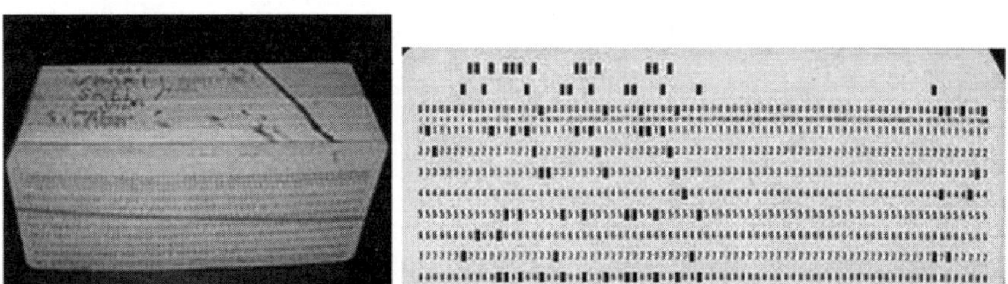

A program deck using 80 column punched cards and a single punched card
(Photo courtesy Wikipedia.org)

An IBM 1401 was the input/output computer of IBM 704. Each user prepared a program with data and placed a header card with a user ID and computer resources needed. A computer operator assembled a batch of users' programs and data and fed them to IBM 1401's card reader. IBM 1401's card reader read program and data cards and stored their contents on a magnetic tape. IBM 704 read the programs in the tape. A batch monitor scheduled these jobs, executed them on IBM 704, and wrote the results on tape. IBM 1401 read this tape and printed the results on sheets of paper using its line printer. These sheets with the results were put in output boxes to be picked up by users.

IBM 704 was an expensive machine, costing over a million dollars. Reading programs and writing the results using slow electro-mechanical devices connected to it was uneconomical. That was why the cheaper 1401 was used for I/O, and tapes were used as a shared secondary store between IBM 704 and 1401. Reading a tape was relatively fast and did not waste 704 time. The overlap of 1401 and 7044 operations reduced the overall computing time of a batch of programs. The entire effort in the early days of computers was to optimise the use of computer resources and minimise idle time. Users' time was not considered as precious. The batch processing, from the point of view of users, wasted their time as running their program took a few hours, and in the end, they would often find a silly syntax error in the program, and the computer aborting it. Getting one successful result using the computer often took many days.

Batch processing frustrated users. I remember a student asking me whether the computer was working for her or she was working for the computer! The situation improved with the advent of FORTRAN as it simplified programming. The availability of FORTRAN led to more users wanting to use computers, and by 1959, the IBM 704 system at MIT was saturated and was replaced by IBM 709, which was twice as fast. Batch processing continued, and users' frustration increased.

John McCarthy joined the faculty of MIT in 1959 and was unhappy as he had to wait a long time to get his programs working. He wrote a note to Professor Phillip Morse, the Director of the computer centre, articulating the need to allow interactive debugging of programs by users of IBM 709. His idea was to enable several programmers to have concurrent access to the computer via remote teletypewriters and let them share its resources and debug and execute their programs. This idea of "time-sharing" a computer was in the air in the late 1950s and was independently suggested by many, including John Backus, Bob Bemer, W.F. Bauer, and Christopher Strachey. McCarthy's articulation, however, persuasively argued the merits of time-sharing and led to its implementation at MIT.

COMPATIBLE TIME-SHARING SYSTEM

The Director of the MIT's computer centre requested his deputy, Fernando Corbatò, to explore the possibility of implementing time-sharing on the IBM 709. Corbatò started writing a program called a "Time-sharing Supervisor" in the spring of 1961. His idea was to give a set of users teletypewriters using which they would write and debug programs. The time-sharing supervisor (occupying 5K words of memory) would run users' programs sequentially, giving each user approximately 200 ms. 200 ms was enough to do significant program development. Initially, the system had three interactive users, each with a teletypewriter. The Time-sharing supervisor serviced users one after another in a round-robin fashion.

MIT asked IBM to modify the 709 system's hardware to partition the main memory of 32K words into two parts—5K words to store the time-sharing supervisor and 27K words to store a user's programs and to ensure that if a user's program attempted to write in the supervisor's partition, it would be trapped. This memory protection feature was a novel idea. Another hardware modification was to provide an interrupt feature that would stop a user's program after a specified period and swap it to secondary memory. The third was to trap a time-sharing user's program if it tried to perform I/O. At that time, the IBM 709 had only magnetic tapes as secondary memory, and disks were not yet available. Each time-sharing user was allocated two exclusive tapes to store program files and dump the running program from the main memory when the allocated time expired. The time-sharing supervisor would read the program from a user's tape into the main memory when its turn came, execute it for 200 ms, and write the program and the result back on tape. Besides executing the programs of the three users who were time-sharing the computer, the supervisor also ran programs from the batch. Only one user's program was in the main memory at a time. The system was called the Compatible Time-Sharing System (CTSS) to specify that it allowed batch processing and time-sharing. This system was running by November 1961. Corbatò wrote most of the supervisor, assisted by Daggett and Daley. CTSS enormously improved users' productivity as they could debug their program interactively and execute it if it was correct. Users realised the power of interaction with the computer, and all users demanded time-shared access to the computer. MIT upgraded IBM 709 to IBM

7090, a transistorised version of 709, with an additional 32 K words memory, by the summer of 1962. The extra memory stored the time-sharing supervisor. 32 K words were available for users' programs and data. An IBM 1301 disk drive replaced the tapes to swap users' programs and data, making the time-sharing system faster. Disk also allowed users to share their files. The computer centre added an IBM 7750 terminal controller that could support up to 32 teletypewriters and some modems. A seminal paper titled "An Experimental Time-Sharing System" was presented at the Spring Joint Computer Conference by Corbatò, Daggett, and Daley in 1962 [1]. They wrote in this paper that once a user got used to interacting with a computer, a delay of even 30 seconds in the computer's response time made them impatient. Surprisingly, users who were waiting a day to get a result in a batch system, complained when they had to wait for a minute to get a response in an interactive system! The use of a teletypewriter was not very convenient. The limited main memory size was another severe constraint.

In 1963, MIT replaced IBM 7090 with IBM 7094, a transistorised machine with all the upgrades necessary to run CTSS and support 32 time-sharing terminals. Corbatò's team demonstrated CTSS in a summer workshop with over 50 well-known computer scientists as participants. Project MAC, supported by the US government's Advanced Research Project Agency (ARPA), bought an IBM 7094. This computer ran an improved version of CTSS. CTSS continued to work till 1973 successfully with several improvements.

Fernando Corbatò (Corby) with IBM 709 in the background
(Photo thanks to galacticjourney.org)

EPILOGUE

CTSS is a landmark in the development of operating systems. It allowed users to interact with computers for the first time. CTSS had many pioneering programs that included RUNOFF, the first text formatting utility (forerunner of word processing); QED, the first text editor for users' programs (ancestor of vi editor); RUNCOM, which executed a list of commands in a file (forerunner of UNIX shell command), MAIL, the first messaging system among users of the system, and the first system to authenticate users with a password. Multics OS followed CTSS at MIT. CTSS influenced the development of many Operating Systems for almost fifteen years. About UNIX, Dennis Ritchie, its developer, remarked, "It is, in fact, a modern implementation of MIT's CTSS" [2]. A comprehensive history of CTSS was edited by David Walden and Tom Van Vleck [3] and published by the IEEE Computer Society.

REFERENCES

[1] F.J. Corbato`, M.M. Daggett, and R.C. Daley, An Experimental Time-Sharing System, Proceedings of the Spring Joint Computer Conference, Vol. 21, 1962, pp. 335–344 http://larch-www.lcs.mit.edu:8001/~corbato/sjcc62/

[2] https://gunkies.org/wiki/Compatible_Time-Sharing_System

[3] David Walden and Tom Van Vleck, Compatible Time-Sharing System (1961–1973), IEEE Computer Society, 2011. https://history.computer.org/pubs/2011-06-ctss.pdf

16

Who Invented Packet Switching?

PROLOGUE

Disputes on the priority of inventions have been frequent. Tesla claimed priority over Marconi as the inventor of the radio based on a patent he had filed in the US in 1897, three years before Marconi. Both Marconi and Tesla had died by the time the US Supreme Court awarded the patent on the invention of the radio to Tesla. In an article [1] co-authored by Leonard Kleinrock, the authors stated, *"Leonard Kleinrock at MIT published the first paper on packet switching theory in July 1961 and the first book on the subject in 1964"*. Donald Davies and Paul Baran disputed it, claiming priority. This anecdote is about the dispute.

WHAT IS PACKET SWITCHING?

From the early days of telecommunications until the mid-1960s, telephone companies primarily used Public Switched Telephone Networks (PSTN) for voice calls between subscribers. PSTN used a technology called *circuit switching* in which a dedicated circuit is established between a calling subscriber and a called subscriber for the entire duration of a telephone call. Circuit switching does not use the communication lines efficiently as the line is reserved for the exclusive use of the subscribers even when a subscriber is silent. This method was necessary for voice communication as a slight delay during voice transmission disturbs the flow of conversation.

In telegraph and teletype communication, slight delays are irrelevant. This type of communication uses the store and forward method, in which messages are queued in intermediate switching centres and forwarded to the recipients when a circuit is available. Notice that this system does not break up messages. This method of communication is called *message switching*.

The situation changes when a computer is accessed remotely from a terminal using a telephone line. The traffic from the terminal is in bursts. For example, in interactive computing, a user's typing speed is slow, and the communication line is often idle. In circuit switching, the communication line does not carry traffic almost 90% of the time. In computer-to-computer communication also, data is sent in bursts. Unlike audio, digital data can tolerate delay. Circuit switching is thus inefficient for data traffic between computers.

When a file is to be sent from one computer to another in a network of computers, it is broken into *packets* of around 1000 bytes. Each packet is labelled with a serial number, addresses of the source and the destination computer, a chunk of data, error detecting bits, and despatched. When a packet arrives at an intermediate computer in the network, this computer examines the packet and sends it along the best available path toward the destination computer. Packets belonging to a file may arrive at the destination computer in a different serial order. The destination computer collects all the packets and rearranges them in the correct order using the serial number of the packet. The advantage of this method is that once a packet reaches a computer, the path it traversed is freed. Thus, many independent files may be broken into packets and share the communication paths, thereby utilising the total capacity of the communication system. This method is called *packet switching*.

PAUL BARAN'S INVENTION

Paul Baran joined the RAND Corporation (primarily financed by the US Department of Defence) in 1959. At that time, the cold war between the US and the erstwhile USSR was at its peak. A project was assigned to him by the US Air Force to examine the vulnerability of the US communication system in case there was a surprise enemy attack. Paul Baran examined the existing communication systems: the telephone system run by AT&T and short-wave radio. The telephone system was a decentralised circuit that could break down in a bombing attack. A Hydrogen bomb blast would blank out the short-wave radio. It was thus necessary to design a reliable communication system that would be robust. He suggested a distributed mesh network to interconnect transceivers. In addition, he proposed that all messages (including voice) transmitted between two transceivers be digitised and broken up into "short message blocks" of 1024 bits. Each block would have, in addition, the addresses of the sender and the receiver, a serial number, and error-detecting bits. He suggested sending the blocks along any available path (assuming some routes may be damaged and not available) and reassembling them at the destination. He simulated the system and found it to be effective. He published his results as a series of research monographs [2]. He unsuccessfully tried convincing AT&T to adopt his idea of breaking messages into blocks and designing the telephone system as a mesh network.

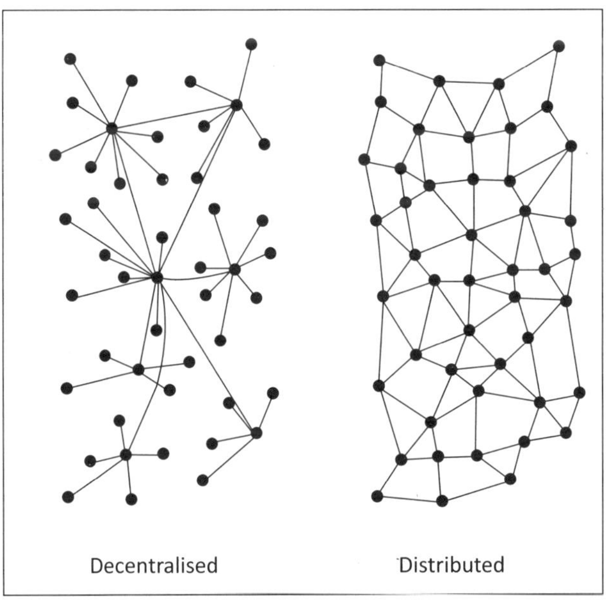

Decentralised and distributed networks. Dots are transceivers, and lines are communication links (Figure courtesy of computersciencewiki.org)

DONALD DAVIES INVENTION

Donald Davies [3] was a UK National Physical Laboratories (NPL) researcher. He visited MIT in 1965 and saw the time-shared computer system in operation. He noted that terminals were connected to the system using dedicated telephone lines. The system used the telephone lines inefficiently as the traffic was bursty with long idle periods. He wondered why multiple users were also not time-sharing the telephone line. On his return to NPL, he pursued his idea of time-sharing communication lines by digital data and invented packet switching independently, unaware of the work of Paul Baran. Davies coined the word *"packet"* for data blocks after consulting linguists. He and his team implemented packet switching using 1024-bit packets and connected several computers in NPL. Scantlebury, a member of his team, presented a paper on packet switching at a conference in Gatlinburg, USA, in 1967, attended by Lawrence Roberts of ARPA [4]. Roberts liked the packet-switching idea and adopted it in designing the ARPANET. Computer scientists generally agreed in the 1970s that Paul Baran and Donald Davies invented packet switching independently. For instance, in a paper titled *"The Evolution of Packet Switching"* by Roberts [5] in 1978, Baran and Davies are credited for inventing packet switching, and Kleinrock's work is not mentioned.

Paul Baran **Donald Davies**
(Photos courtesy Wikipedia)

LEONARD KLEINROCK'S RESEARCH WORK

Leonard Kleinrock obtained a Ph.D. from MIT in 1963. In his thesis titled *Message Delay in Communication Nets with Storage*, published in 1963, he analysed queueing delays in a message switching system operated by Western Union Telegraph Company for processing telegrams. He assumed exponentially distributed message lengths with no upper bound in his thesis. He also assumed Poisson distributed message arrivals and devised formulae on queueing delays in the switching network. It was a seminal thesis on queues in message switching that was later expanded and published as a book [6]. He did not discuss breaking up a message into fixed-length packets, even though it would have been a simple extension of his more complex analysis of variable-length messages.

THE CONTROVERSY OF THE "FIRST INVENTOR" OF PACKET SWITCHING

In 1996, Kleinrock claimed on his website that he was the first inventor of packet switching based on his Ph.D. work. Roberts supported his claim, even though in his paper [5] published in 1978, he had not credited Kleinrock for packet switching. When Davies noticed Kleinrock's claim, he sent him an email to find out on what basis he claimed priority and got a reply that it was based on a section in his book [6] published in 1974. Davies also corresponded with Baran. Subsequently, Davies wrote a paper in The Computer Journal [7] and instructed his son to send it for publication after his death as he was already old and ill and did not want to enter a controversy during his last days [8]. The paper extensively analysed Kleinrock's work, and Davies concluded: *"My contention is that the work of Kleinrock before and up to 1964 gives him no claim to have originated packet switching, the honour of which must go to Paul Baran. The passage in his book on time-sharing queue discipline, if pursued to a conclusion, may have led to packet switching, but it did not".*

EPILOGUE

Based on my analysis of the publications, I conclude that Paul Baran invented packet switching but did not implement one. Donald Davies independently invented packet switching and implemented it in a local area computer network. Leonard Kleinrock did seminal research on queueing theory in message-switched networks where the messages he examined were of variable length.

REFERENCES

[1] Barry M. Leiner et al., Brief History of the Internet, 1997. https://www.internetsociety.org/internet/history-internet/brief-history-internet/

[2] Paul Baran, The Beginnings of Packet Switching: Some Underlying Concepts, IEEE Communications Magazine, July 2002, pp. 42–48.

[3] Donald Davies, https://en.wikipedia.org/wiki/Donald_Davies

[4] W. Isaacson, The Innovators, Simon and Schuster, 2014, pp. 242–246.

[5] L.G. Roberts, The Evolution of Packet Switching, Proceedings IEEE, Vol. 66, No. 11, 1978, pp. 1307–1313.

[6] Leonard Kleinrock, Communication Nets, Stochastic Message Flow and Delay, McGraw-Hill, 1964.

[7] D.W. Davies, An Historical Study of the Beginnings of Packet Switching, *The Computer Journal*, Vol. 44, No. 3, 2001, pp. 152–162.

[8] K. Hafner, A paternity dispute divides net pioneers, New York Times, November 8, 2001.

17

The First Data Base Management System

PROLOGUE

We all encounter database management systems (DBMS) daily without realising it. Indian Railway Catering and Tourism Corporation (IRCTC) stores data on all available tickets in every class on all trains in a database. When you want to reserve a ticket to travel by train, a Data Base Management System (DBMS) accesses this database to determine if the requested ticket is available. If yes, it is issued to you, and the DBMS updates the database. One of the largest databases in the world, Aadhaar, is maintained by the Unique Identification Authority of India. A DBMS queries it. In this anecdote, I will recount when the idea of a DBMS originated and what the first such system in the world was.

Scientists and engineers used early computers for numerical computing in which processing power provided by the CPU was more important than the size of secondary storage. The need to store large volumes of data was felt only when companies started using computers for routine commercial data processing, called Electronic Data Processing (EDP). Early uses of EDP were in payroll preparation, inventory control, accounts receivable, billing, and similar clerical processing. In the 1950s, the only available mass storage system was a magnetic tape drive, and data was input using punched cards. Programs could access data in a tape drive only sequentially. A master file, such as an inventory file, is sorted using an item code as a key and stored in a tape. A clerk punched a card whenever a company's store received an item or issued one. These cards were sorted at the end of the day using the item code as a key and stored in a transaction tape. A program updated the data on the master tape by using the transaction tape. Programs were thus closely linked to how a computer stored data. Programming was challenging as the storage capacity of the main memories of typical computers used for EDP in the 1950s was about 16 KB, and programming was in assembly language.

The first major revolution in EDP was the arrival of addressable disk storage, which provided direct access to any record stored in a disk using a key. Even though IBM invented disk storage in 1956 (the first disk store had a capacity of 5 MB and cost US$ 50,000), it was only commonly available and affordable around 1960. Even then, only experienced programmers could use the disk's addressing capability to retrieve records, as support from the operating systems of that era to access a disk sector directly was lacking.

ADVENT OF INTEGRATED DATA STORE (IDS)

In 1963, General Electric Company (GE) decided to initiate a project called MIACS (Manufacturing Information and Control Systems) using its computer system, GE235, which had a disk drive. GE had many factories manufacturing electrical equipment such as switchgear, motors, and transformers. GE planned to use MIACS to track data on various assemblies, sub-assemblies, and components used during manufacturing. Charles W. Bachman led the programming systems group and decided to develop MIACS using GE's high-level language named GECOM and assembly language for time-critical parts of the system. Disks stored all necessary data. Bachman was an early pioneer in business data processing. It is interesting to recount how Bachman joined GE's data processing group.

When Bachman was attending college, the Second World War broke out. He joined the US Army in 1944, and the army assigned him to the anti-aircraft corps in the South West Pacific area. He used the fire control computers of 90 mm guns during this assignment. Bachman was discharged in 1946 and joined Michigan State College, where he obtained a Bachelor's degree in mechanical engineering in 1948. He subsequently joined the University of Pennsylvania for a Master's degree in mechanical engineering. To his surprise, he found that the course was an evening course for working professionals. He attended day classes at the university's Wharton School of Business with MBA students and learnt about problems in management but did not complete the course. He obtained a Master's in mechanical engineering in 1950 and soon joined Dow Chemicals. After a few years as an engineer and manager, he migrated to its data processing department in 1957 and became its head. Dow Chemicals ordered an IBM 709, one of the largest computers made by IBM, in 1959. In those days, IBM provided only the essential system software and encouraged users to form groups to interchange ideas and write application programs. The IBM users' group, SHARE, cooperatively developed many application programs. (The first program I wrote in 1957 was for IBM 704 using SHARE assembly language, which was better than the assembly language provided by IBM). Bachman was an active member of SHARE and developed a Report Generator program called 9PAC that was very popular. Unfortunately, due to financial problems, Dow Chemicals cancelled their order of IBM 709. Bachman had made many contacts when he was a member of SHARE, and one of them was GE's data processing head. Consequently, he joined GE in 1960 in their data processing department.

Charles Bachman
(Photo courtesy Wikipedia)

Bachman found that while developing MIACS, the application programmers found it difficult to write programs to access data stored in disks and manipulate them. In 1963, Bachman proposed interposing Integrated Data System (IDS) software between application programs and files stored in disks, namely, the database, to ease application programming. Application programmers used the data stored in the database by calling IDS [1], which accessed the database and returned the requested data in the appropriate format. Thus, application programs were relieved of the task of low-level programming to access disk sectors where records were stored and insulated from the details of how and where the disk stored data. If a programmer altered the physical placement of files stored in the database, IDS would change the metadata. IDS enabled the *data independence of programs*, one of the most essential functions of a DBMS. IDS also provided some other features we associate nowadays with DBMS, including data integrity. A later version of IDS had a data description language.

CHARLES BACHMAN GETS THE TURING AWARD

IDS, the first DBMS in the world, was successfully implemented in 1965. In 1973, Bachman was given the Turing Award by the Association for Computing Machinery, USA, for his "outstanding contributions to database technology." He was the first Turing Award winner without a Ph.D. and the first to get it for work related to business data processing. He was among the few awardees who spent his entire professional life in the industry.

Bachman was the chairman of the Database Task Group of CODASYL (Committee on Data Systems Languages), which had drawn up the specifications of COBOL (Common Business Oriented Language). This group evolved the standard of what was known as the CODASYL network data model DBMS. It specified the inter-relations of data in a database as linked records. For example, one set of records might contain records of students and another set of departments. A system of pointers linked students' records with the records of their departments. Programmers had to navigate using the pointers to retrieve the desired data. The task of a database programmer as a 'navigator' was explained by Bachman in his Turing award lecture [2].

EPILOGUE

The work of Bachman and his group on IDS influenced the network model of DBMS developed by the Database Task Group of CODASYL. IDS introduced many terms used in DBMS, such as data definition language, data manipulation language, schema, and data independence of programs. The network model was promoted as a standard in the 1970s and 80s and adopted by many computer companies. However, IBM had its own model of DBMS called IMS (Information Management System), a hierarchical data model. IBM was a dominant mainframe computer manufacturer in the 1960s up to the late 1980s, with the result that IMS dominated the market until a new model of DBMS called the Relational data model came in the late 1980s. The most remarkable fact about IDS is that computers whose main memory was less than 100 KB supported it in the 1960s. Another noteworthy feature of IDS is that its successor, IDMS, was used in many mainframes and supported by Computer Associates till 2014!

REFERENCES

[1] Thomas Haigh, How Charles Bachman Invented the DBMS, a Foundation of Our Digital World, Communications of the ACM, Vol. 59, No. 7, July 2016, pp. 25–30.

[2] Charles W. Bachman, The Programmer as a Navigator, (Turing Award Lecture), Communications of the ACM, Vol. 16, No. 11, November 1973, pp. 653–658.

18

CDC 6600—Cray's First Supercomputer

PROLOGUE

Remington Rand, famous for its office machines in the 1950s, decided to enter the computer industry when Eckert Mauchly Computer Corporation (EMCC) approached it for financial support. It acquired EMCC in 1950 and followed up by acquiring Electronic Research Associates (ERA), a struggling computer company based in St. Paul, Minnesota, in 1952. ERA was making small computers named ERA 1103. Remington Rand merged with Sperry Corporation, which was named Sperry-Rand in 1955. It spun off its computer operations as the Sperry-UNIVAC division. There was rivalry for research and development funds from Sperry-UNIVAC between the engineers of erstwhile EMCC and those from ERA. ERA engineers felt that Sperry-UNIVAC ignored their requests. A group of ex-ERA engineers led by William Norris, including William Drake, Arnold Ryden, and Seymour Cray, decided to form their own company named Control Data Corporation (CDC) in St. Paul. They raised capital of half a million dollars from their contributions, public share offerings, and financiers. CDC's operations started in 1957 in the workshop of Cedar Engineering, a defunct aircraft company,

William Norris
(Photo courtesy alchetron.com)

based in St. Paul. One of Norris's best decisions was to persuade Seymour Cray to join him in founding CDC. Cray, a gifted engineer, and an excellent computer architect, had obtained a Bachelor's degree in electrical engineering in 1949 and a Master's degree in applied mathematics in 1951, both from the University of Minnesota and immediately joined ERA.

CDC initially struggled to survive. Fortunately, it got a contract of $2.5 million from the US Department of Defence to build high-performance computers. Under Cray's leadership, CDC built a computer named CDC 1604 and delivered it to the US Naval Graduate School in January 1960. It was one of the first computers built in the USA that used transistors. It was meant primarily to solve problems in science and engineering. It had a word size of 48 bits and a fast floating-point arithmetic unit. Over fifty CDC 1604s were delivered by 1964 to defence research laboratories and universities.

In the 1960s, IBM dominated the mainframe computer market, and its competitors had to find niche markets to compete with it. Cray wanted to make CDC a leader in building high-performance computers for scientists and engineers and not compete with IBM in business data processing. While CDC grew and became profitable, bureaucracy gradually crept into the organization. Cray wanted to be primarily a designer of computers, and he found the new atmosphere stifling innovation. He requested Norris to allow him and a small engineering group to shift away from the headquarters to a nearby location to build the next CDC computer. He wanted this computer to be a high-performance computer that would outperform the fastest computer built by IBM. Norris was at first reluctant but agreed when Cray threatened to resign. Cray explored during September 1961 various places around St. Paul to locate a new design and development laboratory and selected Chippewa Falls, a small dairying town in rural Wisconsin, around hundred and fifty kilometres from St. Paul [1]. Chippewa Falls, not coincidentally, was where Cray was born. CDC chose a site and began building a laboratory for CDC 6600. The design team estimated that a prototype of 6600 would be ready only after two to three years. Thus, the CDC management decided to develop and market a successor to 1604, called CDC 3600, that would be compatible with it but would be faster and have a larger memory. CDC released CDC 3600 in June 1963.

CDC 6600 DESIGN

Cray handpicked a small group of talented engineers, including James Thornton, Les Davis, Dean Roush, Garner McCrossen, and Paul Kristensen, as lead engineers. While the building in Chippewa Falls was getting ready, the 6600 design team moved to a different location in St. Paul to allow them to work without interruptions. Cray aimed to build a computer that would be the fastest in the world and at least two to three times faster than IBM's fastest computer, 7030. Cray was convinced that an architecture compatible with 1604 would not be able to meet the high speed he aimed. The team had to explore new architectural ideas. He and his team also knew that the germanium transistors used in 1604 would not meet their goal. Fortunately, Fairchild Semiconductor had just then announced silicon transistors based on what they called planar technology. It was faster than germanium transistors used in 1604, and the team chose it to build the logic circuits of 6600. The silicon planar transistor had a switching time of less than 3 nanoseconds. At that time, Fairchild was also designing the first integrated circuits. Cray's team thought of using it but felt it was risky to use integrated circuits, which still had teething troubles. The team found that a bottleneck in increasing the speed of arithmetic circuits was the delay caused by wires interconnecting transistors on printed circuit boards, and it was necessary to pack transistors as closely as possible on boards [1]. Another delay was due to the wires interconnecting logic boards on the backplane. Reducing these wire lengths required innovative *packaging* of logic boards. Transistors switching at high speed dissipated considerable heat and needed a good cooling system. Roush, a mechanical engineer in the team, designed a refrigeration system using Freon gas compressors and heat exchangers to cool the logic circuit packages. Cray called it good *plumbing*. It was impossible to build high-speed computers by just increasing the clock speed. The architecture had to be highly *parallel* to speed up the computer. In other words, a new architectural design had to be evolved that would overlap several operations performed by a computer, such as input/output, retrieval of data/programs from the main storage, and arithmetic operations of the Central Processing Unit (CPU) while executing a program [2]. The computer should also perform several instructions simultaneously in parallel.

THE ARCHITECTURE OF CDC 6600 [2]

A unique feature of 6600 architecture was the addition of 10 Peripheral Processing Units (PPU) that relieved the CPU from performing all functions related to input/output, job scheduling, and workflow. The PPUs, each with 4096 words (12 bits per word) memory and a shared processor, performed these tasks. PPU0 was the master that controlled all the other PPUs. It also hosted the operating system, relieving the CPU from this responsibility. CPU performed its primary task of computing at high speed, and PPUs did all other jobs. Unlike most computers with consoles that had numerous blinking neon tubes displaying the status of the computer, 6600 had two Cathode Ray Tubes (CRT) to display them in alphanumeric form. One of the PPUs was used to drive the CRTs.

On one side, PPUs communicated with the main memory of 6600 and, on the other side, with 12 channels that communicated with input/output units that included drums, disk drives, tape drives, card reader/punch, printer, and the CRTs of the operator's console.

CDC 6600 stored 128 kilowords (60 bits per word) in memory. A word accommodated one floating-point number, or four 15-bit short integers, or two 30-bit integers, or ten 6-bit characters, or two 30-bit instructions, or four 15-bit instructions. The memory had several banks that allowed data retrieval from it in 425 nanoseconds.

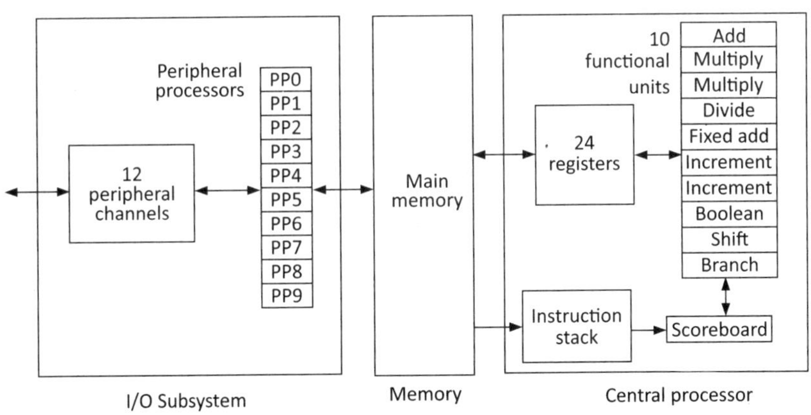

Figure 18.1 Block diagram of CDC 6600
(Courtesy people.engr.ncsu.edu)

The processor retrieved 16 instructions from the memory and kept them in its instruction stack. Many programs in science and engineering use loops in which the same set of instructions are repeatedly used. If these instructions are retrieved from the memory and kept in the instruction stack, they can be executed without accessing memory, thereby increasing the speed of calculations. There were 10 high-speed functional units, as shown in the Figure 18.1. The processor carried out several instructions simultaneously due to the availability of multiple functional units. This parallel execution increased the speed of computation. The scoreboard register held information on the free/busy status of the functional units to facilitate scheduling tasks for these units.

There were 24 registers in the CPU. Of these, 8 registers that were 60 bits long were used to store data to be used in arithmetic operations and storing intermediate results. Placing the registers in the CPU minimised memory access, which was slow compared to the processing speed. Besides these, there were 8 address registers and 8 increment registers, each 18 bits long. Programs used these registers to address large arrays.

Simplicity was Cray's second nature. There were only 64 instruction codes that simplified the logic design of the processor. Nowadays, such computers are called Reduced Instruction Set Computers (RISC). It is also jokingly called Really Invented by Seymour Cray (RISC). Only two instructions could access the main memory. They were to load data to registers in the processor from the memory or to store results from the registers to the memory.

Seymour Cray
(Photo courtesy cgl.ucsf.edu)

The CPU had a 10 MHz clock–three times faster than the existing computers in the market. Add time was 0.3 microseconds, multiply time was 1 microsecond, and divide time was 3.4 microseconds. The CPU consumed 30 kW.

PACKAGING AND PLUMBING

As I mentioned earlier, packaging and cooling were essential to achieve the very high-speed Cray and his group aimed for. Reducing wire lengths was critical. The team designed each printed circuit board to minimise wire lengths. The designers packed two circuit boards in a cordwood package (See Figure 18.2). The cabinets housing the computer circuits were arranged as four wings in four directions at right angles to one another (See Figure 18.2) to reduce the wire lengths between the modules. The wiring interconnecting the modules housed in the cabinets was at the centre. The computer used 400,000 transistors dissipating enormous heat. Cooling was necessary to prevent the computer from burning. Roush, a mechanical engineer in the group, designed a cooling system using Freon refrigerant with one compressor and a heat exchanger housed at the end of each computer wing. The computer was highly reliable, with Mean Time Between Failures (MTBF) greater than 2000 hours [3].

A Cordwood module

An artist's impression of CDC 6600
See the four wings at right angles

Figure 18.2
(Photos courtesy Wikipedia.org)

SOFTWARE

Cray and his team focused on hardware development and paid less attention to software. The computer had no support for virtual memory or paging. Thus, the OS design was relatively simple. Cray's group wrote a rudimentary Operating System (OS) known as COS (Chippewa OS), a simple batch job control system. CDC's Los Angeles group developed SPIROS (Simultaneous Processing OS). SPIROS was, however, full of bugs, and CDC withdrew it. Subsequently, CDC's Sunnyvale, California group developed SCOPE (Supervisory Control of Program Execution) with device control and file support. SCOPE was the main OS of 6600. Later, CDC marketed a Network OS (NOS). As mentioned, PPU0 ran the OS, relieving the CPU from the housekeeping chores. An assembly language COMPASS (COMPrehensive ASSembler) available for CDC 3600 was adapted to CDC 6600. Besides these, CDC 6600 had a FORTRAN 66 compiler. Users wrote most application programs in FORTRAN 66.

EPILOGUE

CDC announced the availability of CDC 6600 in August 1963. When Thomas Watson Jr., IBM's chairman, heard this, on 28 August 1963, he wrote to his top management group the following [4]: *"Last week CDC had a press conference during which they officially announced their 6600 system. I understand that in the laboratory developing this system there are only 34 people 'including the janitor'. Of these 14 are engineers and 4 are programmers and only one person has a Ph.D., a relatively junior programmer. To the outsider, the laboratory appears to be cost conscious, hardworking and highly motivated.*

Contrasting this modest effort with our own vast development activities, I fail to understand why we have lost our industry leadership position by letting someone else offer the world's most powerful computer."

When Cray heard about Watson's memo, he commented, "It seems like Mr. Watson has answered his own question," meaning IBM had bloated.

Probably after seeing Watson's scathing memo, the IBM marketing team announced a non-existent IBM 360/Model 92 and claimed that it was as fast as 6600. IBM's announcement led to the cancellation of some orders for 6600 and temporarily reduced orders for 6600. Norris was furious and filed an antitrust case against IBM in a federal court. IBM was afraid it would lose the case and settled it out of court after 4 years by transferring ownership of its services company to CDC and cash that amounted to $80 million [5].

CDC delivered the first two 6600s to Livermore and Los Alamos laboratories in early 1965. CDC sold a little over a hundred computers in this series to government laboratories and universities primarily to solve science and engineering problems. CDC 6600 cost between $2.5 million and $6 million depending on the configuration. It was the fastest computer in the world from 1964 to 1969 until CDC 7600 succeeded. CDC 7600 was 10 times faster and was the fastest computer in the world until Cray 1 overtook it in 1975.

The development of 6600 and its successors, called "supercomputers," was possible in the US because of the cold war in the 1960s. Weapons developers and cryptographers wanted to buy the fastest computer available with little consideration of cost. The US government laboratories and universities that had projects funded by the Department of Defence were the primary buyers of these multi-million dollar computers. As I mentioned earlier, CDC sold nearly a hundred CDC

6600 supercomputers to these institutions. Contrast this large sale with Atlas computer, a high-speed computer built in the UK, that sold only 3 machines.

REFERENCES

[1] James E. Thornton, The CDC 6600 Project, Annals of the History of Computing, Vol. 2, No. 4, October 1980, pp. 338–348.

[2] James E. Thornton, Design of a Computer—The Control Data 6600, Scott, Foresman and Company, Glenview, Illinois, 1970.

[3] Dag Spicer, Control Data 6600: The Supercomputer arrives, *Dr. Dobb's Journal,* https://web.archive.org/web/20170605132007/http://www.drdobbs.com/control-data-6600-the-supercomputer-arri/184404102

[4] https://www.computerhistory.org/revolution/supercomputers/10/33/62

[5] https://en.wikipedia.org/wiki/Control_Data_Corporation

19

IBM System/360—Birth of a Computer Family

PROLOGUE

IBM released the model 1401 computer in 1959, which soon became a best-seller among business users. Simultaneously, IBM continued developing the 7000 series of computers for scientific users who required numeric-intensive computers. IBM 7094 was the latest in the series, released in 1962.

The 1400 series of computers were developed at the Endicott Laboratories, whereas the 7000 series computers were developed at the Poughkeepsie Laboratories. The groups in these two laboratories were competing for resources, and often, they seemed like two different companies!

Endicott Laboratories was planning a series of computers as an upgrade path of 1401 for business users starting with 1410. Poughkeepsie was planning series 8000 computers to succeed in the 7000 series. These computers were incompatible; software developed for 1401 would not run on 7000 series computers. Besides these, IBM sold model 1620, a small decimal computer for scientists and engineers, and model 1800, a real-time computer for process control. With this wide range of incompatible computers, IBM found that the cost of developing application software was increasing. There was also incompatibility in peripherals such as tape drives and disks that required separate interface designs for various models of computers. Besides these problems, the variety of spares inventory was becoming unmanageable. IBM had to train the marketing group and maintenance engineers on multiple computers.

The top management, headed by T. Vincent Learson, was concerned about these problems and felt that supporting multiple computers would reduce IBM's profitability. It wanted clarity on the future path IBM should take. It was also unhappy with the unhealthy competition between Poughkeepsie and Endicott Laboratories. As a first step, Learson transferred Bob O. Evans, the product manager at Endicott, to manage the Poughkeepsie development group. Evans examined the 8000 series proposal of Poughkeepsie steered by Fredrick Brooks and found that it was not on the right growth path and cancelled its development. When Brooks balked, Learson sent Jerrier Haddad as a referee to resolve the dispute. He backed Evans and recommended the termination of the 8000 series computer design.

Meanwhile, the management was also unhappy with the 1410 and its successors as a growth path. To decide on the future direction to be taken by IBM for the next ten years, Learson's assistant, Donald Spaulding, suggested forming a group of twelve top managers and engineers in all divisions, including marketing. It was named SPREAD (Systems, Programming, Research, Engineering, and Development), jokingly referred to as "Spaulding's Plan to Reorganize Each and All Divisions," with John Haanstra as chairman and Evans as vice-chairman [1]. IBM formed the group in November 1961 and asked it to complete its work by December and submit a report to the top management. They held meetings in a Connecticut motel to protect the group from distractions.

T. Vincent Learson
(Photo courtesy ibm.com)

Bob O. Evans
(Photo courtesy nap.edu)

SPREAD REPORT

The group submitted an audacious 26-page plan to Learson on December 28, 1961. Its main recommendation was to discontinue all the computer models that IBM was currently manufacturing. In their place, introduce a new *family* of compatible computers with a wide range of speeds, memory sizes, and peripherals. They recommended a unified architecture of the computers in the family. Programs written for the low-end model of the computer would run without change on the higher-end models and vice-versa, allowing users to upgrade or downgrade computers as their requirements increase or decrease without rewriting software. The report stated that there will be no distinction between computers for business data processing and scientific computing, as most customers run both types of applications. They recommended developing a unified set of input/output and secondary storage systems. The interfaces to the peripherals would be uniform for all models. This feature would allow customers to keep the peripherals while upgrading the processor. As the architecture of the new family of computers would be radically different from the existing computers, they would be incompatible, and existing computer programs may not run on the new computers. They also suggested a unified high-level language to replace FORTRAN and COBOL. A language called PL/1 was developed and released in 1966.

The group estimated the research and development cost to introduce the new family of computers to be $500 million—the highest amount invested by any private computer company in R&D. They suggested building a factory to manufacture the electronic circuits for the new range of computers.

The top management committee of IBM, chaired by Thomas Watson Jr., discussed the proposal in detail. There were conflicting views and trepidation about taking such a risky step, particularly as the existing products, the 1401 and 7000 series, were leaders in the market. It became clear that IBM would not grow with a haphazard variety of computers. Watson made the final decision and approved the SPREAD report. IBM decided to go ahead with developing a unified family of computers.

IBM asked Evans to plan the New Product Line (NPL) and kept the entire plan confidential to prevent competitors from snooping. Evans requested Fred Brooks (with whom he had an earlier disagreement on the 8000 series proposal) and Gene Amdahl of the Research and Development Division to be the lead architects of the NPL.

Gene Amdahl
(Photo courtesy alchetron.org)

Fred Brooks
(Photo courtesy Wikipedia.org)

THE ARCHITECTURE OF THE NEW PRODUCT LINE (NPL)

Numerous new ideas emerged while designing the architecture of the new family of computers named NPL. All existing IBM computers used 6 bits to code characters and 4 bits to code decimal numbers. Six bits had severe limitations as it could not code lowercase letters, numerous special characters, and non-English characters. The architects decided to use 8 bits to code characters, allowing representation of $2^8 = 256$ characters. They named the coding system EBCDIC (Extended Binary-coded Decimal Interchange Code). A string of 8 bits was called a *byte*. A byte packed two decimal digits. The designers decided to allow every byte in the memory to be addressable. In the original design, the maximum memory size was 16 Mbytes, which was huge in the 1960s. The architects divided the address into two parts to allow a large addressable memory without increasing the computer's word length. One part was called the base address stored in a register. The processor added a displacement specified in an instruction to the base address to obtain the effective address. The machine's word size was 32 bits, with one byte used to code instructions. The architects planned standard instructions for decimal and floating-point binary arithmetic for 32-bit and 64-bit floating-point numbers. Besides these, they added numerous logic instructions. A new feature was the idea of including 16 general-purpose registers to store data or addresses depending on the instruction. These registers were also used to store operands and results in arithmetic operations. The designers planned separate specialised computers called channels to handle data communication to secondary stores, input, and output units. This idea relieved the central processor of controlling slow devices and allowed peripheral devices to be independent of the computer model. In other words, a peripheral could be used with any member of the computer family. IBM planned six models of the computer with varying capabilities. The IBM management decided to build the smallest models at the Endicott Laboratory and the four largest at the Poughkeepsie Laboratories. IBM gave these models arbitrary numbers to guard against competitors guessing IBM's plan.

The architects discussed at length what technology to use for building the processor. In the 1960s, integrated circuits were already in production. The architects felt that integrated circuit technology was immature. Discrete transistor circuits used in the existing product line would become obsolete. A gifted engineer, Eric Bloch, invented a new technology called Solid Logic Technology (SLT), a conservative alternative to integrated circuits. In this "hybrid" technology, components such as transistors, resistors, and capacitors were "grown" on a ceramic substrate and interconnected using thin wires printed on the ceramic [3]. IBM built a factory in upstate New York to fabricate SLTs.

Architects of NPL faced a significant challenge of making all the family members compatible to allow programs written for any computer in the family to run on any other member. Architects solved this problem by designing the computer's control unit, which decodes operation codes and sends control signals to various computer units, using a microcode stored in a fast microcode memory. Maurice Wilkes, EDSAC's designer, had proposed using microcode. This generalised control method, called microcode-based control, accommodated a variety of instruction sets of the NPL series of machines. Besides this, existing customers of the IBM 1400 and 7000 series wanted their programs to run on the new computers to preserve their investment in software. Architects solved this problem by invoking a separate microcode memory appropriate for the instruction sets of those computers. This technique, called emulation, was faster than simulating the earlier machines on NPL.

A new line of secondary memories was designed and fabricated. IBM redesigned the Tape drives to record data on nine tracks to store 8-bit bytes and a parity bit. IBM laboratory at San Jose designed high-capacity, high-speed disk drives. IBM built special-purpose computers (called channels by IBM) to control tapes and disks.

SOFTWARE FOR NPL

Fred Brooks led the software development effort. The main goal was to design a "universal" Operating System (OS) that would be appropriate for the whole family of computers. Implementing this OS was the most significant challenge, as the lower models in the series had limited memory. The OS was to be multi-programmed; in other words, many programs would be in a queue, and the OS would schedule a ready-to-run program to run on the processor. Multi-programming would minimise the idle time of the processor. The software group underestimated the time required to develop the OS. Whereas IBM laboratories built the hardware as scheduled, and the time to announce the new family of computers approached, the software was not ready. As the delay increased, IBM assigned more programmers, which grew to over 1000. In Brook's view, this did not help. Brooks later wrote a classic book [4] stating that adding programmers to a late software project was "like throwing gasoline on a fire". Ultimately, a simple but buggy disk OS with a million lines of code was ready when IBM 360 was released. The original estimate for developing the OS was $40 million. It eventually cost $500 million, the single largest expenditure in the development of System/360.

NAMING NPL

Towards the time NPL was to be announced, a search for naming it began. IBM gave the responsibility to the advertising department. After brainstorming, the group suggested the name System/360. They chose 360 to indicate that the new family of computers covered the entire 360 degrees of a compass, meaning that customers can use System/360 for any size job. The slash in the name had no significance; the advertisers thought it "looked good" following System.

ANNOUNCEMENT OF SYSTEM/360

By mid-1963, IBM had firmed up most of the architecture of the System/360 family, but no computer was working. Meanwhile, Honeywell Computers announced the Honeywell 200 in December 1963, which used integrated circuits and was two to three times faster than the 1401. It cost the same as 1401 and could run programs written for 1401 unchanged. IBM started losing customers, and IBM's sales force became jittery and wanted IBM to announce System/360. Thomas Watson Jr. decided to announce the new family on April 7, 1964, simultaneously at 165 locations worldwide, attended by about 100,000 persons. IBM did not announce the topic of the meeting. It arranged a special train to take the attendees (that included the press and big customers) from the Grand Central Station in New York. Watson Jr. addressed the biggest meeting held in Poughkeepsie. He announced IBM's computer family idea that would allow customers to upgrade their computers without having to rewrite application software. A portion of the press release [2] stated: *"System/360 includes 19 combinations in its central processors of graduated speed and memory capacity. Incorporated with these are more than 40 types of peripheral equipment, which store information and enter it into and retrieve it from the computer. Built-in communication capability makes System/360 available to remote terminals, regardless of distance."*

IBM announced six models, 30, 40, 50, 60, 62, and 70, of System/360. A non-working mock-up model of System/360 was on display. The sheer audacity of IBM's plan amazed the entire press corps and computer professionals. IBM announced the delivery date of the computers as April 1965.

IBM System/360 Model 30. Left to Right: Tapes, Console, CPU Disk drives
(Photo courtesy Wikipedia.org)

RELEASE AND RECEPTION OF SYSTEM/360

Tom Watson Jr. recalled that: *"The expenses of the project were indeed staggering. We spent three-quarters of a billion dollars just on engineering. Then we invested another $4.5 billion on factories, equipment and the rental machines themselves. It was the biggest privately financed project ever undertaken"* [2]. Watson Jr. had bet the company on the success of System/360.

Fortunately, the reception of System/360 was fantastic. IBM received over 2000 orders within the first two months. The first IBM System/360 Model 40 was delivered in April 1965, and the Model 30 in June 1965. Models 60 and 62 were merged as model 65 and delivered in November 1965, and finally, model 70 was renamed 75 and delivered in January 1966. Eight more models followed over the years. System/360 made IBM the undisputed leader of the mainframe era. By the end of 1966, between seven and eight thousand System/360s were installed, and IBM was manufacturing 1000 units per month with yearly revenue of $4 Billion [2]. In the next six years, IBM's revenue jumped to $75 Billion with a profit of $1 Billion per year. Watson's gamble handsomely paid off.

One of the significant shortcomings of the early models of System/360 was that the OS did not support interactive time-sharing, which was becoming popular. IBM rectified this lacuna in model 67 in May 1966. However, IBM's Time-Sharing Operating System was clumsy and not widely used. The University of Michigan developed the Michigan Terminal System (MTS) for IBM 360/67 in 1967. MTS was a better time-shared OS, and many academic institutions adopted it.

EPILOGUE

System/360 was the engine of IBM's growth for the next thirty years. The marketing blitz by IBM left the competition far behind, and IBM ruled the mainframe computer market. The legacies of System/360 are compatible series of computers allowing program portability, microcode, byte, byte addressing, 32-bit word length, General Purpose Registers in CPU, Program Status Word, and specialised I/O computers. Its main failing was a poorly designed OS that needed to support virtual memory and time-sharing in the early models. The time-sharing OS released later for the bigger 360 models was clumsy.

Seven companies whose combined market share was less than that of IBM, called *the seven dwarfs* (Burroughs, UNIVAC, NCR, Control Data Corporation, Honeywell, RCA, and General Electric), fought back against the introduction of System/360 in different ways [5]. RCA decided to copy the architecture of 360 and used integrated circuits that made their machines called the SPECTRA series faster. It could not compete with IBM as IBM had a vast, well-trained marketing team, a loyal customer base, and huge sales volume with better performance at a lower price. Honeywell mimicked earlier IBM machines. It built computers, both smaller and larger than Honeywell 200. Burroughs and NCR designed their series of compatible computers. Burroughs designed the 500 series computers and NCR the Century series. CDC decided to produce computers for the niche market of high-performance computers for use by scientists and engineers. UNIVAC became a shadow of its old self and sold machines mainly to airlines. General Electric collaborated with MIT and Dartmouth College and made good time-shared computers. The revenues of RCA and GE dwindled by the early 1970s. RCA sold its computer division to Sperry Rand, which owned UNIVAC, and GE sold its computer operations to Honeywell. IBM and the BUNCH (Burroughs, UNIVAC, NCR, CDC, and Honeywell) were the computer companies left.

Meanwhile, a new class of low-cost computers called minicomputers was evolving with the introduction of PDP-8 by Digital Equipment Corporation (DEC) on March 22, 1965. Minicomputers addressed a different market segment. Anecdote 13 describes the DEC story.

REFERENCES

[1] Bob O. Evans, System/360: A Retrospective View, Annals of the History of Computing, Vol. 8, No. 2, April 1986.

[2] Chuck Boyer, The 360 Revolution, IBM Publication.

[3] https://www.chipsetc.com/the-ibm-slt—solid-logic-technology.html

[4] Frederick Brooks, The Mythical Man-Month, Addison-Wesley, 1974.

[5] Martin Campbell-Kelly et al., Computer—A History of the Information Machine, Routledge, NY, 2018.

20

Neural Networks

PROLOGUE

Computers displaying intelligent behaviour have fascinated and also alarmed humans. Artificial Intelligence (AI) history is replete with very optimistic promises and hype about the development of intelligent computers, followed by disillusionment and despair. Journalists publicise and sensationalise small advances in AI. Researchers in AI are also responsible for some of the hype. As soon as Alan Newell, J. C. Shaw, and Herbert Simon wrote a promising program to play chess in 1957, Simon predicted that "within ten years, a digital computer will be the world's chess champion." It took forty years before that happened. Simon also said, "Within ten years, a digital computer will discover and prove an important new mathematical theorem". This prediction is yet to happen. In an interview with *Life* magazine in 1970, Marvin Minsky, another AI pioneer, stated that "in three to eight years, we will have a machine with the intelligence of an average human being." The over-optimism of AI researchers and the non-delivery of promises resulted in periods known as *AI winters*, during which government funding for AI research dwindled. Two incidents precipitated the first AI winter between 1974 and 1980. In 1960, Rosenblatt designed a single-layer neural net called Perceptron and trained it to recognize patterns. It was over-publicised and touted as an analog of the human brain. Marvin Minsky and Seymour Papert wrote a book titled *Perceptrons*, which showed that single-layer neural nets had severe limitations. Soon after that, research funding in neural nets ebbed. A Russian-to-English machine translation project floundered in 1966. An evaluation of AI research by Sir James Lighthill in the UK in 1973 was critical of AI research outcomes. The failure of Perceptrons to meet its hype and that of the machine translation project led to the first AI winter.

As we will see in this anecdote, neural network research recovered in 1986 with the advent of multi-layered neural networks. It led to the development of Large Language models in 2023 and the current resurgence of neural network-based AI.

NEURAL NETWORK MODEL [1]

The human brain consists of billions of nerve cells called neurons that communicate with one another using what are known as synapses. Dendrites accept external stimuli from organs, sending electrical impulses to the neuron's cell bodies. These impulses travel through the network of neurons via axons (See Figure 20.1). The neurons decide whether to ignore the impulses or send them on.

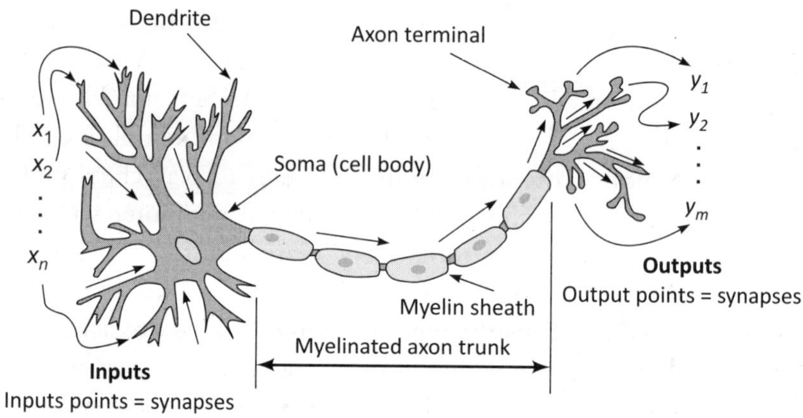

Figure 20.1 Model of a neuron
(Figure courtesy Wikipedia)

Walter McCulloch, a philosopher turned research physician, worked at the Neuropsychiatric Institute at the University of Illinois at Chicago in 1943. His area of research was the structure of the brain. Walter Pitts was a prodigy and taught himself mathematics, logic, and philosophy by frequently going to the public library in Detroit. When he was twelve, to escape from bullies on the streets of Detroit, he spent three days in the public library studying the classic book *Principia Mathematica* by Alfred Whitehead and Bertrand Russel. He detected some errors in it and wrote to Russel. Russel invited him to come to England

and work with him. He was too young and poor to accept the offer. Later, he heard that Russel was visiting the University of Chicago. Pitts joined the university as a janitor and attended Russel's and other mathematics lectures. McCulloch observed Pitts' activities, realised his genius, adopted him as his protégée, and asked him to live with him in 1939. Over the next few years, they collaborated to write several seminal papers on modelling neurons and neural networks. The McCulloch-Pitts mathematical model of a neuron is given in Figure 20.2.

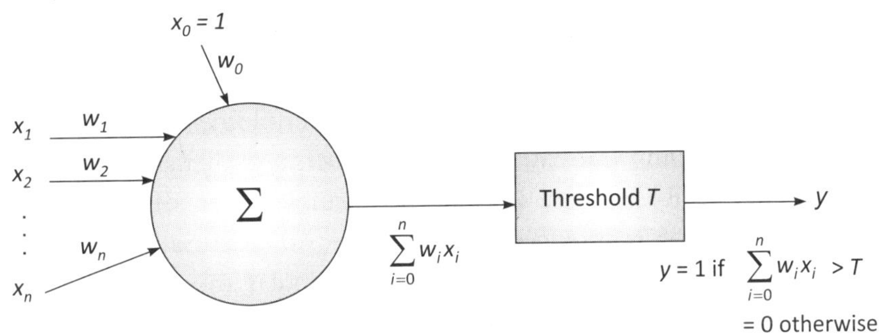

Figure 20.2 McCullough-Pitts mathematical model of a neuron

The electrical impulses to a neuron are modelled as inputs x_1, x_2 …, x_n, multiplied by a set of weights w_i. An input x_0, called bias, is set to 1. If the sum of $w_i x_i$ for $i = 0$ to n exceeds a threshold T, the neuron fires and gives an output y, else 0. In the model, the x's are binary numbers.

Warren McCulloch **Walter Pitts**

(Photographs courtesy Wikipedia)

PERCEPTRON [2]

Frank Rosenblatt was employed as a research psychologist at the Cornell Aeronautical Laboratory (CAL) in Buffalo, New York, after obtaining a Ph.D. in psychology from Cornell University in 1956. He studied the model of neurons suggested by McCulloch and Pitts. He built an electronic digital system to simulate a network of neurons (an artificial neural network (ANN)) in 1957 and called it *Perceptron.* A Perceptron had an input layer, a single layer of artificial neurons, and an output layer. Rosenblatt trained the Perceptron by adjusting the vector of weights $w_1, w_2, \ldots, w_n$ to obtain a desired output vector $d_1, d_2 \ldots, d_n$ for a given input vector $x_1, x_2, \ldots, x_n$. The inputs and outputs are binary vectors. An array of bits, one bit per pixel, represents an image. Rosenblatt trained a Perceptron to separate images into two sets based on a distinguishing characteristic. For example, he was able to separate circles from rectangles. In mathematical terminology, a Perceptron is capable of classifying linearly separable vectors. As digital components were expensive, Rosenblatt built only a single layer of neurons in Perceptron. The Perceptron was touted as an artificial "brain" and over-publicised by the popular press. The popular media implied that Perceptron could solve many complex recognition problems.

Marvin Minsky and Seymour Papert debunked the myth of the Perceptron by showing that it had severe limitations in a book of the same title they wrote in 1969 [3]. They analysed how Perceptron learnt. They showed, theoretically, that it is impossible to train a Perceptron to learn the exclusive OR function. The book dampened research funding for artificial neural networks (ANN).

MULTI-LAYERED NEURAL NETWORKS

Several researchers recognized the limitations of single-layer neural networks. Following this, many research groups worldwide started exploring neural networks with two or three layers of neurons interconnected in various patterns. The layers between the output and input layer of Perceptron were called "hidden layers". Researchers also improved the neuron model by replacing the simple threshold T in the McCulloch-Pitts model with a non-linear activation function. A neuron fired if $\left\{ f\left(b + \sum_{i=1}^{n} w_i x_i \right) \right\} > T$, where b is a bias and f is a non-linear function. Training an ANN consisted of adjusting the weights w_i until it could recognize a desired pattern. As computing power was limited, training ANNs was slow and expensive. Several groups worldwide independently developed the back-propagation algorithm to train multilayer ANNs. They were, however, impractical due to the complex computation required for training.

David Rumelhart, Geoffrey Hinton, and Ronald Williams achieved a breakthrough in 1986. In a research paper published in *Nature*, they explained how the back-propagation algorithm uses the hidden layers to find features in the input data and allows succeeding layers to use these in recognition tasks [4].

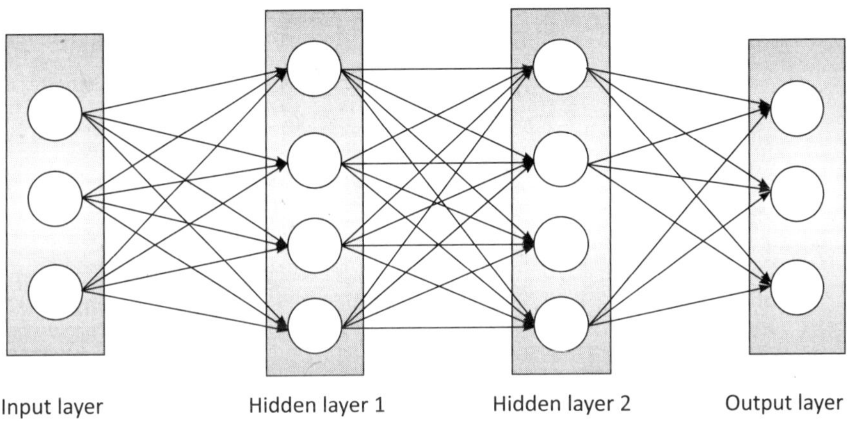

Figure 20.3 A multi-layered neural network

Yann LeCun, a French computer scientist, joined as a post-doctoral fellow in 1987 with Hinton, a professor at the University of Toronto. He worked with Hinton's group for a year and researched on ANNs. In 1988, LeCun joined AT&T Bell Laboratories and continued research and development on ANNs. He led a group that trained a multi-layered ANN to recognize handwritten US postcodes called ZIP codes (similar to India's PIN code) in 1989. This project was one of the first to use ANNs in a practical problem. His group continued working on ANNs and trained a multilayer ANN to recognize characters in handwritten cheques widely used in US banks [5].

After these initial successes in the late 1980s, further research in ANNs slowed down as training simple ANNs with existing computers was laborious and expensive. Training an ANN with more than two hidden layers was laborious and difficult. Training needed more data. Only in 2006 did Hinton and his associates find a systematic training method for many-layered ANNs. Meanwhile, Yann LeCun, Yoshua Bengio, and several other researchers proposed and experimented with a variety of ANNs known as Convolutional Neural Nets, Recurrent Neural Nets, Neural Nets with Long- and Short-term Memory, and

Generative Adversarial Networks. These ANNs differ in the type of activation function and the configuration of arcs connecting neurons. These ANNs use training schemes specific to them and are appropriate for recognizing different types of inputs, such as handwriting, speech, and images. For their pioneering work on ANNs, Hinton, LeCunn, and Bengio received the Turing Award in 2018.

Geoffrey Hinton **Yann LeCun** **Yoshua Bengio**

(Photographs courtesy Wikipedia)

DEEP NEURAL NETWORKS [6]

Training these multi-layered ANNs, called *deep neural networks*, was too slow and impractical until GPGPUs (see Anecdote 55), which are very fast and work in parallel, were available. GPGPUs could quickly solve linear algebraic equations that arise while training ANNs. Cloud computing arrived and hosted GPGPUs that could be used "on-demand". The Internet provided oodles of data. YouTube offers vast quantities of video data. Digitised speech data were available from audiobooks. Images were available from facial data collected by the US Department of Defence, Flickr, Facebook, and the Internet. These developments led to *deep learning,* the process of training multi-layered ANNs (also known as *deep neural nets*) to recognize text, image, audio, and video data.

Soon, many companies, such as Google and Microsoft, started researching ANNs. In 2015, DeepMind, an AI company in the UK, trained an ANN to play the Chinese board game GO, called AlphaGO, that beat the world GO champion Lee Sedol (See Anecdote 9). The latest success of ANNs is ChatGPT, a generative large language model, that can converse fluently in any subject (See Anecdote 72).

Deep ANNs have two significant flaws. Many deep ANNs cannot explain how they solved a problem. Solutions obtained by some deep

ANNs are not robust. In other words, a small perturbation of inputs can sometimes lead to incorrect recognition. These flaws could lead to legal and ethical problems. Suppose a self-driving car trained by a deep ANN meets with an accident, causing the death of a human. In that case, it is difficult to fix responsibility. An incorrect recognition of a face at a crime scene may send an innocent person to prison. Research is in progress to rectify these problems but has yet to mature.

EPILOGUE

In the perception of the general public, industry, and governments, AI has oscillated between periods of exuberance and despair. AI has transformed from an area of academic study to one of the mainstream technologies impacting our daily lives.

Among AI researchers, the two schools of AI–writing programs mimicking human problem solving versus creating a model of the human brain and training it had their ups and downs. Deep neural networks and deep learning belong to the second school and are now ruling AI research (2024). Almost human-like capability exhibited by generative Large Language Models such as ChatGPT and Google's Gemini has alarmed both their creators and the public. There is a public outcry to regulate their development, even some demands to ban further research and development in this field of AI (AI is now synonymous in public perception with deep neural nets and their training). In my opinion, these are extreme reactions, and I believe that humankind is wise enough to adapt to the new reality of AI.

REFERENCES

[1] Andrey Kurenkov, A Brief History of Neural Nets and Deep Learning, https://www.skynettoday.com/overviews/neural-net-history

[2] Frank Rosenblatt, The Perceptron—a perceiving and recognizing automaton, Report 85-460-1, Cornell Aeronautical Laboratory, 1957.

[3] Marvin Minsky, Seymour Papert, Perceptrons: An Introduction to Computational Geometry, MIT Press, 1969.

[4] David E. Rumelhart, Geoffrey E. Hinton, and Ronald J. Williams, Learning representation by Back-propagating errors, Nature, Vol. 323, October 1986. www.iro.umontreal.ca

[5] Y. Le Cun et al., Backpropagation Applied to Handwritten Zip Code Recognition, Neural Computation, Vol. 1, No. 4, pp. 541–551, 1989.

[6] Ian Goodfellow, Yoshua Bengio, and Aaron Courville, Deep Learning, MIT Press, 2016.

21

BASIC and the Dartmouth Time-sharing System

PROLOGUE

Dartmouth College is a liberal arts college established in Hanover, New Hampshire, USA, in 1769. It was a small men's college in the 1960s with an enrollment of around 3000 with 2500 undergraduates. About 2000 students were in humanities and social sciences. It had a small computer centre headed by Thomas Kurtz, a mathematics department faculty member. In 1962, he, along with John Kemeny, a colleague, persuaded the college administration to expand the computing facilities and introduce a course on computing to all students, including those in humanities and social sciences. In their eloquent letter to the President of the university [1], they wrote, *"Whether a student will ever use a computing machine or not, his life is likely to be affected by such machines, and hence, he should know something about their capabilities and limitations. In this sense, contact with electronic brains is as essential as learning how to use the library."* The college approved their suggestion. However, to implement it, they encountered two problems. The first was existing programming languages, such as FORTRAN and Algol, were too complex to teach humanities and social science students. The second was that the available computers were batch-processing systems. They were difficult to use. Batch processing requires students to write a program, punch it on cards, and submit it to a computer operator. The operator assembles a batch of programs and feeds them to the computer. The students receive the printed results in a few hours. Very often, the program would have an error that required the program to be modified, and a student had to go through the cycle of punching corrections on cards and re-submission. Often, students needed three or more attempts to get results. This process wasted students' time and de-motivated many students to learn programming. Kurtz and Kemeny wanted to solve both of these problems.

BASIC PROGRAMMING LANGUAGE

The most popular programming language in the 1960s was Fortran. Algol was another language standardised by an international group of computer scientists. It had a better syntactic structure. Fortran had efficient compilers supported by IBM and was adopted widely. Conversely, major computer vendors did not support Algol, and the available compilers were inefficient. Kemeny and Kurtz considered using a subset of Fortran to teach programming to students. Fortran was designed to be used by scientists and engineers, and its syntax rules were complex for humanities and social science students to learn. The same was true of Algol. These shortcomings of Fortran and Algol motivated Kurtz and Kemeny to explore designing a new language that would be easy to learn and use by humanities and social science students. They developed a language they named BASIC (Beginners' All-purpose Symbolic Instruction Code) with a small set of instructions and simple syntax rules. BASIC combined some valuable features of Fortran and Algol. I give below a part of a BASIC program to add alternate numbers of a string of numbers X(1), X(2), X(3), ... X(50):

```
10 FOR I = 1 TO 50 STEP 2
20 LET S = S + X(I)
30 NEXT I
```

Observe that each statement has a unique number as a label. This labelling simplified editing. A programmer may add a new statement using an intermediate number. In the program above, single letters name variables. In the first version of BASIC, variable names were at most two characters long: a letter followed by a digit. Kurtz and Kemeny felt it was adequate for small programs. The use of LET in statements was to remove any confusion students may have if they write X = X+1. The other commands were READ, PRINT, GOTO, IF, THEN, DATA, GOSUB, RETURN, DIM, DEF, and REM for remarks.

Arithmetic operations available were: +, –, *, /, and up arrow ^ for exponentiation. Numbers were classified as real (those with fractional parts) and integers in Fortran and Algol. In BASIC, all numbers were reals. This feature simplified writing programs.

DARTMOUTH TIME-SHARING SYSTEM (DTSS)

Thomas Kurtz visited the Massachusetts Institute of Technology (MIT) in early 1962, where the first time-shared operating system called Compatible Time-Sharing System (CTSS) for the IBM 7090 mainframe computer designed by Fernando Corbató was in operation (See Anecdote 15). It was a complex system meant for a large group of researchers and not suitable for use by novices. During this visit, he met Professor John McCarthy, who had motivated the development of CTSS. When Kurtz told McCarthy about Dartmouth's plan to teach programming to beginners, he responded, "Why don't you use a time-sharing system" [2]. He told Kurtz that time-sharing was feasible on a small computer and mentioned a time-sharing system developed by Bolt, Beranek, and Newman (BBN), a company in the Boston area, for a small PDP-1 computer. Kurtz returned to Dartmouth and, along with Kemeny, wrote a proposal to the National Science Foundation (NSF) to support the development of a suitable programming language and a time-sharing system to teach programming to undergraduates at Dartmouth College. They also persuaded the college administration to fund the project partially and explored the market for suitable computers. They selected the GE-225 computer as a suitable computer. Kurtz and a student went to GE's factory in Phoenix, Arizona, in the summer of 1962 and discussed the project with the engineers there [2]. When they returned, they decided that a combination of two computers, GE-225, to compile and execute programs, and DATANET-30, a front-end computer for communication with teletype terminals and schedule programs, would be appropriate. The two computers were to share a disc to send and receive data (See Figure 21.1).

The college sent a letter of intent to buy the systems to GE in April 1963. Meanwhile, Kurtz and Kemeny and student programmers started to learn how to program the system.

In parallel, Kemeny used a GE-225 computer nearby to write a compiler for BASIC. In January 1964, NSF agreed to grant US$ 500,000 for the project. GE also gave Dartmouth a significant discount to buy the computers. The computers arrived in late February 1964 and became operational in March 1964. Immediately, a group of around a dozen students, mostly senior undergraduate students in mathematics, worked along with Kemeny and Kurtz to design a time-shared operating system for it. Kemeny and Kurtz's decision to take the students' assistance to write an operating system was bold, as in those days, computer vendors or professional programmers hired by customers designed complex operating systems.

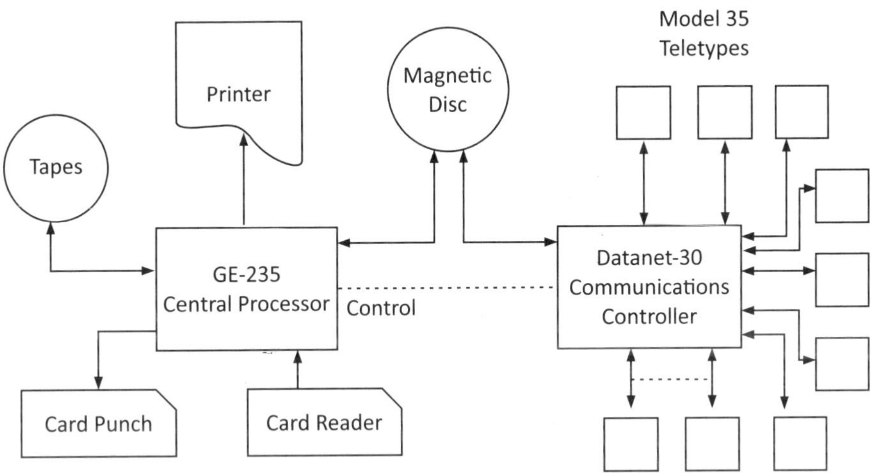

Figure 21.1 Schematic Diagram of System Hardware

Schematic of Dartmouth Time-Sharing Computer System

The dashed line connecting Datanet-30 and GE-235 is for control signals

(Figure courtesy Wikipedia)

The two-computer configuration proved a good choice from several points of view [3]. The front-end computer DATANET-30 was the executive that allocated time slices to users and managed the scheduling of programs ready for execution. Execution of programs took place in the mainframe GE-225 system. Execution errors of programs running in GE-225 would not damage the job scheduler in the front-end computer. The mainframe computer received control signals via a special path (See Figure 21.1) from the front-end computer. The system transferred data between the two computers via a shared disk. The system's efficiency increased dramatically due to separating tasks between DATANET-30 and GE-225. Users spent most of their time typing programs on the teletypewriter, examining results, and thinking how to proceed. These tasks typically took minutes, and only the inexpensive DATANET-30 was used during this time, with several users typing programs. Simultaneously, the more expensive GE-225 executed several users' programs, each program for a few seconds, and placed the results in the shared disk. The results were taken by DATANET-30 and printed on the teletypewriters of users. GE-225 was thus efficiently used to cater to many users.

The student programmers worked hard, and DTSS became operational on May 1, 1964, with two teletypewriters that could be used simultaneously with the system. When GE saw the successful operation of the time-sharing operating system, it was pleasantly surprised and replaced the GE-225 with a more powerful GE-235 at no extra cost. GE's idea was to collaborate with Dartmouth to develop the system further and use it in GE's data centre operation.

Thomas Kurtz **John Kemeny**

(Photos courtesy Wikipedia.org)

In a few months, around 30 teletypewriters were using the system simultaneously. One of the main objectives of DTSS was to provide immediate feedback to a student as soon as he submitted a program for execution. The designers aimed at a response time of around 10 seconds as they wanted a student to have the illusion that the computer was working solely for him. All statements in BASIC had a line number to simplify editing. Commands to DTSS did not have a line number. The commands were simple English commands. For example, NEW to name a program and store it in memory, LIST to display a program in memory, SAVE to store a program on the disk, RUN to compile and execute a program in memory, OLD to copy a previous program stored in the disk to memory, RENAME to change the name of a program in memory, UNSAVE to clear a program from the disk. Students thought that these commands were part of BASIC language. BASIC and DTSS were intertwined so well that students did not realise that an operating system was managing the execution of their programs.

EPILOGUE

When GE saw the successful operation of DTSS at Dartmouth College, it saw a commercial opportunity to sell time-shared computers. In January 1965, two students from Dartmouth installed DTSS and BASIC on GE-235 and DATANET-30 at GE's factory in Phoenix, Arizona. GE renamed the combination of these two computers as GE-265 and started using it in 25 of their data centres that catered to over 50,000 users.

Besides BASIC, these systems had Algol and Fortran. Over the next few years, GE implemented DTSS in more powerful mainframes and was highly successful in marketing and using these computers in their data centres.

Upgraded versions of DTSS were implemented over several years at Dartmouth on more powerful GE computers. By 1969, Dartmouth added terminals at Dartmouth and several high schools in the neighbouring areas that catered to over a hundred users.

Dartmouth group improved BASIC, and new versions with better features appeared over several years. Many mini-computer vendors adopted BASIC. When the Altair 8800 PC appeared in 1974, Bill Gates and Paul Allen wrote a version of BASIC (not Dartmouth BASIC) interpreter for this PC, and Microsoft was born (Incidentally, Bill Gates learnt to program when he was a student in high school by using BASIC on a GE time-shared computer).

As many versions of BASIC started appearing in the market, the American National Standards Institute (ANSI) standardised BASIC in 1978. BASIC was popular until the late 1980s and gradually died as better languages appeared.

REFERENCES

[1] The 1960's Dartmouth College, https://www.dartmouth.edu/its-tools/archive/history/timeline/1960s.html

[2] Thomas E. Kurtz, BASIC: In History of Programming Languages, Association for Computing Machinery, Editor Richard L. Wexelblat, June 1978, pp. 515–537.

[3] John G. Kemeny and Thomas E. Kurtz, Dartmouth Time-Sharing, Science, October 11, 1968, pp. 223–228.

22

From ELIZA to Alexa—History of Human-Computer Conversation

PROLOGUE

Alan Mathison Turing was born on 23 June 1912 in the UK. He obtained a Bachelor's degree from Cambridge University in 1934 and a Ph.D. from Princeton University in 1938. Turing made three landmark contributions during his scientific career. In 1936, he published a paper titled "On Computable Numbers," in which he proposed a model of a universal computing machine popularly known as "The Turing Machine." He proved that numbers exist that this machine cannot compute. This paper demonstrated the theoretical limitations of computers. In 1940, he found a method of breaking the German Enigma code [1] and designed a machine that broke it. Enigma code-breaking contributed to the Allied victory in the Second World War. The last was the paper "Computing Machinery and Intelligence" [2], which appeared in Mind, a little-known philosophical magazine, in October 1950. He starts the article with the sentence, "*I propose to consider the question "Can machines think?" This should begin with the definitions of the meaning of the terms "machines" and "think.*" He argues that the common usage of these words is vague, and a machine cannot answer the question as posed. He replaces the question by postulating an imitation game. He proposed a game between a computer that imitates a man, a woman, and an interrogator. A wall separates the interrogator from the computer and the woman. The interrogator types his questions using a teletypewriter. These are randomly routed to either the computer or the woman. The answers are typed and relayed back to the interrogator. Suppose after a reasonably long question-answering session, the interrogator cannot decide which answers are from the computer and which are from the woman. In that case, the woman and the computer are indistinguishable. In other words, one may conclude that the computer is intelligent. Turing believed that in fifty years, computers would pass his test.

Alan Turing
(Photo courtesy Wikipedia)

Computer scientists have extensively debated the Turing test, and the current consensus is that it is a significant milestone in the development of Artificial Intelligence (AI) but does not fully capture the nuances of human intelligence. However, the idea of a human-computer conversation captured researchers' imagination in AI. It led to the development of several computer-based natural language question-answering systems.

ELIZA PROGRAM [3]

Joseph Weizenbaum, a Massachusetts Institute of Technology professor, wrote one of the earliest programs in 1966 to mimic a natural language conversation between a human and a computer. He designed a list-processing language called SLIP and embedded it in MAD (Michigan Algorithmic Decoder). Weizenbaum wrote a program using this language on MIT's Time-shared IBM 7094 computer. Weizenbaum called this program ELIZA after the flower seller Eliza Doolittle in Bernard Shaw's play Pygmalion (later adapted as the popular musical My Fair

Lady) in which Professor Henry Higgins takes a bet that he will teach flower seller Eliza Doolittle to speak proper English in an upper-class accent. ELIZA program learns to converse gradually through several interactions, just like Shaw's character Eliza Doolittle. ELIZA mimicked a non-directive psychotherapist—an approach in which a therapist tries to let a patient figure out their problem by framing questions based on a patient's response. Weizenbaum aimed to program a computer to respond in natural language by analysing a natural language input. I reproduce a typical conversation with ELIZA in Figure 22.1.

Patient: Men are all alike.

Computer: In what way?

Patient: They're always bugging us about something or the other.

Computer: Can you think of a specific example?

Patient: Well, my boyfriend made me come here.

Computer: Your boyfriend made you come here?

Patient: He says I'm depressed much of the time.

Computer: I am sorry to hear you are depressed.

Patient: It is true I am unhappy.

Computer: Do you think coming here will help you not to be unhappy?

Patient: I need some help, that seems certain.

Computer: What would mean to you if you got some help?

Patient: Perhaps I could learn to get along with my mother.

Computer: Tell me more about your family.

Patient: My mother takes care of me.

Computer: Who else in your family takes care of you?

Patient: My father.

Computer: Your father?

Conversation continues ...

Figure 22.1 Sample of ELIZA's Conversation

ELIZA used the fact that people use a small number of keywords in most conversations. ELIZA stores sentence templates whenever a keyword appears. For example, a reference to a member of one's family, such as "my mother" or "my sister," results in the computer printing the response "Tell me more about your family." Often, ELIZA reverses a patient's statement, as in the computer's response, "Your boyfriend made you come here?" to a patient's statement, "Well, my boyfriend made me come here", in the above example. Several simple rules to transform sentences made ELIZA seemingly an intelligent conversationalist and fooled many ordinary people into believing another person was answering the questions. Weizenbaum wrote a book [4] based on his observations of people who used ELIZA. He was startled to see how people using ELIZA became emotionally involved. Even his secretary, who had seen him develop ELIZA, asked him to leave the room when she conversed with it!

Joseph Weizenbaum
(Photo courtesy Wikipedia)

HUMAN-COMPUTER DIALOG SYSTEMS [5]

Weizenbaum's research kindled the interest of many researchers, and they wrote natural language processing programs to mimic human-computer dialogs. Kenneth Colby of Stanford University wrote a program called PARRY in 1972 that simulated a conversation of a paranoid schizophrenic with a doctor. Colby gave five psychiatrists a transcript of PARRY's responses and the responses from a human patient and asked them to separate PARRY's responses from those of the actual patient. The psychiatrists separated the two responses only 48% of the time—almost like guessing. Colby demonstrated a conversation between ELIZA and PARRY at the International Computer Communication Conference (ICCC 72), which is interesting to read [6].

JABBERWACKY, a program developed by the British programmer Rollo Carpenter in 1988, was the subsequent significant development in dialog systems. By then, PCs had arrived, and developing interactive dialog systems was easier and cheaper. It was the first system that combined natural language processing with machine learning. JABBERWACKY analysed a user's input, identified keywords, and created a database of input-output responses over a series of interactions. A machine learning system used this to improve its responses. JABBERWACKY became popular and is available on the Internet even now.

Michael Mauldin coined the term chatterbot in 1994 for human-computer dialog systems. Chatterbot was later abbreviated as *chatbot.* He wrote a dialog system named JULIA, which ran on the Internet Relay Chat (IRC) system. JULIA's responses were humorous or clever and made JULIA famous. Chatbot entered dictionaries around 2000. The Oxford Dictionary defines *it as a computer program designed to simulate conversation with human users, especially over the Internet.*

In 1991, Creative Labs released a chatbot named DR. SBAITSO (Sound Blaster AI Text to Speech Operator), which mimicked a psychologist and used a straightforward text-based dialog system. It was capable of giving spoken answers, but the system that was released gave answers as text. Speech-based dialogs became popular later in interactive systems designed to answer customer queries.

Richard Wallace of Lehigh University developed the next notable system named ALICE (Artificial Linguistic Internet Computer Entity) in 1995 for use on the Internet. It was a rule-based system that used a natural language processor with a database of 41000 keywords. One of its exciting features was its use of linguistic deflection in answering queries. For example, if you asked, "Why are apples Red?", it responded, "Does everything have to have an explanation?" ALICE was rewritten and improved, and the latest version uses an AI markup language to specify conversation rules. It was a remarkable system in its time and won the Loebner Prize (a prize given to a most human-like dialog system) in 2000, 2001, and 2004. The perfume retailer CyberScent used ALICE technology for online customer support. Spike Jonze, a movie writer and director, cites ALICE as the inspiration for his highly acclaimed movie *Her*, in which the hero falls in love with a chatbot named Samantha.

VOICE ASSISTANTS

Bell Labs, IBM, and academic researchers in universities pioneered speech recognition and synthesis research in the 1960s. Very powerful integrated circuits were available by 2001, which led to the commercial availability of robust speech recognition and synthesis systems. Chatbot developers used these extensively.

ActiveBuddy Inc. designed one of the first voice-based intelligent chatbots named SMARTERCHILD in 2001. It had access to an extensive database and used this to answer queries such as the results of football matches, stock prices, weather, arrival and departure times of airlines, etc. It was available on America Online (AOL) Instant Messenger and Windows Live Messenger. It inspired the design of many interactive voice-based customer relations systems.

SIRI was one of the first voice assistants integrated with smartphones and devices using Apple's iOS. Apple Computers released it in 2010. SRI International collaborated with the Federal Polytechnic of Lausanne and Nuance Communications and developed the voice recognition and response technology that SIRI used. An advanced neural network developed by Nuance Communications trained it. SIRI is quite sophisticated and can obey commands such as: Hey Siri, call my mom, remind me tomorrow to send greetings to Tom, and what will the weather be like tomorrow? It answers questions such as "What is the height of Mount Everest?" by using the information available on the Internet. SIRI finds it challenging to recognize foreign accents. It ostensibly stores many conversations (anonymously) to train the system, worrying many privacy advocates.

IBM developed a notable Voice Assistant named WATSON in 2011. IBM WATSON beat the champions Brad Rutter and Ken Jennings in a "Jeopardy!" television game on 16 February 2011. In this game, a player guesses the question from its answer. Later, doctors used IBM WATSON to diagnose illnesses and engineers to design systems.

Microsoft released the Voice Assistant CORTANA in 2014. CORTANA worked with both Windows OS, Android, and iOS. Microsoft integrated CORTANA with its Bing search engine. It answered questions, scheduled appointments, and could converse in several languages, including Chinese. Microsoft discontinued it in 2021.

Amazon released an intelligent voice-based chatbot named ALEXA in 2014. Amazon bought a Polish speech synthesiser company, Nona, in 2013 and designed ALEXA using its technology. ALEXA uses AI and natural language processing for speech recognition and synthesis. Amazon built a smart speaker (a combination of a microphone and a speaker which Wi-Fi or Bluetooth could connect to a computer) named *Echo*, which is used as the primary device for voice-based interaction with a smartphone/computer running on Android, iOS,

Linux, or Windows. A user wakes up ALEXA using the command (also called a *hot word*) "*Hey Alexa*". Echo is used to answer real-time queries on the weather, stock prices, and sports scores. It can also be commanded to play music, set alarms, stream podcasts, read audiobooks, and control smart devices. It understands several languages: English, French, German, Italian, Spanish, Portuguese, Japanese, Hindi, and Arabic. Industry estimates that Amazon employs around 10,000 people in the ALEXA group, and it costs approximately $200 million to develop the system. As of 2019, Amazon sold 100 million ALEXA-enabled smart speakers.

The media reported that Amazon routinely records user interactions (ostensibly to train the system) without users' consent and uses it for marketing. Amazon vehemently denies this statement.

Google released GOOGLE ASSISTANT, a chatbot similar to ALEXA, in 2016 for Android-based smartphones. It uses AI extensively and accepts both voice and text commands. It is also adapted to work with several other operating systems. It answers questions, plays games, schedules appointments, adjusts device settings, and carries out many other daily tasks. In a recent update, Google announced that it identifies objects using the phone's camera, supports e-commerce, and can be used to send money. Customers may also use GOOGLE ASSISTANT as a smart speaker, like ALEXA. There are concerns about the privacy of GOOGLE ASSISTANT users.

EPILOGUE

Chatbots developed by companies for customer interaction proliferated with advances in AI, natural language processing, and the advent of social media platforms. Since early 2016, chatbots have answered customer complaints and queries. Human interaction has almost disappeared, to the chagrin of several customers, including me. Interactions with chatbots can often be exasperating. Over 500,000 chatbots covering a wide area, including marketing, health care, entertainment, education, and many other fields, are now active.

REFERENCES

[1] Imperial War Museum, UK, How Alan Turing Cracked the Enigma Code. https://www.iwm.org.uk/history/how-alan-turing-cracked-the-enigma-code#:~:text=With%20the%20help%20of%20captured,of%20all%20German%20naval%20signals.

[2] A.M. Turing, Computing Machinery and Intelligence, Mind, 59, pp. 433–60, October 1950.
https://academic.oup.com/mind/article/LIX/236/433/986238

[3] J. Weizenbaum, ELIZA—A Computer Program for the Study of Natural Language Communication between Man and Machine, Com. ACM, Vol. 9, No. 1, Jan. 1966, pp. 36–45.
https://dl.acm.org/doi/10.1145/365153.365168

[4] J. Weizenbaum, Computer Power and Human Reasoning, W. H. Freeman, San Francisco, 1976.

[5] E. Adamopoulou, and L. Moussiades, Chatbots: History, Technology, and Applications, Machine Learning and Applications, Vol. 2, December 2020, Elsevier.
https://www.sciencedirect.com/science/article/pii/S2666827020300062#b107

[6] V. Cerf, PARRY encounters ELIZA. Based on a demonstration at ICCC 1972.
https://datatracker.ietf.org/doc/html/rfc439

23

Electronic Payment Systems

PROLOGUE

In 1949, Frank McNamara dined at an expensive New York restaurant, and to his embarrassment, he had left his wallet at home. Fortunately, his wife rescued him. It made him invent a Diner's Club Card with his business partner Ralph Schneider in 1950. The system he invented was to enroll frequent diners as members of the Diner's Club, which issued cards that the members could use to pay restaurant bills instead of cash. Diner's Club persuaded several popular restaurants in New York to accept Diner's Club cards. Members paid the cost of meals by presenting their cards to the restaurant. The restaurant owners collected the amount due from the customers' Bank. The Bank charged a small commission from its customers for each transaction.

In 1958, American Express started issuing what is now known as credit cards to their customers and convinced many merchants to accept payment with these cards, guaranteeing payments to the merchants. Bank of America followed in 1958, first in Fresno, California, and later all over California. It expanded in 1966 to include banks in all the states in the United States and was renamed Visa Card. Other banks did not want to be left behind when they found that the credit card was a profitable business. They cooperated and created the Mastercard, accepted nationwide in the United States in 1967.

In 1960, IBM asked Forrest Parry to embed a magnetic tape strip storing the owner's identification data in their identity card. While he was struggling to find a technique to embed the magnetic tape, his wife, who was ironing clothes, suggested that he should try a hot iron. Parry ran a hot iron over a magnetic strip placed on a plastic card and was pleasantly surprised to see that it stuck permanently to the card, and the data in it was intact.

This magnetic strip technology, with the strip on a plastic credit card storing data relevant to the card's owner, was adopted by credit card companies in the 1970s. Banks gave merchants Point of Sales (PoS) terminals. When customers presented their credit card, the merchant requested them to enter their Personal Identity Number (PIN) on the PoS and swiped the card. Telephone lines transmitted the data stored in the card from the merchant to the card company, and the transaction was approved if the PIN and the card data matched. Soon, debit cards followed. The Bank debited a customer's bank account when she paid a merchant. By the 1980s, credit and debit card payments took off with the expansion of specialised intermediaries such as Visa and Mastercard, which settled accounts between banks and credit card holders worldwide.

Frauds by duplicating data on magnetic stripes increased in the early 1980s, leading to newer card technology using embedded microprocessors in 1984. Contactless cards using Near Field Communication (NFC) technology appeared in the early 2000s. Credit and debit cards heralded the beginning of electronic payment systems.

AUTOMATED TELLER MACHINE (ATM)

John Shepherd-Barron was working in De La Rue, a printer, in England. One evening in 1965, he found no cash in his wallet. It was after banking hours. He wondered why there should not be a cash dispenser outside banks to withdraw money after banking hours, similar to chocolate dispensers. He and his team designed a machine that accepted specially printed cheques marked with a carbon-14 radioactive material to ensure security and dispensed a fixed amount. Each customer had a Personal Identification Number (PIN), which she entered on the cash dispenser after inserting the cheque to withdraw cash. Shepherd-Barron proposed a 6-digit PIN but found that his wife could easily remember only up to 4 digits. Therefore, he decided on a 4-digit PIN, which still survives! He sold his idea to Barclay Bank, which installed the first cash dispensing machine, later called ATM, on 27 June 1967 in its Enfield branch, limiting the maximum cash withdrawal to £10. Within a few days, a Swedish bank installed an ATM called Bankomat, designed by Matior. After a few months, Westminster Bank in England installed ATMs designed by Smith Industries named Chubb MD2. Soon, ATMs spread all over Europe. The first ATMs designed by Docutel, a Texas Company, were installed in the USA in September 1969 by the Chemical Bank in New York.

ATM designers used microprocessors in the machines in 1972. Microprocessors added many more features to ATMs. Soon, Banks networked ATMs with their computer systems. Further innovations in networking allowed customers to withdraw money from any ATM regardless of which Bank owned it.

SWIFT SYSTEM

In the 1970s, international inter-bank financial transactions were settled manually by messages sent over a Telex network. The First National City Bank of New York (now Citibank) controlled the system. European banks were wary of a single entity control. Carl Reuterskslöld, an earlier employee of American Express, decided to establish an international computer-based cooperative system based on a common standard to settle inter-bank financial transactions. He established the Society for Worldwide Interbank Financial Telecommunication (SWIFT) as a cooperative venture with 239 banks in 15 countries as founding members in 1973, with headquarters in Brussels. Logica, a telecommunication consultant, designed the communication system, and Burroughs Corporation installed the computers. The system was ready in 1975, and the first transaction using the network took place in 1977. Banks in the United States became members of SWIFT in 1979. It is an example of international cooperation in banking and has grown, incorporating new technologies as soon as they matured.

ONLINE PAYMENT WITH MINITEL

Minitel was a pioneering system rolled out by the French Telecom in 1982 (See Anecdote 49). Each subscriber got a Minitel terminal connected by the French Telecom company. Customers could send/receive messages, shop online, obtain information on train timings, and many other services currently available on the World Wide Web with Minitel. The Telephone company charged payments for goods and services to the subscribers' telephone bills. Minitel was a pioneering online e-commerce and payment system.

MONDEX CASH CARD

The idea of a stored value card (sometimes called a digital wallet) was invented in 1990 by Tim Jones and Graham Higgins, who were employees of the NatWest Bank in the United Kingdom. Their idea was to let the card owners withdraw money from their Bank and store it in the card's memory. The card became a *digital wallet.* A customer and a merchant inserted their respective cards into the terminal. A customer transferred money from his card to the merchant's card by entering the amount and his PIN. The card's memory stored the previous ten transactions. Customers recharged the card from ATMs or from cooperating banks.

This idea was feasible as microprocessors had become inexpensive and were used in the cards. The NatWest and Midland banks implemented it in 1995 in the UK. In July 1996, 17 cooperating banks spun off Mondex cards into a separate entity called Mondex International. Mastercard acquired Mondex in September 1996. The card use spread internationally and was popular in the early 2000s. However, when smartphones arrived, payment was more convenient with smartphones, and Mondex cards died in 2008.

PAYPAL DIGITAL WALLET

When the World Wide Web appeared in 1993, technologists wondered whether it could be used for commerce. As early as 1994, Pizza Hut created a website that allowed its customers to order a Pizza from a menu and pay cash on delivery. Early browsers were insecure and unsuitable for financial transactions. Netscape, a pioneer in web browser design, released encryption software to ensure secure communication between a client and a server, called Secure Software Layer Protocol (SSL 2.0) in 1995. It had some flaws, and version 3.0 was released in 1996. This software was the basis for financial transactions over the Web. Credit Card transactions began on the Web in 1995.

Max Levchin **Peter Thiel**
(Photos courtesy Wikipedia)

In September 1995, Pierre Omidyar founded AuctionWeb (later renamed eBay), letting customers list items for sale and sell to the highest bidder. The purchaser paid by mailing a physical cheque, as credit cards were unsuitable for individual transactions. In 1998, Max Levchin, a security specialist, and Peter Thiel, a financier, started Fieldlink (later renamed Confinity) to provide secure software for hand-held devices such as Palm Pilot. The company was unsuccessful, and they were looking for alternate business models and saw a business opportunity to enable small payments for purchases on eBay. Confinity switched to providing a digital wallet to customers to allow small payments over the Web. Meanwhile, Elon Musk and his associates had started a company named X.com with the same objectives as Confinity. The companies merged and named PayPal in 2001, with Thiel as its managing director. Anyone with a valid email ID and phone number could become a member of PayPal and create a digital wallet to deposit money using their credit/debit card and pay from it. Interestingly, when PayPal started, it encouraged members to join by crediting $10 to a member's account! Soon, customers used PayPal to make most of their payments on eBay. PayPal earns revenue by charging a small commission for making a payment. Membership multiplied in step with the growth of eBay. PayPal went public, and eBay acquired it in 2002 for $1.5 billion in eBay shares. PayPal became an independent subsidiary of eBay. It improved its services in step with the evolution of new technology. When smartphones appeared, customers could create PayPal wallets on their smartphones and pay from one smartphone wallet to another.

PayPal became profitable and the dominant multinational player in the e-payment market. By 2022, its subscriber base grew to 435 million, its turnover to approximately $1350 billion, and its profit exceeded $ 2 billion.

MOBILE PAYMENT SYSTEMS

The arrival of mobile phones revolutionised e-payment. One mode of payment was to store credit/debit card data in the phone and pay merchants by placing the phone near a PoS terminal that used Near Field Communication (NFC). The terminal read the credit/debit card information, the amount payable, and a customer's PIN and debited their card. Many systems appeared pioneered by Philips, Sony, Samsung, and others starting in 2002. Many others, including Visa, Mastercard, and American Express, introduced NFC cards in 2008. NFC cards are current.

The need for a NFC-enabled PoS terminal was eliminated in 2011 by the advent of the QR code scanning system. In this method, a consumer scanned the merchant's QR code with their smartphone and entered the amount due. The customer's wallet was debited and credited to the merchant's wallet. This mode of payment was pioneered in China by Alipay and adopted later by Tencent. Over 80% of all mobile payments in China used QR codes by 2018. The National Payment Corporation of India (NPCI), a not-for-profit company set up by the Reserve Bank of India with the Indian Banks' Association, launched BharatQR in 2017 to make payments from and to banks and to wallets. It works alongside the QR codes of card companies. In 2020, PayPal also adopted QR code-based payments.

Another pioneering mobile payment method was M-Pesa. Mobile phone operators Vodafone and Safaricom introduced M-Pesa in Kenya and other African countries where formal banking and smartphones had not penetrated in 1997. The user deposited money with the mobile operator, who credited it to the mobile phone. A sender transferred funds by a PIN-enabled SMS to a recipient's phone. The recipient could collect the amount from the mobile operator. The operator charged a small commission for sending and collecting money.

Google pioneered the App on smartphones for payment in 2011 with its Google Pay wallet. Currently, many wallet Apps, including Apple Pay, Samsung Pay, and Paytm, are widely used for mobile payments.

UNIFIED PAYMENT INTERFACE (UPI) IN INDIA

India pioneered mobile phone payments by introducing a Unified Payment Interface (UPI) in 2016. It is a centralised platform operated by the NPCI that connects consumers' bank accounts with numerous payment Apps such as Paytm, PhonePe, Google Pay, and BHIM. These apps permit transferring money instantly from any bank account linked to UPI to anyone by using their mobile phone linked to UPI or their QR code. NPCI secures UPI payments by two-factor authentication. Payment is instantaneous in real time. Most UPI transactions are free. They work across numerous banks. NPCI charges merchants a small fee between 0.4% and 1% of the transaction amount. The impact of UPI has been phenomenal as it has catered to millions of users, such as street vendors, providing them with secure cashless transactions.

EPILOGUE

Electronic payments have come a long way, starting with credit cards in the 1960s. Nowadays, all e-commerce payments are made by credit or debit cards using a secure Internet connection. Mobile payment Apps have proliferated. Systems such as UPI in India are leading towards a cashless society. One need not fear pickpockets; only mobile phone snatchers!

REFERENCES

[1] Karl Montevirgen, How money moves in the era of digital payment systems. https://www.britannica.com/money/types-of-payment-systems

[2] David Shrier, German Canale, and Alex Pentland, MIT Connection Science Report.
https://www.getsmarter.com/blog/wp-content/uploads/2017/07/mit_mobile_and_money_payments_report.pdf

[3] The History of Mobile Payments
https://xsreviews.co.uk/editorial/the-history-of-mobile-payments/

24

Expert Systems

PROLOGUE

In Anecdote 20, I mentioned the advent of the first AI winter between 1974 and 1980 due to the excessive uncalled-for hype following the invention of Perceptron and its severe limitations. The first AI winter was also due to the failure of the natural language translation project and the Lighthill report of 1973 that criticised AI research.

AI research recovered in 1981 when the Japanese government massively funded the Fifth Generation project to design highly parallel computers to solve AI problems. This project coincided with developing Expert Systems (ES) to solve several problems requiring human expertise. The first significant ES called DENDRAL, which predicted the structure of organic molecules from their mass spectra, was developed by Feigenbaum and his team at Stanford University in 1968. Many useful ESs followed, and ES became economically significant, and many companies developed and marketed these systems. It became a billion-dollar industry. However, AI researchers soon realised that these systems took a lot of work to maintain and had limitations. In particular, it was challenging to gather expert knowledge. Everyday knowledge, not explicitly stated, known as *common-sense knowledge,* took a lot of work to collect and codify. Progress in expert systems slowed down. The disillusionment with expert systems led to the second AI winter in 1987, which lasted until 1994.

By 1994, two significant developments had occurred that led to the resurgence of research funding and industry participation in AI. The computing power of computers increased by orders of magnitude due to the arrival of parallel computers with huge primary and secondary memories. The Internet came of age, and massive multimedia data stored on the World Wide Web became available. Cloud computing emerged with the advent of the Internet and provided access to enormous computing power "on-demand". These developments led to several highly publicised successes. Notable among them are IBM Deep Blue beating Gary Kasparov, the world chess champion in 1997, IBM Watson beating champions Brad Rutter and Ken Jennings in the word game Jeopardy! on the US national TV in 2011, and DeepMind's AlphaGo beating Lee Sedol, the world GO champion, in 2016. In 2022, the generative large language model-based ChatGPT of OpenAI demonstrated its capability to converse naturally with humans. DALL-E, another generative AI system, could draw pictures from a short description. ChatGPT (Anecdote 72) and conversational chatbots such as Google's Gemini have amazed and alarmed humans. Not a day passed in 2024 without an article or news item in the papers expounding on the fantastic capability of AI. Hype yet again!

EARLY AI PROGRAMS MIMICKING HUMAN PROBLEM-SOLVING [1]

Early AI researchers' attempted to demonstrate the intelligence of computers by writing programs mimicking human problem-solving behaviour, primarily *deductive logic*, and finding heuristics to solve problems. AI researchers' favourite areas were proving theorems in mathematics, playing board games, performing algebraic manipulations, solving elementary problems in calculus, and general problem-solving. Newell, Shaw, and Simon wrote a program called Logic Theorist in 1956 that proved 38 of the 52 theorems in the famous book *Principia Mathematica* by Alfred Whitehead and Bertrand Russell and found new and elegant proof for a theorem. H. Gelernter developed a geometry theorem-proving program in 1958. Newell and Simon simulated the thinking of humans to develop a general logic problem solver in 1959. James Slagle wrote a heuristic program that could perform symbolic integration in 1961. In 1964, Danny Bobrow demonstrated that a computer could solve an algebra problem using a natural language statement. The same year, Bertram Raphael wrote a question-answering program based on a logical representation of knowledge. Another significant development was Macsyma (Project MAC's Symbolic

Manipulator), a general-purpose algebra system developed in 1968 and still used after continuous improvement.

EXPERT SYSTEMS [2]

In 1964, Edward Feigenbaum of Stanford University was convinced that computers could demonstrate intelligence by inductive reasoning as well as deductive reasoning, which was the popular paradigm in AI at that time. Inductive reasoning is making broad generalizations from a set of observations. He talked to Joshua Lederberg, a Nobel Laureate who was then working on a project to determine whether life-precursor molecules such as amino acids are on Mars by analysing the data from a mass spectrometer in the Mars probe. Lederberg sought the assistance of Carl Djerassi, a professor of organic chemistry at Stanford, who guided a team of expert interpreters of data obtained from mass spectrometers to determine the structure of organic molecules. Feigenbaum and Bruce Buchanan interacted with Djerassi's group and designed a computer program that predicted the structure of organic molecules from their mass spectra. The program was named DENDRAL (Dendritic Algorithm—tree-like exhibiting spreading roots and branches). DENDRAL codified the knowledge of expert organic chemists as a set of *if-then* rules. Feigenbaum's group compared DENDRAL's performance with that of the postdoc organic chemists and found it was not very good initially. However, when they added more rules based on additional knowledge obtained from the chemists, it became as good as those of the postdocs in the laboratory. In 1968, Feigenbaum, Buchanan, and Lederberg wrote a paper describing DENDRAL, the first Expert System (ES). Based on this and later work, Feigenbaum emphasised the need for expert knowledge to develop an intelligent system [3]. Knowledge engineering is the methodology of extracting knowledge from experts and codifying it. He also enunciated three requirements of ES: *knowledge extraction, explanation, and flexibility*. When an ES recommends an action based on its inputs, it should be able to explain why it recommended that action. If an ES developer adds new knowledge, it should be possible to modify the ES easily using it.

Edward Feigenbaum
(Photo courtesy Wikipedia)

Edward Shortliffe developed a significant ES called MYCIN at Stanford University in the early 1970s over five years. It assisted physicians in identifying bacteria causing severe infections and recommending the appropriate antibiotic dosage. Its knowledge base had around 600 rules. It had a conversational interface for doctors, an explanation module, and a facility to modify the knowledge base. It performed reasonably well as judged by experienced physicians. In 1983, Daniel Bobrow and Gerald Dejong designed an ES called PROSPECTOR that assisted geologists to analyse geological data and predict the presence of valuable mineral deposits. It was a notable system as knowledge extraction was difficult.

JAPAN'S FIFTH GENERATION PROJECT

The Japanese Ministry of International Trade and Industry (MITI) started a 10-year project called the Fifth Generation Computer Systems (FGCS), with a budget of $450 million in 1982 to design massively parallel computers, promote logic programming, emphasising the use of Prolog, and natural language processing. The Japanese project led to the funding of parallel computer development and AI research in many parts of the world including the US (Strategic Computing Initiative) in 1983 with a budget of $1 billion, the UK (Alvey) in 1984 with a budget of £ 375 million, European Union (ESPIRIT) in 1982 with a budget of 1.2 billion Euros, and India (Knowledge-based Computer Systems, KBCS) in 1985 with a budget of ₹140 million and UN assistance of $ 5.2 million.

All these projects gave an impetus to research and development of ES, parallel computers, and AI, in general, worldwide. In India, several ESs were developed, including an ES shell (a software tool for creating an ES) named Vidwan by the National Centre for Software Technology in the late 1980s. KBCS also funded research in natural language processing in Indian languages and parallel computers.

INDUSTRY ADOPTION OF EXPERT SYSTEMS

Observing the success of ESs such as MYCIN and PROSPECTOR, ES was embraced by the industry in the early 1980s [4]. DEC engineers developed a significant ES called R1/XCON in 1982 to configure computer systems, saving hundreds of thousands of dollars. Several companies started developing ES and marketed them. By the mid-1980s, two-thirds of the FORTUNE 500 companies used ES in one or more business areas. In 1986, Intellec Corporation designed and marketed an ES shell successfully.

Expert Systems were used in health care, primarily assisting doctors in diagnosis. Finance and banking used ESs for credit scoring, risk assessment, and investment advice. Manufacturing and engineering used ESs in fault diagnosis, process optimization, and quality control. The oil and gas industry used ES in oil exploration, pipeline fault detection, and risk analysis. Telephone companies used ES to detect faults in telephone systems. The aerospace industry used ES in mission planning, fault diagnosis, and ensuring the safety of operations. ESs were employed in customer support by several companies. Lawyers used them in analysing contracts, checking compliance, and guidance on adhering to regulations. Tutoring systems also used them. ES became a billion-dollar industry, the first commercial success of AI.

EPILOGUE

After the initial success of ES, its developers discovered that expert knowledge was expensive and challenging to gather and codify. ES was also difficult to modify as new knowledge became available. The excessive optimism on the utility of ES waned in the late 1980s. However, ES continues to be used in medical diagnosis and by many industries, particularly in troubleshooting complex engineering systems.

REFERENCES

[1] Edward A. Feigenbaum, and Julian Feldman, Computers and Thought, McGraw-Hill, New York, 1963.

[2] David C. Brock, Learning from Artificial Intelligence's Previous Awakenings, AI Magazine, Vol. 39, No. 3, pp. 3–15, Fall 2018.

[3] Edward A. Feigenbaum and Bruce G. Buchanan, DENDRAL: and Meta-DENDRAL: roots of knowledge systems and expert system applications, Artificial Intelligence, Vol. 59, pp. 233–240, 1993.

[4] Bruce G. Buchanan, A (Very) Brief History of Artificial Intelligence, AI Magazine, Vol. 26, No. 4, 2006, pp. 53–60.

25

The Birth of Unix

PROLOGUE

The first time-sharing system, CTSS, implemented on an IBM 709 at the Massachusetts Institute of Technology (MIT) by Fernando Corbató and his team in 1961, made users realise that interaction with the computer during program development increased their productivity (See Anecdote 15). Corbató and his team designed in early 1963 an improved CTSS that used a transistorised IBM 7094 with two 32K (36-bit word) central memory banks. One bank stored the time-sharing supervisor and the other bank users' programs. It also had a drum and disks as secondary memory for swapping users' programs and data. In addition, IBM provided a switching system that connected 32 users' teletype terminals to the computer. J.C.R. Licklider (earlier a faculty member at MIT) had moved to the Advanced Research Project Agency (ARPA) of the US Department of Defence. ARPA supported research in Universities to help improve defence preparedness of the USA. Licklider was a proponent of better human-computer symbiosis to enhance productivity and creativity. After a meeting with Professor R.M. Fano of the Electrical Engineering Department at MIT, he encouraged Fano to submit a proposal to ARPA for funding research at MIT to design a computer system that will work very much like an electrical utility. In other words, users can log on to this computer from anywhere, use its processor and storage "on-demand", and pay for what they use. Fano submitted a proposal in January 1963 titled Project MAC (Multi-Access Computer) to ARPA, and ARPA approved it in July 1963 with a grant of US$ 2.2 million per year for three years.

PROJECT MAC AND MULTICS

Project MAC started by buying an IBM 7094 system identical to the one in MIT's computer centre and implemented CTSS to enable interactive program development by Project MAC staff. Soon, MAC staff wanted another computer with hardware tuned to implement an improved time-shared operating system (OS). After discussions with several computer vendors, the group decided to buy General Electric's GE 645 computer as GE was willing to modify its architecture to suit the development of time-shared OS. Work started implementing an OS called Multics (Multiplexed Information and Computer Service) [1]. The software group wrote Multics using PL/I—a powerful high-level programming language that IBM developed. It was one of the first attempts to write an OS in a high-level language. AT&T's Bell Telephone Laboratories joined the project in November 1964 by contributing technical staff and funds. AT&T also bought a GE 645 to implement Multics for their use. AT&T assigned full-time Ken Thompson, Dennis Ritchie, Doug McIlroy, J.F. Ossanna, Stuart Feldman, and Robert Morris to the development of Multics. GE delayed delivery of GE 645 with the requested hardware modifications to Bell Labs and it arrived only in January 1967. The Bell Labs' Multics group used CTSS on IBM 7094 remotely from their laboratories in New Jersey for program development. Multics specification was very ambitious, and despite having a staff of over 100 programmers, progress was slow. AT&T's management had second thoughts on the project on two counts. One was the long delay, and the second was whether Bell Labs' research team should be working on OS, which was of no direct relevance to AT&T's business. Thus, AT&T's management ended its participation in Multics development in April 1969.

GENESIS OF UNIX

The Bell Labs team of programmers was deeply involved in developing Multics. The team was highly impressed by the convenience of using CTSS and Multics interactive time-shared systems. It eased program development and allowed the sharing of files among team members, which created a fellowship among them. They wanted a similar programming environment in Bell Labs. In 1969, they started exploring and implementing a simpler time-sharing OS despite knowing there

Ken Thompson and Dennis Ritchie
(Photos courtesy YouTube)

would be no support from the management. Ken Thompson found an unused PDP-7 computer in the laboratory and started implementing an OS much simpler than Multics but having many of its essential features, such as time-sharing and shared-file system in the summer of 1969. His team, which included Ritchie and Canaday, called the system Unics (Un-multiplexed information and computing service) intended as a joke because it supported only one user initially—Thompson—in contrast to Multics. The name later morphed to Unix. The most innovative feature the team implemented was a hierarchical filing system and treating devices as files. Thompson wrote the OS in the assembly language of PDP-7 and was ready by the end of 1969. Having successfully designed a reasonably powerful OS with only 4200 lines of code that occupied 16KB of memory, Thompson and Ritchie wanted to improve it. As OS development was not on the agenda of AT&T, they used deception. They wrote a proposal to the management that they would develop an interactive text editor for typists to write AT&T's patent applications and requested Bell Labs to buy a PDP-11 computer. A PDP-11 arrived in late 1971, and they rewrote Unix for it. PDP-11 was used interactively in time-shared mode by three to four typists and was a hit as it was simple to use and enormously improved their productivity. The features implemented in this version of Unix included a simple line editor, a text processor, some games, utility programs such as dump and restore disk images on tape, interactive BASIC, FORTRAN, and a language named B. B was derived from BCPL (Basic Combined Programming Language) a language designed by Martin Richards of the Multics group at MIT. Ritchie later improved the language B to C, which he developed to write Unix. He re-wrote Unix in C in 1973. It was an important decision as it made Unix portable to other computers. When Unix became stable, Thompson and Ritchie felt it was time to publicise it. They wrote a paper describing the design of Unix in the

Communications of ACM in 1974 [2]. It attracted the attention of OS designers, and requests started pouring in from many organizations for a copy of Unix code. These requests put AT&T in a dilemma as a court order did not allow it to sell software. As a compromise, AT&T announced that it would distribute Unix source code free with no support and collect $100 for postage and the cost of tapes. Bell Labs team quipped about Unix—"no advertisement, no support, no bug fixes, payment in advance".

EPILOGUE

The Unix team was not allowed by AT&T lawyers to circulate bug fixes or OS enhancements to those who received the tapes. Thus, the users banded together and formed a Unix users' group named Usenix. They circulated among themselves and to Bell Labs group bug fixes and enhancements improving Unix. Unix groups also came up worldwide and contributed to improving it.

On a request by his manager, Thompson wrote **grep** (**g**lobally search for **r**egular **e**xpressions and **p**rint) in 1974, which searches a text and picks up a specified character string. Users continuously added similar simple programs. The popularity of Unix stems from its building-block approach that allows a set of simple programs, such as grep, to be "piped" to produce sophisticated results. Its philosophy that *everything is a file* permits it to perform standard operations on different file types, hardware devices, and even system processes.

The University of California, Berkeley (UC Berkeley) designed an improved version of Unix called Unix BSD (Berkeley Software Distribution) in 1978 based on AT&T's Unix (version 6) while Ken Thompson spent a sabbatical year at UC Berkeley during 1975–76. UC Berkeley freely distributed Unix BSD. By 1980, the US government removed the ban on AT&T selling software, and it formed a subsidiary—Unix Systems Laboratory to license Unix. This company filed a case in 1992 against UC Berkeley for patent infringement. UC Berkeley consequently rewrote Unix BSD, removing most of AT&T's code. Bill Joy, a student at UC Berkeley, was primarily responsible for this rewrite and improving Unix BSD. In 1982, he co-founded Sun Microsystems with three partners and designed and manufactured Motorola 68000-based workstations with Unix OS. Soon, many workstation companies sprouted, and all used Unix-like OS. Unix and its clones became standard OS, and many companies implemented versions such as HP-Unix and Ultrix on mini-computers. Cray, a supercomputer manufacturer, also adopted Unix in Cray YMP and its later supercomputers.

Meanwhile, 80386-based PCs were becoming popular. 80386 Unix BSD was available but not widely used. Not aware of this, Linus Torvalds, a student in Finland, designed a version of Unix from scratch for 80386 PCs in 1991 and made it open-source. Except for Windows OS on PCs, all other computers, such as Apple, use Unix or its descendants today.

REFERENCES

[1] Multics https://multicians.org

[2] D.M. Ritchie and K. Thompson, The UNIX Time-sharing Operating System, Communications ACM, Vol. 17, No. 7, pp. 365–75, 1994.

26

Project MAC—Towards a Computing Utility

PROLOGUE

Massachusetts Institute of Technology (MIT) had an IBM 704 computer used as a batch processing machine in 1959. When John McCarthy joined the faculty of MIT in 1959, he was unhappy that he had to wait long to get results from the computer. He wrote a note to the computer center director articulating the need to allow interactive debugging of programs by IBM 709 users. His idea was to enable several programmers to have concurrent access to the computer via remote teletypewriters and let them share its resources, debug, and execute their programs. His note resulted in the Compatible Time-Sharing System (CTSS) developed by Fernando Corbató and his team in 1961 (See Anecdote 15).

Meanwhile, J.C.R. Licklider, a professor of psychology at MIT, had worked with interactive analog computers. When he tried using a digital computer for a more complex simulation, he found his productivity poor working with a batch processing non-interactive computer. This experience convinced him that a symbiotic relationship between computers and their users would increase productivity. In 1960, he wrote a paper titled Man-Computer Symbiosis [1] in which he stated:

"In the anticipated symbiotic partnership, men will set the goals, formulate the hypotheses, determine the criteria, and perform the evaluations. Computing machines will do the routinizable work that must be done to prepare the way for insights and decisions in technical and scientific thinking."

He advocated the development of interactive time-shared computers to achieve this goal. When CTSS became operational, he was one of its happy users.

Experience with CTSS convinced McCarthy about the inevitability of interactive time-shared computers in the future. He let his imagination run riot and expanded on his idea of interactive time-shared computers. In a lecture [2] he gave in 1961 during the centenary celebration of MIT, he said:

"If the computers of the type I have advocated become computer of the future, then computing may someday be organized as a public utility just as the telephone system is a public utility. ...... The computer utility could become the basis of a new and important industry."

GENESIS OF PROJECT MAC AT MIT

A conference on computers and communications was held in Virginia during the third week of November 1962. Robert Fano, a professor of electrical engineering at MIT, and Licklider attended it. Licklider left MIT, and after a stint at Bolt, Beranek, and Newman (BBN), a consulting company, he joined as director of the Information Processing Techniques Office (IPTO) of the Advanced Research Projects Agency (ARPA) of the Department of Defence (DoD) of the US government. IPTO was disbursing funds to universities to conduct research in frontier areas of computers and communications. At the end of the conference, Fano and Licklider took a train back to Boston on November 21, 1962, a day before the US Thanksgiving holidays. During this journey, Fano and Licklider had a long conversation on the future of computing and various research ideas. Licklider said that IPTO could fund MIT around $3 million a year for three years if MIT wrote a proposal to do advanced research in the areas of operating systems for interactive time-shared computers and artificial intelligence. As we saw earlier, Licklider was a champion of man-computer symbiosis, and he had used CTSS. Licklider was confident that MIT would productively use the massive funding. Fano was trying to reorient his research in the electrical engineering department from information theory to computers as he realised that computer research had a bright future and that MIT should play a leadership role in this area. He worked hard during the long weekend from November 22 to 25 and was ready with an outline of a proposal on November 26, 1962. The proposal had three goals. The first was to develop an interactive time-shared computer system that would support many users, leading to a computer utility. The second was to educate the community of researchers to use this system. The third was to support education and research at MIT in related areas. Fano discussed the gist of his proposal with the President of MIT, who asked him to go ahead. The project titled MAC stood for Machine Aided Cognition/Multiple Access Computer. The idea was that a multi-access computer was a means to an end, namely, human cognition, which was the project's broad objective [3]. MIT sent a proposal to IPTO on January 1, 1963. IPTO approved it on March 1, 1963, and released $2,200,000 on July 1, 1963.

Robert Fano
(Photo courtesy Wikipedia)

MAC PROJECT STARTS

Licklider suggested to Fano that MIT convene a summer meeting to create awareness among academics and industry researchers about time-shared computers and their advantages. Fano invited a group of around 60 participants to visit MIT during July–August 1963 and use CTSS, which was now running on a transistorised IBM 7094 computer with two banks of 32 Kword main memory, a swapping drum, disks, and a terminal controller that could support 32 terminals. The participants included active and well-known researchers in computing at that time. Nathaniel Rochester and Gene Amdahl from IBM, Donald Knuth from Stanford, Alan Perlis from Carnegie Mellon, Maurice Wilkes from Cambridge University, and Douglas Engelbart from Stanford Research Institute, among others, attended this event. This meeting was an eye-opener to many participants, convincing them about time-shared computers.

The next step was to start designing an advanced OS for a time-shared computer that would ultimately be the operating system of a computer utility. The computer centre at MIT had installed an IBM 7094 with two main memory banks (each with 32 K words (36-bit words)), large disks and drums for program swapping, and an enhanced input/output controller. Additional hardware had improved CTSS. Project

MAC bought an IBM 7094 system identical to it. A user was allowed to log on to one of the two computers. Access to the computers was from over 100 teletypewriters. These teletypewriters were connected to a private branch exchange at MIT to enable access to either system. Teletypewriters were placed not only in MIT but also in the homes of some faculty and outside the Boston area. Project MAC connected two graphics terminals with a light pen for input and a PDP-1 computer to the IBM 7094. This system was crucial in further software development.

MULTIPLEXED INFORMATION AND COMPUTING SERVICE (MULTICS)

A primary goal of Project MAC was to design a computer utility. A computer utility was to provide [4]:

- Continuous remote terminal access to computing service as a regular mode of usage similar to that available to telephone users.
- A reliable file system that allows users to store their single copy of programs and data confidently. Allow users to share files selectively.
- Service users requiring both small and extensive resources with equal efficiency.
- Provide a variety of programming environments and human interfaces.
- Flexible to accommodate technological improvements and changing user requirements.

An operating system to meet the above objectives was called Multics, and one of the goals of Project MAC was to design and implement it.

HISTORY OF THE DEVELOPMENT OF MULTICS

As we saw, project MAC started in July 1963. It spent the first year buying an IBM 7094, implementing CTSS, and coupling it with an identical system in MIT's computer centre. This system was now ready for software development. Meanwhile, Fernando Corbató (who had joined Project MAC) and his team started looking for an appropriate computer to implement Multics. In August 1964, Project MAC selected General Electric (GE) model 645 computer for developing Multics after exploring available computers in the market. Project

MAC selected the GE 645 computer as it was willing to modify the hardware to accommodate special requirements to implement Multics and be a partner in the project. GE designed a generalized Input/Output controller that could easily handle disks, drums, tapes, and teletypewriters. GE also added a 4 M-word (36-bit word) high-speed drum. It modified the main memory controller to facilitate designing a time-shared operating system.

Multics development started in August 1964 using IBM 7094/CTSS. The Multics program was divided into many modules. The Multics team wrote a 3000-page document containing the detailed specifications of each module. A small group was assigned to each module and the groups worked in parallel. The developers decided to write Multics using PL/I, a general-purpose, high-level, machine-independent language developed by IBM. They chose PL/I as it was a powerful programming language and portable. It was one of the early attempts to write an operating system in a high-level programming language.

In November 1964, Bell Telephone Laboratories (BTL) partnered to develop Multics. BTL sent some of its best software developers, including Ken Thompson and Dennis Ritchie, to join the Multics team. GE delivered the GE 645 computer in January 1967, and Project MAC shifted Multics development to it from IBM 7094. Multics was a highly ambitious operating system, and on average, around 300 persons were engaged in developing it from 1965 to 1969. The OS developers planned to complete Multics by 1967, but it was delayed, as is common with complex software projects. ARPA reviewed the MAC project in 1968, and many expected that funding would be stopped [5]. ARPA, however, recommended the continuation of the project. Meanwhile, BTL became impatient as they installed GE 645 with the hope that Multics would run on it. Consequently, BTL withdrew from the project in April 1969. The first version of Multics started running on GE 645 system in October 1969. The total funding provided by ARPA for Project MAC between 1963 and 1970 was US$ 25 million [5].

EPILOGUE

Multics was a pioneering attempt to design a secure time-shared operating system. It met most of the goals set for it. Current operating systems include many of the ideas and features of Multics. Multics, however, did not become a standard operating system. Thompson and

Ritchie designed Unix, a popular, standard operating system today, based on their experience working on Multics development.

Honeywell bought General Electric's computer division that had designed GE 645 in 1970.

Honeywell continued to support the Multics project. GE 645 was improved by Honeywell, named 6180, and released in 1973 with Multics. Honeywell sold around 80 computers with Multics between 1969 and 2000.

MIT's Information Processing Centre used GE 645 and its successor Honeywell 6180 with Multics from 1969 to 1988. Besides the Multics project, MAC supported many computer-related projects from 1963 to 1974, when it closed.

REFERENCES

[1] J.C.R. Licklider, Man-Computer Symbiosis, IRE Transactions on Human Factors in Electronics, Vol. HFE 1, March 1960, pp. 4–11.

[2] J. McCarthy, Time-Sharing Computer Systems, in Management and the Computer of the Future, Editor M. Greenberger, MIT Press, 1962, pp. 221–236.

[3] R.M. Fano, The MAC System: the computer utility approach, IEEE Spectrum, January 1965, pp. 56–64.

[4] F.J. Corbato, J.H. Saltzer, and C.T. Clingen, Multics—The first seven years, Proceedings, Spring Joint Computer Conference, 1972, pp. 571–583.

[5] T. Van Vleck, Multics, Project MAC, https://multicians.org/project-mac.html

27

The First Packet-Switched Wide Area Network—ARPANET

PROLOGUE

October 4, 1957, was a historic day on which the erstwhile USSR launched Sputnik, the first artificial satellite. The US administration was shocked as they had always thought they were technologically superior to the USSR. Launching a satellite required a very powerful rocket that the USSR could use to launch a nuclear-armed ballistic missile threatening the USA. There was an immediate reaction in the USA to fund research not only to launch a satellite but also to defend the USA from any nuclear attack. Advanced Research Projects Agency (ARPA) was established in 1958 by the US Department of Defence (DoD) to carry out research in advanced technologies by primarily outsourcing research projects relevant to DoD to universities and research-oriented companies.

LICKLIDER'S IDEA

J.C.R. Licklider, who worked in Bolt Beranek and Newman Inc. (BBN) in Cambridge, Massachusetts, was invited in October 1962 to join ARPA as the head of the Information Processing Techniques Office (IPTO). Licklider was a psychologist who dabbled in computers. In the 1960s, computers were mostly batch-processing machines that did not allow interaction between users and computers. He firmly believed that the potential of computers could be fully realised only through close interaction between computers and humans and wrote a classic paper in March 1960 entitled "Man-Computer Symbiosis" [1]. In this paper, he argued that humans can postulate hypotheses and formulate models, whereas computers can calculate and remember. Humans must evaluate the results obtained from computers, modify the model appropriately, and compute it again. Interaction between humans and computers is essential to expedite this iterative process leading to discoveries.

MIT built the first time-sharing interactive computer in 1961. Commercial time-shared systems followed. In October 1963, Licklider wrote a memo: "Intergalactic Computer Network" that proposed interconnecting computers spread worldwide, enabling scientists to cooperate by sharing their ideas and computing resources. Ivan Sutherland succeeded Licklider at IPTO in 1964 and worked for a year, and Robert Taylor succeeded him in 1966.

J.C.R. Licklider
(Photo thanks fergusson.edu)

GENESIS OF ARPANET

IPTO had funded several projects to build and buy time-shared computer systems for many universities across the US. Robert Taylor read Licklider's report on Intergalactic Networks. The report convinced him of the need to interconnect computers funded by IPTO not only for him to access them from a single terminal in his office but also to permit the centres to exchange software and access one another's computers to improve research productivity. He requested the ARPA director to sanction a million dollars for this project, which was immediately approved. Taylor invited Lawrence G. Roberts, working at the Lincoln Laboratory of MIT, in January 1967 to manage the networking project. Roberts' task was to interconnect widely separated computers funded by ARPA using the existing telephone system. Roberts tried to convince the directors of the computer centres funded by ARPA to cooperate in interconnecting the computers to create the ARPANET and explained the advantages of resource sharing. They were reluctant as they felt that substantial resources of their computers would be used up in managing the communication between computers, slowing down their machines. Wesley Clark, one of the members of Roberts' group, suggested that a separate minicomputer named

Interface Message Processor (IMP) be used at each computing node to manage the communication chores, relieving the mainframe computers from this task. This idea was acceptable to the computer centre heads.

In the ACM Symposium on Operating Systems Principles held in Gatlinburg, Tennessee in October 1967, Roberts presented a paper [2] explaining the advantages of networking time-shared computers and the functions of the IMPs that would connect these computers using leased telephone lines. IMPs would buffer messages, check transmission errors, request data re-transmission if there was an error, and take routing decisions. Roberts was concerned about the inefficient use of leased telephone lines in transmitting digital data. At the same Symposium, Roger Scantlebury, a member of a group headed by Donald Davies of the National Physical Laboratory, Teddington, UK, presented a paper [3] on connecting computers using *packet switching* that used telephone lines efficiently to transmit "bursty" digital data. Roberts was sure after listening to his talk that ARPANET should use packet switching. He soon found out that the packet switching idea had been described extensively by Paul Baran of RAND corporation in a set of reports. Roberts read Baran's reports and discussed how ARPANET could use packet switching with Baran. Roberts decided to network computer centres at the University of California, Los Angeles (UCLA) headed by Leonard Kleinrock, Stanford Research Institute (SRI) at Santa Monica (near San Francisco) led by Douglas Engelbart, University of California at Santa Barbara (UCSB) headed by Glenn Culler, and the University of Utah headed by David Evans. An IMP was to be installed at each of these centres to connect the computers. UCLA had an SDS Sigma 7 computer. Leonard Kleinrock and Larry Roberts were Ph.D. students at MIT and shared an office while they were there. Kleinrock had

Robert Taylor **Larry Roberts**

(Photo thanks to Wikipedia)

developed a queuing theory model of message-switching networks as a part of his thesis. Roberts was aware of this and requested Kleinrock to analyse the planned packet-switched network and its feasibility. SRI had an SDS 940 computer, and Engelbart had done pioneering work on interactive computing. UCSB had an IBM 360/75 running OS/MVT time-shared OS. Culler and Fried, two professors there, had done pioneering work on computer-aided education with the time-shared system. The University of Utah had a DEC PDP-10 with TENEX time-sharing OS and an excellent computer graphics research group led by Ivan Sutherland. Observe that the computers were diverse with different OSs, and it would have been tough to interconnect them without IMPs.

FOUR NODE ARPANET

As soon as IPTO decided to interconnect computers using IMPs and packet switching, a tender was floated on 29 July 1968, giving rough specifications of the requirements of an IMP. Major companies such as IBM and CDC were not interested in building IMPs. The final two contestants were Raytheon and BBN. The proposal of BBN was detailed and impressed IPTO. BBN was awarded the tender on 7 April 1969 for a million dollars to build and install four IMPs. BBN was to deliver and install an IMP at each of the four centres in monthly intervals starting at UCLA in September 1969. BBN selected ruggedised Honeywell DDP-516 computer to build the IMPs. It built each IMP with an interface with adequate buffering to connect to any computer. BBN wrote the IMP management software in the assembly language of the Honeywell machine. It delivered the first IMP to UCLA on 30 August 1969, the second one to SRI on 1 October 1969, the third to UCSB on 1 November 1969, and the last to Utah on 1 December 1969. As soon as BBN delivered an IMP to UCLA, Charlie Klein, a student of Kleinrock, wrote a program to log into the computer at SRI via IMP. He successfully transmitted the letters L and O from UCLA to SRI. As soon as he typed the third letter G, the system crashed. Thus, LO was the first message transmitted on the ARPANET! He fixed the bug, and the first login to the SRI machine was successful on October 29, 1969. By 21 November 1969, the first link via two IMPs at UCLA and SRI started working. This software made it simple to connect other IMPs as soon as they were installed and tested. By 5 December 1969, the first four nodes of the ARPANET started exchanging messages.

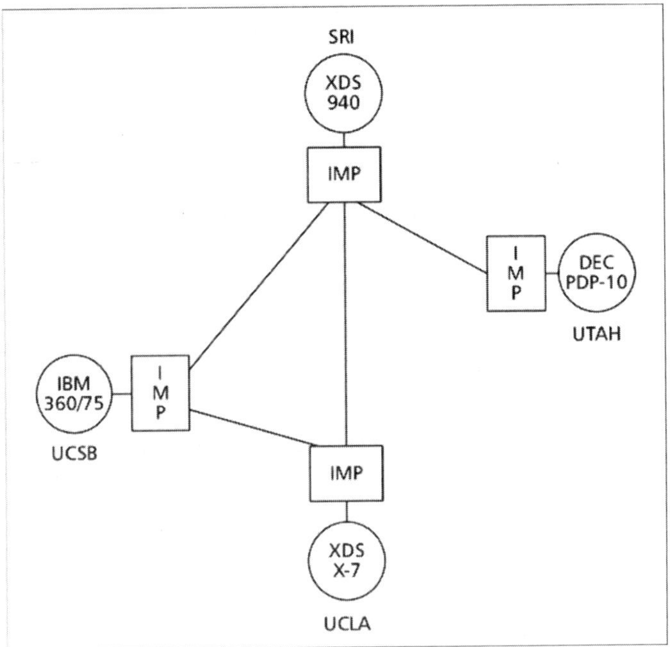

The first four nodes of ARPANET

EPILOGUE

Once the researchers connected the four computers, a Network Control Program was implemented in 1970, allowing the systematic data exchange among the computers. Subsequently, researchers wrote software for remote login, file transfer between computers, and email. Interestingly, the most popular use of the network was email! Soon, the network expanded to the east coast of the USA with an IMP at BBN. In 1971, a satellite link connected ARPANET to the University College, London. Many computer centres joined rapidly, and by August 1972, there were 29 computers in ARPANET.

A landmark event was the public demonstration of ARPANET at the International Conference on Computer Communications (ICCC) held in Washington DC in October 1972, where the ARPANET team installed 50 terminals, and delegates were able to log on to any computer in the ARPANET, write programs, send mail, and transfer files. By 1975, the ARPANET was declared operational and handed over to the Defence Communications Agency with 57 host computers.

REFERENCES

[1] J.C.R. Licklider, Man-Computer Symbiosis, IRE Transactions on Human Factors in Electronics, Vol. HFE 1, March 1960, pp. 4–11.

[2] L.G. Roberts, Multiple Computer Networks and Intercomputer Communication, ACM Symposium on Operating Systems Principles, Gatlinburg, Tennessee, USA, October 1967.

[3] D.W. Davies et al., A Digital Communication Network for Computers Giving Rapid Response, *ibid.*

28

The ALOHAnet—The First Random-Access Wireless Network

PROLOGUE

After obtaining a Ph.D. in Electrical Engineering from Stanford University in 1958, Norman Abramson continued there as a faculty member until 1965. He then taught at the University of California, Berkeley, in 1966 and Harvard University in 1967. Abramson got an offer of a Professorship from the University of Hawaii in 1968. He took a big gamble [1] in moving from a "first-tier" university to a not-so-well-known university. In 1969, the US Department of Defence (DoD) funded research in "second-tier" universities to broaden human resource availability. Abramson learnt about this decision and went to the Advanced Research Project Agency (ARPA) of DoD in Washington, DC, and submitted a proposal to research wireless data communication at the University of Hawaii. To make the proposal acceptable to the sponsors and the university, Abramson and his colleagues Wesley Peterson, Thomas Gaarder, Franklin Kuo, Shu Lin, and Edward Weldon proposed to build a system to remotely access and time-share the IBM mainframe computer at the main campus of the University at Honolulu from the smaller campuses in the islands of Oahu, Kauai, Maui, and Hawaii all within a radius of about 300 km. The telephone system in the Hawaiian islands was unreliable, so the group proposed to build a wireless network using ultra-high frequency (UHF) radio. Information

Processing Techniques Office (IPTO) of ARPA, whose director was Robert Taylor and deputy director Lawrence G. Roberts, accepted the proposal and allocated substantial funds to Abramson's group.

ALOHANET DESIGN

The project's primary goal was to allow several remote terminals to access the mainframe computer (that was the hub) sharing a UHF radio channel. One solution was to share the UHF band by allocating non-overlapping frequency bands to each terminal. This allocation would allow the terminals to use the mainframe independently. However, the bandwidth for each terminal would be small, slowing down communication. Allocating an independent link to each terminal would be wasteful for digital communication as terminals send data in bursts. The research group decided to use packet communication, pioneered by ARPANET, and share the radio channel using the ALOHA (Additive Links On-line Hawaii Area) protocol (Incidentally, Aloha is a Hawaiian word for love, affection, peace, compassion, and mercy used as a greeting in the Hawaiian islands.) The US Federal Communication Commission permitted the research group to operate two radio channels centred around 407.35 MHz and 413.475 MHz with 100 KHz bandwidth for data communication. The group decided to use one of the bands to transmit data from the terminals to the hub, namely the mainframe computer (called the inbound channel) and the other band to transmit data from the mainframe to the terminals (called the outbound channel). Any terminal wanting to send data to the hub used the inbound channel. The channel was "random access," as any terminal can send data on it at any time it chooses. Packets transmitted by the terminals to the hub include, besides data, error-detecting bits to allow the hub to check to see that the received data is error-free. Errors may occur due to a noisy channel or another terminal sending a packet simultaneously to the hub on the channel, causing collision. If a receiver gets a packet without error, the hub sends an acknowledgment to the sender on the outbound channel. If the sender does not receive an acknowledgment within the time taken for the packet to reach the hub and return, plus error-checking time, it assumes that the hub has not correctly received the packet due to collision. The sender then waits for a random period and re-sends the packet. Usually, the second attempt would succeed. If not, the sender picks another random period, and the packet is re-sent. If, after numerous attempts, the sender fails (which is rare), it simply gives up. This simple protocol is called *pure Aloha.*

In the system designed by Abramson and his group, called ALOHAnet, the terminal at each node was connected to a Terminal Control Unit (TCU). The TCU broke a message from the terminal to the hub into packets and implemented the Aloha protocol. The packet transmission rate was 9600 bps. The system was operational in late 1969, and Abramson published a paper describing it in 1970 [2]. As the channel is shared, the system becomes inefficient when the number of terminals increases. Abramson's group theoretically calculated that the channel's utilization efficiency was only 18.4%.

Norman Abramson
(Photo courtesy Wikipedia)

Lawrence G. Roberts, who had become the director of IPTO that funded the Aloha network research, was a technically savvy bureaucrat (he had a Ph.D. from MIT) and took a lot of interest in the study done by Abramson's group. He analysed why the Aloha system was inefficient. He modified the Aloha protocol to another protocol called *slotted Aloha.* In slotted Aloha also, the radio channel is shared by all the terminals. Channel time, however, is divided into slots. Each time slot equals the packet transmission time from a terminal to the hub. Any terminal that wants to send a packet waits till the beginning of a time slot. Collision may occur if two or more terminals try to transmit a packet at the beginning of the same time slot. He showed that this technique doubled the efficiency of utilisation of the system [3].

ALOHA SYSTEM JOINS ARPANET

In 1972, ARPANET was rapidly growing, connecting universities in the US mainland. Abramson was visiting Roberts in his office in Washington, DC, to discuss technical and funding aspects of ALOHAnet. During their discussion, Roberts had to leave his office to attend an urgent call. Abramson saw on the blackboard a diagram showing various centres that were to be provided Interface Message Processors (IMP) for connecting to the ARPANET. On impulse, Abramson took a chalk piece and inserted IMP for ALOHAnet, and the date for installation as

December 17 [4]. As the relationship between Abramson and Roberts was quite close and informal, Abramson had written on the board without Robert's permission. His idea was to connect ALOHAnet with ARPANET. By the time Roberts returned, Abramson had forgotten about his writing on the board, and there was no discussion with Roberts on this topic. Two weeks before December 17, 1972, Abramson was pleasantly surprised when he received a message asking him to prepare space to install an IMP. Abramson's group connected ALOHAnet to ARPANET via a dedicated satellite channel using the IMP.

PACNET

Advanced Technology Satellite-1 (ATS-1), the first experimental geosynchronous multi-purpose satellite, was launched in 1966 and allowed communication with VHF transponders. In 1973, Abramson's group requested the use of this satellite to create an experimental computer communication network connecting the University of Hawaii with NASA Ames research centre in California, the University of Alaska, Tohoku University in Sendai, Japan, the University of Electro-Communication in Tokyo, Japan and the University of Sydney in Australia. Low-cost earth stations were established in each of these centres. This network, called PacNet, used pure Aloha protocol to exchange data among these six centres and operated at 9600 bps. When PacNet was operational, it was connected to ARPANET. Thus, ARPANET became international [4].

EPILOGUE

The seminal idea of ALOHAnet is random access by terminals of a shared broadcast channel for packet communication. Robert Metcalfe of Xerox PARC spent a month in 1972 with Abramson's group. understanding the system (See Anecdote 38). On his return, he modified the idea of random multiple access of a broadcast medium used in ALOHAnet to develop the Carrier Sense Multiple Access with Collision Detection (CSMA/CD) protocol to communicate among computers connected to a local area network and called it the Alto ALOHA network. Later, it was renamed Ethernet. Abramson group's idea of randomly accessing a shared broadcast medium was used in the Carrier Sense Multiple Access with Collision Avoidance

(CSMA/CA) protocol of Wireless networks in 1985. The idea was employed again by mobile telephone networks to send messages.

REFERENCES

[1] Norman Abramson, A History of Computer Communications:1968–88, (oral history), http://www.historyofcomputercommunications.info/Individuals/abstracts/norm-abramson.html

[2] Norman Abramson, ALOHA system: Another alternative for computer communications, Fall Joint Computer Conference, 1970, pp. 281–85.

[3] Robert G. Lawrence, ALOHA packet system: With and Without Slots and Capture, Computer Communications Review, Vol. 5, No. 2, pp. 28–42, April 1975.

[4] Norman Abramson, The ALOHAnet—Surfing for Wireless data, IEEE Communications Magazine, December 2009, pp. 21–25.

29

A Concise History of Robots

PROLOGUE

Robots have captured the imagination of humans from ancient times. The Czech science fiction dramatist Karel Capek coined the name robot in the play RUR (Rossum's Universal Robots), which he wrote in 1920. In this play, a fictional Rossum Corporation develops a cheap biological humanoid machine called "robot" (derived from the Czech word robota—forced labour) and manufactures them on a secret island. As Rossum Corporation manufactures more robots, their prices drop, and they are enslaved by humans and ordered to do all manual labour. The enslavement of robots creates a human race with little work, and they question their purpose in life. Soon, robots get angry, organize themselves, and kill all humans. The play was famous and was performed worldwide.

The play added the word robot to the English dictionary. The Oxford English dictionary defines a robot as "a machine capable of carrying out a complex series of actions automatically, especially one programmable by a computer". In science fiction, a robot is "a machine resembling a human, moves as humans do, and performs human-like functions automatically".

Isaac Asimov, a famous science fiction writer, was inspired by Capek's play and, in his story *Runaround*, written in 1942, introduced three laws of robotics. The first law states that a robot may not cause harm to humans by its actions or inactions. The second law requires a robot to obey humans unless it violates the first law. The third law requires a robot to ensure its survival as long as it does not conflict with the first two laws. Later, he added a fourth (often called zeroth) law that superseded the three laws. It requires that a robot shall not harm humanity or, by inaction, allow humanity to be harmed. These laws have inspired all science fiction writers and humanoid robot designers since.

One of the earliest robots was built by William Grey Walter, a physiologist, during 1948–49, before the advent of computers. He called them Elmer and Elsie, which used analog electronic circuits to simulate neurons. They were in the shape of tortoises, had light sensors, moved very slowly toward a light source, and recharged themselves when their batteries were low.

Nowadays, a machine, to be called a robot, must be programmable, sense its surroundings, and perform a physical activity such as moving an object. There are three broad categories of robots.

1. *Industrial robots* that perform routine, repetitive actions, such as in automobile assembly lines.
2. *Service robots* that perform services such as stacking items on shelves, delivering items, cleaning rooms, cleaning sewage drains, aiding surgeons in complicated surgeries, and move in inaccessible or hazardous environments.
3. *Humanoid robots* that resemble humans capable of autonomous limb movement and action, speak, hear, and obey commands.

INDUSTRIAL ROBOTS

George Devol was born in 1912 in Louisville, Kentucky. A self-educated electrical engineer and a serial inventor, he saw the repetitive, tedious manual tasks performed in the assembly line of automobile companies and wanted to automate them. In the early 1950s, computers had arrived, and he got an idea to design a programmable machine that could pick up and place objects. Devol designed it and applied for a patent in 1954 for a "programmed article transfer device that makes available for the first time a more or less general purpose machine that has universal application for a vast diversity of applications where cyclic digital control is desired." He obtained a patent in 1961. Devol started looking for a company to manufacture a machine using his patent. Most were not interested. He fortuitously met Joseph Engelberger, an engineer and entrepreneur, at a cocktail party in 1956 and told him about his invention. Engelberger immediately saw its potential and was interested in carrying forward Devol's idea.

George Devol **Joseph Engelberger**
(Photos courtesy Wikipedia)

The two formed a company, Unimation, in 1956, and their first product was Unimate (a name suggested by Devol's wife, Evelyn). After some struggle trying to convince companies to buy their product, Devol was able to sell a Unimate to General Motors in 1961. The robot stored its program in a drum memory. It had an arm with pressure sensors to pick items. General Motors used it to pick hot door handles of cars and drop them to cool before the next operation on the assembly line. Unimate was licensed to companies in Europe and Japan. Japanese companies were enthusiastic about industrial robots and quickly adopted them in automobile assembly plants.

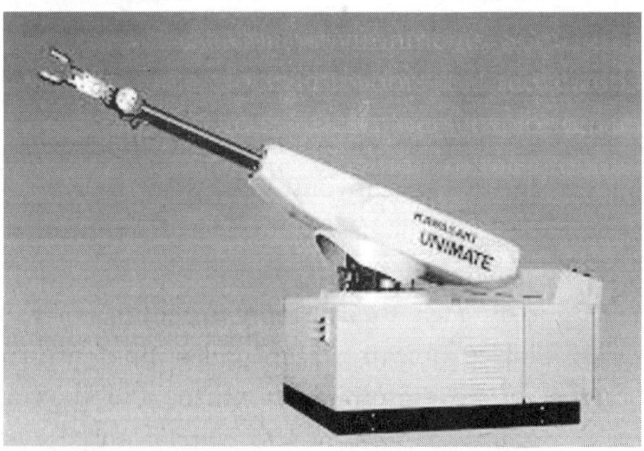

Unimate Robot licensed to Kowasaki
(Photo courtesy Kawasaki)

Researchers at MIT and Stanford subsequently developed advanced computer-controlled electro-mechanical sensor-guided arms during the 1960s and 1970s. Advanced industrial robots soon used electronic eyes to track the movements of a robot arm that could move in several dimensions. In 1976, Victor Scheinman built a servo-controlled arm while he was a student at Stanford University. He joined Unimation and made a robot called PUMA (Programmable Universal Machine for Assembly) in 1978. PUMA's arm could move in three dimensions and work on fast assembly lines. Since its introduction, PUMA and its clones, which were more nimble, have been extensively used in automobile assembly lines, electronic printed circuit assembly, and several other industries all over the world. Over the years, industrial robots have improved by incorporating better environmental sensing with cameras, laser guidance, improved actuators, and better computer programs that allow finer control of movements. It is estimated that over 3 million industrial robots are in operation worldwide, primarily in the automobile and electronics industries. Japanese companies are now world leaders in manufacturing and using industrial robots.

Besides assembly lines, pick-and-place robots are used in many fields, including biology laboratories. Biology laboratories use small robotic arms to handle test tube arrays and pipetting reagents precisely in a specified sequence.

SERVICE ROBOTS

Service robots perform helpful tasks for individuals or organizations, often in hazardous environments. Some examples are hospital carts that assist nurses, logistics robots that move and stack material, autonomous vacuum cleaners, mars rovers exploring terrains, volcano exploration robots, deep sea exploration robots, robots that assist surgeons, robot vacuum cleaners, robot security patrol, self-driving cars, and intelligent assistants in departmental stores. They are autonomous, mobile, smart, and can sense their environment. The history of their development is a collection of individual landmark robot designs, some of which I will describe in what follows. I have not described self-driving cars as their history is long and tortuous, and I cannot do justice to their history in this short anecdote.

Shakey was the first general-purpose mobile robot designed and developed by a team of over a dozen engineers at the Artificial Intelligence Center of the Stanford Research Institute between 1966 and 1972. The Defence Research Projects Agency (DARPA) funded the project. The project combined research in computer vision, natural language processing, logical reasoning, and physical action. Shakey used its camera, sonar range finder, radio link, collision detection sensors, and onboard processor. The team discussed various Greek and Latin names for it. One of the members suggested *Shakey* as it was tall and had a tendency to shake while moving.

Shakey Robot in 1972
(Photo courtesy Wikipedia)

The HelpMate autonomous mobile robot
(Photo courtesy NASA)

Shakey responded to voice commands to travel from a given point to a destination, turn on or off light switches on the walls of rooms, open and shut doors, climb up a block of wood, and push objects. The actions to be performed were pre-programmed. It was a pioneering effort that laid the groundwork for the design of mobile robots. It received extensive coverage in the popular press when it was released. Carnegie Mellon University's Robot Hall of Fame inducted Shakey into its collection.

HelpMate was a pioneering robot that could navigate autonomously through hospitals, including calling and using lifts without any guidance system, such as electrical tracks embedded in the corridor. It was built over a decade, starting in 1985, by Transition Research Corporation, a small research-oriented company, with funding from the US National Aeronautical and Space Administration (NASA). It could carry up to 100 kg and transport medicines, laboratory specimens, medical records, meal trays, and radiology films as ordered by nurses using a keyboard mounted on the cart. It navigated using cameras and later with laser beams (lidar). The *Haidilao* Chinese restaurant chain has employed similar technology recently (2018) to take food ordered by customers from the kitchen to a customer's table. Its vision system detects obstacles, including moving people, and navigates between rows of tables. Many of the functions in the kitchen are also automated with pick-and-place industrial robots.

Dante was a tethered walking robot with eight legs designed by a large team of researchers at Carnegie Mellon University (CMU) during 1990–92. NASA and NSF funded it. It could climb steep slopes and survive in the harsh environment of a volcano in Antarctica. It rappelled down the slope of an active volcano, Mount Erebus in Antarctica, and collected gas samples emanating from the hot lava for study by volcanologists. It was followed by *Dante II*, another walking robot, in 2020 designed at CMU, which collected gas samples from the floor of the crater of Mount Spurr volcano in Alaska.

Spirit and *Opportunity* were another notable pair of robots sent to explore Mars. Designed and launched by NASA, both landed in separate locations on Mars in January 2004. They were planned to be active for 90 Martian days but lasted much longer: *Spirit* until 2010 and *Opportunity* until 2018. They were 1.5 m tall, 2.3 m wide, and 1.6 m long. The rovers were six-wheeled with a suspension to allow them to remain on the ground while navigating the rough Martian surface. Each wheel had its drive motor and could travel at 10 mm/sec. They would stop every 10 seconds, observe the surroundings for 20 seconds, and send images to the Earth station. They were solar-powered.

Mars Explorer Rover

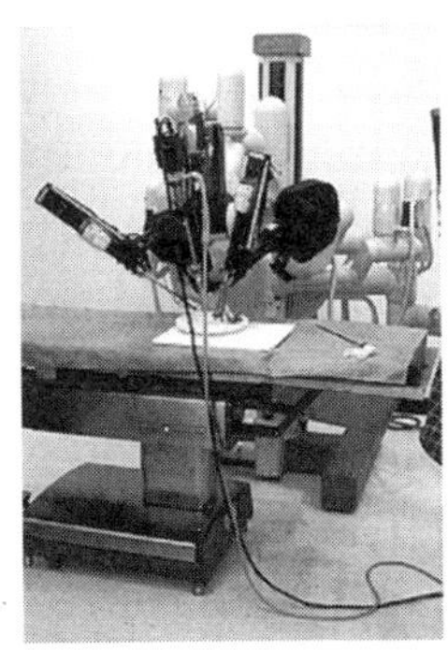

Da Vinci Robot Surgical unit

(Photos courtesy Wikipedia)

Da Vinci surgical robot was designed by Gary Guthart, Joseph Rosen, and Larry J. Scott of the University of California, San Francisco, in 1999. The US Federal Drug Administration (FDA) approved its use in 2000. It is manufactured and marketed by Intuitive Surgicals. Since its introduction, it has been used in millions of surgeries worldwide. It consists of three main parts: a surgeon's console, a vision system, and a patient's cart. A patient lies on a cart and up to four robotic arms are introduced through small incisions around the organ to be operated. The arms hold surgical instruments that a surgeon controls. The arms have better dexterity than human arms and compensate for any hand tremors of a surgeon. A surgeon sits at his console and has a 3D view of the area to be operated. The surgeon manipulates the robotic arms using hand and wrist movements.

Robotic surgery is used primarily on minimally invasive procedures in prostate surgery, gynaecology, gall bladder removal, kidney surgery, and even heart valve-related surgery.

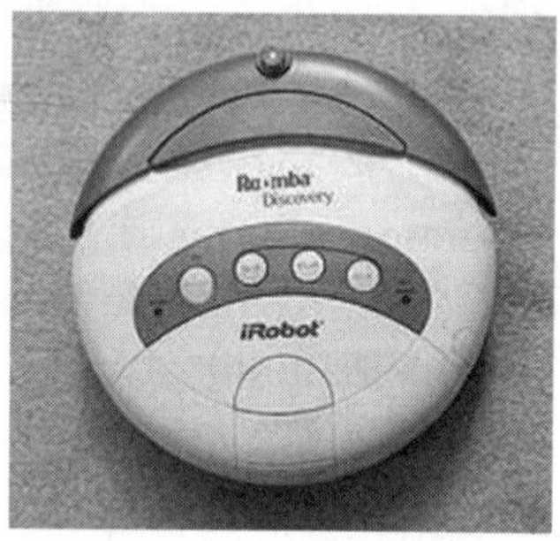

Roomba vacuum cleaner
(Photo courtesy Wikipedia)

Roomba is a room-cleaning robot manufactured by iRobot, a company based in Bedford, a suburb of Boston. It was founded in 1990 by three MIT roboticists, Colin Angles, Helen Greiner, and Rodney Brooks. The group pioneered research in small autonomous mobile robots used in bomb disposal and those that can work in rugged terrains. In 2002, iRobot designed a room-cleaning robot named Roomba, which found a ready market. Since then, around ten generations of Roombas have been marketed, each adding novel features. Recent models have a vision system to avoid obstacles and prevent it from falling down stairs, floor mopping, control by a mobile phone app, and the ability to seek a power outlet when its battery is low. Around 40 million Roombas have been sold worldwide. A basic model is available in India for around ₹17,000.

HUMANOID ROBOTS

A robot that resembles a human body with a head, torso, two arms, and two legs is known as a humanoid robot. Some of them have eyes and a mouth. Waseda University in Japan built the first humanoid robot, WABOT 1 (WAseda roBOT), during 1970–73. It could control its limbs, see and talk in Japanese, and grip and carry objects. It was followed by WABOT 2, built during 1980–84. WABOT 2 was explicitly designed to play an electronic keyboard musical instrument. It could play and also accompany a musician.

WABOT-I
(Photo courtesy Waseda University)

ASIMO
(Photo courtesy Wikipedia)

In 2000, Honda, a Japanese automobile company, built *Asimo*, a humanoid robot that could walk, talk, hear, see, and recognize faces, objects, and gestures. It interacted with humans and walked at a speed of around 1.6 km/hour. In appearance and actions, it was impressive. An improved model made in 2007 could climb stairs. It was named Asimo in honour of Isaac Asimov. Honda took it around the world to show off its capabilities. It conducted the Detroit Symphony Orchestra in 2008. The first model was 130 cm tall, weighed 54 kg, and could work for about 30 minutes on a full charge of its Li-ion battery. Honda made about 100 units in 4 models. Honda produced the last model in 2011.

ROBOTIC DOG

Aibo is a robotic dog made by Sony in Japan. Aibo in Japanese means companion. Sony released 5000 Aibos in June 1999, priced at $ 2500, and sold them out within 20 minutes of their release. Aibo can respond to its name, wag its tail, roll over, play fetch ball, sit, shake hands, act sad or happy, and recognize its master. Its personality grows over time. All the actions are programmable in its built-in processor. Sony built four generations of Aibos until 2006 when it was discontinued. Sony resurrected it in 2010 with a fifth-generation improved model, which is still available for around $ 2900.

Aibo—Sony's Robotic dog
(Photo courtesy Wikipedia)

EPILOGUE

In the popular imagination, robots are machines built in the image of man. Many fictional robots such as R2D2, C-3P0 of Star Wars, T-800—the Terminator, The Iron Man, and Ava in Ex Machina have bolstered this imagination. In the real world, they are mundane. The most numerous robots, around 3 million, are industrial robots, which do not resemble humans. They, however, are the most important, increasing the productivity of humans and performing hazardous tasks. Service robots such as Roomba, HelpMate, and da Vinci surgical assistants have also demonstrated their utility. Companies have made humanoid robots, but they have yet to become human assistants. However, they may soon be able to provide companionship to older people just like Aibo does. Autonomous self-driving cars are reaching maturity after five decades of research worldwide but are not yet on the roads. The field of robotics is an exciting multi-disciplinary research area that requires teams of mechanical engineers, control systems engineers, electronics engineers, computer scientists, and human factor engineers.

REFERENCES

[1] Volker Graefe and Rainer Bischoff, From Ancient Machines to Intelligent Robots—A Technological Evolution, Ninth ICEMI–2009. https://ieeexplore.ieee.org/document/5274297

[2] Hans Moravec, Robot Technology, Encyclopaedia Britannica. https://www.britannica.com/technology/robot-technology

[3] Matt Simon, The Wired Guide to Robots, Wired Magazine, April 16, 2020 https://www.wired.com/story/wired-guide-to-robots/

[4] Piper Thomson, An Exhaustive History of Robotics, August 30, 2019 https://www.g2.com/articles/history-of-robots

30

System R—The First Relational Data Base Management System

PROLOGUE

In the late 1960s and up to the late 1970s, organizations used two Data Base Management Systems (DBMS) models. Database Task Group of CODASYL (Committee on DAta SYstems Languages) promoted a model, called the network model, as the industry standard. In the network model, records in the database were linked as a complex web using pointers. IBM promoted the other model called Information Management System (IMS). It was a hierarchical model in which database records were arranged as trees. Neither model had any sound theoretical underpinning and required extensive training of programmers for proper use. They were, however, well supported by the computer industry and were efficient in terms of the use of computer resources. A programmer had to "navigate" the database using the links connecting the records to retrieve a desired record.

Edgar F. Codd, a researcher at IBM's San Jose Research laboratory in California, was unhappy with the complexity of these DBMS. He started research on database theory, culminating in a landmark paper he published in the Communications of ACM titled "A Relational Model of Data for Large Shared Databanks" in 1970 [1]. In this paper, he suggested organizing data as a set of tables called Relations. Each relation consists of a set of records, one record per row. Each record has several items (or fields), and one or more is a unique key. A group of relations relevant to an application constitutes a relational database. Unlike the earlier systems, this model did not explicitly include "connections" between records. In a Relational database, table information was combined by comparing attribute values across tables. Codd also proposed a relational calculus to manipulate relations and retrieve desired record(s) from the database. The ACM, USA gave him the Turing Award in 1981 "for his fundamental and continuing contributions to the theory and practice of database management systems."

Edgar F. Codd
(Photo thanks alchetron.com)

SYSTEM R

Codd's work attracted the attention of another group of around 30 researchers led by Donald Chamberlin, working in the same IBM Research laboratory in 1973. This group started implementing an experimental Relational Data Base Management System (RDBMS) called System R. It was not intended as an IBM-supported product but was to be a proof-of-concept of RDBMS. The group's design did not strictly follow Codd's theory, and Codd chose not to associate with this group in their implementation efforts. As the first step, the System R group developed a query language from 1973 to 1975 to retrieve data from RDBMS. They wanted the query language to be English-like, which non-professional users and professional programmers could learn easily. It used verbs such as CREATE TABLE, UPDATE TABLE, SELECT, DELETE, etc. It was called Structured English Query Language (SEQUEL). Donald Chamberlin and Raymond Boyce described SEQUEL in a paper they presented at an ACM Workshop [2] in 1974.

Donald D. Chamberlin
(Photo courtesy computerhistory.org)

Raymond F. Boyce
(Photo courtesy alchetron.com)

In this paper, they described in detail the syntax and semantics of the language. They gave statements for creating Relations as tables and querying them using SEQUEL. Chamberlin's group wrote the SEQUEL interpreter in PL/1 (the standard IBM high-level language of the 1970s), and some parts were in assembly language. They found that SEQUEL was a trademark of Hawker Sidley Aircraft Company. Consequently, they abbreviated it as SQL. The patent office did not patent software in those days. IBM was also quite liberal in allowing their researchers to publish their work. At the insistence of the paper's referees, Chamberlin and Boyce also gave the complete syntax of SEQUEL in BNF (Backus-Naur Form) notation. This paper led to many companies copying the syntax and semantics of SQL in later years and SQL becoming a de-facto ISO standard for querying RDBMS.

The next phase of the development of System R was during 1976 and 77. In this phase, the group led by Chamberlin implemented a full-function multi-user version of System R on an IBM mainframe computer using VM/CMS, a developer-oriented operating system. They also optimized the SQL system to reduce the retrieval time by compiling frequently asked queries as machine code.

The final implementation phase was between 1978 and 1979, during which Chamberlin's team installed System R in user sites not as an IBM-supported product but as experimental sites. The sites were at Pratt and Whitney Aircraft Engines and Upjohn, a pharmaceutical firm. Users liked SQL and quickly adapted to the use of RDBMS. Compared with the IMS, System R was less efficient. This inefficiency was offset by the ease of designing a database using relations and retrieving desired data using SQL. The training time required to design RDBMS and learn SQL was considerably less than designing using IMS.

In a classic paper titled "A History and Evaluation of System R", authored by Chamberlin and 16 authors that appeared in the Communications of ACM in 1981 [3] the authors recount the development of System R over the period 1973 to 1979.

In the 1970s and 80s, IBM was primarily a hardware company dominating the mainframe market. IBM promoted software only if it increased hardware sales. It would have taken considerable resources to implement System R on the then most popular OS of IBM, MVS (Multiple Virtual Storage), and market it. IBM was thus lukewarm about making System R a product on their mainframes because IMS was doing very well in the market, and the management was reluctant to promote a rival product. Meanwhile, the computer scene was rapidly changing with the advent of minicomputers followed by PCs and powerful workstations. Oracle was promoting RDBMS and SQL on many computer models as it was a software company and hardware-neutral. RDBMS with SQL was rapidly gaining users due to its simplicity. As hardware became powerful and cheaper, efficiency was not a significant consideration. Ease of use was. In response to the new competition, IBM released IBM SQL/DS RDBMS in 1981 for their operating systems DOS/VSE and VS/CMS, which ran on their smaller computers. DB2 followed this for MVS mainframe computers in 1983. Only in the 1990s did IBM develop DB2 that ran on other operating systems such as OS/2, UNIX, MS Windows, and Linux.

EPILOGUE

During the development of System R, many seminal contributions in transaction processing emerged. A significant contribution was the design of algorithms to prevent interference between concurrent database users. It resulted in the formal definition of ACID (Atomicity, Consistency, Isolation, and Durability) properties of all database transactions by Jim Gray. His work involved profound theoretical ideas and resulted in the classic 1000-page book "Transaction Processing: Concepts and Techniques" written by him and A. Reuter. Gray received the Turing Award in 1998 for his "seminal contributions to database and transaction processing research and technical leadership in system implementation."

Jim Gray
(Photo thanks to ACM Sigmod.com)

IBM was very liberal in allowing the researchers to publish their work (without patenting) related to System R, which resulted in over 40 papers in Conferences and Journals. These publications influenced many startup companies to implement and market RDBMS and SQL systems. Notably, as mentioned earlier, Larry Ellison, Bob Miner, and Ed Oates started Software Development Laboratories in 1977. The company's name was changed to Oracle in 1983. They were impressed by Codd's work on RDBMS and System R implementation. Using the published literature, they created their version of RDBMS and SQL called Oracle RDBMS. Unlike System R, which was oriented towards IBM's mainframes, Oracle RDBMS was written in C and thus machine-independent. It quickly captured the RDBMS market for PCs, minicomputers, and later mainframes. In 2023, there were around a dozen RDBMS companies, most modelled on System R. Even though IBM's computer scientists did all the seminal research and implementation of RDBMS, today, IBM is a minor player in the RDBMS market as it chose to support IMS for too long.

REFERENCES

[1] E.F. Codd, A Relational Model of Large Shared Data Banks, Communications of ACM, Vol. 13, No. 6, June 1970, pp. 377–87.

[2] D.D. Chamberlin and R.F. Boyce, SEQUEL: A Structured English Query Language, Proceedings ACM-SIGMOD Workshop on Data Description, Access, and Control, ACM Press, 1974, pp. 249–264.

[3] D.D. Chamberlin and 16 other co-authors, A History and Evaluation of System R, Communications of ACM, Vol. 24, No. 10, October 1981, pp. 632–46.

31

Who Invented Email?

PROLOGUE

One of the "killer applications" of the Internet is email. It has now become the most common mode of communication. The postal mail system, used for centuries, is rarely used nowadays for communication and is derisively called *snail* mail.

The Oxford Dictionary defines email as: "Messages distributed by electronic means from one computer user to one or more recipients via a network".

The Cambridge Dictionary defines email as: "the system for using computers to send messages over the internet".

Observe the significant difference. Oxford Dictionary does not use the word internet.

I asked the question, "Who invented email?" to Google. On October 2, 2019. I received the reply given below:

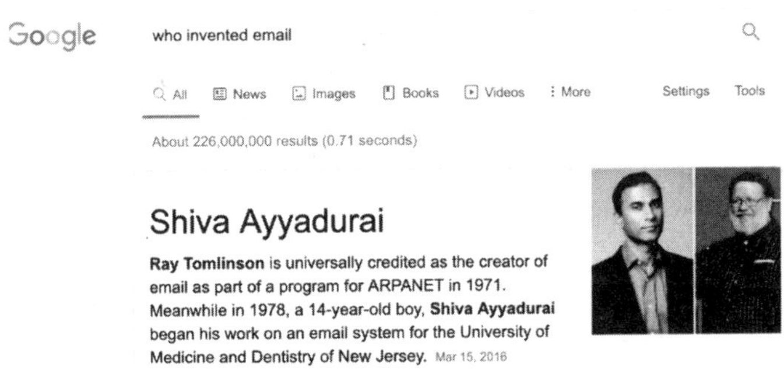

Screenshot from Google

(I have omitted the irrelevant part of the answer in the above screenshot. The picture on the left is that of Ayyadurai, and the one next to him is that of Tomlinson)

I repeated the question to Google on November 20, 2023. It gave the following answer:

"Perhaps the most widely accepted story about who really invented email centers around another MIT graduate named Ray Tomlinson. He created an electronic messaging system for ARPANET (or the Advanced Research Projects Agency Network), which was a precursor to the Internet."

(I have omitted the picture of Tomlinson to save space)

I was puzzled, and I dug into history to find the answer. I present what I found in what follows. It is up to you to decide who invented email.

TOMLINSON'S CLAIM [1]

Tomlinson claims that during the summer and autumn of 1971, he was part of a small group of programmers in Bolt, Beranek, and Newman Inc. (BBN), a company in Cambridge, Massachusetts, USA, that was developing a time-sharing operating system (OS) called TENEX for DEC PDP 10. He was improving a local inter-user mail program called SNDMSG that allowed a user of PDP 10 to compose, address, and send messages to other PDP 10 users' mailboxes. A similar program, CTSS Mail, was written as early as 1965 for the Compatible Time-Sharing System at MIT by Tom Van Vleck and Noel Morris. A mailbox is a file with a particular name that allows other users to write at its end but not read it or overwrite what is already in it. In other words, your mail is sent and written in the recipient's mailbox, but you cannot read or delete what is already in their mailbox. Tomlinson remembered that he had worked on an experimental file transfer program called CPYNET that was used to transfer files between computers connected to a network. It occurred to him that SNDMSG could incorporate code from CPYNET to send material to a mailbox file in a remote computer connected to a network in addition to sending mail to mailboxes in local computers. He added the CPYNET code with some modifications to the protocol with the SNDMSG code to send messages to remote computers. To address a recipient in a remote computer, he placed an @ sign between the receiver's (login) name and their host computer's name. It would be something like naomi @ comp_abc. The first message he sent was between two computers located side by side connected by the ARPANET. The message was from him to himself. When the mail program worked, he released it to colleagues who started using it to send messages to their colleagues connected to the ARPANET. He sent the first set of messages in 1971. The next release of TENEX OS in 1972 included the SNDMG program with network mail capability. ARPANET programmers later replaced the CYPNET protocol with a better File Transfer Protocol with mail transfer features. They continuously improved the mail transfer protocol after that. Larry Roberts, who was managing the ARPANET, encouraged his colleagues to use email and wrote a program to manage it. Soon, email became the most common application of the ARPANET.

AYYADURAI'S CLAIM [2]

Shiva Ayyadurai was a 14-year-old high school student in New Jersey. He was admitted to a special programme for gifted students to learn computer programming at the Courant Institute of Mathematical Sciences in New York in 1978. Soon after, Ayyadurai joined the University of Medicine and Dentistry of New Jersey (UMDNJ) computer center as a summer research student at the request of his mother, Meenakshi, who was working as a mathematician at the university. When he joined, Les Michelson, who was in charge of the computer facilities at UMDNJ, gave him the challenging task of developing an inter-office mail system to be used by doctors, secretaries, office workers, and medical students who were not computer savvy. The inter-office paper-based mail system had the following interlocked parts (as explained by Robert Field in [2]): Inbox, the Memo ("To: ","From:", "Date:", "Subject:", "Body:", "Cc:", "Bcc:"), Forwarding, Composing, Drafts, Edit, Reply, Delete, Priorities, Outbox, Folders, Archive, Attachments, Return Receipt, Carbon Copies (including Blind Carbon Copies), Sorting, Address Book, Groups, and Bulk Distribution. Ayyadurai designed and developed (during 1978 and 1979) a computer program that replicated all the functions of UMDNJ's existing inter-office paper-based mailing system. He wrote the program in FORTRAN IV as he had learnt this computer language at the Courant Institute. The program had 50,000 lines. He named it EMAIL because it electronically emulated the existing paper-based mailing system. Another reason was that FORTRAN IV allowed only uppercase letters for names, and the OS he used allowed only five characters for program names. EMAIL used the HP IMAGE/1000 database system. The university had a variety of computers connected to a wide-area network, and users could send an email from any computer to any other computer in the network. The staff of UMDNJ extensively used EMAIL for inter-office communication as it was easy to use and reliable. In 1982, Ayyadurai obtained the copyright for EMAIL and its user manual. (There was no software patenting law in 1982). ARPANET existed in 1978, but UMDNJ was not connected to it. As a high school student, Ayyadurai was probably unaware of ARPANET. He submitted his work to the Westinghouse Science Contest for high school students as "a High-Reliability Network-wide, Electronic Mail System" and won an award.

CERTIFICATE OF COPYRIGHT REGISTRATION

This certificate, issued under the seal of the Copyright Office in accordance with the provisions of section 410(a) of title 17, United States Code, attests that copyright registration has been made for the work identified below. The information in this certificate has been made a part of the Copyright Office records.

REGISTER OF COPYRIGHTS
United States of America

FORM TX
UNITED STATES COPYRIGHT OFFICE
REGISTRATION NUMBER
TXu 111-775

EFFECTIVE DATE OF REGISTRATION
8 30 82
Month Day Year

DO NOT WRITE ABOVE THIS LINE. IF YOU NEED MORE SPACE, USE A SEPARATE CONTINUATION SHEET.

1 TITLE OF THIS WORK ▼
EMAIL
PREVIOUS OR ALTERNATIVE TITLES ▼
Computer program for Electronic Mail System
PUBLICATION AS A CONTRIBUTION If this work was published as a contribution to a periodical, serial, or collection, give information about the collective work in which the contribution appeared. Title of Collective Work ▼

If published in a periodical or serial give: Volume ▼ Number ▼ Issue Date ▼ On Pages ▼

2 a NAME OF AUTHOR ▼
Mr. Shiva Ayyadurai
DATES OF BIRTH AND DEATH
Year Born ▼ 1963 Year Died ▼
AUTHOR'S NATIONALITY OR DOMICILE
Domiciled in ▶ United States
WAS THIS AUTHOR'S CONTRIBUTION TO THE WORK
Anonymous? ☐ Yes ☒ No
Pseudonymous? ☐ Yes ☒ No
NOTE
NATURE OF AUTHORSHIP Briefly describe nature of the material created by this author in which copyright is claimed. ▼
Created and Wrote entire text of the computer program.

Copyright certificate issued for Shiva Ayyadurai's email program.

EPILOGUE [3]

Ray Tomlinson developed a messaging system in 1971 and sent messages between two computers connected to the Internet. He was also the first to introduce the @ symbol used in email addresses. Shiva Ayyadurai developed a complete email system that emulates a manual office mailing system in 1978. This system, however, was only capable of sending and receiving email in a private wide area network of UMDNJ. He copyrighted the name EMAIL in 1982. Together, these constitute the email system that all of us use today.

REFERENCES

[1] Tomlinson on how he invented a mailing system for the ARPANET. www.raytheon.mediaroom.com
[2] University of Medicine and Dentistry of New Jersey, Computer group: www.historyofemail.com
[3] Discussion in Quora www. quora.com/who-invented-email

32

The First Commercial Microprocessor—Intel 4004

PROLOGUE

A group of engineers led by Robert Noyce and Gordon Moore, who worked earlier at Fairchild Semiconductor, started Intel in July 1968. Intel is a major manufacturer of integrated circuit chips today. When it began, Intel concentrated on manufacturing memory chips using a technology known as Metal Oxide Silicon (MOS). Intel foresaw that magnetic core memory, the dominant main memory of computers in the 1960s, would soon be replaced by semiconductor memory as it was faster, and its cost was bound to come down. Additionally, MOS memory chips were easy to manufacture due to their regularity of structure. As a startup, Intel had cash flow problems and accepted contracts to design and fabricate custom integrated circuit chips besides manufacturing memory chips.

Nippon Calculating Machine Corporation, a Japanese company, was manufacturing and selling desktop calculators, primarily in foreign markets, in the 1960s using the brand name Business Computers (Busicom). A unique feature of Busicom calculators was a small line printer that could be attached to it. Early models used small-scale integrated circuit chips, making the calculator bulky and expensive. The manager of the calculator group asked, in late 1968, a design group led by Masatoshi Shima to redesign the calculator using Large-Scale Integrated Circuits (LSI) to reduce the cost of the system and make Busicom calculators competitive in the market with Sharp, a sizeable

Japanese company, dominated the calculator market at that time. Sharp used custom LSIs made by Rockwell Semiconductor Systems, a well-established integrated circuit manufacturer in California, in its calculators. Shima's group designed the calculator using eight LSI chips. Busicom decided to outsource manufacture of these LSI chips to Intel.

TED HOFF'S DESIGN

A three-member team from Busicom, led by the manager of the project Masuda, came to Intel in June 1969 to negotiate a contract to manufacture the LSI chips they designed. Shima made the presentation and explained the functions of the LSI chips. He stated that the calculator would be programmable with the program stored in a Read Only Memory (ROM) chip. It was to be exclusively designed for Busicom and not sold to any other user. Intel agreed to undertake the project. Busicom followed up with a formal contract in September 1969.

Intel assigned the Busicom project to Marcian "Ted" Hoff, manager of its Applications Research Department, with Stanley Mazor as his co-designer. Hoff's primary experience was in systems design rather than in chip design. The Japanese team explained, over considerable time, their reasonably complete design to Hoff and Mazor. Hoff felt Busicom's design was too complicated and expensive to implement [1]. The chips required many pins and were incompatible with the standards of Intel chips. Hoff had worked with Digital Equipment Corporation's PDP-8 computer. PDP-8's compact instruction set and simple implementation impressed Hoff. He suggested that the team redesign the calculator using the logical structure of a computer, such as PDP-8, that could be programmed to mimic a calculator. Such a design would allow flexibility to add features to Busicom's calculator. Hoff refined his design from August 1969 to October 1969 with some assistance from Mazor [1]. He proposed a system with four chips: a 2048-bit ROM chip to store the calculator's program, a 320-bit Random Access Memory (RAM) to store data to be processed, a 4-bit Central Processing Unit (CPU), and a 10-bit Shift Register as an interface for input and output. These chips used 16 or 18 pins IC packages that were standard in the industry. The most complex chip was the CPU, which Hoff estimated would require around 2000 transistors. Shima was reluctant to change his design as his team had spent considerable time designing and debugging these chips [2]. His design used eight chips and non-standard 36 or 40-pin packages for the ICs. Shima and Hoff presented their designs to a group of Intel and Busicom executives, and the executives selected Hoff's design for implementation.

Ted Hoff
(Photo thanks to Wikipedia)

Masatoshi Shima
(Photo thanks to kytoprize.org)

IMPLEMENTATION OF HOFF'S DESIGN

Shima accepted his management's decision and started working with Mazor to clean up Hoff's rough design. They completed the logic design, and Shima returned to Japan in December 1969. He began work on programming the CPU chip and documenting the design. Shima went to Intel in April 1970 after completing his job to examine the progress Intel had made in fabricating the chips. He was shocked when he found that Intel had made no progress. Hoff had been taken away from Busicom's project and assigned to another project. In any case, Hoff was not competent to design the logic circuits and chip layout. He was a systems designer who was very good at examining the broad picture and suggesting an appropriate solution. Intel needed competent logic designers who could translate Hoff's system design to chip design. In April 1970, Intel recruited Federico Faggin to design and fabricate the four chips of the Busicom calculator. Faggin earned a doctorate in physics in 1965 from the University of Padua in Italy. After working for a few years in Italy, he joined Fairchild Semiconductor in 1968, where he and a colleague invented silicon-gate technology for fabricating high-density, high-performance Metal Oxide Silicon (MOS) integrated circuits. He was also an expert logic designer.

When Faggin joined the Busicom project, he found that the logical design of the chips had yet to begin, and he had to start from scratch. Shima and Mazor explained the architecture of the chips to him. Faggin began designing the four chips [3]. He worked 12 to 16 hours a day to complete the already delayed project. Shima was at Intel until

November 1970 and assisted Faggin by working out the chips' logic design and layout and developing tests to verify the design. Faggin numbered the four chips as 4001(ROM), 4002 (RAM), 4003 (Shift Register), and 4004 (CPU). The 4001 ROM stored 256 bytes, and the 4002 RAM stored 40 bytes. The 4003 Shift Register was 10 bits long and was to be used to scan the keyboard, printer, and display of the Busicom calculator.

The most complex chip in this set was the 4004 CPU chip. It was a microprocessor that used 4-bit data width, a 4-bit adder, an 8-bit accumulator to store partial sums, 16 4-bit registers, 45 instructions, and a 740KHz clock. It took 850 microseconds to add two 8-digit numbers. The chip required 2300 transistors.

Federico Faggin

Stan Mazor

(Photos thanks to Wikipedia)

Faggin designed these chips, and they were fabricated by March 1971 and sent to Busicom for testing and incorporation in their calculator. Shima and his colleagues had already developed boards to use the chips. As soon as they started receiving the chips from Intel, they built calculators and similar machines and sold around 10,000 units to NCR, which had a contract with Busicom.

Early Intel 4004 chip in a ceramic package

(Photo thanks to Wikipedia)

MARKETING THE MICROPROCESSOR

Even though Busicom was successful in marketing calculators and associated equipment, such as cash registers and billing machines that used the 4000 series chipset, it soon found that its competitors were lowering the prices of competing machines. Busicom requested Intel in May 1971 to reduce the price of the 4000 series chips. Hoff, Mazor, and Faggin persuaded Intel's management to agree to lower the price of the chips provided Busicom was willing to waive the exclusive rights contract that prevented Intel from selling the chips to other companies. In July-August 1971, Busicom waived exclusive rights to the chipset for a negotiated price reduction. Intel could now sell the 4-chip set, named MCS-4 (Microcomputer System 4-bit), to anyone.

When Intel obtained the rights to sell MCS-4 to anyone, Hoff, Faggin, and Mazor tried convincing the marketing group that the chipset was versatile and could be used not only in calculators but also as controllers in many systems. Faggin designed a system to test chips using MCS-4, demonstrating its versatility. Intel's management was unsure whether Intel should venture into the systems business with the new chips when stabilizing its memory business. Arthur Rock, the chairman of Intel's board, convinced the board that Intel should enter the systems business. Intel's marketing group was also not confident until Ed Gelbach joined as marketing director in mid-1971. Gelbach was confident in marketing MCS-4. Besides, he also foresaw that sales of microprocessors would increase the sales of memory chips, which was then Intel's main product. A two-page advertisement titled "Announcing a New Era of Integrated Electronics" was released in the November 1971 issue of Electronics News, a trade journal. It described the MCS-4 chipset and its applications for digital control. Intel followed up by demonstrating the applications of the chipset at the Fall Joint Computer Conference and distributing data sheets and application notes. The demonstration was a roaring success. The microprocessor was now a new integrated circuit in the market, heralding a new era of embedded control systems and microprocessor-based computers.

WHO INVENTED THE FIRST MICROPROCESSOR?

The credit for inventing the first microprocessor, Intel 4004, has been widely debated [3]. Marcian "Ted" Hoff gets the credit for its invention.

It is not the whole story. The motivation for the design came from Busicom, and Shima of Busicom stayed with the project from its beginning to its end, participating in the conception, design, testing, and use of 4004. Ted Hoff conceived the idea of a programmable single-chip processor. Mazor was his sounding board and collaborator in his design effort. Faggin did the most challenging part of the work by performing the detailed logic design and fabricating the 4004 chip using silicon-gate MOS technology he co-invented at Fairchild Semiconductor. Finally, the genius of Gelbach successfully marketed the invention to the world.

EPILOGUE

The successful completion of the 4004 microprocessor gave Intel the confidence to design more powerful microprocessors. Based on a contract with Computer Terminals Corporation, Hoff and his group developed an 8-bit processor named 8008, which Intel fabricated in April 1972 [4]. It was followed by 8080, an improved version of 8008 in April 1974, 8085 in March 1976, and 8086, a 16-bit processor in June 1978. Intel soon found that software tools were essential to use these processors in systems. It developed various tools and application notes that encouraged users to design complex systems using these processors. Over the years, Intel has become a highly successful manufacturer of a wide variety of microprocessors, from 80486 to the current (2024) Core i9- 14900HX, 24 core processor. It sold its memory manufacturing unit in 2020.

REFERENCES

[1] Marcian E. Hoff, Designing the First Microprocessor, IEEE Solid State Circuits Magazine, Winter 2009, pp. 22–28.

[2] Federico Faggin, The Making of the First Microprocessor, IEEE Solid State Circuits Magazine, Winter 2009, pp. 8–21.

[3] William Aspray, The Intel 4004 Microprocessor: What Constituted Invention? IEEE Annals of the History of Computing, Vol. 19, No. 3, 1997, pp. 4–15.

[4] Robert N. Noyce and Marcian E. Hoff, A History of Microprocessor Development at intel, IEEE Micro, February 1981, pp. 8–21.

33

History of Computer Games

PROLOGUE

Playing games on a computer is as old as computers. Alexander Douglas wrote the first program, called OXO, for playing the game *naughts and crosses* (also known as *Tic-Tac-Toe* in the US) in 1958 for the EDSAC at Cambridge University, as a part of his Ph.D. thesis, primarily to illustrate human-computer interaction. Researchers wrote programs to play *board games* such as checkers and chess in the mid-1950s on mainframe computers of that era to mimic human intelligence. They were the beginning steps in the then-emerging area of artificial intelligence (See Anecdote 9). Mainframe computers of the 1960s and 70s were not conducive to playing another genre of games known as *action games*. An interactive computer with a display is essential to play currently popular genres of computer games such as action games, adventure games, first-person shooter games, role-playing games, war games, survival games, massively multiplayer online role-playing games, and many more games requiring immersion in virtual worlds.

Steve Russell and his colleagues wrote the first interactive video game program, *Spacewar!*, for the DEC PDP-1 computer at the Massachusetts Institute of Technology in 1962. *Spacewar!* simulated a fight between two spaceships, "the needle" and "the wedge", travelling in the gravity well of a star. Two players with console switches controlled the ships, and the goal was to destroy the opponent's ship. DEC distributed the program's source code, and the game became very popular at all PDP-1 installations, including the one at IIT/Kanpur.

From this humble beginning, video games have rapidly progressed through several phases. Games designed in the early 1970s, known as *Arcade Games,* were played on coin-operated machines installed in bars and restaurants, primarily in the US and Japan. These games soon moved to homes in the mid-1970s and were played using hand-held consoles that controlled images on TV screens. When home PCs appeared in the early 1980s, video games moved to them. When PCs became powerful with 3D graphics in the 1990s, the games became more complex with intricate storylines, 3D visualisation, and audio. The demand for 3D graphics hardware surged as the gaming industry grew, leading to improved graphics chips and lowered prices. In the mid-1990s, hand-held home video game consoles incorporating powerful built-in microprocessors with excellent 3D graphics appeared. These consoles had buttons that game players used to control the progression of the games displayed on the large TV screens at home. Competition among companies such as Sony, Microsoft, and Nintendo that manufactured gaming consoles has led to the development of powerful graphic chips. Concurrently, developers designed a variety of games to use these consoles starting in the mid-2000s. The Internet revolution led to the development of multiplayer games on computer networks. Cloud computers stream games to less powerful home computers and consoles. When reasonably priced smartphones came in 2007, games moved to them. The emergence of Virtual Reality (VR) goggles has led to the development of immersive games in virtual worlds.

ARCADE GAMES

Arcades in the US had coin-operated pinball machines in the 1960s, which attracted visitors to bars and restaurants to play with them. A friend invited Nolan Bushnell, an entrepreneur, to play *Spacewar!* on the PDP-1 at Stanford University. Soon after playing it, Bushnell decided to develop its arcade version. He and his partner Ted Dabney designed a coin-operated arcade machine in 1971 to play *Computer Space*, the arcade version of *Spacewar!* It was not very popular, as casual arcade users found the game rules intimidating. Bushnell saw a ping-pong game developed for the Magnavox TV at a trade show and felt he could modify it as an arcade game. He and Dabney started Atari, a company for manufacturing arcade video game machines, in June 1972. Bushnell gave Allan Alcorn the task of developing an arcade machine to play ping-pong. Alcorn had recently joined Atari after graduating with an Electrical Engineering and Computer Science degree from the University of California, Berkeley. Alcorn devised a digital circuit using transistor logic and connected it to a home TV set to allow two people to play video ping-pong. The design realistically simulated a ping-pong game with sound effects when a paddle, represented by a small line, strikes a ball. It also had a scoring system. The first player who scored 11 points was declared the winner. Bushnell and Dabney were impressed by the system, manufactured it, and named it PONG. Arcades installed PONG in November 1972. A customer could play video ping-pong by inserting a 25-cent coin into PONG. The game was a hit as the rules for playing it were simple. Eight thousand PONGs were installed by 1974. Each PONG earned, on average, $35 to $40 per day, giving Atari a steady revenue stream.

Atari's PONG was a landmark in computer gaming history. It popularised electronic arcade games, which became a big industry. Atari soon designed the popular games *Breakout*, in which a player bounces a ball through a wall, breaking it, and *Asteroid*, in which a player guides his spaceship through a field of asteroids, blasting them and avoiding collisions. Arcade games spread internationally, particularly in Japan.

Allan Alcorn

PONG machine

(Photos courtesy Wikipedia)

The Japanese companies Taito and Namco designed arcade game machines with new games. Taito released *Space Invaders* in 1978, and Namco released *Pac-man* in 1980. In *Space Invaders*, a player controls a spaceship to defend Earth from a swarm of alien invaders by shooting them down while avoiding their attacks. Taito and Namco sold hundreds of thousands of these game machines. *Pac-man* (originally called *Puck-man* in the Japanese version and changed to *Pac-man* as

Puck sounded similar to a swear word in English!). In *Pac-man*, a player moves a character through a maze to eat dots while avoiding being eaten up by ghosts. Nintendo released another classic game, *Donkey Kong*, in 1981, in which a player guides Mario to rescue his kidnapped girlfriend, Pauline, from the clutches of the angry ape Donkey Kong. These games led others to create first-person shooting games and maze games. Arcade games proliferated, and the golden age of arcade games lasted until 1983. In 1983, the game market crashed as too many uninteresting games flooded the arcades. Simultaneously, many arcade games migrated to home gaming consoles, reducing the number of visitors to arcades. There was a revival in the 1990s with 3D graphics games and adventure games that used special game control devices such as a steering wheel. However, Western societal changes led to the arcade's closure in the early 2000s. Arcades, however, were popular in Japan and East Asia until COVID-19 struck in 2020, leading to the closure of many arcades. A revival is afoot with virtual reality machines that provide gamers with immersive experiences.

MAGNAVOX ODYSSEY

Ralph H. Baer, an electronics engineer, was the head of the Equipment Design Division of Sanders Associates, a defence electronics equipment manufacturer. In August 1966, while waiting for a bus, he got the idea to use a home TV to play games in addition to passively watching programmes. His idea was to design a low-cost *game box*, costing around $25, that could control the beam on the TV display and allow viewers to play games. The R&D director of Sanders allowed him to pursue his idea and allocated a small budget even though it had no relevance to Sanders' primary business. By August 1967, the prototype was ready. Baer and colleagues designed many prototypes and games using the game box, including ping-pong. The final product was ready in November 1967. Sanders was a defence contractor and was not interested in entering the retail business to market the game box and searched for a partner. Magnavox, a television manufacturer, agreed in January 1971 to manufacture and sell it. Magnavox engineers added more games, including basketball, volleyball, and several others totalling 28 games, and modified the game box. Magnavox finally marketed this game box in November 1972.

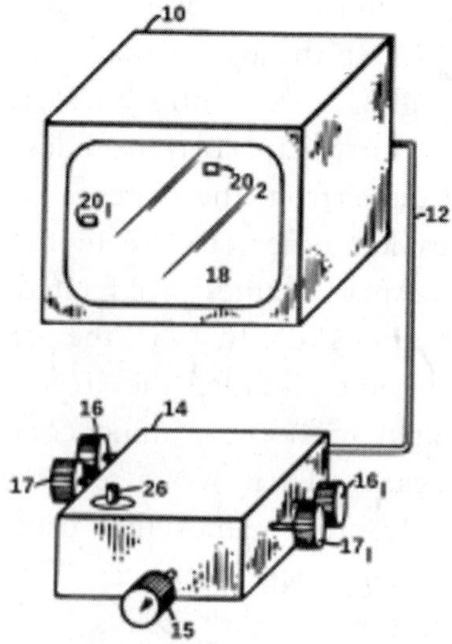

Ralph Baer **Patent Drawing of Odyssey**

(Pictures courtesy Wikipedia)

It was named *Magnavox Odyssey* and cost $99.95. Over the next three years, Magnavox sold 300,000 units. The game box was the first *video console* to control images on a TV screen. The game box was the beginning of the *video game* industry. Baer is now called the "Father of Video Games" and was awarded the US National Medal of Technology in 2004. Sanders and Magnavox patented the game box. Over the years, they sued emerging video game companies, including Atari, for patent infringement whenever any games were similar to those in *Odyssey.* Sanders and Magnavox earned over $100 million from the patent suits until 1990, when the game box patent expired.

ATARI VIDEO CONSOLES

In 1974, Atari designed a video console version of PONG using an LSI chip to reduce the cost. Sears, a retailer, sold over 150,00 units just before Christmas 1975 for $98.75 each.

Low-cost microprocessors emerged in the late 1970s. Atari designed a hand-held video console system (VCS) using MOS Technology's 8-bit microprocessor 6507 in 1977. It was programmable and had a built-in game cartridge (a ROM) for storing games. Atari sold VCS with a joystick, paddle controllers, and a game cartridge with *Pong, Pac-Man,* and *Combat.* The price of a console was around $ 190. Atari sold thirty million units during its lifetime up to 1992. Atari reduced the price of VCS and planned to recoup the cost from the sales of games. This strategy failed as many independent game designers flooded the market with low-cost game cartridges for Atari's VCS. Many of these games were of poor quality and led to the video game market crash in 1983. Atari was also guilty as it released the game *ET*, an adaptation of the famous movie ET, in 1982, whose video quality and storyline were poor. Atari buried 700,000 game cartridges, including ET, in a landfill in New Mexico in 1983, eventually leading to Atari's closure.

ENTRY OF JAPANESE COMPANIES

The video console market revived in the US in 1985 when the Japanese company Nintendo Electronic Systems (NES) entered the scene. It designed a proprietary console that could load only its game cartridges. NES also designed the game *Super Mario Bros* (a game in which a player guides a fat plumber, Mario, to rescue Princess Peach from the evil king Bowser in the Mushroom Kingdom), which became a best-seller and sold 430 million copies. Super Mario Bros was the beginning of the *Mario* series of games. Soon, Sega, another Japanese gaming company, entered the market and produced the *Sega Genesis* console and the popular games *Sonic the Hedgehog, Phantasy Star*, and *Streets of Rage.* NES and Sega were competing vigorously and dominating the video console market until 1994, when Sony entered the scene with its PlayStation, which had cutting-edge 3D graphics and revolutionised the gaming industry. Independent game developers designed many classic games such as *Tomb Raider, Spiderman, Gran Turismo 2, Doom, Grand Theft Auto, and Quake* that used the 3D features of PlayStation. Sony sold over 100 million PlayStation 1s. The next model, PlayStation 2, was released in 2000 and sold 155 million units, a record. Sony cleverly allowed PlayStation 2 to be used as a CD music player and DVD video player, making it a "home entertainment system". Soon, Microsoft entered the gaming console market with its Xbox in 2001. It bundled many games with the console hardware. Many independent game developers also developed games for it. The sales were, however, disappointing as Microsft sold only 24 million Xboxes. This business was loss-making, and Microsoft's OS business subsidised it.

The game console market continued to thrive, with game designers developing thousands of games for these consoles. Many generations of video game consoles have appeared, including PlayStation 3, PlayStation 4, and PlayStation 5. Each generation pushed the boundaries of 3D graphics performance and the types of games. Microsoft competed with the Xbox 360 in 2005, the Xbox One in 2013, and the Xbox Series X and S in 2020. NES also released a console called Wii in 2006. It was less powerful than Sony and Microsoft's but provided new features like Internet connectivity and motion control. It bundled a viral game, *Wii Sports*, with its earlier best-sellers such as *Super Mario, Legend of Zelda, Pokemon, and Metroid.* It sold 100 million units within a year of its launch.

Xbox S controller

PlayStation 4 controller

(Photos courtesy Wikipedia)

Since 2010, a new era of streaming games from the cloud with services such as PlayStation Now and Xbox Game Pass has emerged.

With broadband connections and almost universal availability of the Internet, the genre of games called Massive Multiplayer Online Games and its descendants have emerged. In this scenario, a group of gamers play a game interactively on the Internet and social networks such as Facebook. Popular games include *Fortnite, Mario Kart 8, Diablo 4, Call of Duty: Warzone,* and *Farmville.*

PERSONAL COMPUTER GAMES

Atari released 400 and 800 computer models with 8-bit processors for the home computing and gaming market in 1979. Atari ported the popular arcade games *Frogger* (guiding a frog to cross a road with heavy traffic), *Centipede* (shooting a centipede that divides in multiples), and *Pong* to these computers. Commodore released a low-cost Commodore64 home computer in 1982, which could display colour and became very popular, selling around 15 million units. Independent game producers emerged and produced games for it. In the UK, BBC Micro and Sinclair ZX Spectrum dominated the home computer market with many games. With the emergence of the IBM PC in 1981, game developers designed many games in the MS-DOS environment. IBM bundled its PCs with Microsoft's *Adventure* and *Flight Simulator*. These were crude games as the graphics were primitive. The emergence of low-cost IBM PC clones in 1985 led to a flood of games developed by independent developers for MS-DOS. Playing games at home was one of the major applications of around 24 million home computers in the USA. The new generations of PCs in the 1990s had excellent 3D graphics and sound cards and added special peripherals for gamers. Many of the popular games on video consoles were ported to these PCs. Independent game producers increased as the PC market was huge and most of them used Microsoft OS. Games were distributed first on floppy discs, then on CDs, and nowadays over the Internet. Professionals estimate that there are over 500,000 game developers worldwide, and over 60% of them develop games for PCs.

The popularity of video games and the massive demand for realistic 3D game-playing environments led to the growth of companies designing and manufacturing high-performance graphics hardware used as co-processors in PCs and game consoles. Graphic card manufacturers such as NVIDIA thrived (See Anecdote 65). IBM's graphics processor developed for PlayStation 3 was modified and used as a floating point accelerator in IBM's Roadrunner PetaFLOPs high-performance computer (See Anecdote 69). Graphics processors solve large sets of simultaneous algebraic equations at petaflops speed. These processors are used to train large neural networks used in current AI systems.

GAMES ON MOBILE PHONES

As soon as mobile phones became popular, manufacturers started designing games for them. The first game was *Snake,* developed by Nokia for its feature phone in 1997. The next phase was when Japanese mobile phones were connected to the Internet by NTT Docomo in 1999, which allowed Japanese gaming companies to adapt some of the simple popular games to mobile phones. There was a big revolution in 2007 when Apple introduced the iPhone and an App Store, allowing anyone to sell software for iOS devices easily. Many games, such as

Angry Birds and *Cut the Rope,* appeared. Game developers and the number of games grew by leaps and bounds when the Google Play store for Android-based smartphones started in 2012. As smartphone ownership grows geometrically worldwide, game developers expect the revenue from mobile phone games to overtake the revenue from console and PC games. The main challenge in developing mobile games is the small screens on mobiles and the need for control devices. Developers have innovatively used touch-sensitive screens and accelerometers in phones to control games. Console manufacturers have started designing mini consoles with mobile processors to port many low-cost mobile games.

EPILOGUE

In 2022, the worldwide video game market revenue was US$ 183 billion, of which $92 billion was for mobile games (www.statista.com). Market analysts estimate that one-third of the people in the world play computer games now. The earnings of the video gaming industry have overtaken the combined revenues of the music and film industries. Many games are shooting and war games. Psychologists are concerned that this may increase the aggression of children playing these games. Game addiction is another concern. Educational games and solving puzzles have great value but are not a lucrative market. Developing and marketing games is a new industry that is not capital-intensive. It is a fertile area for innovative, imaginative game developers worldwide.

REFERENCES

[1] History of Video Games – Four Decades of Video Entertainment https://cdn.hackaday.io/files/1649347056536256/History%20of%20Video%20Games-Four%20Decades%20of%20Video%20Entertainment.pdf

[2] Robert Dillon, The Golden Age of Video Games, CRC Press, 2016.

34

Xerox PARC and Alto Personal Computer

PROLOGUE

In 1970, Xerox was an extremely successful copier manufacturer with an annual revenue of $ 1.6 billion. Its president, C. Peter McColough, decided to open a new research center far away from its headquarters in Rochester, New York, so that it could invent future technologies without day-to-day pressures. Xerox leased a building in Palo Alto, California, near Stanford University. The selection of this location was an excellent decision as students and faculty of Stanford University could interact with the scientists at the research center named Xerox Palo Alto Research Center (Xerox PARC). The broad mandate given to the centre was to develop "the office of the future". The center's director gathered a compact group of brilliant researchers, granting them considerable work freedom. The head of the computer systems division, Bob Taylor, who was earlier a manager at the Advanced Research Projects Agency (ARPA) of the Department of Defence of the US government, had funded many university projects and had met and heard many young promising researchers. He recruited a group of brilliant computer scientists, including Alan Kay, Butler Lampson, Robert Metcalfe, and Charles Thacker. They later got the ACM Turing award for the research work they had initiated at Xerox PARC. Besides these, there was also a galaxy of computer scientists that included David

Boggs (Ethernet), Richard Shoup (SuperPaint), Alvy Ray Smith (Paint program), John Warnock (Adobe Illustrator), Chuck Geschke (Page description language), Adele Goldberg (Smalltalk), and Lynn Conway (VLSI design) to mention a few. I have written the inventions they made at Xerox PARC in the parentheses next to their names. These researchers were free to pursue their passion and "invent". The research group discussed all ideas threadbare in an atmosphere of constructive criticism. Xerox PARC scientists credit Bob Taylor as a great research manager who catalysed their research, and fully supported and insulated them from the bureaucracy.

XEROX ALTO PERSONAL COMPUTER

One of the projects Alan Kay dreamed up was to develop what he called Dynabook. His dream was to invent a personal laptop computer with interactive capabilities. In the 1970s, the technology of integrated circuits had not advanced enough to put an entire computer in a notebook-sized device. However, Lampson and Thacker liked his idea, and the three of them teamed up to design and develop a Personal Computer (PC), the first of its kind in the world. They named it Alto, and it was ready in 1973. The most crucial innovation in Alto was the use of a bitmapped display along with a mouse that had been invented by Doug Engelbart the previous year along with Bill English (who had shifted to Xerox PARC). Engelbart's primitive mouse was improved and used in Alto. The group also introduced the idea of multiple overlapping windows and icons. Alto's users used to point to icons to initiate programs. The designers incorporated the concept of windows, icons, mouse, and pointer in Alto. The Alto designers conceptualized it as a PC on every office worker's desk. As the workers were expected to communicate and cooperate, the designers mooted the idea of networking computers. The project to network Altos led Metcalfe and Boggs to invent the Ethernet protocol to communicate among computers connected to a cable. A word processor was an essential requirement for every office. Charles Simonyi developed Bravo software, the first WYSIWYG document preparation program, providing multi-fonts on Alto's bitmapped display. It used the mouse extensively to point to words for editing. In 1972, the object-oriented language Smalltalk was designed and implemented on Alto by Alan Kay, Adele Goldberg, and their group. Another pair of computer scientists, Chuck

Geschke and John Warnock, developed a page description language called Interpress meant for Desktop Publishing (DTP). Another notable work done at Xerox PARC by Lynn Conway was creating graphics tools for drawing integrated circuit sketches on Alto's display. She and Carver Mead (who was visiting from Caltech) collaborated to develop a structured VLSI design methodology and wrote a famous book on VLSI design. The Altos in Xerox PARC were networked, and the scientists used email extensively. The concept of Remote Procedure Call (RPC) was invented by Bruce Nelson and Andrew Birrell and, with that, distributed computing [1].

Xerox PARC Alto Personal Computer
(Photo thanks to Wikipedia)

From our current perspective, the Alto was too expensive as a PC. When Thacker and his group designed Alto, it used MSIs and LSIs as microprocessors were unavailable. Charles Thacker noted that it cost $12,000 to make and would have cost $40,000 if marketed in 1975. Xerox did not develop Alto as a product. Xerox PARC built around 2000 Altos, of which Xerox offices used 1000, 500 given to Universities, and the rest used in-house [2].

STEVE JOBS VISITS XEROX PARC [3]

Jeff Raskin, who worked for Apple on the team designing the Macintosh computer, had seen Alto and its capabilities. He requested Steve Jobs to visit Xerox PARC and see the path-breaking research they were doing. In December 1979, Steve Jobs and his team visited Xerox PARC, and Jobs was astounded to see the graphical user interface and how Alto used a mouse. He immediately saw that these technologies would become part of future PCs. He wanted a deeper technical discussion by his team with Xerox PARC engineers. Even though the engineers at Xerox PARC were not very enthusiastic, the management of Xerox struck a deal with Apple to share the technology in return for 100,000 Apple shares at $10 each. (The million-dollar investment in shares later appreciated to over a billion dollars). Xerox PARC researchers gave the technical information the Apple team requested. Apple team refined the mouse, made it reliable and cheap, improved the icons, and made the system more user-friendly and cost-effective. Apple implemented Windows, icons, mouse, and pointer technology in Mcintosh, and it was a hit. Apple released the Macintosh in January 1984 at an affordable price of $2,495.

When Microsoft also followed with Windows OS in November 1985, Steve Jobs accused Bill Gates of stealing his idea, to which Bill replied, "*Well Steve, I think there is more than one way of looking at it. I think it is more like we both had this rich neighbour named Xerox, and I broke into his house to steal the TV set and found out that you had already stolen it*". Apple filed a case against Microsoft for copying the Graphical User Interface (GUI) concept. However, a US court dismissed it. The court opined that a patent or copyright cannot protect the GUI and the desktop metaphor. Seeing the success of Apple using its technology, Xerox entered the PC market with Xerox Star. It was too late; the system was expensive, not as good as Apple's, and failed in the market.

XEROX LASER PRINTER

Another notable invention at Xerox PARC was the laser printer. Gary Starkweather, an engineer in the Webster research centre of Xerox, had a brilliant idea of converting a Xerox copier to one that would directly print material displayed on a computer's screen. His managers considered his idea ridiculous and wanted him to do something more useful. He secretly continued his work and built the printer parts but not the interface to the computer. He requested a transfer to Xerox PARC, where the managers did not consider any idea bizarre. He pursued his passion in this environment and designed a prototype laser printer in 1971 named SLOT (Scanned Laser Output Terminal). Lampson and his group in 1972 developed a character generator and a digital control system for the printer. This development resulted in a laser printer that was attached to Alto. Subsequently, Xerox transformed it into a product—Xerox 9700 in 1977—the first commercial laser printer in the world.

EPILOGUE

Industry leaders criticised Xerox management for not commercialising the technologies developed at Xerox PARC. Many ex-employees profited from it. Metcalfe started 3Com and monetised Ethernet and networking technologies. Warnock started Adobe Systems, which created the Postscript page description language based on his research at Xerox PARC. Simonyi, who had developed Bravo at Xerox PARC, joined Microsoft and developed office software. Xerox's top management focussed on copiers and did not see the potential of emerging technologies. The only technology that they profited from was the laser printer. In 2002, Xerox PARC was spun off from Xerox as an independent company and re-named PARC.

REFERENCES

[1] Tekla S. Perry and Paul Wallich, Inside the PARC: the "information architects", IEEE Spectrum, October 1985, pp. 62–75.

[2] The Xerox Alto: A Personal Retrospective (Talks by Charles Thacker and Butler Lampson) YouTube.

[3] The Xerox PARC Visit, https://web.stanford.edu/sites/mac

35

CP/M and Gary Kildall

PROLOGUE

When Intel announced the first single-chip microprocessor 8008 in 1972, there was tremendous enthusiasm, particularly among hobbyists excited about building their computers using this chip. Gary Kildall taught computer science at the Naval Postgraduate School located at Monterey in California in 1972 and was a part-time consultant to Intel. He was impressed by the capability of 8008, designed a high-level language PL/M (Programming Language for Microcomputers), and wrote a compiler for it. PL/M was the first language meant explicitly for microprocessors and had many low-level features that allowed access to specified bytes in memory, I/O ports, and processor interrupt flags. PL/M had no I/O routines, and an Operating System (OS) was required to execute it on microcomputers. Intel was not willing to support Kildall in designing and writing an OS. Killdall, however, felt that it was necessary to develop an operating system and started working on one.

DEVELOPMENT OF CP/M OPERATING SYSTEM

Kildall needed a microcomputer development system to write an Operating System. He persuaded Intel to give him a development system. Kildall bought a floppy disk drive that IBM had recently developed and integrated it with the development system. In 1974, he wrote in PL/M a disk operating system named CP/M (Control Program for Microcomputers) for Intel 8008 on this system. During the early seventies, several manufacturers started building microcomputers using Intel 8008. To make CP/M portable across different manufacturers' computers with varying memory sizes, Kildall had the brilliant idea of splitting CP/M into two parts. One part, called the Basic Input-Output System (BIOS), was machine-specific, and the other part, consisting of a Basic Disk Operating System (BDOS) and a Console Command Processor (CCP), was machine-independent. Hence, for a new machine, only BIOS had to be written. CP/M became the de-facto standard OS for almost all PCs manufactured between 1974 and 1980.

STARTING OF DIGITAL RESEARCH INC. (DRI)

Kildall was, at heart, an academic. His wife Dorothy convinced him to start a company to market CP/M. The company was named Intergalactic Digital Research, and Kildall later renamed it Digital Research Inc. (DRI). It began in his large house in Pacific Grove in northern California. By 1981, 300 different models of computers used CP/M, and DRI's yearly revenue was over $5 million.

IBM COMES CALLING

IBM decided to enter the PC market in 1980. It took a policy decision to outsource the development of software. Among the software it required was a high-level language. BASIC was the most popular language during the initial days of PCs. Microsoft developed a BASIC interpreter in 1975, considered the best available on the market. Consequently, IBM went to Seattle to negotiate the purchase of BASIC from Microsoft. BASIC required an OS to run. CP/M was the de-facto standard OS for microcomputers. Consequently, Bill Gates of Microsoft suggested that IBM contact Kildall at DRI for the OS. Gates knew Kildall as they were both from Seattle, and Gates had used the mainframe computer at the University of Washington in Seattle as a schoolboy while Kildall was the computer's system administrator. Gates had visited Kildall at his home, and there was even some discussion on DRI acquiring Microsoft, but there was no serious follow-up [1]. Gates phoned Kildall to say that a valuable customer was coming to negotiate the purchase of CP/M. He did not disclose that the customer was IBM, as he had signed a non-disclosure agreement.

As it happened Kildall had a prior commitment to deliver software to an important customer. He flew to meet his customer as an amateur pilot with his own plane. When he was away, the team from IBM came to DRI, and Kildall asked his wife and business partner Dorothy to negotiate the sale of CP/M with IBM. In 1981, IBM was the largest computer company in the world with a turnover of billions of dollars, whereas DRI was a pigmy in comparison. IBM's team included corporate lawyers. It was standard practice of IBM to request its vendors to sign a non-disclosure agreement. Dorothy and DRI's lawyers balked as they felt the non-disclosure agreement was one-sided. IBM's team was upset as most vendors signed the agreement as it was a routine procedure. Dorothy wanted her husband to be present for the negotiations.

Dorothy and Gary Kildall
(Photo thanks to computerhistory.org)

MICROSOFT CLINCHES OS DEAL WITH IBM

The IBM team was in a hurry to conclude an agreement and returned to Microsoft to find a solution. Meanwhile, Microsoft discovered that a small company, Seattle Computer Products (SCP), had developed an OS called QDOS (Quick and Dirty Operating System), a clone of CP/M for Intel 8086—a 16-bit computer (At that time, CP/M was available only for 8-bit computers). Microsoft negotiated with SCP and bought the source code outright for $75,000 with the condition that Microsoft could modify and resell it. Bill Gates and his team visited IBM in November 1980 and agreed to develop an OS they named PC-DOS for the IBM PC. Gates, a brilliant businessman, foresaw that there would be clones of IBM PC and negotiated a deal to licence the OS to IBM for $50,000 with the provision that it would be *non-exclusive* and that he could licence it to other manufacturers as MS-DOS. IBM agreed, provided that the strict deadline for delivery of the OS, which was July 1981, was met and the project kept top secret.

Microsoft hired Tim Paterson, the programmer who had developed QDOS for SCP. Gates and his team, along with Paterson, modified QDOS, wrote PC-DOS, and met the deadline of July 1981. Meanwhile,

Kildall, when he saw a copy of PC-DOS, was shocked that it had many similarities with CP/M and threatened to sue IBM for copyright infringement (In the early 1980s, software patenting was nonexistent, and copyright laws had no clarity for software). After protracted correspondence, IBM agreed to give its customers the choice to use either CP/M or PC-DOS. However, the licence fee fixed by IBM for CP/M was $240 compared to $40 for PC-DOS. Kildall could have sued IBM for its partiality, but being an academic at heart and not litigious refrained from doing so. Most customers chose PC-DOS. Microsoft renamed PC-DOS as MS-DOS for IBM PC clones, and it became the standard OS for PCs and sold millions of copies. SCP threatened to sue Microsoft as it had not disclosed that QDOS was to be sold to IBM. Microsoft settled the case out of court in 1986 for $1 million.

Computer magazines call Kildall "one who would have been Gates" but lost the opportunity as "he went flying" when IBM came calling. Kildall refutes this in his memoirs [1], claiming that he negotiated with IBM later but was unsuccessful as IBM did not agree to his terms. There has been a long controversy about whether PC-DOS was a substantial copy of CP/M, as claimed by Kildall and refuted by Gates. A forensic analysis comparing the two codes claims that PC-DOS was not a copy of CP/M [2].

EPILOGUE

Even though Kildall lost the IBM contract, he sold DRI to Novell in 1991 for $120 million. He continued to be technically active and developed systems to interface optical disks with PCs and file systems for CD-ROMs. Despite his enormous contributions to microcomputer software, Microsoft overshadowed him due to his mistake of not clinching the IBM deal. In 2014, IEEE recognized his contributions to computer science by placing a plaque [3] outside the house where DRI started. Gary Kildall died in 1994 at the age of 52 in an accident.

REFERENCES

[1] Kildall, Scott and Kildall, Kristin(eds.), "Computer Connections: People, Places, and Events in the Evolution of the Personal Computer Industry" Archived in Computer History Museum, USA. Free download from computerhistory.org.

[2] Zeldman, Bob, Did Bill Gate Steal the Heart of DOS? IEEE Spectrum, July 2012.

[3] Legacy of Gary Kildall: The CP/M IEEE Milestone Dedication—YouTube video.

36

Cryptography

PROLOGUE

Cryptography is converting or encrypting *plaintext* into an unintelligible text, called a *ciphertext,* using a *secret key*. One can only get the original plaintext from the ciphertext if the secret key is known. Cryptography is derived from the Greek word *Kryptos,* which means hidden. Cryptography has been used since ancient times. Julius Caesar, the Roman emperor (44 BCE), did not trust couriers who carried messages from him to his generals in remote places as they may be captured while travelling or maybe bribed to leak the messages. He encrypted the messages by replacing each letter in the message with a letter *n* letters away from it in the alphabet. Using the English alphabet, if *n* = 3, the letter A will be replaced by E, B by F, ….., and Z by D. If a message is STARTATTACK, the encrypted message would be WXEVXEXXEGO. The value of *n,* the encryption key, will be known only to trusted persons and will be changed periodically. This encryption method is called *Caesar encryption.* It is insecure because if an enemy captures even a few messages, he can easily guess the value of *n*. This type of encryption is called *symmetric or private key* encryption. The sender encrypts a message with a private key given to the receiver. The receiver decrypts it using his copy of the key. *Cryptology* is the science of designing encryption and decryption methods. Persons who invent encryption methods that are difficult to crack are known as *cryptographers*. Those who find ways to decrypt ciphertext are called *cryptanalysts* or, in popular language, code breakers. Code breakers access several ciphertexts and analyse them to guess the key used to encrypt, and use it to decrypt the ciphertext.

Cryptography became critical during the World Wars. During the Second World War (1939–45), Germans used Enigma, an electromechanical machine, to rapidly encrypt messages sent to their naval and front-line commanders. German defense forces distributed secret code books to all field commanders and changed the Enigma key daily to avoid decryption by the Allies who read wireless messages. Enigma codes were tough to break. Polish spies were able to smuggle some Enigma machines. A Polish cryptanalyst Marian Rejewski built an electromechanical machine called *Bombe* in 1938 to decrypt German messages just before the Second World War began. It was unreliable. When the war started, Poland sent Bombe to Britain, and British code breakers led by Alan Turing built an improved version of Bombe. Bombe was used to decode several German messages with the help of the code books captured from the Germans and detailed analysis of messages, which generally began with a weather report. With this intelligence, the Allies knew precisely where German submarines in the Atlantic Ocean were heading and the instructions German top brass gave to the field commanders and acted appropriately. Tommy Flowers and colleagues built a special-purpose electronic computer named *Colossus* in 1944 to break another German cipher named *Lorenz*. War historians estimate that the efforts of the British code breakers helped the Allies shorten the war by two years and ultimately win.

THE FEISTEL ENCRYPTION ALGORITHM

In the late 1960s, IBM established a cryptographic research group led by Horst Feistel at its Yorktown Heights research laboratory in New York, foreseeing the need to encrypt data stored in computers and transmitted by telephone lines. In 1971, IBM received a request from Lloyds Bank in the UK to design a remote cash dispensing machine. IBM decided to encrypt data sent between the bank's computer and the cash dispenser using the Lucifer encryption algorithm developed by Feistel's group. Lucifer encryption algorithm splits plaintext, normally a sequence of ASCII characters, into blocks of 128 bits. Each block is encrypted one after the other. The algorithm splits a 128-bit block into two 64-bit blocks, L_0 and R_0 (See Figure 36.1). R_0 is encrypted using a function F with a secret 64-bit key K_0, and the result Exclusive ORed (bit by bit) with L_0, resulting in R_1. The resulting L and R are flipped. This step constitutes one round of the Feistel encryption. This round is repeated *n* times with a different key in each round, where *n* is a variable number (usually 16), resulting in a ciphertext. Note that the last round also flips L and R. The ciphertext is decrypted by applying the encryption procedure in reverse (See Figure 36.1) using the same sequence of keys in reverse. The only way to break the Feistel cipher is to try all possible sets of 16 keys, each 64-bit long, which is an arduous task even for the fastest computers.

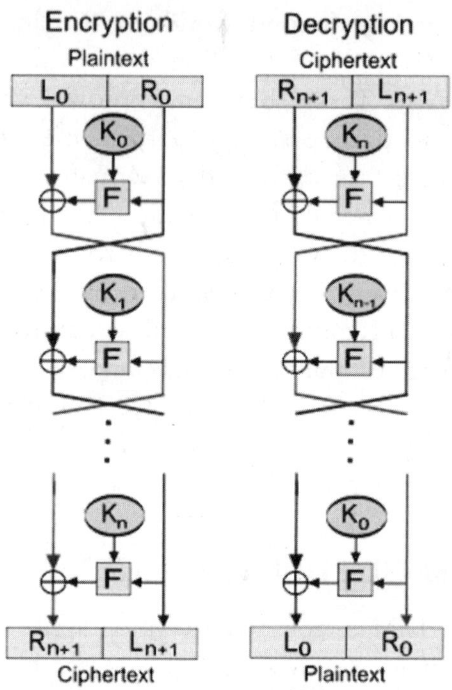

Figure 36.1 Feistel encryption and decryption
(Figure courtesy Wikipedia—Amriki)

DIGITAL ENCRYPTION STANDARD (DES)

In August 1974, the US National Bureau of Standards (NBS) invited cryptographers worldwide to submit cryptography algorithms for adoption as the national standard by the US government. IBM submitted Lucifer, and NBS selected it as the standard. However, the US government's National Security Agency (NSA) was uncomfortable with this encryption because it was too strong. NBS and IBM researchers modified the Feistel algorithm to the Digital Encryption Standard (DES) algorithm. The main changes were to reduce the block size from 128 to 64 bits and the key length from 64 to 56 bits. Another encryption function, S, replaced F to strengthen the encryption from an attack known as a differential attack. Experts opined that the NSA intentionally reduced the key length to enable it to decrypt the ciphertext and designed S to allow the NSA a back door entry to examine messages. NBS dismissed these allegations. Hardware designers could quickly build an integrated circuit chip to implement DES. DES was widely adopted. DES chips encrypt plaintext and decrypt ciphertext. Software implementation of DES was slow. The widespread use of DES led academics to explore cryptography, and many research papers on DES appeared. The 56-bit key length made DES insecure as computers became faster. In 1998, the Electronic Frontier Foundation (EFF) built a DES cracker nicknamed Deep Crack, which cracked DES-encrypted text by brute force in 56 hours. Deep Crack made DES insecure, and NBS suggested Triple DES that applied the DES algorithm three times with three different 56-bit keys, effectively increasing the key length to 168 bits. Triple DES became the standard until the Advanced Encryption Standard (AES) replaced it in 2000.

ADVANCED ENCRYPTION STANDARD (AES)

In 1997, the National Institute of Standards and Technology (NIST)—the renamed NBS—invited proposals worldwide for a new standard symmetric encryption algorithm with the condition that the algorithm should be public and only the key secret. The other conditions were that it uses 128, 192, or 256-bit keys and 128-bit blocks as input, is easy to implement in hardware, and has no secret (called back door) entry for decryption. By mid-1998, several experts shortlisted and scrutinized fifteen proposals from nine countries. NIST organized three conferences for the proposers to present their algorithms. Cryptographers extensively analysed the algorithms. Finally, an algorithm named *Rijndael* (pronounced Rain doll), designed by two Belgian cryptographers, Vincent Rijmen and Joan Daemen, was declared the winner in 2001. It is now the Advanced Encryption Standard (AES).

Vincent Rijmen
(Photo courtesy Wikipedia)

Joan Daemen
(Photo courtesy www.ru.nl)

AES encryption splits plaintext into 128-bit blocks, and each block is encrypted using the AES algorithm. The algorithm substitutes bits in the 128-bit block with others and permutes the result. Both substitution and permutation use a secret key. These operations constitute one round of encryption. AES repeats the encryption round ten times using the 128-bit key. The result is the ciphertext. The AES algorithm increases the number of rounds for longer secret keys. The ciphertext is decrypted by applying the algorithm in reverse. The AES algorithm is fast and can be implemented in an integrated circuit chip. AES can also be efficiently coded even in 8-bit microcontrollers. Most computers nowadays have built-in AES instructions to encrypt messages and store data in databases.

PUBLIC KEY ENCRYPTION

The main problem with symmetric encryption is the difficulty in sharing the secret key between the sender and the receiver. The secret key must be sent to the receiver using a communication medium different from that used to transmit messages. For instance, if senders use a telephone line to send messages, they should employ a courier to send the key. If sender S has 1000 receivers, each receiver must have a different secret key. S must maintain a database of the keys in a secure medium. S must change the keys periodically to ensure security and distribute them. If S adds more receivers, they must be issued new keys securely, and the keys database must be updated. If S is an e-commerce company with millions of customers and new customers added every minute, creating keys, distributing the keys, maintaining the key database, and periodically changing the keys would be impractical. This difficulty is called the *key distribution problem* in symmetric key encryption. The consensus among cryptographers over 2000 years was that the key distribution problem was unsolvable.

The difficulty of solving the key distribution problem fascinated Whitfield Diffie. He travelled around the US, passionately espousing the importance of solving this problem. After his talk at the IBM Thomas Watson Research Laboratory, he learnt about Professor Martin Hellman of the Electrical Engineering Department of Stanford University's research on the same topic. Diffie immediately went to Stanford and joined Hellman as a doctoral student in 1975. The discipline of a doctoral course requiring him to take classes and submit assignments on time did not suit his temperament. He dropped out but continued his research with Hellman. Ralph Merkle soon joined them. While he was an undergraduate student at the University of California, Berkeley, in 1974, Merkle invented an inelegant solution to the key distribution problem as a part of a class project. His solution was for a sender and receiver to exchange millions of puzzles and agree upon a secret key by solving these puzzles. He wrote a paper explaining his solution and submitted it to the Communications of ACM (a renowned computer science journal), which rejected it because the reviewer did not fully comprehend the nuances of the solution. Merkle joined Hellman and Diffie in 1975. The three of them brainstormed and invented a solution to the key distribution problem in 1976 based on ideas from the number theory. Hellman and Diffie published a paper titled "New Directions in Cryptography" in the IEEE Transactions on Information Theory describing an algorithm now called the Hellman-Diffie key exchange algorithm. The algorithm used a one-way (non-reversible) mathematical function to exchange numbers between a sender and a receiver on an insecure communication channel and arrive at a mutually agreed secret key. Their method solved a centuries-old problem that cryptographers thought was unsolvable. They received the Turing Award for their breakthrough research in 2015.

Merkle's paper was re-reviewed by ACM and published in the Communications of ACM in 1978 with an apology note by the journal's editor.

Even though it solved the key distribution problem, the Hellman-Diffie-Merkle method was difficult to implement. The difficulty of implementing the Hellman-Diffie-Merkle method led researchers to explore simpler ways. Ronald Rivest, Adi Shamir, and Leonard Adleman working at MIT, invented a better algorithm called the RSA public-key algorithm in 1977. This algorithm allocates two keys to each organization that wants to communicate with one another. One is called a *private key*, and the other a *public key*. Organizations publish their public key on their website. Sender S, wanting to send a secure message to receiver R, encrypts it using R's public key. R decrypts it using its private key. The beauty of this method is that there is no key distribution.

Martin Hellman

Whitfield Diffie

Ralph Merkle

(Photographs courtesy Wikipedia)

A snooper can decrypt the encrypted message sent to R only if she knows R's private key. Because keys are hundreds of digits long, it is practically impossible to crack a ciphertext. For better security, organizations change their key pairs periodically.

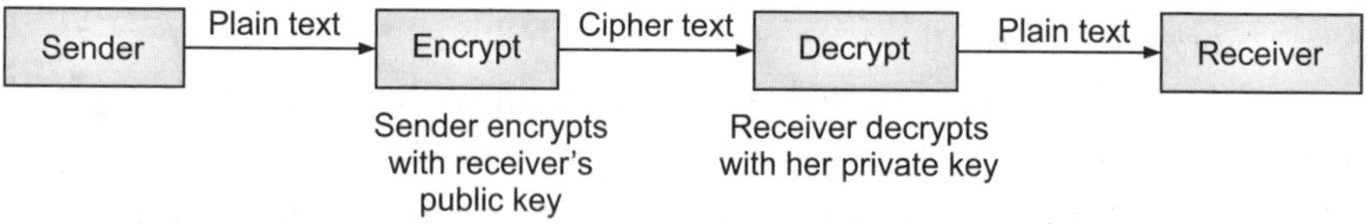

Public key Encryption

Public key encryption has another interesting property. Sender S may encrypt a message with his/her *private key* and send it to a receiver R. R can decrypt this encrypted message by using S's *public key*. Because only S knows his/her *private key*, R can be sure that the sender is S. It is equivalent to a signed message from S. This is the basis of what is known as a *digital signature*.

Ronald Rivest

Adi Shamir

Leonard Adleman

(Photos courtesy Wikipedia)

The RSA algorithm depends on the fact that it is easy to multiply two prime numbers but very difficult to find the two prime numbers given their product.

Another group of cryptographers, James Ellis, Clifford Cocks, and Malcolm Williamson, working at a top-secret defence laboratory in the UK, had independently solved the key distribution problem. They invented the public key encryption method in 1975. Their approach was kept under wraps by the UK Ministry of defence and was declassified only in 1997. These cryptographers were unrecognized for an invention that pre-dated the RSA algorithm.

In his column on mathematical games in the *Scientific American* magazine of August 1977, Martin Gardner gave a message encrypted using RSA that a codebreaker could crack only by factoring a 129-digit product of 64-digit and 65-digit primes. Rivest offered a prize of $100 to the successful codebreaker. Rivest estimated that it would take 40 quadrillion (10^{15}) years with the then-existing methods of factoring and the speed of computers. In 1992, Derek Atkins, a computer science student at MIT, requested volunteers over the Internet to cooperatively crack the code. Over 600 volunteers joined and cracked Gardner's encrypted message in eight months. RSA designers realised that the encryption key of 129 digits (~462 bits) was insufficient. Currently, RSA uses longer 2048-bit keys.

Another public key encryption method, called Elliptic Curve Cryptography (ECC), using the properties of elliptic curves, defined by the equation $y^2 = x^3 + ax + b$, was independently invented by Victor Miller in 1986 and Neal Koblitz in 1987. ECC is more efficient than RSA. It uses shorter key sizes and is preferred for mobile devices, cryptocurrencies, and the Internet of Things. Public key encryption requires what is known as a Public Key Infrastructure (PKI) to authenticate the public keys of organizations by issuing certificates. Governments issue certificates through their agents. The Internet ensures secure communication between a website and its client by a protocol called HTTPS, an abbreviation of hypertext transfer protocol secure. When this protocol is used, the communication between a website and its user is encrypted and secure. A lock icon indicates it. All commonly used web browsers support HTTPS.

EPILOGUE

Encryption technology has revolutionized the usage of computers. Widespread use of the Internet and a plethora of applications such as e-commerce, secure e-mail, secure monetary transactions with credit/debit cards, unified payment interface (UPI), cryptocurrency such as bitcoin, and blockchains would not have been possible without encryption methods invented in the 1970s.

Quantum computers are emerging, and they are a threat to existing cryptographic techniques. Research on quantum cryptography is in progress to ensure better security. Presently (2024), quantum computers are in the experimental stage in laboratories, and none is in production. Thus, they are not a threat to encrypted communication.

REFERENCES

[1] Landau, S., Designing Cryptography for the new Century, Communications of ACM, Vol. 35, No. 5, pp. 15–128, 2000.

[2] Stallings, W., *Cryptography and Network Security*, 3rd edition, Pearson Education Asia, New Delhi, 2003.

[3] Rajaraman, V., *Essentials of E-Commerce Technology*, PHI Learning, New Delhi, 2009.

37

Computer Graphics—The Utah Teapot and Animated Hand

PROLOGUE

The Whirlwind computer (See Anecdote 4), designed for real-time simulation for the US defence department in 1951, was the first computer to attach a large Cathode Ray Tube (CRT) as an output device for displaying signals received from Radars and point to a location on the screen using a device called a light pen. SAGE computers, based on Whirlwind, designed for air-defence used CRT displays. The Tata Institute of Fundamental Research (TIFR), Bombay, built a CRT output system in 1959 and attached it to the TIFRAC computer. It could display characters and waveforms [1].

Analog computers built in the early 1950s had CRT displays as their output unit. An analog computer programmer could vary the parameters of differential equations solved using them and immediately see the effect of the changes on the CRT screen. This interactive capability immensely helped a user to design systems. Digital computers were too expensive in the 1950s to permit single-user interaction. The first interactive digital computer, TX0, was built at MIT's Lincoln Laboratory in 1956 (See Anecdote 13). It had a large CRT display (12-inch diameter, Resolution 512 × 512 Pixels).

Ivan Sutherland joined MIT's Lincoln Laboratory as a doctoral student in the Electrical Engineering Department in 1960 after obtaining a Master's degree at Caltech. He was looking for a project and decided to develop programs to draw and process two-dimensional drawings on the CRT display of TX-2 (a successor of TX-0) built by researchers in the Lincoln Laboratory of MIT. TX-2 was a transistorised computer with a 36-bits word length and allowed interaction using a CRT display and a light pen. Sutherland developed a program named *Sketchpad* that ran on TX-2 and drew lines, rectangles, circles, ellipses, and other geometric objects on its CRT display. A light pen was available along with the display, and he used it to point to the objects and manipulate them. This project was the beginning of graphics processing on computers [2].

Ken Olsen at the Digital Equipment Corporation (DEC) designed a computer named PDP-1 in 1960 (See Anecdote 13). It was a transistorised version of TX-0 and had a 12-inch CRT display and a light pen. DEC donated a PDP-1 to MIT's Electrical Engineering Department in 1961. Students could experiment with it. Steve Russel, a Master's student, and colleagues wrote an interactive game called *Spacewar!* using PDP-1, one of the earliest computer games. These were the earliest developments in computer graphics.

Ivan Sutherland

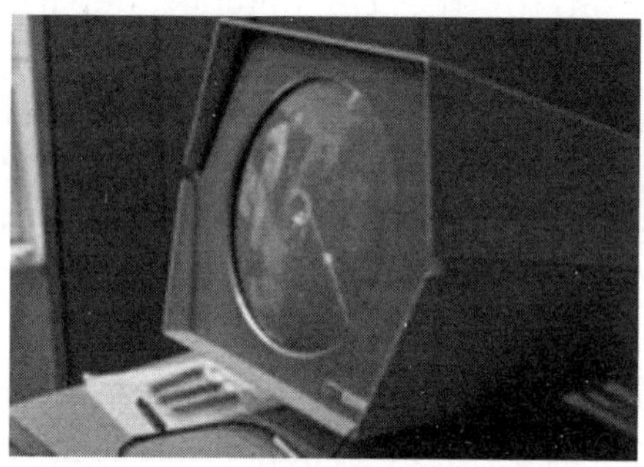

CRT Display used in *Spacewar!*

(Photos courtesy of Wikipedia)

COMPUTER-AIDED DESIGN

In the mid-60s, multi-user time-shared computers began appearing, which allowed interaction with computers. Automobile and aircraft companies found CRT display useful as an output device to display 2D drawings and manipulate them. General Motors [3] and Boeing pioneered using computers for engineering drawing and utilised them in design. William Fetter and Verne Hudson of Boeing coined the phrase computer graphics. Computer graphics require good displays with fast response time. IBM pioneered and built the model 2250 graphics terminal. It was expensive and cost around $280,000. It could be attached to IBM's scientific computer, IBM 1130, and the IBM 360 series computers. Only large companies such as Boeing and General Motors could afford these terminals. These companies developed software to draw engineering drawings and display 3D pictures of car bodies. Pierre Bézier of Renault automobiles invented the use of curves in 3D modelling, which led to displaying realistic surfaces.

A significant development was the advent of the Tektronix 4010 storage tube CRT terminal. It was relatively inexpensive, costing around $5,000, and gave an impetus to research in computer graphics. Research on the display of realistic images began with the advent of this terminal.

IBM 2050 graphics terminal (See Light pen) **Tektronix 4010 terminal**

(Pictures courtesy Wikipedia)

3D GRAPHICS

David Evans was a professor in the University of California, Berkeley Electrical Engineering Department during 1960–65, working primarily in computer architecture. The University of Utah invited him in 1965 to establish a Computer Science Department. He decided to reorient his interest and started research in computer graphics. He could persuade Ivan Sutherland, who was teaching at Harvard University, to join him. Together, the two established one of the best groups of doctoral students in computer graphics worldwide and invented a slew of techniques to realistically render 3D graphics images and animations during the late 1960s and the 70s. They found that devices to render realistic 3D images were woefully inadequate and decided to establish a company to manufacture graphics computers. The company, Evans and Sutherland, started operations in Salt Lake City, Utah, in 1968. It designed and manufactured state-of-the-art graphics computers.

3D graphics requires a realistic display of three-dimensional objects on the screen of a CRT, which is two-dimensional. Researchers in Utah invented numerous techniques in 3D graphics, such as hidden surface removal, shading, ray tracing, lighting, and texture mapping. Martin Newell, a Ph.D. student at Utah, was bubbling with ideas on realistically rendering 3D shapes. He searched for an object for modelling that reflected light and had irregular surfaces and textures. One afternoon, he was drinking tea (being British) with his wife Sandra and talking about his search for an object to model. On the spur of the moment, she proposed the ceramic teapot they were using [4]. It was an odd-shaped pot with a handle, a spout, and a ceramic reflective surface. It was a challenging object to model. Newell immediately drew the shape on a graph sheet and used it as a model. He wrote a program to display it on a Tektronix graphics terminal. His colleague Jim Blinn did not like the shape and flattened it. The Utah teapot was born in 1975. He and his colleagues used the model extensively in their research, and it became a benchmark in 3D graphics rendering research. Many of his colleagues in the Utah group found the intricate object useful for modelling. Newell felt it would be a valuable benchmark for other researchers and publicised the specifications. In the closed community of graphics researchers, the teapot became a standard. Anyone with a new idea in computer graphics tested it on the Utah teapot. The Utah teapot came full circle when a 3D printer used its 3D model to build a physical teapot!

A modern rendering of the Utah teapot model
(Photo courtesy Wikipedia)

COMPUTER ANIMATION

From early childhood, Edwin Catmull had dreamed of becoming an artist to create Walt Disney's animated cartoons. He soon discovered his talent was not in drawing and decided to join the University of Utah, where he obtained a BS in physics and computer science in 1969. Upon graduation, he joined Boeing as a programmer. Two years later, he was laid off in a mass retrenchment. He decided to return to the University of Utah, started his post-graduate studies in computer science, and joined David Evan's graphics group. As a project in a computer graphics course in 1972, he decided to model and animate a hand on a computer [5]. It was a very ambitious project as computer graphics was in its infancy and graphics hardware was primitive. His animation consisted of rotating his left hand. Catmull made a plaster model of his left hand and drew 350 triangles and polygons on it. This model was used to represent the surface of his hand on a computer's display. He then wrote a three-dimensional animation program that displayed the hand's swiveling, opening, and closing. It was the world's first computer animation program. Fred Parke, another Ph.D. student who created a computer animation of his wife's face, assisted him. Hollywood science fiction movie *Futureworld* used Catmull's hand animation snippets in 1976. Catmull completed his doctoral degree in 1974. He joined the New York Institute of Technology and established a computer graphics group there to continue his work on 3D animation. George Lucas, a Hollywood film producer, persuaded him in 1979 to join the graphics division of Lucas films named Industrial Lights and Magic (IL&M), whose aim was to use computer graphics in movies. Catmull, along with Alvy Ray Smith and a group of talented engineers, developed an excellent graphics computer, and another group developed software for animation. IL&M was spun off as a separate company named Pixar, with Catmull as President and Smith as Vice-President. Pixar was losing

Edwin Catmull
(Photo courtesy Wikipedia)

A scene from the Disney movie Toy Story
(Photo courtesy Toystory.disney.com)

money and was looking for an investor. Pixar approached Steve Jobs, who had left Apple Computers and started NeXT Computers, which was not doing well in the market. Jobs was impressed by Pixar's graphics computer and animation software and bought it for $5 million in 1986. He encouraged Pixar to innovate and funded it despite losing millions of dollars. Pixar, however, was winning awards for its animated movies. A notable computer-animated short film named *Tin Toy* was produced by Pixar and directed by John Lasseter. The film tested the Photo-realistic Renderman software developed by the Pixar software group led by Catmull. A partially completed *Tin Toy* was shown at the SIGGRAPH annual convention in August 1988 to a standing ovation from graphics professionals assembled there. Hollywood Motion Pictures Academy awarded it an Oscar for "Best Animated Short Film" in 1988. It was the first computer-generated animated movie. It attracted the attention of the Walt Disney production company, which signed a contract with Pixar in 1991 to make a full-length feature film titled *Toy Story*, directed by John Lasseter, using computer animation software. The movie was released in 1996 and was a hit. It earned $394.4 million worldwide on a production budget of $30 million, and Pixar made a huge profit. Another computer-animated film, *Finding Nemo*, followed it in 2003 and made $940.3 million on a budget of $94 million. Since then, Hollywood has released many computer-generated full-length movies. Disney acquired Pixar in 2006.

GRAPHICAL USER INTERFACE

David Canfield Smith [6] was a doctoral student at Stanford University during 1967–75. He initially started work in Artificial Intelligence but did not make much progress. Alan Kay had just joined Stanford, and in a conversation, he remarked, "I don't want to make a smarter computer; I want to use computers to make people smarter". This statement was etched in Smith's mind. He requested Alan Kay to be his thesis adviser. When Kay shifted to Xerox PARC, Smith started working there part-time, continuing his thesis. Xerox PARC was building the Alto computer, and Smith began working on the Graphical User Interface (GUI) for it along with Kay and others. He invented the idea of graphical icons as part of the interface and developed appropriate symbols. As Alto was conceived as part of Xerox PARC's paradigm of the "office of the future," the icons designed depicted a folder, file, trash bin, etc., pictorially. Steve Jobs visited Xerox PARC, saw a demo of the windows, icons, mouse, and pointer used by Alto, and adopted them in Apple's computers (See Anecdote 34). Alan Kay and his group developed an object-oriented language called Smalltalk, oriented towards graphics. Smith used Smalltalk to design the GUI.

SCIENTIFIC VISUALISATION

Richard Hamming, a famous computer scientist, remarked that the purpose of computing is insight, not numbers. A ream of numbers does not provide insight; graphical representations such as bar charts and pie charts do. 2D graphics programs convert tables of numbers to these visual representations. Giving the results of computer simulations of physical and biological systems as 2D and 3D graphics greatly enhances scientists' understanding of the functioning of these systems. Graphics software displays the results of simulations as waveforms with time as an independent variable. The effect of changing parameters of a simulation model may be immediately seen in an interactive computer when the waveforms change. Graphics software can display 3D models of complex molecules and rotate them slowly, and the effect of chemical reactions on their structures may also be simulated and displayed. Aircraft designers use animation programs extensively to illustrate turbulent flows around aircraft wings and body, which facilitate the design of the 3D shapes of the wings and the body. Graphics are also extensively used in drug design and medical imaging.

STANDARDISATION IN GRAPHICS

Computer Graphics quickly became an important research topic in academia, and the Association of Computing Machinery (ACM), USA, established a Special Interest Group in Graphics (ACM SIGGRAPH). In 1977, a group of ACM SIGGRAPH experts developed the first standard for graphics called the 3D core graphics system, which became the foundation for further developments in graphics. Researchers contributed numerous graphics routines to a library that expedited developments in this area. The most productive group of researchers [7] at the University of Utah, led by Evans and Sutherland in the 1970s, made notable contributions to this library.

Jim Clark, an alumnus of Utah, later founded Silicon Graphics, a company that manufactured graphics workstations in 1982. In the late 1980s, it became well-known for its excellent graphics hardware and software. In 1991, Silicon Graphics began developing a language-independent graphics standard for 2D and 3D graphics called Open GL (Graphics Language) and released it in June 1992. Open GL has a library of primitives that is machine and OS-independent. Graphics programmers have used them extensively since then.

EPILOGUE

Real-time graphics applications require many floating-point arithmetic operations for rendering and shading. Evans and Sutherland's graphics computers implemented these using numerous medium-scale integrated circuits, which were expensive. When computer games using graphics became popular with the advent of PCs in the early 1980s, add-on graphics cards appeared. Soon, the market for these cards expanded, and simultaneously, the number of transistors integrated on a single integrated circuit chip increased, enabling the circuitry of an entire card to be put in a chip called a Graphics processing unit (GPU). GPUs became popular as an add-on to CPUs. Graphics has now become an integral part of computation.

GPUs could solve simultaneous linear equations used in graphics programs. NVIDIA, a pioneer in this area, released more powerful GPUs and a programming system allowing them to be used as a general-purpose chip, GPGPU. GPGPUs have now become important components of supercomputers and are used extensively to train artificial neural networks (ANN). ANNs are employed in the DALL-E program that generates graphic images from natural language descriptions.

REFERENCES

[1] Suryanarayana Rao, P.V., Character Display System for use as a Digital Computer Output, Review of Scientific Instruments, Vol. 30, pp. 749–50, 1959.

[2] Ivan Sutherland, The TX-2 Computer and Sketchpad, *Lincoln Laboratory Journal*, Vol. 19, No. 1, pp. 82–84.
https://www.ll.mit.edu/sites/default/files/page/doc/2018-05/LookingBack_19_1.pdf

[3] Fred K. Krull, The origin of Computer Graphics within General Motors, IEEE Annals on the History of Computing, Vol. 16, No. 3, pp. 40–56.

[4] Trevor English, The Teapot that Became the Standard in Computer Graphics. https://interestingengineering.com/innovation/the-teapot-that-became-the-standard-in-computer-graphics

[5] A computer-animated hand, https://en.wikipedia.org/wiki/A_Computer_Animated_Hand

[6] David Canfield Smith, https://en.wikipedia.org/wiki/David_Canfield_Smith

[7] Computer Graphics and Computer Animation—A Retrospective Overview. https://ohiostate.pressbooks.pub/graphicshistory/chapter/4-3-university-of-utah/

38

The First Local Area Network

PROLOGUE

Xerox Palo Alto Research Centre (PARC) built the first desktop Personal Computer, Alto, in 1973 (See Anecdote 34). The Centre planned to give each scientist an Alto and wanted to interconnect them for easy communication. Xerox PARC had also built the prototype of a laser printer, and they wanted all the Alto users to share it. Xerox PARC recruited Robert Metcalfe in 1972 for his expertise in networking. He had worked on the ARPANET at the Massachusetts Institute of Technology as part of his doctoral thesis work. One of his tasks was to connect Xerox PARC to the ARPANET. There was a delay in acquiring an Interface Message Processor essential to connect Xerox PARC to the ARPANET. Meanwhile, Metcalfe's manager asked him to design and implement a network connecting Altos and the laser printer. Metcalfe started thinking about this problem and wanted to arrive at an elegant solution.

METCALFE AND ALOHANET

Metcalfe had registered as a Ph.D. student at Harvard University but did most of his work with the ARPA networking group at MIT. When he submitted his thesis to Harvard in June 1972, there was an oral examination, and the committee rejected his thesis as, in their opinion, it was primarily implementation-oriented. The thesis needed more mathematics and theory to deserve a Ph.D. Meanwhile, Metcalfe accepted a job offer from Xerox PARC. He informed his employer about his failure. Despite this, Xerox PARC asked him to come and join and work on his degree. He was committed to attending the first International Conference on Computer Communications (ICCC) in Washington, D.C., scheduled to be held in October 1972, which showcased ARPANET. He flew to Washington, D.C., and stayed with his friend Steve Crocker. He could not sleep due to jet lag [1] and saw the Proceedings of the 1970 Fall Joint Computer Conference on a shelf. Flipping through it, he came across a paper by Norman Abramson and his group at the University of Hawaii titled *The ALOHA System—Another Alternative to Computer Communication* that described how a time-shared mainframe computer in Oahu, one of the islands in Hawaii, could be accessed from terminals distributed in other islands using a shared UHF radio communication channel. In the ALOHA protocol, a terminal sends data to the computer using the UHF channel and waits for an acknowledgment. If it did not receive an acknowledgment, it assumed that another terminal was also sending data and there was a collision on the radio channel. Both terminals would then wait for different random intervals and re-send the data on the radio channel, and ultimately, there would be successful transmission. As the number of terminals increased, collisions increased, and access to the computer slowed down (See Anecdote 28). The paper's theoretical component modelled the system using what Metcalfe thought were unrealistic assumptions to make the mathematics tractable.

As soon as he returned to Palo Alto, Metcalfe requested Abramson to permit him to visit Hawaii to study the ALOHA system. Abramson readily agreed, and Metcalfe's manager allowed him to visit Hawaii for a month. He researched the ALOHA system and got some insight into how many users can use a shared communication link in a disciplined way. He modified his Ph.D. thesis to include a mathematical model of the ALOHA system with realistic assumptions. He was examined orally at Harvard in June 1973, and his revised thesis was accepted.

INVENTION OF ETHERNET

With the insight gained after studying the ALOHA network, Metcalfe returned to the problem assigned to him, namely, network Alto computers and the laser printer. He had worked on the ARPANET, which used packet communication to send data between computers on a cable. He decided to use packet communication between computers and a television co-axial cable to interconnect the computers. The cable running on the ceiling of the building was to act as a broadcast medium. Metcalfe's communication protocol broke the data to be sent from one computer to another into several packets called frames. Each frame consisted of a preamble (for synchronization and to check if the cable is busy), the address of the source computer, the address of the destination computer, data to be sent (called payload), and bits to check whether any errors occurred during transmission of the frame. He decided to limit the maximum data length in a frame to about 1500 bytes, break up the message sent by a source computer into a sequence of frames, and send the frames one after another and assemble them at the destination computer. The computer that wanted to transmit a frame listened to the cable to determine whether any signal was already present (Carrier Sense). The protocol sent the frame in the cable if no signal was detected. As the cable is accessible to all the computers (Multiple Access), any other computer could also have found no signal in the cable and decided to transmit a frame simultaneously. If two or more computers simultaneously put their frames in the cable, there would be a collision. The sender will detect collision if it senses a sudden increase in signal level in the cable. The sender would then back off for a random interval and retransmit the frame in the cable, hoping there would be no collision. If there is a collision, it will back off again and attempt to send the frame after double the random interval. Metcalfe worked out theoretically that a collision-free transmission would occur within a short interval. He called his protocol CSMA/CD (Carrier Sense Multiple Access with Collision Detection) and the network ALOHA Alto Net. Later, Metcalfe decided to rename it Ethernet as the network was to connect Altos and any other computer and peripherals. He chose the word Ether as, in the early days of electromagnetic transmission, scientists (incorrectly) postulated that electromagnetic waves needed a medium called Ether to carry them. He wrote a note to his manager describing his idea on May 22, 1973, and his manager asked him to go ahead with the project.

Preamble	Destination address	Source address	Frame type	Data packet	Check bits
8 bytes	6 bytes	6 bytes	2 bytes	46 to 1500 bytes	4 bytes

An ALOHA Alto data packet (Later called Ethernet Frame)

IMPLEMENTATION OF ETHERNET

Metcalfe looked for a partner with expertise in circuit design and tapping a television cable to connect computers to it. He found that Richard Boggs, a part-time Stanford University student with the requisite knowledge, was looking for a project at Xerox PARC. They teamed up and designed the circuit board, called a Network Interface Card, to connect Alto to the broadcast cable. They found insufficient space in the board for a clock needed to drive the circuits and decided to use the Alto's system clock instead. Alto's system clock ran at 2.93 Mhz. Thus, the speed of the first Ethernet was 2.93 Mbps, even though it could run much faster. They demonstrated the system in mid-1975 with 100 Altos and a laser printer connected to the network.

Robert Metcalfe

David Boggs

(Photos courtesy Wikipedia)

Xerox applied for a patent for Ethernet in 1975 and obtained it in 1978. In 1976, Metcalfe and Boggs published the seminal paper "Ethernet: Distributed Packet Switching for Local Computer Network" in the Communications of ACM [2]. ACM gave the prestigious Turing Award to Metcalfe for the invention of the Ethernet in 2022.

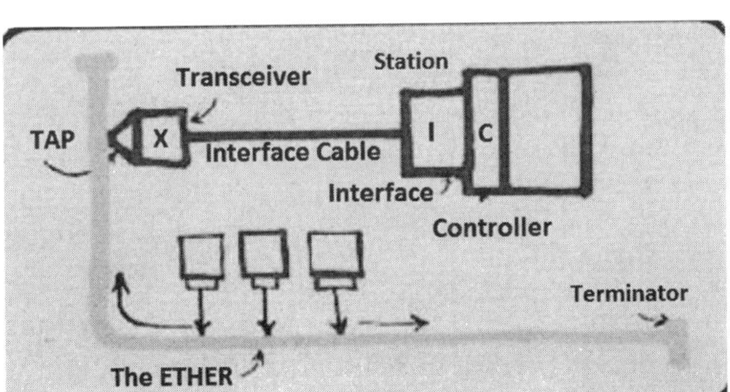

Ethernet concept figure drawn by Metcalfe and Boggs

STANDARDISING THE ETHERNET PROTOCOL

Metcalfe left Xerox PARC in 1979 to co-found 3Com Corporation with some partners to market network products. He persuaded Digital Equipment Corporation, Intel, and Xerox to standardise the Ethernet Protocol, including the frame structure. They agreed, and a standard called DIX Local Area Network (LAN) protocol with 10 Mbps speed emerged. It became an industry standard in 1980. Metcalfe also persuaded the IEEE Local and Metropolitan Network (LAN/MAN) standards committee to examine the DIX protocol standard and develop an IEEE standard. The IEEE committee developed the IEEE 802.3 LAN protocol standard in 1985 based on the DIX standard. In 1985, a new IEEE standard 802.3a that used a thinner co-axial cable with 10Mbps speed, also called 10BASE2, was announced. As technology progressed, IEEE announced Ethernet standards for 100Mbps and 1 Gbps.

EPILOGUE

With advances in integrated circuits, switches have become inexpensive. Thus, network designers interconnect computers with switches to form LANs rather than shared cables, as in early Ethernets. These LANs are called switched Ethernet and do not use CSMA/CD protocol, as the switch can connect directly to any two computers using their addresses. There is no Ether in Ethernet. Only the frame structure of the Ethernet standard remains in current LANs.

REFERENCES

[1] Robert Metcalfe, Oral History, Computer History Museum. https://www.youtube.com/watch?v=zKz07DdaKzw

[2] Robert M. Metcalfe and David R. Boggs, Ethernet: distributed packet switching for local computer network, Communications of ACM, Vol.19, No.7, July 1976.

39

Apple I and Apple II—Birth of the First Commercial Personal Computers

PROLOGUE

Homebrew Computer Club was an informal computer hobbyist group started in March 1975 by Gordon French and Fred Moore in Menlo Park, California. It was a popular club where many hardware designers met to exchange their experience in design with the Intel 8008 microprocessor released in 1972 and its successors, such as MOS Technology's 6502. Some members were building computers with these new chips. One of the first hobbyists' computers, the MITS (Micro Instrumentation Telemetry Systems) Altair 8800 microcomputer, was designed using an Intel 8080. MITS sent it to the Homebrew computer club for review. The computer used toggle switches to input data and LED display as output. Programming was tedious as the binary machine code was input using switches, and the output was displayed as a binary string on the LED display.

Steve Wozniak (known as Woz) attended the first meeting of the Homebrew computer club along with his friend Steve Jobs, where Altair 8800 was on display. Woz worked at Hewlett Packard Company designing calculators and building electronic circuits as a hobby in his spare time. Steve Jobs befriended Woz, who was five years younger than him. Both went to the same school, and their common hobby was building electronic circuits and playing pranks. However, their personalities were different. Woz was shy and inarticulate but was a wizard in designing electronic circuits and software. On the other hand, Jobs was an extrovert, a born salesman, and driven by ambition to succeed.

SINGLE BOARD COMPUTER

Woz was not impressed by the Altair 8800 and felt he could do much better. He started designing a computer using Motorola 6502 and thought it needed a much better input and output system than switches to input data and LED to display output. He planned to build a machine with interfaces to attach a standard keyboard for input, a TV to display alphanumeric output, and an audio cassette recorder as a secondary memory. As a wizard in designing digital systems, he built the system with a few chips, mounted them on one printed circuit board, made the system work, and demonstrated it at the next meeting of the Homebrew computer club. He distributed the circuit diagram of his board and described its design to the members in detail. The club members were impressed to see the computation output displayed on a TV screen.

Steve Jobs (left) and Steve Wozniak demonstrating Apple I at the Homebrew Computer Club (Photo courtesy Apple)

Jobs was excited and averse to Woz giving away the design. Being business savvy, he suggested they start a company to market the product. He convinced one of the members of the Homebrew club, Paul Terrel, who ran The Byte Shop in Mountain View, California (that sold electronic components to hobbyists), to buy 50 computer boards designed by Woz as soon as they were ready.

APPLE COMPUTER COMPANY STARTED

When they found a buyer, it was time to start a company. Jobs and Woz started a company on April 1, 1976. They named it Apple Computers. Jobs chose the name Apple as he was on a fruit and vegetable diet and had just returned from an Apple orchard. He felt Apple sounded "fun, spirited, and not intimidating" [1]. Rob Janoff designed the Apple logo [2]. The bite taken out of the apple in the logo was to make it look more like an apple and not some other round fruit such as an orange. Janoff used the rainbow colours in the original logo to indicate that the computer could display colour.

Jobs sold his Volkswagon van and Woz his scientific calculator and raised $1300 capital to buy components to build the boards. Jobs and Woz started the company in Jobs' parents' garage, and Woz primarily designed and wired the first 50 computer boards [3]. Jobs bought the necessary components at competitive prices. The board used a 1 MHz 6502 CPU, 4KB RAM (expandable to 8KB), interfaces to attach a keyboard, a colour TV, and a cassette tape as secondary memory. A ROM on the board had a system monitor program, utilities, and a BASIC interpreter. Jobs sold each board for $500 to the Byte Shop, which added a 33% margin and sold it for $666.66. It was an instant hit with hobbyists. Customers attached a keyboard and a TV monitor to run BASIC programs and play some games. Apple I was the first personal computer commercially marketed. Apple built only 200 boards. Today, Apple I boards have become collectors' items, and an auction of a board in September 2018 fetched $375,000!

An Apple I board
(Photo courtesy to oldcomputers.net)

APPLE II ENTERS MARKET

Observing the popularity of Apple I boards and perceiving its superiority over existing computers such as the MITS Altair 8800, Steve

Jobs saw a business opportunity to make a full-fledged personal computer using the board. Jobs and Woz did not have the capital to expand the company. Jobs soon found a financier, Mike Markkula, who not only invested $250,000 to develop Apple II but also helped with his experience in business and engineering. He became Apple's third partner and later assisted the company in going public. Markkula insisted that the computer must have an excellent look to convince customers that professionals designed it. He remarked that people often judge a book by its cover design! Apple designed an attractive beige-coloured moulded plastic case with an integrated full-function keyboard to accommodate the board. Jobs also decided that the computer would not have a cooling fan, as it, besides being noisy, is also less reliable than electronic circuits. He hired Rod Fort, whose expertise was in designing an efficient switched-mode power supply that did not require a fan for cooling.

Apple II computer
(Photo courtesy oldcomputers.net)

Apple II was similar to Apple I. It used a Motorola 6502 microprocessor, 4 KB dynamic RAM expandable to 48 KB, a ROM to store the monitor program, a BASIC interpreter, and some computer games. It had an interface to connect to a colour monitor or an NTSC TV set and displayed 40 characters per line and 24 lines in upper case only. It also had an audio cassette tape interface. Apple expected users to connect their monitors and cassette tapes. Apple sold the 4 KB RAM model for US$1298 and the 48 KB model for US$ 2638. Apple sold the first computer on June 10, 1977. By the end of 1977, Apple sold about 7,000 Apple IIs. The standard configuration was a 9-inch monochrome monitor, game paddles, and a cassette deck.

Apple II with monitor, game paddles, and cassette tape secondary memory. The original Apple logo is shown on top
(Photo courtesy Wikipedia)

Apple II was a very successful computer, and the Macintosh, which had a graphical user interface and was a lot more sophisticated, followed. It was priced high at $2500 compared to the Apple II's price of $1395 in 1984. Apple continued to sell the Apple II, and its successors were continuously improved and sold till 1993 with more memory, added hardware such as hard disks, and an extensive software library. During its 16-year life, 6 million Apple IIs were sold, with 1 million sold in 1983.

EPILOGUE

Soon after the release of Apple II in June 1977, it had two competitors. In September 1977, Tandy Corporation released a computer named TRS 80 and sold it through Radio Shack, an electronic components and kits retailer. It used Zilog's Z80, an 8-bit microprocessor with 4 KB dynamic RAM, a monochrome 12-inch display, and a cassette recorder as secondary memory. It also had a BASIC interpreter with floating point capability. Its most attractive feature was its price of $400 for the system without a monitor and $600 with a monitor. It out-sold Apple II in the early days due to its low cost. Tandy discontinued it in 1980 and sold other successor models for many years.

Another competing computer was the Commodore PET (Personal Electronic Transactor) 2001, marketed in October 1977. It used a 6502 microprocessor, 4 KB memory, a monochrome display (40 lines, 25 characters per line), cassette tape secondary memory, a small keyboard, and Microsoft BASIC. PET sold for $795. Customers criticised PET for its small, unreliable keyboard, which was improved later. Commodore sold PET to many high schools in the USA.

Personal Computer Trinity of 1977 (Left to Right: Commodore PET 2001, Apple II, TRS 80) (Photo courtesy Wikipedia)

Professionals mark 1977 as the year of birth of commercial Personal Computers and refer to the three computers as the "1977 Trinity".

REFERENCES

[1] Walter Isaacson, Steve Jobs—an authorized biography, Simon & Schuster, New York, 2011.

[2] The Evolution and History of the Apple Logo Design and Meaning, https://inkbotdesign.com

[3] Steve Wozniak (with Gina Smith), *i*Woz, W.W.Norton, New York, 2006.

40

Cray-1—A Computer Architecture Marvel

PROLOGUE

Control Data Corporation's 6600, designed by Seymour Cray, was the fastest computer in the world when CDC released it in 1965 (See Anecdote 18). It remained so till 1969, and CDC sold 100 CDC 6600s at an average price of $ 2.5 million. Cray followed this up with CDC 7600, which was ten times faster than CDC 6600. CDC sold 75 units of CDC 7600 at the base price of $5 million. It was the fastest computer in the world till the mid-1970s. Cray designed CDC 8600 next, a multi-processor version of 7600. It did not perform as per expectations and was unreliable. So CDC decided not to release it.

Meanwhile, James Thornton, who had earlier worked with Cray, independently designed CDC STAR-100, which used a new idea known as *vector processing* (A vector is an array of values treated as a unit. For example, the intensity of pixels along a display's row). In vector processing, arithmetic operations are performed on two vectors using an idea similar to that of an assembly line in manufacturing. A vector arithmetic unit with N stages is N times faster than a scalar arithmetic unit operating on a single pair of numbers. In STAR-100, two vectors stream from the main memory to a vector arithmetic unit, and the result streams back to the main memory. This method is called *memory-to-memory vector processing*. The vectors may be of any length. Even though the vector arithmetic speed was high, the long time to access vectors from memory constrained the overall computation speed. Another deficiency of STAR-100 was its slow scalar arithmetic unit. STAR-100 was not cost-effective. CDC sold only three STAR-100s. Advanced Scientific Computer (ASC) manufactured by Texas Instruments (TI) also used memory-to-memory vector processing. ASC's scalar speed was low. TI sold only seven ASCs.

CRAY RESEARCH STARTS

Seymour Cray requested CDC to let him design a machine from scratch that would be the fastest computer in the world. CDC could not find resources to sustain another project besides STAR-100 and rejected Cray's request. Cray decided to leave CDC and start his own company, Cray Research. He persuaded six colleagues, including Lester Davies and Dean Roush, to join him. The break-up of Cray Research from CDC was cordial. CDC invested $250 million in Cray's venture. Given his reputation, it was easy for Cray to raise the necessary capital from Wall Street to start his company. Cray Research was incorporated in 1972 and began operations in Chippewa Falls, adjoining CDC's factory.

THE ARCHITECTURE OF CRAY-1

Cray began designing Cray-1 with a clean slate. He liked the vector processing idea of STAR-100 but not its implementation. Cray decided to provide storage for vectors in the Central Processing Unit (CPU) and perform vector operations using them. However, he had to limit the vector length (the number of elements in a vector) to 64 as the cost of providing vector registers in the CPU was high. Limiting vector length was not a significant disadvantage, as many problems used short vectors. In addition, it was clear to Cray that unless the speed of calculating with scalars was also high, the computer's overall performance would be slow because not all program operations are vectorizable. Cray chose an 80 MHz clock (the fastest CPU clock in 1972) so that all calculations, including those using scalars, could be performed fast. There was one clock pulse every 12.5 nanoseconds. The word size was 64 bits. All floating-point numbers were 64 bits long, which provided high precision in floating-point calculations with 14 mantissa digits. The features of the Cray-1 processor are given as follows:

Cray-1 Processor Features
80 MHz Clock
64 bits per word
64 bits floating-point numbers
12 Pipelined Functional Units (Add, Multiply, Reciprocal) for both scalars and vectors
128 Instruction Types
16 and 32 bits long instructions
128 Instruction registers (32 bits long)
72 Address registers (24 bits long)
72 Scalar registers (64 bits long)
8 Vector registers (64 words long, 64 bits word)
160 Megaflops speed

Cray used the instruction registers to pre-fetch instructions from the memory and store them in the processor. Pre-fetching instructions reduced the need to access memory to execute short instruction sequences. A unique feature of the Cray-1 CPU was 8 vector registers, each 64 words long. Vectors were pre-fetched from the main memory and stored in these registers to perform arithmetic operations using stored data. Another impressive feature of the Cray-1 processor was called vector chaining. Vector chaining streamed the results of the vector add operation to a vector multiplier. This feature increased the processing speed as multiply followed add in many programs.

The primary memory size was 1 million words with 64 bits per word and an additional 8 bits for Single Error Correction and Double Error Detection (SECDED), which made data access from the main memory highly reliable. Cray organized the main memory as 16 independent banks access from which were interleaved. Cray accessed one word from the memory every clock tick.

The input/output section was rudimentary. Cray-1 was a number cruncher with most input/output units, such as tape and disks, connected to a front-end computer. Cray used the front-end computer as an operator console. Cray used a Data General's Eclipse computer as the front-end computer with early Cray-1s. Cray designed and sold a 16-bit mini-computer as the front-end with later models. Many users bought IBM, CDC, or DEC computers as front-ends. Cray-1 had 12 input/output channels connected to the main memory. An I/O channel retrieved one 64-bit word from the memory every 100 nanoseconds. Cray connected fast disks and the front-end computer to the channels.

TECHNOLOGY OF CRAY-1

To work at a high speed, Cray decided to use integrated circuits to build both the CPU and the main memory. Cray used high-speed small-scale integrated circuits with less than a dozen gates each, manufactured by Motorola, in its CPU. It used memory chips, each storing 1024 bits, manufactured by Fairchild Semiconductor, to build the main memory. The designers mounted these integrated circuit chips on 6 inches-wide, 8 inches-long, five-layer printed circuit boards. They mounted over 200 chips on each board. This design generated enormous heat as an 80 MHz clock drove the circuits. Cooling was essential to prevent the circuits from going up in smoke!

COOLING OF CRAY-1

Roush, the designer of the cooling system of CDC 7600, designed an innovative cooling system for Cray-1. He inserted a copper plate between pairs of circuit boards. This plate carried the heat generated by the boards. Pipes carrying cold Freon were mounted on the edges of these plates to cool the circuit boards. The hot Freon went to a refrigeration system. The design of the cooling system was complicated. In an early system, the aluminium tubes carrying Freon leaked. Freon had some oil that spread on the copper plate and shorted the connectors of the integrated circuits. Solving this leakage problem by selecting appropriate cooling tubes delayed the fabrication of Cray-1 by six months! [1]

THE PHYSICAL DESIGN OF CRAY-1

The Cray-1 system implemented many innovative ideas to achieve its high speed. A critical problem was keeping the wires' lengths interconnecting the circuit boards short. The cabinets of Cray-1 were arranged in the shape of a C (See Figure 40.1) to achieve this. The wires were painstakingly soldered to the back-plane by well-trained ladies. (I learnt while visiting the Cray factory that each Cray was hand-wired and carried a brass plaque engraved with the names of the ladies who wired it). The power supply and the refrigeration system were in cabinets at the bottom of Cray-1 surrounding it. These were upholstered; many called it the "world's most expensive love seat" [1].

3D rendering of Cray1 with humans to scale

Cooling system of Cray-1

Figure 40.1

(Figures courtesy of Wikipedia.org)

The input to the power supply was 208 Volts at 400 Hz. The computer used a motor-generator set to obtain this supply. Cray chose a 400 Hz supply as it reduced the size of the transformers in the power supply and simplified filtering of the ripples in the rectified DC voltage. Credit is due to Lester Davies, the chief engineer, who supervised the implementation of Cray's ideas. The team that designed Cray-1 had only around 35 members.

Cray-1 weighed 5000 kg, used 100 km of wiring, and consumed 115 kW. The average cost of Cray-1 was $ 8 million. The speed of supercomputers is customarily quoted as millions of floating-point operations per second (megaflops). Cray-1's speed was 160 Megaflops—the fastest in the world in 1976. It was the fastest computer in the world till 1982.

Lester Davies

(Photo courtesy of Chippewa.com)

CRAY-1 SOFTWARE

Only two persons worked on Cray-1 software. One engineer designed the Operating System (OS) and the other the languages [2]. Cray-1's software was rudimentary. Cray-1 had a simple multi-programmed batch OS called COS that supported up to 63 jobs. It received job requests and data files from the front-end computer. The front-end computer received the results of the computation.

Instructions to add, subtract, and multiply vectors, called vector instructions, were implemented as machine instructions. Cray Assembly

Language (CAL) used these vector instructions. Cray programmers wrote a Fortran compiler using these vector instructions. This compiler converted all innermost loops of programs (without any branching instruction) into one that could use vector instructions and was called "*Vectorising* Fortran". This version of Fortran was the primary language used to program science and engineering problems. Compilers ran on the front-end computer.

Later models of Cray implemented a Unix OS called UNICOS tailored for Cray-1. Los Alamos Scientific Laboratory and Lawrence Livermore Laboratory collaborated and designed a time-shared OS called Cray Time-Sharing System (CTSS) for Cray-1. The users of Cray-1, an elite group, developed many application programs. This group cooperated and exchanged programs. Slowly, an excellent library of application programs for Cray-1 evolved. These were checked by the programmers at Cray Research and distributed to customers. Later models of Cray that continued to have Cray-1's architecture used this program library.

EPILOGUE

Cray delivered the first Cray to Los Alamos Laboratory in March 1976. As it was the middle of the year, the laboratory did not have ready cash [2]. Cray Research offered to install Cray for a trial period of six months on the condition that if Los Alamos was unhappy with the machine, Cray Research would take it back. Los Alamos found that data retrieved from the memory were sometimes incorrect. Cray modified the memory to incorporate error detection and correction. Subsequently, Los Alamos Laboratory ordered five Cray-1s. Lawrence Livermore Laboratory bought the next Cray-1. The Cray-1s at Los Alamos and Lawrence Livermore Laboratories were primarily used to design nuclear weapons. The first official customer of Cray-1 was the National Centre for Atmospheric Research, Boulder, Colorado, which modelled and simulated weather phenomena. It bought Cray-1 in 1977 for $ 8.86 million and used it till 1989. Another major customer was the US National Security Agency, which used it for cryptography. Universities in the US and Europe used them to simulate complex physical systems. General Electric used it to design nuclear power plants. Several improved models of Cray-1 followed. It was the most successful supercomputer, and Cray installed 80 Cray-1s world wide.

As customers could use Cray-1 to design nuclear weapons, it was called a dual-use technology product by the US government and was subject to export controls. Cray Research could only sell Cray-1 to overseas customers with export clearance from the US government.

REFERENCES

[1] Richard M. Russell, The Cray-1 Computer System, Communications of the ACM, Vol. 21, No. 1, January 1978, pp. 63–72.

[2] YouTube Video, Cray-1 Supercomputer 30th Anniversary, Computer History Museum.

41

The First Inter-Networking Project

PROLOGUE

ARPANET project demonstrated the reliability of packet-switched networks. By 1972, 50 computers spread all over the US, and computers at the University College, London, were connected using IMPs (See Anecdote 27). There was trepidation among the bureaucrats of the US Department of Defence (DoD) that they were financing the ARPANET project, which was used for a purpose not directly related to defence needs. ARPA began two projects it could justify as directly relevant to DoD to alleviate this feeling. One project, PRNET, was started in 1973. This project designed a Packet Radio System (PRS) to demonstrate how wireless packet data communication can take place among mobile computers placed in trucks, tanks, etc., on a battlefield. The other was packet data communication between ground stations via a satellite. This project was relevant to DoD as a seismic data collection centre called NORSAR (Norwegian Seismic Array) was set up in Kjeller near Oslo to monitor the erstwhile Soviet Union's underground nuclear tests. NORSAR sent data by satellite to a ground station in the US, connected to a terrestrial data collection network. This satellite communication system was also to be used for communication among computers. This project was called SATNET. The next logical project was to connect PRNET, SATNET, and ARPANET. A successful connection of three disparate networks, whose only commonality is packet switching, would be a spectacular demonstration of inter-networking. This project had steadfast support from the DoD. Robert Kahn, who had earlier worked at Bolt Beranek and Neuman (BBN) on designing the IMPs of the ARPANET, joined the Information Processing Techniques Office (IPTO) of ARPA in 1972 and was leading this project.

PACKET RADIO NETWORK (PRNET)

Packet switching with wireless signals was first used in the ALOHAnet in Hawaii by Norman Abramson and his group in 1971. ALOHAnet allowed terminals located on the Hawaiian Islands to access the mainframe computer located on the main campus of the University of Hawaii (Anecdote 28). Packet switching had not been used to communicate between *mobile* computers. The objective of the PRNET project was to investigate the feasibility of using packet-switched radio to communicate among computers placed in mobile vans. Mobile vans may go through tunnels that would blackout wireless signals, and the system should be able to recover from such events. Arrays of ground-based repeaters were used to enhance signal strength and route the signals among the mobile computers. Stanford Research Institute (SRI), with BBN and Collins Radio as partners, coordinated the project. SRI provided the vans and computers with appropriate software, BBN the networking technology, and Collins Radio the packet radio equipment. The system used spread spectrum wireless technology for reliable data transmission in an electromagnetically noisy environment. The system could transmit data at a speed of 100 to 400 kbps. An experimental system was ready in 1973 that successfully transmitted data among mobile computers and with SRI. The system was fully operational in September 1976 when the research group found that a computer mounted in a van driven on a highway in the San Francisco Bay Area (with long bridges and tunnels) could communicate reliably with other vans and a computer in SRI.

SRI packet radio van with a computer used in PRNET
(Photo thanks to Wikipedia—SRI)

SATNET

Roberts of IPTO initiated this project in 1971 to connect ARPANET to the packet network at NPL, which Donald Davies designed. Due to political reasons explained by Peter Kirstein [1], this did not fructify. Roberts decided to connect the University College London's (UCL) computer centre headed by Peter Kirstein to ARPANET using a communication satellite link that ARPA had with NORSAR and a cable connection to London.

In 1973, a commercial satellite provided by COMSAT became operational and provided a 64 kbps link to earth stations. Multiple earth stations across Europe, covering England, Germany, Norway, and Italy, could receive the satellite signal. Roberts proposed that all these earth stations can share this link using packet switching. Kahn, who succeeded Roberts in IPTO, carried through this project with BBN, COMSAT, Linkabit Corporation, UCLA, UCL, Norwegian Defence Research Establishment, and the UK's Royal Signals and Radar Establishment. Each earth station had a simple message processor. At the end of this project, communication could take place reliably among the SATNET participants.

INTERCONNECTING ARPANET, PRNET, AND SATNET

ARPANET, PRNET, and SATNET were disparate in their interfaces, packet sizes, data transmission speed, and packet labelling. In June 1973, Robert Kahn wanted to interconnect these three systems, which was quite challenging.

The first step was to design a *gateway* for each network to connect with the other network. The next step was to develop a net-to-net connection protocol. Kahn requested Vinton Cerf, who was on the faculty of Stanford University, to carry out the project. Cerf started a series of meetings attended by his graduate students, Kahn, and computer scientists from SRI and Xerox PARC to find a solution to the inter-networking problem. Among the people who participated in these meetings was Gerard LeLann from France, who was on sabbatical at Stanford University. He had worked on the French computer networking project, the Cyclades, led by Louis Pouzin.

Louis Pouzin
(Photo thanks to Wikipedia)

Cyclades project, unlike ARPANET, did not have separate IMPs to manage networking functions. The computers in the network exchanged what Pouzin called *datagrams*, which had, besides data, addresses of the sending computer and the receiving computer and error-detecting bits. These datagrams sent from a host computer would travel independently to the receiving computer, which would assemble them. The computers at the two ends were responsible for the error-free transmission of datagrams. This idea was attractive to interconnect disparate networks.

Vinton Cerf **Robert Kahn**

(Photos thanks to Wikipedia)

Cerf and Kahn designed a protocol for inter-networking based on inputs provided by Pouzin. The protocol satisfied four requirements listed below:

1. Each network was treated as an independent entity.
2. *Gateways* (nowadays called routers) were interposed between the networks to control the transmission of packets between them.
3. The transmission of packets was "best effort". If a packet was lost in transit, the receiver detected it and requested the sender to retransmit it. In other words, the sending and receiving computers, called hosts, assumed the responsibility for error-free communication.
4. Communication of packets among networks was not globally controlled.

The first version of the protocol, called *Transmission Control Program (TCP v1)*, was published by Vinton Cerf and Robert Kahn [2] in May 1974. Meanwhile, the International Working Group (INWG), formed in 1972 and chaired by Cerf to design protocols for inter-networking, was also working in parallel and met many times [3]. The formulation of the first version of TCP gained numerous ideas during discussions in INWG meetings.

An improved version, TCP v2, followed TCP v1. In August 1977, Jon Postel suggested layering the Transmission Control Program into two independent parts with clean communication between them. His suggestion divided TCP into two parts: TCP (Transmission Control Protocol) and Internet Protocol (IP)—TCP/IP v3. This protocol gives each computer or device connected to the network a unique address called its IP address. TCP breaks up a message into packets and attaches the IP addresses of the sender and the receiver, the serial number of the packet, and error-detecting bits. IP routes the packets to the intended receiver using an optimal path through the network. TCP reassembles the received packets into the original message, ensuring there are no errors in the received message. The protocol designers slightly improved TCP/IP v3; a final stable version, TCP/IP v4, became the standard in 1980 and widely adopted in 1983.

EPILOGUE

In 1976, Vinton Cerf left Stanford University and joined ARPA to devote full-time to the inter-networking project. On 22 November 1977, his group conducted a vital experiment to examine whether TCP/IP worked effectively to connect PRNET, ARPANET, and SATNET. A message was sent via PRNET to the ARPANET from a computer in a van moving on a highway in the San Francisco Bay Area. The message reached the east coast of the US and was transmitted by SATNET to the University College, London, from where it was retransmitted to ARPANET and received back by the computer in the van moving in the PRNET. After a round trip journey of 150000 km, the van's computer received the message without a single bit error! This experiment proved the reliability of the networks and the TCP/IP protocol.

REFERENCES

[1] Peter T. Kirstein, Early experiences with the Arpanet and Internet in the United Kingdom, IEEE Annals of History of Computing, Vol. 21, No. 1, pp. 38–44, 1999.

[2] Vinton G. Cerf and Robert E. Kahn, A Protocol for Packet Network Interconnection, IEEE Transactions on Communications, Vol. Com 22, No. 5, May 1974.

[3] Alexander McKenzie, INWG and the Conception of the Internet: An Eyewitness Account, IEEE Annals of the History of Computing, pp. 66–71, January–March 2011.

42

The First Reduced Instruction Set Computer

PROLOGUE

The Advanced Research Projects Agency (ARPA) of the US government gave a project on VLSI design to Professors David Patterson and Carlo Sequin of the Electrical Engineering and Computer Science Department of the University of California at Berkeley (UC Berkeley) in 1980 to explore new microprocessor architecture. The team led by Patterson carried out a statistical analysis of the execution frequency of the instructions in a set of commonly used benchmark programs. The analysis showed that these programs did not use most instructions in the instruction set of existing microprocessors, such as Motorola 68000 and Intel 8086. These programs used only 30% of the instructions 90% of the time. The team also found that decoding circuits used much of the processor chip area due to the complexity of the instructions and addressing modes. The existing microprocessors also required many accesses to the main memory during computation. Numerous accesses to the memory slowed computation as memory access time was much slower than the CPU processing time. Cache memory alleviated the problem to some extent. Based on these results, Patterson and his group designed a microprocessor with just 31 instructions, all equal length, and fewer addressing modes, as opposed to 56 variable length instructions in Motorola 68000. The reduced number and regularity of the instructions made their decoding circuits simple. The designers could use the chip area saved to introduce numerous registers in the CPU, which were used for many arithmetic operations, storing intermediate results, and handling procedure calls. As the number of instructions in their computer was small, they called it a Reduced Instruction Set Computer (RISC). Students at UC Berkeley designed the first RISC processor and fabricated an experimental chip in 1982. At the same time, students of Professor John Hennessy at Stanford University also had a similar idea and designed a RISC processor named MIPS (Microprocessor without Interlocked Pipeline Stages). Hennessey and Patterson later collaborated to write the classic textbook "Computer Architecture: A Quantitative Approach"[1]. In recognition of their pioneering work, they were jointly awarded the ACM Turing Award in 2017. The citation for both of them was:

"For pioneering a systematic, quantitative approach to the design and evaluation of computer architectures with enduring impact on the microprocessor industry."

John Hennessy **David Patterson**

(Photos courtesy acm.org)

Please observe that the Turing Award did not recognize their work on RISC as John Cocke, an IBM researcher, proposed RISC much earlier. His work on RISC computer architecture was confidential to IBM and unknown to Patterson and Hennessy. John Cocke received the Turing Award in 1987, thirty years before Hennessy and Patterson, for his work on RISC computers and concurrent work on compiler optimization. The Turing Award citation of John Cocke was:

"For significant contributions in the design and theory of compilers, the architecture of large systems and the development of reduced instruction set computers (RISC); for discovering and systematizing many fundamental transformations now used in optimizing compilers including reduction of operator strength, elimination of common subexpressions, register allocation, constant propagation, and dead code elimination."

GENESIS OF IBM 801—THE FIRST REDUCED INSTRUCTION SET COMPUTER

In 1974, IBM Thomas J. Watson Research Centre at Yorktown Heights in New York began a project to design a digital telephone exchange. The exchange specified that it should handle an average of three hundred calls per second in real-time. Each call to be handled by the exchange required 20,000 instructions to be processed. The telephone exchange computer was to process 6 million instructions per second (MIPS). However, as the design team led by John Cocke did not know much about the actual instructions required for call handling, they decided to build a computer to cater to the worst-case scenario. They aimed at a 12 MIPS computer—a very high-speed computer in 1974! The nature of the instructions to be processed was quite different from a general-purpose computer. For instance, there was no need for floating-point arithmetic. Another critical decision the team took was to write all programs in a high-level language PL.8, a subset of PL/1, a popular language developed by IBM in 1964. The design of the machine progressed rapidly, but IBM lost the telephone exchange contract and abandoned the project in 1975. However, John Cocke used the ideas and experience gained by the team during the design effort, built a fast minicomputer, and named it IBM 801, somewhat unimaginatively, as 801 was the building number in which they worked.

John Cocke
(Photo courtesy of youtube.com)

DESIGN DECISIONS [2]

One of the studies that had been carried out by IBM using instruction execution traces of a variety of programs on its earlier mainframe computers, such as the IBM 370 series, was that LOAD, STORE, BRANCH, FIXED-POINT ADD, and COMPARE were the most frequently executed instructions consuming over 50% of the computing time. IBM found that about 40 instructions took 90% of the execution time of programs. Cocke decided to have a small number of instructions in IBM 801 and added an instruction only if it paid for itself by its frequency of use. Another study carried out during the design of IBM 801 showed that having separate instruction and data caches increased the bandwidth between the memory and CPU, enabling the computer to attain 12 MIPS speed. Only two instructions accessed memory, one to load data from the memory to a register and the other to store data from a register to the memory (Nowadays, this type of CPU architecture is called Load-Store architecture). The computer performed all arithmetic operations using operands stored in several CPU registers. Instructions of IBM 801 were simple, short, and of uniform length, unlike many existing machines in which the instructions were complex and long, with many addressing modes (Cocke called his design a Regular Instruction Set Computer). Earlier computers used long and complex instructions because accessing instructions from memory was slow, and designers wanted to reduce the number of instructions in a program and, consequently, the number of memory accesses. Complex instructions also simplified the design of compilers. In IBM 801, programs accessed most instructions from the fast instruction cache, and the penalty of having more instructions in a program was low.

Another idea was pipelining instruction execution, which was possible as all instructions were of uniform length and took almost equal time to execute. With pipelining, while the control unit fetched one instruction, another was decoded and fetched data from a register, the third executed the instruction, the fourth stored the result in a register, and the fifth wrote back the result from the register to the data cache. Each of these steps took only one clock cycle. Pipelining acted as an assembly line, thereby improving the instruction throughput to one instruction per clock cycle. The pipeline throughput would be upset if an instruction to be executed by a program was not the next instruction in a sequence, which happens if the instruction is a branch instruction. The pipeline would also be upset if the data needed to execute an instruction is unavailable. Cocke and his team developed techniques to alleviate these problems using extra hardware and compiler transformations. The RISC idea worked due to advances in compiler design that enabled the designers to write optimizing compilers that efficiently used the available hardware. IBM built 801 in 1978, four years before UC Berkeley RISC. In 1978, the IBM 801 was IBM's fastest experimental computer [3].

EPILOGUE

IBM spun off 801 as IBM ROMP (RISC Office products Microprocessor), used as the processor in IBM PC RT (RISC Technology) in 1986. IBM PC RT was unsuccessful but spurred further development of RISC microprocessors, leading to IBM RISC System/6000. Soon after, IBM partnered with Motorola and Apple, the AIM alliance, to build a single-chip RISC microprocessor in 1993 used in Apple Power Macintosh 6100. Almost all IBM computers, including the IBM Blue Gene supercomputer, use IBM RISC-based processors.

Workstations such as Sun Microsystems, Digital Equipment Corporation, and Silicon Graphics used the RISC architecture processor and its variants developed at UC Berkeley and Stanford. Today, a large majority of microprocessors use RISC architecture. Mobile phones use billions of ARM (Advanced RISC Machines) processors. RISC idea has become so pervasive that even Intel 80×86 series of Complex Instruction Set Computers convert their instructions to RISC-like micro-operations at run time and execute these using pipelining to increase instruction throughput.

REFERENCES

[1] John Hennessey and David Patterson, *Computer Architecture—A Quantitative Approach*, 6th Edition, Morgan Kaufmann-Elsevier, 2017.

[2] John Cocke and V. Markstein, The evolution of RISC technology at IBM, *IBM Journal of Research and Development*, Vol. 34, pp. 4–11, 1990.

[3] George Radin, The 801 Minicomputer, *IBM Journal of Research and Development*, Vol. 27, pp. 237–246, 1983.

43

Invention of the Global Positioning System

PROLOGUE

Global Positioning System (GPS) has become indispensable in our daily life. It is an essential navigation tool that airplanes, ships, and cars use. We use it on our smartphones with Google Maps to locate an address. It is even used to tag some prisoners on bail.

GPS depends on accurate timing signals sent from a constellation of satellites maintained by the Governments of various countries. Most people use the one maintained by the US government. GPS derives the timing signals from atomic clocks placed in the satellites. The constellation of satellites maintained by the USA and Russia covers the entire world. The system supported by the US defence department has a constellation of 27 satellites with four satellites each in six orbits (and three spare satellites) travelling 20,200 km above Earth. Each satellite orbits the Earth once every 12 hours (Currently, the number of satellites in orbit has increased to 31.)

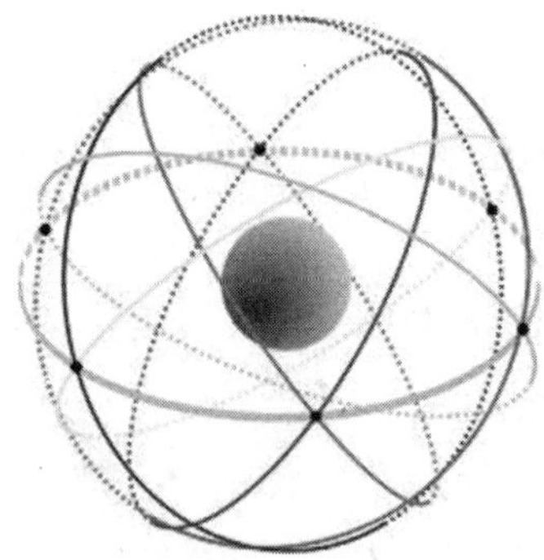

Satellite orbits of GPS
(Photo thanks to Wikimedia)

Four out of the 31 satellites are visible from anywhere in the world. Anyone can use the signals from the satellites free of cost. A GPS receiver measures its distance from a satellite by sensing the timing signal sent from the satellite using radio waves, which travel at the speed of light. To detect its position (latitude, longitude, altitude) and velocity, a GPS receiver utilises the timing signals received from four satellites using a process known as *trilateration* [1, 2].

GPS RELEASED FOR GENERAL USE

Initially, GPS was intended only for use by the US defence forces. In 1983, a Korean Airlines plane, due to poor navigation instruments, strayed into the Soviet airspace and was shot down by the Soviet Union, leading to the death of 269 innocent people. This tragic event persuaded then US President Ronald Reagan to allow GPS for navigation by anyone in the world free of charge. The positional accuracy for civilian use was initially limited to about 100 metres. This restriction was removed by the then US President Bill Clinton in 2000, and positional accuracy of around 4 metres was available to anyone. The accuracy, however, depends on the quality of the GPS receiver and the atmospheric conditions. It is now capable of an accuracy of 30 cm. in ideal conditions with excellent receivers. Even though GPS is freely available now for all to use, the US Department of Defence (DoD) controls it and blacks out the signals in any region at its will, which the US government did in 1999 during the Kargil War. That is why India has its GPS called IRNSS (India Regional Navigation Satellite System), maintained by the Indian Space Research Organization that covers India and the surrounding areas [1].

INVENTORS OF GPS

Three engineers are credited with the invention of GPS [3]. Roger Lee Easton Sr. was the head of the US Naval Laboratory's space application branch. When Sputnik, the first satellite in the world, was launched by the Soviet Union in October 1957, Easton invented a method to accurately track it. He conceived the idea of using very accurate electronic clocks placed in multiple satellites to determine the precise location of an object on the ground.

Roger L. Easton
(Photo thanks to Wikipedia.org)

Easton and his team tested the concept by launching two satellites, TIMed nAvigaTION (TIMATION) I and II, in 1967 and 1969, and two navigation technology satellites, NTS 1 and NTS 2, in 1974 and 1977. Easton obtained eleven patents for various inventions related to GPS. In 2004, he received the US National Medal of Technology and Innovation from the US President "*for extensive pioneering achievement in spacecraft tracking, navigation, and timing technology that led to the development of the NAVSTAR Global Positioning System.*"

Bradford Parkinson, a colonel in the US Air Force with a Ph.D. in Aeronautics and Astronautics from Stanford University, was asked to revive an Air Force programme called 621B that provided latitude, longitude, and altitude information for navigation based on satellite signals. Later, the US government's Department of Defence decided to develop a joint program for navigation purposes, combining the work done by the Navy and the Air Force with the Army as a user.

Bradford Parkinson
(Photo thanks to Wikipedia.org)

Parkinson was in charge of the NAVSTAR GPS joint program office from 1972 to 1978. He replaced the clock in TIMATION with an accurate atomic clock, used the novel radio signal structure from the Air Force program 621B, and the orbital prediction method from another Navy-sponsored system called TRANSIT developed by the Johns Hopkins University Applied Physics Department. This integrated system formed the NAVSTAR Global Positioning System. The citation by the Inventors' Hall of Fame, to which he was inducted in 2004, acknowledges Parkinson "*as the program's first manager; he has been the chief architect of the GPS throughout the system's conception, engineering development, and implementation.*" He is known as the "Father of GPS".

The third person recognized for operationalising GPS is Ivan Alexander Getting, who was the founding president of The Aerospace Corporation in Los Angeles, set up to assist the aerospace efforts of the US Department of Defence. A complex project such as GPS that was very expensive (as it needed many satellites) and used technologies developed by two different branches of the US defence forces, namely, the Navy and the Air Force with their agendas, required a diplomat and a technologist who could steer the project through a labyrinthine bureaucracy.

Ivan Getting was a skilful coordinator and a respected senior engineer. Getting had a deep knowledge of the GPS technology besides his persuasive abilities. The US National Academy of Engineering awarded him the Charles Stark Draper prize with Parkinson for the "*design of GPS, on its operational value, and on planning, negotiations, and reaching agreements with all the system's stakeholders that was critical to its becoming a reality.*" Getting is also credited with proposing a three-dimensional, time-difference-of-arrival position-finding system for navigation.

Ivan Alexander Getting
(Photo thanks eth.org)

Besides these three engineers who were directly responsible for designing and operationalising GPS, a mathematician, Gladys Mae West, who the US Naval Weapons Laboratory employed, is also recognized for proposing the optimal orbits for the GPS satellites.

She used the powerful IBM 7030 'Stretch' computer to process satellite data to determine their exact location. She was inducted into the US Air Force Space and Missile Pioneers' Hall of Fame in 2018 for her programming effort that "*delivered increasingly refined calculations for an extremely accurate geodetic earth model, a geoid, optimized for what ultimately became the Global Positioning System orbit.*"

Gladys Mae West
(Photo thanks to Wikipedia)

EPILOGUE

The US Navy conceptualised the development of a Global Positioning System in 1972. The development effort with all approvals lasted till 1978 when the US launched the first four satellites. It became fully operational with the launch of all 24 satellites (and three spare satellites to substitute if one or more satellites failed) after seventeen years in 1995. An accuracy of around 4 metres was available only in 2000. This timeline illustrates how long an important invention takes to be available for general use. Today, GPS receivers on the ground are inexpensive. A GPS fitted to a car to find its position costs around ₹5000. Free apps that use GPS to detect its position are available on mobile phones. This position information is shown on Google Maps to find out the street address of the location of the mobile phone. Some recent Apps on mobile phones have a voice guidance system that tells a driver the route from location A to location B while they drive a car.

REFERENCES

[1] K.C.T. Swamy, Global Navigation Satellite System and Augmentation, Resonance, Indian Academy of Sciences, Vol. 22, Issue 12, December 2017, pp. 1155–74

[2] How does GPS work? www.physics.org/article-question.asp?id=55

[3] Who Invented GPS? People Behind the GPS, www.geoawesomeness.com

44

Rise and Fall of Workstations

PROLOGUE

With the advent of microprocessors, low-cost personal computers, Apple II, Commodore PET, and TRS-80, using 8-bit microprocessor chips and floppy drives as secondary memory, appeared in the market in 1977 (See Anecdote 39). However, personal computers with high-resolution graphics display, a large main memory of the order of 1 MB, processor speed of the order of a few thousand instructions per second, and secondary memory of the order of 10 MB required by engineers and scientists and other professionals for applications such as the computer-aided design of electronic systems, simulation of aerodynamic systems, design of large structures, and development of complex systems software were not available. The time was ripe to design such systems.

PERQ 1 WORKSTATION

Carnegie-Mellon University (CMU) solicited proposals in the mid-1970s from vendors to provide high-performance personal computers called workstations. CMU characterised personal workstations as ones intended for single users with a high-resolution graphics terminal (preferably 1000 × 1000 pixels), processor speed of one million instructions per second, 1 MB main memory, 100 MB secondary memory, and special transducers [1]. Professional engineers and scientists required such a workstation for numerically intensive simulations, visualization, and computer-assisted design (CAD) of engineering systems such as large-scale integrated circuits, automobiles, and airframes.

Responding to this request, six former CMU alumni and employees, including Brian Rosen, who had worked at Xerox PARC, and Raj Reddy, a professor at CMU, started Three Rivers Computer Corporation (3RCC) at Pittsburgh in 1974 [2]. This company developed a PERQ (Pascal Engine that Runs Quicker) workstation. They built the central processor using integrated circuit arithmetic and logic unit chips (bit-slice chips) rather than a microprocessor. It was micro-coded using a 4 K word (64-bit word) writable control store, had up to 2 MB main memory, 24 MB hard disk, and a floppy disk. Its Input/Output System used a Zilog Z80 microprocessor, a speech synthesiser, secondary memory interfaces, and Ethernet interfaces. PERQ's display was an 8.5 × 11 inch, 768 × 1024 bitmapped monochrome unit. Early models had a graphics tablet. PERQ had an instruction set called Q-code, which was optimized to run Pascal programs and could execute 1 million instructions per second. It initially had a single-user operating system called PERQ OS. Later, the company ported UNIX. A basic configuration with 256 KB memory and 12MB disk cost $ 19,500 at its launch in August 1979. UK's Rutherford Appleton Laboratory ordered the first PERQ on 1 June 1979.

ICL PERQ 1 workstation. The computer and the disk are under the table
(Photo courtesy of Wikipedia)

As early orders for PERQ 1 were from the UK, 3RCC signed a collaboration agreement with ICL, UK, to market PERQs in Europe and later for co-development. It was a popular workstation in Europe in the early 1980s. The company closed in 1986 as it could not compete with other workstation manufacturers such as Apollo Computer, Sun Microsystems, Silicon Graphics, and HP, which started dominating the market in the mid-1980s.

APOLLO WORKSTATION

William Poduska (who had founded Prime Computers) realized that graphics-oriented personal workstations would have a large market and established, along with around a dozen engineers, Apollo Computer Inc. in 1980, with headquarters in Chelmsford, Massachusetts, to design and manufacture them [3]. Poduska and his team felt that a distributed network of workstations with a graphical user interface would interest groups of engineers working cooperatively in CAD, desktop publishers, and software developers. Apollo's first product was the DN100 workstation, which used two Motorola 68000 (16-bit) microprocessors, a high-resolution graphics terminal, and a 20 MB hard disk. A proprietary OS called Aegis, similar to Unix OS, was developed. Apollo used a proprietary token ring network rather than Ethernet to interconnect the workstations. Apollo's network was elegant and faster than Ethernet, allowing easy sharing of programs and data files among the workstations connected to it. Another useful feature was networking of diskless workstations with a server that had a disk. Programs could be booted remotely using the server's disk. Apollo sold numerous workstations to Mentor Graphics (an electronic design automation company), General Motors, Ford, Chrysler, Boeing, and large stock market traders. Aegis was soon improved and replaced by Domain/OS. Over 30 models of Apollo with the prefix DN, which used Motorola 68010, 68020, 68030, and 68040 (32-bit) microprocessors, were manufactured for a decade. From 1980 to 1986, Apollo was a very popular workstation with an average sale of 10,000 units in 1986. The average price of an Apollo workstation was $40,000 in the mid-1980s but rapidly came down later.

One of the notable Apollo workstations was DN 10000, which used a proprietary RISC processor PRISM (Parallel Reduced Instruction Multiprocessing). It was called a Personal Supercomputer as it used 64-bit floating-point numbers, had a speed of around 100 MIPS, and supported 3D graphics. Due to fierce competition from new entrants that lowered the cost of workstations, Apollo lost its dominance in the market. After successive losses in 1987 and 1988, Apollo was sold to HP in 1989 for $ 476 million. HP continued using Apollo's design, calling them HP-Apollo workstations. Model DN 2500 was released in 1989 as a 4 MIPS (Million Instructions Per Second), 4 MB memory workstation for $4000. HP released the last version of Domain/OS in 1992 and discontinued it in favour of a Unix-based OS called HP/UX. HP gradually reduced the production of HP-Apollo workstations and finally withdrew them in 1997.

SUN WORKSTATIONS [4]

Stanford University's computer science department received a dozen Altos donated by Xerox in 1979, and they were networked using Ethernet. Professor Forest Baskett gave a project to his doctoral student Andreas Bechtolsheim to design a workstation with the recently released Motorola 68000 microprocessor that would be faster than Alto and have better graphics processing and display to implement software for CAD of electronics systems. The goal was to design a workstation with 1 MIPS processor, 1 MB main memory, and 1 Megapixel bitmapped display, costing 1 "Megapenny" ($10,000). They were to be a part of the Stanford University Network. Bechtolsheim, along with a group of students, designed a computer with three circuit boards: a CPU board using a Motorola 68000 microprocessor, a board with circuits to process graphical data and control the graphics display, and a third board to connect it to the Ethernet. Workstation designers preferred Motorola 68000 over Intel 8086 as its internal registers were 32 bits long compared to the 16-bit registers of 8086. In addition, Motorola 68000 had many addressing modes that eased programming. The university had an electronic design package to lay out and test the circuits, which hastened the design. Bechtolsheim and his team built ten workstations called SUN (Stanford University Network) in 1981 with university funds. Bechtolsheim tried selling the design to computer manufacturers, but there were no takers.

Two alumni of the Stanford Business School, Vinod Khosla, and Scott McNealy convinced Bechtolsheim to start a company along with them to manufacture and market SUN workstations. As Bechtolsheim was primarily a hardware designer, they asked Bill Joy, who had designed the University of California, Berkeley version of Unix (BSD), to join them. This group of four founded SUN Microsystems in February 1982 in Santa Clara, California, with venture capital funding of $1.7 million from venture capital company Kleiner Perkins [5]. Vinod Khosla was the first CEO of SUN. They cleaned up the computer designed by Bechtolsheim and christened it SUN-1. It had the BSD version of UNIX OS and could be networked using its built-in Ethernet interface.

The marketing of SUN-1 was good, and SUN Microsystems made a profit in the first quarter of its existence in July 1982. It reported a revenue of $8 million in its first year of operation, with 80% of its products sold to universities.

Andreas Bechtolsheim **Vinod Khosla** **Scott McNealy** **Bill Joy**
(Photos of Bechtolsheim, Khosla, and Joy courtesy of Wikipedia.org)
(Photo of McNealy courtesy of linkedin.com)

SUN Microsystems followed SUN-1 by SUN-2, SUN-3, and SUN-3x, which used Motorola 68010, 68020, and 68030, respectively. Meanwhile, the workstation market was getting crowded, with many new players such as Silicon Graphics, DEC, and HP entering it. Despite this, SUN captured more than 20% of the market share as it was reasonably priced and had an excellent graphics processor and display. Between 1985 and 1989, Sun grew at a compound rate of 145% per year. In 1987, it reported sales of a billion dollars.

Meanwhile, other workstation manufacturers were announcing RISC processor-based workstations. Sun decided to use the RISC processor design of David Patterson and his group at the University of California, Berkeley, named SPARC (Scalable Performance Architecture) and fabricated it in collaboration with Fujitsu in 1986. SUN announced SPARC station 1 using a SPARC processor in 1987. Over 50,000 of these were sold by 1990. Sun also designed a new Unix-based OS called Solaris and standardised it for Sun products. Another innovation was the development of the Network File System (NFS) in 1984, which allowed the sharing of files across not only SUN computer networks but also with workstations of different manufacturers. SUN's corporate strategy was to place all its designs in the open domain to let others use them and ultimately make them the industry standard. Accordingly, SUN placed the designs of SPARC, Solaris, and NFS in the open domain. The strategy, mainly opening up SPARC microprocessor design, increased the demand for SPARC microprocessors, reducing its price. SUN had a dominant position in the workstation market by the late 1980s. SUN also competed with Wintel PCs by introducing a low-cost SPARCstation SLC in 1990 for $4995. It encouraged third-party software developers to develop word processors, spreadsheets, database systems, and presentation software for it. The performance of SPARCstation SLC was 12 MIPS and overtook those of minicomputers, leading to the gradual demise of minicomputers. SUN also designed high-performance servers with multiple processors to be part of the SUN network. SUN introduced the last model SUN workstation, named Ultra SPARC, using a 64-bit RISC processor in 1995. Soon, Personal Computers were becoming fast with larger screens and better graphics at a much lower cost as the market proliferated. SUN withdrew the Ultra SPARC series of workstations in 2009, signalling the end of the workstation era.

SILICON GRAPHICS WORKSTATIONS [6]

James Clerk was on the faculty of Stanford University in the late 1970s. Between 1979 and 1982, he and six of his students worked on algorithms for creating and displaying three-dimensional (3D) images on a computer. Based on this, they designed and built a very large-scale integrated circuit chip called a "geometry engine" to display 3D colour images. Clerk left Stanford University in 1982, obtained venture capital, and started Silicon Graphics (SG) in Mountain View, California, along with his students to commercialise their design. Clerk wisely inducted Edward McCracken from Hewlett-Packard as the company's chief executive to run it, and he concentrated on product development.

James Clerk
(Photo courtesy of Wikipedia)

Silicon Graphics Indigo Workstation
(Photo courtesy of wiki.preterhuman.net)

In 1983, SG released its first product, IRIS 10000, a graphics terminal that could be attached to mainframes or minicomputers for manipulating and displaying 3D images. Along with the terminal, SG also sold a 3D graphics software library. Next year, SG released IRIS 1400, a stand-alone 3D graphics workstation that used a Motorola 68000-based processor. It was an expensive ($40,000) colour graphics terminal for displaying 3D images. 3D workstations were in great demand from mechanical engineers designing 3D systems, automobile manufacturers, chemists for rendering and visualising molecules in three dimensions, and filmmakers for producing animated movies. It was an excellent product with a niche market. Other workstation manufacturers were concentrating on lower-cost models. IRIS 2400 followed IRIS 1400 in 1985. It had better graphics and cost $60,000. By 1988, SG captured 50% of the graphics workstation market and had a revenue of $153 million. In 1987, SG decided to use a RISC processor (MIPS) in its workstations. Over the next few years, SG designed a series of high-performance graphics workstations that became legendary and known for their excellence. Notable among them were workstations named Indigo and Octane.

SG tied up with Industrial Light and Magic, a subsidiary of Lucas Films, in 1987. Lucas Films produced numerous animated movies using SG workstations. By 1992, SG was a highly profitable and most reputed manufacturer of 3D graphics workstations and high-performance servers, with an annual revenue of $3 billion. Soon, competition from Apple Computers and commodity personal computers, which were much cheaper and had good graphics, ate into its market. Coupled with several unwise acquisitions, including that of Cray, SG (renamed SGI) slowly but steadily declined. It went bankrupt in 2009, and Rackable Systems, a manufacturer of servers, acquired it. Rackable Systems was renamed Silicon Graphics International Corporation.

OTHER WORKSTATIONS

During the 1980s, many companies entered the burgeoning workstation market and got the nickname "JAWS" (Just Another Work Station) from venture capitalists. One of the earliest workstations was Xerox STAR, based on Alto, released in 1981. Xerox STAR primarily focussed on the office automation market and pioneered a window-based graphical user interface, icons, folders, mouse, file servers, Ethernet, and print servers. It cost around $17,000, failed in the market, and Xerox withdrew it in 1985.

Among the big players in workstations with greater than 20% of the market share were Hewlett-Packard (HP) and IBM. HP designed its own workstations besides HP-Apollo workstations. Among the popular HP workstations was the HP 9000 series 200, released in 1984 [7]. The early models used Motorola 68000 series processors. In the late 1980s, HP started using its own RISC processor, PA-RISC, and its Unix implementation, HP-UX. HP marketed the 9000 series with 300, 400, and 500 models up to the early 1990s. The 400 series was renamed HP-Apollo 400 when HP acquired Apollo in 1989. After the mid-1990s, HP started using IA-64, a 64-bit processor co-developed with Intel. In 2008, HP stopped marketing the 9000 series and withdrew from the workstation market.

HP 9000/435 workstation

IBM RS/6000 workstation boxes

(Photos courtesy of Wikipedia.org)

IBM entered the workstation market late with its IBM RT PC (RISC technology Personal Computer) in 1986. It used IBM's RISC microprocessor ROMP, its version of Unix called AIX, and a 4.3 BSD Unix variant. The average price of an RT PC was $12,000. The use of PC in its name confused the buyers, who thought it was a high-priced IBM PC rather than a Unix workstation. PC RT's sales were poor, and IBM withdrew it in 1991. IBM RS/6000 succeeded it. It used a faster RISC processor named POWER [8]. It ran AIX OS and was well-received in the market. Tilak Agerwala (an alumnus of IIT/Kanpur) led a group that developed IBM RS/6000 and later used it to design IBM's parallel supercomputer Deep Blue, which became famous for beating Gary Kasparov, the world chess champion, in 1997.

EPILOGUE

In early 2000, Intel announced the Pentium processor running with an 800MHz clock, main memory addressability of 64 GB, 1 MB cache memory, and built-in floating-point arithmetic. The disk capacity also increased to a GB. Graphic add-on cards improved graphics performance. Networking became standard with a built-in Ethernet interface card. Many PCs started using Linux. Microsoft OS also improved with a graphical user interface. The distinction between PCs and workstations gradually disappeared. The workstation manufacturers began marketing their processors as servers. SUN, SGI, HP, and IBM servers became parts of high-performance, loosely coupled parallel computers.

REFERENCES

[1] Gordon Bell, Towards a history of (personal) workstations, Proceedings of the ACM Conference on the history of personal workstations, January 1986, pp. 1–17.

[2] https://en.wikipedia.org/wiki/PERQ

[3] https://en.wikipedia.org/wiki/Apollo_Computer

[4] https://en.wikipedia.org/wiki/Sun_Microsystems

[5] https://www.kleinerperkins.com/case-study/sun-microsystems/

[6] https://en.wikipedia.org/wiki/Silicon_Graphics

[7] https://en.wikipedia.org/wiki/HP_9000

[8] https://en.wikipedia.org/wiki/IBM_RS/6000

45

The First Spreadsheet Program for Personal Computers

PROLOGUE

Oxford Dictionary defines a spreadsheet as "*a computer program that is used, for example, when doing financial or project planning. You enter data in rows and columns and the program calculates costs, etc. from it. The individual documents are also called spreadsheets.*"

The idea of writing spreadsheet programs occurred to many programmers when mainframes and time-shared computers began to be used for business data processing [1]. Business Computer Language was an early spreadsheet program written for IBM mainframes in 1962. Another program called LANPAR (LANguage for Programming Arrays at Random) was developed in 1969 by Pardo and Landau and used extensively by several companies, including AT&T and General Motors. Programmers developed similar programs for Time-shared computers. Displays were not commonly available then, so the program printed the results. They were niche products and not widely used.

When Apple II entered the market in 1977, the computing scenario drastically changed as it was an inexpensive computer and could be bought by many. Professionals called Apple a hobbyists' machine as it had only 16KB memory (later expandable to 48KB), and the software available was meagre—a BASIC interpreter and some gaming programs. The time was ripe to develop more useful programs for it.

THE GENESIS OF THE SPREADSHEET PROGRAM FOR APPLE II

Dan Bricklin graduated with a BS in Electrical Engineering and Computer Science from MIT in 1973. He worked as a programmer for three years at the Digital Equipment Corporation with a team developing a word processor for a minicomputer. He later worked for a cash register manufacturer for a year. As he had wanted to start his own business in the long run, he joined the Harvard Business School in 1977.

In a class on finance, the professor illustrated a financial model using a grid drawn on the blackboard and entered numbers and formulae in each box. This grid was called a spreadsheet. When, for instance, a discount rate entered in the spreadsheet changed, the numbers in many boxes changed. Entering the new numbers in the spreadsheet was a laborious task and was done by erasing and re-entering numbers in many boxes. Bricklin, who had worked in the Multics project at MIT that was developing an interactive time-shared system, felt he could do the entire cumbersome calculation using an interactive computer program. He was unaware of the existing spreadsheet programs. He imagined drawing a grid on a large display, entering numbers in each square in the grid, entering formulae, and calculating independently in each grid box. In the summer of 1978, he decided to pursue his idea of writing and marketing a spreadsheet program. As a full-time student, he did not have the time or the resources to create a product. He discussed his idea with a long-time friend, Bob Frankston, who had worked with him in the Multics project at MIT. Bob Frankston also graduated from MIT with a BS in computer science and mathematics in 1970 and SM and EE while working on the Multics project. He was adept at programming the 6502 microprocessor used in Apple II as he had worked for a company trying to build a multiprocessor using 6502.

In September 1978, Bricklin borrowed an Apple II computer from Dan Fylstra (who had also graduated from MIT and later Harvard Business School in 1977) and was a co-founder of Personal Software that published and marketed software products for Personal Computers. Bricklin wrote a prototype spreadsheet program for a finance application on Apple II in BASIC. In his design, he created a grid on Apple's screen, naming the columns using uppercase letters A, B, C, etc., and the rows using numbers 1, 2, 3, etc., entered decimal numbers, and formulae for calculation, pointed to grid boxes using Apple's arrow keys to start the computation. The program instantly performed the calculation. When he changed a number in a box, the spreadsheet instantly changed the value in all the relevant boxes. The program ran successfully on October 8, 1978 [2]. He demonstrated the program to Fylstra and Frankston, and they were highly impressed and immediately decided to develop it as a product for Apple II. The decision to develop the spreadsheet program for Apple II was apt as interaction, good user interface, and display were the program's most essential features, and Apple II provided these. Besides this, Apple II only had a few application programs in 1978. Following discussions among Bricklin, Frankston and Fylstra in November 1978, Fylstra suggested the name *VisiCalc* for the spreadsheet program and all of them agreed. They also agreed that the program would be developed by Frankston and Bricklin and marketed by Fylstra's company, Personal Software. They settled on a royalty to be paid on the sales of VisiCalc by Personal Software to the company to be formed by Bricklin and Frankston.

Bob Frankston and Dan Bricklin. Bricklin is holding a plaque placed on the wall of the classroom at Harvard University, where he got the idea to develop VisiCalc
(Photo courtesy alumni.hbs.edu)

THE DEVELOPMENT OF VISICALC

Bricklin and Frankston started a company, Software Arts, on January 2, 1979. They rented the attic of a house in Arlington near Harvard and installed a terminal connected using a dial-up modem to the Multics time-shared system of MIT. Frankston developed a macro-assembler for the 6502 microprocessor (used in Apple II) on Multics and started writing the VisiCalc programs using this assembler at night as the cost of using the time-shared computer was low at night. He tried to write VisiCalc for an Apple II with 16 KB memory, but he failed and wrote it for an Apple II with 32 KB memory. Frankston also wrote the low-level I/O programs and file system as he did not want to depend on Apple's proprietary software. Bricklin designed the user interface of VisiCalc. One of the early decisions was to use decimal arithmetic as binary arithmetic, even though faster, would lead to some conversion and rounding errors. Bricklin designed reference cards on how to use the system and also sample illustrative examples such as budget preparation and tax returns for users to understand the system while Frankston developed the program.

VISICALC RELEASED

They showed the first version of VisiCalc on Apple II in May 1979 at the West Coast Computer Faire, and an improved version at the National Computer Conference in New York in June 1979.

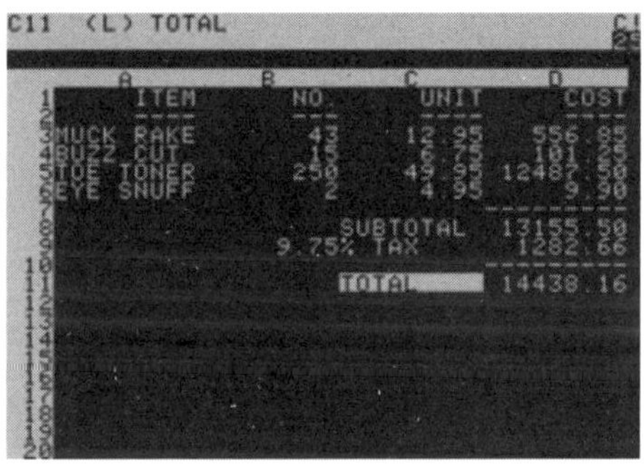

VisiCalc Screen Shot (Courtesy Wikipedia)

Benjamin Rosen, who saw the demonstration, wrote in Morgan Stanley Electronics Letter on July 11, 1979 [2], "*Though hard to describe in words, VisiCalc came alive visually. In minutes people who never used a computer are writing and using the program. .... It is important to stress that the user need not know anything about computers or programming to derive VisiCalc's benefits. You construct a VisiCalc program much as you would define a problem on a sheet of paper or blackboard—except that VisiCalc executes it electronically, rapidly, and accurately; it encourages sensitivity analysis; and it makes possible easy updates and changes. Also, the program you've created, along with their data and results, may be stored on disk and/or printed out as a hard copy.*" He concluded by saying, "*So who knows? VisiCalc could someday become the software tail that wags (and sells) the PC dog.*" His statement was prophetic. Two hundred thousand copies of VisiCalc were sold at $99 per copy in the first two years after its release on October 17, 1979. It increased the sales of Apple II, which became a popular machine with small businesses and home users. Many people bought Apple II just because VisiCalc was available only for it. Steve Jobs said [3], "*VisiCalc was what propelled the*

Apple II to the success it achieved." It was the first "killer application" that made PCs useful for small businesses. Soon, Software Arts released VisiCalc for Commodore PET, Atari 800, and TRS 80 computers. The increase in sales of Apple II with VisiCalc was one of the reasons IBM entered the PC market. VisiCalc was ported to IBM PC when it entered the market in 1981. It became one of its top-selling programs and sold 300,000 copies.

EPILOGUE

From the earlier price of $99, VisiCalc increased the price to $250 for an improved version. In the 1980s, software was not patentable, and soon, there were many imitators of VisiCalc, notably SuperCalc and Multiplan. However, VisiCalc dominated the market and sold 500,000 copies by the end of 1982. Around this time, there was a severe misunderstanding between Software Arts and Personal Software (that had changed its name to VisiCorp), leading to court cases and distracting Software Arts from developing improved versions of VisiCalc. Meanwhile, Mitch Kapor, a former employee of VisiCorp, released the Lotus 1-2-3 spreadsheet program in 1983 that took full advantage of IBM PC's longer word length and memory size compared to Apple II and was superior to VisiCalc. Soon, users switched to Lotus 1-2-3, and VisiCalc rapidly lost its market dominance, became insolvent, and was acquired by Lotus Corporation in 1985.

REFERENCES

[1] Spreadsheet, Wikipedia.org
[2] www.bricklin.com
[3] Steve Jobs about VisiCalc spreadsheet, NHK documentary 1996, Youtube.com.

46

Birth of the IBM Personal Computer

PROLOGUE

International Business Machines (IBM) was the largest multi-national computer company in the world in 1980, with a revenue of $26.21 billion, net earnings of $3.39 billion, and growth of 15%. It was well known for its large, powerful, highly reliable, expensive mainframe computers. The price of the mainframe computer IBM 3081, released in 1980 as the successor of the highly successful IBM 370 series, was $8.7 million.

Besides the big mainframes, IBM sold electric typewriters and small office machines. One of its smallest computers, the IBM 5100 portable computer (not at all portable as it weighed 25 kg), was released in

The IBM 5100 Portable Computer with 5-inch display and cartridge tapes
(Photo courtesy of Wikipedia)

1975. It was a desktop machine with a keyboard, a 5-inch CRT display, a cassette tape drive, 64 KB RAM, and a ROM that stored interpreters for BASIC and APL languages. The processor was a 16-bit processor called PALM (Put All Logic in Microcode). It cost $ 20,000 for the 64 KB model.

The IBM 5100 was followed by the IBM 5110, which was launched in 1978. The main improvement of 5110 over 5100 was additional I/O devices (floppy drives, RS 232 interface, etc.) and a larger character set. The next model in the series was the IBM 5120, released in 1980, which had a larger 9-inch CRT display and two built-in 8-inch, 1.2 MB floppy drives. It also bundled with the hardware, programs for billing, payroll, inventory, accounts payable, accounts receivable, and general ledger accounting. Bill Lowe, Director of the IBM Entry Systems Division, located in Boca Raton, Florida, oversaw the design of the IBM 5100 series machines.

IBM 5120 computer with 9-inch display and two floppy drives
(Photo courtesy of oldcomputers.net)

System/23 Datamaster followed IBM 5120, whose design started in 1978. IBM marketed it to small businesses. It used an Intel 8085 microprocessor with a 4.77 MHz clock, 256 KB main memory, 112 KB ROM, two 8-inch floppy disks, and a 15-inch 24 lines, 80 characters per line display. It had a BASIC interpreter, word processor, and business software similar to the one for IBM 5120. It cost around $ 10,000. A second terminal could be attached to this machine. Designing an upward compatible BASIC delayed the machine's release by a year and was released only in July 1981.

IBM PC PROJECT

Meanwhile, Apple, Tandy, and Commodore released Personal Computers (PCs) at much lower prices, ranging from $600 to $ 1700, and sold thousands. A new home and small business PC market had opened up with an annual sale of $150 million in 1979, growing at 40% per year. In 1980, Atari, a small company manufacturing PCs, sent a proposal to Frank Cary, the then chairman of IBM, that they would design and build PCs for IBM if it wanted to enter the market [1]. Cary passed it on to Bill Lowe, the Director of IBM's Entry Systems Division, to examine it. He, in turn, took it to IBM's management committee, which dismissed it as frivolous. However, as IBM's chairman sent it and the PC market was growing, the management committee asked Lowe to examine whether IBM could design and manufacture its PC. IBM was a massive organization with a labyrinthine bureaucracy. Most new projects took three to four years to complete. A committee member remarked: "*IBM bringing out a personal computer would be like teaching an elephant to tap dance*" and not feasible. The management committee felt that only if IBM could design and market a PC speedily, it should attempt it.

Lowe took the challenge and said he could design and market a PC in one year if given a free hand to make crucial decisions without going through the normal tortuous IBM process. IBM had constituted small independent business units that could take up projects and short-circuit the bureaucracy. One such unit was formed in July 1980 with a small group of a dozen engineers to examine the feasibility of making and marketing a PC in one year. They designed a prototype in a month using off-the-shelf components and demonstrated it. The project was approved, and Lowe set a deadline of August 1981 to release the IBM PC. Meanwhile, Lowe was promoted and transferred (in the usual bureaucratic way) from the Entry Systems Division, and Don Estridge became the head of the group.

The group met regularly and made several strategic decisions that were alien to standard IBM practice. IBM was a vertically integrated company that normally sourced most essential components from within. IBM also developed software in-house. However, Estridge made many strategic decisions to meet the very tight deadline of one year. These were [1]:

1. Design the system in the IBM laboratory, buy well-tested components for the PC hardware from the open market, and manufacture it in IBM's Boca Raton plant.

2. Perform all quality control of hardware in-house.
3. Outsource all systems and applications software. Test and assure the quality of all software bought from outside vendors.
4. Outsource marketing of the PCs to retailers such as Sears-Roebuck and ComputerLand.
5. Set the market price competitive and similar to that of other PCs like Apple.

The IBM team had design experience with the Intel 8085 processor as System/23 Datamaster used it. Hence, they designed the PC using a 4.77 MHz Intel 8088 microprocessor, a hybrid processor with an 8-bit data bus, 16-bit registers, and a 20-bit address. The 20-bit address allowed addressing 1 MB memory and consequently solved more complex problems.

The design team decided to have an open architecture with several expansion slots to allow other vendors to attach peripherals. Unlike other available PCs, IBM PC's memory design included a parity bit for each word to check memory errors. The computer was tested and ready for manufacture in April 1981.

ENTRY OF MICROSOFT

IBM decided to outsource the development of BASIC interpreter, even though it had developed BASIC for the 5100 series machines. From experience, developing a new BASIC in-house would have taken IBM at least two years. This assessment led IBM to Microsoft, which had developed BASIC for other PC vendors. IBM gave Microsoft a contract to design BASIC and the OS. (I have described how Microsoft got the OS development contract from IBM in Anecdote 35). Microsoft signed a contract in November 1980 to deliver the OS and BASIC before July 1981 and to keep the agreement top-secret. IBM PC prototype was sent to Microsoft at Seattle in November 1980. The IBM team visited Microsoft frequently, and IBM tested the software using several IBM-designed tests. Microsoft delivered the PC-DOS OS, BASIC, FORTRAN, Pascal, and a game program in July 1981. Bill Gates pulled a strategic coup by insisting that instead of IBM buying PC-DOS outright, it would pay a royalty for each copy licenced and that Microsoft would be allowed to licence PC-DOS to other PC vendors as MS-DOS. IBM signed this agreement that had far-reaching consequences not expected by IBM then. IBM also licenced EasyWriter word processor and VisiCalc spreadsheet program.

IBM 5150 PC with colour display and full function keyboard
(Photo courtesy of Wikipedia)

IBM PC RELEASE

IBM released 5150 PC at an event at the Waldorf Astoria Hotel in New York on August 12, 1981. IBM chose model 5150 to indicate it was a continuation of the 5100 series computers. IBM PC had a professional look, and its hardware was highly reliable. The system had a keyboard with 83 alphanumeric keys, a numeric keypad, and ten function keys. The keyboard was attached to the central unit by a 6-foot flexible cable, allowing a user to place it on one's lap. It had a 15-inch monochrome or colour display with 80 characters per line and 24 lines. It supported 40KB ROM and 16 KB to 256 KB RAM. It had two diskette drives and 5 expansion slots to connect other circuits and peripherals. The minimum configuration with 16KB RAM without a display cost $1565, and the maximum configuration with a printer and all software cost around $6000. This low price for a computer was unheard of in IBM's history.

IBM releasing the PC was a momentous event and gave legitimacy to PCs. IBM PCs sold fast, registering sales of 13,500 units in the first two months and 750,000 by 1983. It was a popular computer with small businesses, and a saying among managers was that "*No one ever got fired for buying IBM.*" Soon, numerous independent software vendors created a variety of software for the IBM PC, making the PC yet more popular.

EPILOGUE

The consequences of IBM choosing an open architecture, using off-the-shelf components, Intel 8088 as the processor, and outsourcing OS to Microsoft were profound. By June 1982, Columbia Data Products made the first IBM PC compatible (also called IBM PC Clone), followed by Compaq and many others. The clones could use the same components as IBM, use a similar design, and did not develop an OS as it was available from Microsoft. They were cheaper and ate into IBM's market share. Microsoft became dominant in the software industry. IBM introduced its own OS called OS/2 in 1987, but Microsoft's Windows OS overtook it. PCs and other small computers started to dominate the market, and IBM lost its pre-eminent position in the computer industry. Was IBM's decision to set a one-year deadline to manufacture the IBM PC that led to many consequential decisions, including using an open architecture, sourcing off-the-shelf components, and outsourcing OS to Microsoft, a strategic error?

REFERENCES

[1] Jimmy Maher, The complete history of IBM PC, https://arstechnica.com/gadgets/2017/06/ibm-pc-history

47

Osborne 1—The First Portable Computer

PROLOGUE

Alan Kay had dreamed of a computer in 1972, which he named Dynabook, which was to be "A personal computer for children of all ages." It was to be like the tablet computer that we use today. Technology was not available in 1972 to realise his dream. However, his colleagues at Xerox PARC liked his idea, resulting in the Alto personal computer (See Anecdote 34). Alto was not portable. When 16-bit microprocessors appeared in 1978, his colleagues at Xerox PARC, Douglas Fairbairn, Adele Goldberg, and Larry Tesler, resurrected the idea of a portable computer that one could take anywhere. They built a portable computer called Xerox NoteTaker [1] in 1978 that they said was "designed as a personal tool to be its user's constant companion. NoteTaker could be accommodated in a case with dimensions 53 cm (L) × 35 cm (W) × 18 cm (H) and weighed 22 kg. The CPU was an Intel 8086 (16-bit processor) using a 5MHz clock and 256 KB RAM (quite large in 1978). It had a monochrome 17.8 cm (diagonal) touch-sensitive display (640 × 480) pixels, a 340 KB floppy drive, a mouse, a 300 bps modem, an Ethernet card, and a rechargeable battery (2 to 3 hours). The OS was Smalltalk. It cost $5000. They made only ten prototypes. The design team tried hard to convince Xerox management to produce and market it. Xerox management initially showed some interest but decided not to produce it, and consequently, it died.

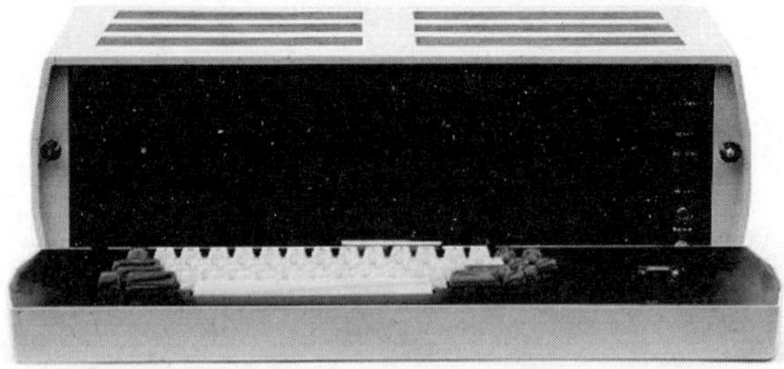

Xerox Notetaker (Photo courtesy history-computer.com)

OSBORNE 1 PORTABLE COMPUTER

Adam Osborne visited Xerox PARC sometime in 1979, and he was excited when he saw the NoteTaker and decided to build one and market it. It is interesting to look at his background and what brought him to Xerox PARC.

Adam Osborne [2] was born in 1939 in Bangkok, Thailand, to a British father and a Polish mother. When war broke out, his parents moved to India as Adam's father, Arthur Osborne, was a devotee of Sri Ramana Maharishi of Thiruvannamalai in Tamil Nadu. Adam Osborne was admitted to a boarding school in Kodaikanal, a hill station in Tamil Nadu, and studied there until he was eleven. He could converse fluently in Tamil. The family moved to England in 1950, and Adam Osborne completed his schooling there. He obtained a Bachelor's degree in chemical engineering from Birmingham University in 1961. Following his girlfriend, Osborne moved to the United States and received a Ph.D. in chemical engineering from the University of Delaware in 1968. His thesis required extensive programming, and he became computer savvy. Subsequently, he joined the Shell Oil Company in California but was not very happy working there and left in 1971. The decade of 1970s was an exciting time in northern California. Intel launched 8008 in 1972, and some hobbyists started building computers using it. Osborne had a flair for writing and lucidly explaining complex technical subjects. He established a publishing company, Osborne Associates, in 1972. Osborne wrote technical manuals for several computer companies. In 1976, he authored the first book on microcomputers titled "Introduction to Microcomputers" and published it. I remember to have bought one as it was an inexpensive paperback book printed using newsprint. His book became instantly popular, sold over 300,000 copies, and was translated into many languages. He wrote successive volumes on various aspects of microcomputers and persuaded others to write books related to microprocessor hardware and software. By 1977, there were around 40 titles. McGraw Hill Publishing Company acquired his company in 1979 for a few million dollars. He was looking to enter new avenues with cash in hand, and the Xerox PARC visit was opportune. In 1980, he met Lee Felsenstein, a hardware designer, at the West Coast Computer Faire and convinced him to join his company, Osborne Computer Corporation, to build a portable computer.

Osborne 1, a portable computer, was released in April 1981. The size of the computer was 22.9 cm (height), 52.0 cm (length), and 22.7 cm (depth). The keyboard folded, and the computer became a box that could be carried like a briefcase and weighed 10.7 kg. It had no built-in battery. It worked when plugged into the main power. One could easily tuck the computer under an airline seat (Nowadays, this computer is described as "luggable" as it is heavy). It used Zilog Z80 (an 8-bit processor) with a 4 MHz clock as its CPU, 64 KB RAM, 4 KB ROM, two 5.25 inch floppy disks (102KB each), RS 232 interface, IEEE-488 interface, a modem interface, 5 inch - 52 characters - 24 lines monochrome display and a fold-down 69 key detachable keyboard doubling as the computer's lid. Osborne described the performance of the computer as adequate for most purposes. The most attractive feature of Osborne 1 was its bundled software. The software consisted of CP/M OS, WordStar word processor, SuperCalc spreadsheet, Microsoft BASIC, CBASIC of Digital Research, Mailmerge for email, and dBase II.

Osborne 1 Portable Computer (Photo thanks to history-computer.com)

Osborne 1 advertisement. The person on the right is carrying an Osborne 1 computer.

The computer with the software cost $1795. It was considered a bargain at that time as the software itself, if licensed separately, would have cost around $1500.

OSBORNE EFFECT

Professionals welcomed Osborne 1. Osborne sold 100,000 units in the first six months and approximately 10,000 per month after that. Osborne made a strategic mistake by prematurely announcing a better model he named Osborne Vixen before it was ready. The distributors stopped ordering Osborne 1 in anticipation of the new model, and some cancelled their orders. Osborne was left with a large inventory of unsold Osborne 1. There was a sudden cash crunch, and Osborne could not raise working capital. The company collapsed and declared bankruptcy in 1983. Announcing a new model prematurely, leading to customers cancelling orders of an existing model and postponing buying decisions, was called *the Osborne effect.*

Osborne argued in 1984 in his biography [3] that the reasons for closing down his company were more complex. His company was undercapitalised. Sales of Osborne 1 hugely surpassed his expectations. The company bought components for cash, whereas distributors delayed payment. The company could not get bank advances, leading to severe cash flow problems. At the same time, two companies, Kaypro and Compaq, announced portables. One of them, Compaq, announced the release of an IBM PC-compatible portable computer using MSDOS. Computers using CP/M OS were going out of fashion. All these conspired, leading to Osborne Computer Corporation closing down.

Adam Osborne
(Photo thanks alchetron.com)

SOFTWARE PUBLISHING

Adam Osborne was not one to easily give up. He saw an opportunity in software publishing. He felt that the software systems being sold were overpriced and needed to be more affordable. His idea was to price them similar to books and market them through bookstores. In 1984, he founded Paperback Software International Ltd. He wrote popular software such as the word processor NewWord, database software VP-info, and spreadsheet program VP-Planner. Osborne placed the software disk inside the manual cover, which explained how to use the software. The software was reasonably priced at around $100, whereas similar software by big companies cost $500. In 1987, Lotus 1-2-3 filed a case accusing that Osborne's VP-Planner had the same look and feel menu interface as their product and violated Lotus's copyright. While the case dragged on, it was difficult for Osborne to get venture capital to expand his company. Lotus won its suit in 1990. The loss of the suit led to the closure of Paperback Software.

EPILOGUE

In 1992, Osborne was diagnosed with a brain disorder that led to mini-strokes. He came to Kodaikanal to stay with his sister Katya Douglas (who had settled down there) and briefly ran an India-based publishing venture [4]. Adam Osborne died in 2003 at the age of 64.

REFERENCES

[1] Xerox NoteTaker, Wikipedia https://en.wikipedia.org/wiki/

[2] Jack Schofield, Adam Osborne – Obituary, The Guardian, 27 March 2003.

[3] Adam Osborne with John C. Dvorak, Hypergrowth: The Rise and Fall of the Osborne Computer Corporation, Idthekkethan Publishers, Berkeley, California, USA, 1984.

[4] Anand Parthasarathy, Osborne: Pioneer in portable computing, The Hindu, March 26, 2003.

48

CSNET, Merit Network, and BITNET

PROLOGUE

Starting as a network of four computers in 1969, ARPANET became a network of 50 computers in 1972 when it was publicly demonstrated at the International Conference on Computer Communications as a wide area packet-switched network. ARPANET grew to 213 computers in 1981. ARPANET became more of a communication network among scientists, allowing them to exchange emails, transfer files, and share news through newsgroups (See Anecdote 27). In addition, the ARPANET project also led to the development of a non-proprietary TCP/IP protocol to interconnect disparate networks (Anecdote 41). Many universities could not join ARPANET as the IMPs cost was high, and DoD could not fund them. Researchers in computer science departments in many universities felt disadvantaged as they could not interact with their colleagues in other universities, whereas those connected by ARPANET could. Lawrence Landweber of the University of Wisconsin at Madison took the initiative and called a meeting in May 1979 of computer science professors of eleven universities in the USA, a representative of the National Science Foundation (NSF) of the US government, and a representative of ARPANET to explore how a larger community of computer scientists can get services similar to that provided by ARPANET. At this meeting, the group decided to request that NSF fund the formation of a computer science network and connect it to the ARPANET. This meeting was the beginning of the

NSF getting involved in networking university researchers, ultimately leading to NSFNET, which replaced ARPANET as the backbone of the worldwide Internet.

CSNET

In November 1979, Lawrence Landweber, Peter Denning of Purdue University, David Farber of the University of Delaware, and Anthony Hearn of the University of Utah, on behalf of a consortium of 11 universities spread all over the USA, submitted a proposal to the NSF to fund the creation of a computer science network. Initially, NSF was skeptical as it felt that it was a parallel ARPANET, management policy needed to be clarified as many universities were involved, and it was an infrastructure project that would reduce funding of basic research, which was NSF's primary mission. The consortium rewrote the proposal with the help of Vinton Cerf of ARPA to implement TCP/IP in their computers (that ARPA agreed to give), connect CSNET to ARPANET using a digital packet network provided by Telenet (a private provider), provide CSNET services to the universities connected to ARPANET, create a Phonenet with dial-up telephones for email and file transfer to smaller centres with low budget, and work out entry and usage charges of all members. They submitted the revised proposal to NSF in November 1980. NSF accepted the proposal in January 1981 and agreed to give a grant of US$5 million with the condition that NSF would appoint a manager for the first two years to coordinate this multi-institutional project and that CSNET would be self-supporting in 5 years. NSF divided the work among the cooperating Universities, with significant responsibilities taken by the University of Wisconsin, Purdue University, and the University of Delaware. Telenet, a packet-switched network provider, was contracted to connect the centres and a gateway provided to ARPANET [1]. By early 1982, the network had 24 sites; by 1984, the number of sites had grown to 84. As promised to NSF, connection and usage charges for members of CSNET were determined, and by 1986, CSNET became self-supporting, with 165 universities

Lawrence Landweber
(Photo courtesy Wikipedia)

and some industries as members. The universities were not only in the USA but also in many countries in Europe and Asia.

MERIT COMPUTER NETWORK

In 1966, the three major state universities in the state of Michigan in the USA (the University of Michigan (U-M), Ann Arbor, Michigan State University (MSU), East Lansing, and Wayne State University (WSU), Detroit met to discuss how they could cooperate to share their computer resources to enhance education and research in their state [2]. With support from the then governor of Michigan, George Romney, a non-profit corporation named Michigan Education and Research Information Triad (MERIT) was formed in 1966. The state of Michigan agreed to give start-up funding of US$ 400,000 provided MERIT could get a matching grant from another source. MERIT sent a proposal to NSF requesting it to support their networking initiative. NSF reviewed the proposal and granted $400,000. With a total grant of $ 800,000, MERIT started operations in August 1969, with U-M agreeing to house and fund the initial staff of MERIT.

Between 1966 and 1970, U-M computer centre staff carried out a project titled CONversational COMPuters (CONCOMP) with ARPA funding. In this project, U-M staff interfaced a Digital Equipment Corporation's (DEC) PDP-8 minicomputer with the IBM 360/67 mainframe computer in the university computer centre and wrote software to allow multiple terminals connected to PDP-8 to time-share IBM 360/67. U-M computer centre staff also wrote Michigan Terminal System (MTS), a time-sharing operating system for IBM 360/67 that many universities extensively used. MERIT built on this experience of U-M staff.

The first project undertaken by MERIT in 1969 was to connect the mainframes at U-M, WSU, and MSU using Communication Computers (CC), similar to IMPs of ARPANET, and a packet-switched network. Applied Dynamics, a Michigan-based company, was given a contract for around $300,000 to build the CCs and interface them with the mainframes at the three universities. Applied Dynamics chose DEC PDP-11s as the CCs. Applied Dynamics, MERIT staff, and the university's computer center staff worked closely and implemented a network connecting IBM 360/67s at UM and WSU by December 1971. MSU connected its CDC 6500 to the network in October 1972. The network of these three universities started services including email, file transfer, remote login, and remote batch processing by early 1973, four years after ARPANET. In 1976, the network was connected to Telenet, allowing dial-in by clients anywhere in the US and abroad to the computers in the network and use their services. In 1978, Western Michigan University (WMU), which had a DEC PDP-10 computer, wanted to join the network. WMU connected its computer with a new communication computer, a cheaper version of PDP-11, and a DEC VAX computer running Unix OS in the Electrical Engineering department of U-M to create a five-computer network. MERIT was renamed Merit Networks as it was no longer a Triad. In 1983, TCP/IP software became the communication software of the Merit network and it was ready to be connected to the ARPANET. In 1985, another state university in Michigan, Oakland University, and in 1987, Eastern Michigan University, Central Michigan University, and Michigan Technological University joined the Merit network, and the network became a regional network using TCP/IP. Merit continues to operate, providing various computer communication services.

BITNET

Faculty and university students connected to ARPANET, CSNET, and Merit started routinely using email and file transfer, whereas those not in any network felt disadvantaged. Ira Fuchs, director of the computer center at the City University of New York (CUNY), and Greyden Freeman of the computer center at Yale University got together to find a way of providing similar facilities, particularly to the liberal arts professors, in their universities [3].

Ira Fuchs
(Photo thanks Wikipedia)

Greyden Freeman
(Photo thanks yale62.org)

Both CUNY and Yale had mainframe IBM computers with the software Remote Spooling Communication System (RSCS) and a Network Job Entry (NJE) protocol that allowed IBM computers to communicate using a leased telephone line. In May 1981, they connected their computers and exchanged emails and files without having to develop any new software. They called this network BITNET (Because It's Time NETwork). Soon, many universities in the US North East, primarily with IBM mainframes, joined BITNET. The entry cost was low as the only requirement was to lease telephone lines and get one more member to connect to them. Each member in BITNET stored emails and files it received from its closest neighbour and forwarded them to the next computer in the chain towards the destination address. By 1983, 20 universities were on BITNET, and the membership increased to around 400 by 1984. With the increase in membership, BITNET Information Centre (BITNIC) was started with funding from IBM to administer and answer user queries. When IBM funding ended in 1987, BITNET members contributed to continue BITNIC. Non-IBM computers, many of them DEC VAX computers, joined BITNET with the appropriate communication protocol. Eric Thomas, a student of Ecole Supérieure d'Electricité in Paris, developed a software named LISTSERV for BITNET in 1986. This software maintained and managed emailing lists without human intervention. It also automated the administration of discussion groups and mass mailings and maintained a searchable index of previous discussions.

By 1990, BITNET had around 500 US universities and 1400 universities in 49 countries worldwide as members. TCP/IP protocol was being standardized around this time. In 1991, BITNET was merged with CSNET, and the new network was called the Corporation for Research and Educational Network (CREN). CREN continued to function till 1996 and shut down with the emergence of the Internet.

EPILOGUE

NSF, which was earlier reluctant to fund infrastructure projects, changed its policy after the success of CSNET. This policy change led to increased basic research output due to better communication and collaboration among university computer scientists. Merit, funded partially by NSF, also became a successful regional network. Both these projects had started with seed funding from NSF and became self-supporting. This experience led NSF to fund a much more extensive country-wide network that eventually became the backbone of the Internet.

REFERENCES

[1] Peter J. Denning, Anthony Hearn, and C. William Kern, History and Overview of CSNET, SIGCOMM 83: Proceedings of the Symposium on Communication Architectures and Protocols. Association for Communication Machinery, pp. 138–45.

[2] Eric M. Aupperle, Merit—Who, What and Why, Library Hi Tech, Vol. 16, No. 1, 1998.

[3] David A. Grier, Martin Campbell, A Social History of BITNET and LISTSERV, IEEE Annals of the History of Computing Vol. 22, Issue 2, April–June 2000, pp. 32–41.

49

Minitel: The French Online Marketplace

PROLOGUE

In the late 1970s, French President Valery Giscard d'Estaing felt that France was behind in telecommunications and information technology. The penetration of telephones in France was much lower than in other Western countries. France was importing most of its computer-based systems. He requested Simon Nora and Alain Minc, two members of his government, to investigate why France was falling behind and to suggest solutions. In 1978, they wrote a report titled "The Computerization of Society" that was far-sighted. In this report, they argued that telecommunication and informatics were converging, leading to many novel applications that would profoundly affect societies and that France must be prepared for this revolution. They coined the word télématique (telematics in English) and suggested that France must digitize its telephone network and facilitate entrepreneurs to provide information services over this network [1]. The President ordered the state-run Post, Telegraph, and Telephone Company (PT&T) to study the report and devise a telematics system for the French. In 1983, the engineers of PT&T rolled out a uniquely French system called Minitel that allowed ordinary people to access more than 26,000 online services such as news, booking train tickets, chatting online, buying groceries for same-day delivery, getting weather reports, and casting horoscopes. These online services were over a decade before any other country provided similar services! In this Anecdote, I will trace the birth, growth, and death of (now forgotten) Minitel, the world's first online digital marketplace that was the envy of the world in the 1990s and is a blip in the history of computing.

Cover of Nora and Minc report

MINITEL SYSTEM

The Minitel system consisted of a landline telephone to which a dumb terminal comprised of a monochrome videotext display and a keyboard were connected (See picture). Besides letters and digits, the keyboard had function keys for some simple operations. The terminal had a built-in low-speed modem to connect it to the telephone line. Subscribers could use the telephone independently for regular calls. To access a service using the terminal, a user dialed a number on the phone. A program stored in the PT&T network switch answered the call with an audio tone. On hearing this tone, the user hung up the telephone and switched to the Minitel terminal and typed a short mnemonic code.

Minitel Terminal
(Photo courtesy Wikipedia)

For example, to book a train ticket, the sequence of actions would be: dial 3615 followed by the code SNCF (the code for French Railways) on the Minitel keyboard. As soon as a subscriber typed the mnemonic code, the Minitel system established a connection via Transpac, the French (packet-switched) Public Data Network between the host computer of the service provider and the client's Minitel terminal. This connection allowed a user to interact with the service provider. Small service providers used a service bureau's computer or that provided by PT&T.

MINITEL BUSINESS MODEL

The initial problem faced by PT&T was to induce customers to adopt Minitel. It hit upon the brilliant idea of dispensing with printed telephone directories, usually given free with telephones, and instead providing it as a service on Minitel. An electronic telephone directory could be accessed from Minitel using a simple natural language interface. It was up-to-date and easy to search. The cost of printing, distributing, periodically updating, and answering directory inquiries was slightly less than that of a Minitel terminal. PT&T ordered thousands of Minitel terminals from French companies such as Alcatel and Matra. Every subscriber got a free Minitel terminal along with a phone. The telephone instrument and the terminal were the property of PT&T, and the subscriber surrendered them if they discontinued the service. A subscriber plugged in the terminal to the telephone, and the terminal was ready for use. All public telephone kiosks and offices also had Minitel. The French government provided several government services, such as applying for a university and driving licences on the Minitel system. These services induced telephone subscribers to use Minitel.

As the number of Minitel terminals increased, entrepreneurs saw an opportunity to provide services. Services such as dating, chat rooms, horoscope casting, tax advise, and stock price bulletins started appearing. The barrier to the entry of vendors was low as PT&T did not levy any up-front charges. PT&T added the charges for the information service provided by a vendor to a customer's telephone bill (based on the connected time of the terminal to the provider's host), subtracted a percentage as service charges, and remitted the collected amount to the vendor. Vendors were relieved of billing and collecting payments for their services from customers. This assistance was a great boon to small vendors. When Minitel users increased, smartcard readers were attached to Minitel to allow direct payment to vendors for more expensive services such as plane tickets.

Another notable aspect of customer billing was that the bills did not specify the service used, thereby preserving the privacy of the service a customer accessed [2]. Vendors were paid a consolidated amount for their services by PT&T each month and did not know the customers. This procedure was valuable to many customers as some of the most popular services on Minitel were *messageries roses*. These were chat rooms that had pornographic content and became notorious. They were widely advertised and highly profitable.

PRESTEL SYSTEM

The Minitel system was not the first videotex system. In the mid-1970s, the British Post Office (now British Telecom) experimented with a videotex system. Research engineer Sam Fedida of the British Post Office designed the system. He modified a television set, added a keyboard to create a videotex terminal, and connected it to the telephone network to access a database on a minicomputer in 1974 [3]. It was named Prestel and introduced as a service in 1979. British Telecom's business model mainly addressed corporate customers. A customer bought a terminal from British Telecom to access a host computer system maintained by it. The host provided services such as a mailbox, stock market quotes, currency exchange rates, etc. The terminal cost was high, and British Telecom charged for host access. It was not economical for an individual subscriber and did not become popular. At its peak, it had only 90,000 subscribers. In an ironic twist, Sam Fedida's son Clive Fedida, who was managing commercial operations of British Telecom, decided to close the service in 1994.

Apart from Prestel, many countries have tried to introduce Minitel-like services. Belgium, Netherlands, Germany, and Italy had similar systems that did not become as popular as Minitel as their business model was different. None of them gave free terminals—most of them centralized databases. A system called 101 online was introduced in the San Francisco area by French Telecom using Minitel. It failed because users had to buy Minitel terminals, and vendors used an inflexible centralized database [4].

EPILOGUE

There were a few thousand Minitel connections when the French PT&T introduced Minitel in 1982. As the number of services available increased, Minitel's popularity rapidly grew, mainly because the terminals were free to subscribers. By 1986, there were 1.4 million Minitel connections, which peaked at around 10 million in 1999. That year, there were 25 million system users out of the French population of 60 million. Around 26,000 services were offered, with 10,000 companies registered as Minitel vendors. During the first eight years of operation, the Minitel service made a profit of 3.5 Billion French Francs. The number of connections started declining in 2000 as the World Wide Web became popular. The monochrome alphanumeric terminal became "unfashionable". French Telecom allowed users' PCs to be used instead of the Minitel terminal, providing the same services. By 2000, the Internet was conquering the world, and with the emergence of the World Wide Web, organizations offered many online services on the Web. The number of Minitel users declined in 2009, and users returned their Minitel terminals. The system started losing money, and the French Telecom company retired the service in 2012, thirty years after it began.

REFERENCES

[1] Julien Mailland and Kevin Driscoll, Minitel: The Online World France Built Before the Web, IEEE Spectrum, June 2017.

[2] Minitel, Wikipedia, https://en.wikipedia.org/wiki/Minitel

[3] Britain's Prestel, iml.jou.ufl.edu/Carlson/History/Prestel.htm

[4] Julien Mailland, 101 online: American Minitel Network and lessons from its failure, IEEE Annals of the History of Computing, Vol. 38, Issue 1, January–March 2016.

50

Caltech Cosmic Cube and Successors

PROLOGUE

In May 1981, Geoffrey Fox, who was a professor of physics and dean of educational computing at the California Institute of Technology (Caltech), attended a seminar on Very Large Scale Integrated Circuits by Professor Carver Mead of the Electrical Engineering Department in which he described how several tasks could be carried out concurrently by an integrated circuit chip. At that time, Fox was trying to solve problems in lattice dynamics, which required intensive computation and took several hours to solve in Caltech's VAX 11/780. He figured he could break up the lattice dynamics problem into several parts and solve it concurrently, as there was very little interaction between them. Fox and his team simulated a four-processor computer on VAX 11/780 and could solve a miniature version of the problem. In September 1981, he approached Charles Seitz of the Electrical Engineering Department and requested that he and his team consider building a computer with several processors that could solve problems concurrently. Seitz and his team evinced interest in Fox's proposal and started to work on the architectural design of a computer that could concurrently solve large problems. They chose what is now known as a message-passing parallel computer architecture, one of the first such design ideas. The Caltech team used the term concurrent computer to emphasise that it broke up its programs into a set of concurrent processes.

MESSAGE-PASSING PARALLEL COMPUTER

The general idea for solving problems on a message-passing parallel computer is to break up the problem into several tasks and determine which tasks could be carried out concurrently and which require results from other tasks to proceed further. Once this is done, the tasks are allocated to computers to maximise their concurrent execution. Whenever a task scheduled in a computer (CE_n) requires the result of a task running on another computer (CE_k), the result is sent by CE_k as a message to CE_n. The CEs in the parallel computer cooperate to solve the problem. Standard programming constructs are currently available to program message-passing parallel computers in languages such as Fortran and C. If T is the time needed to run a program on a single computer, the time required to run it on a parallel computer with N computers, in an ideal case where there is no interaction between tasks, will be T/N. However, as most programs require some interaction among tasks, the time will be ET/N, where E is greater than 1. E will increase as the interaction between the tasks increases.

CALTECH CONCURRENT COMPUTER [1]

Seitz and his team selected Intel 8086 as the processor for the concurrent computer as it was the only chip in the market in 1981which had a companion floating point chip 8087. Floating point calculations are essential for solving problems in science and engineering. The clock speed of the computer was 5 Mhz. The team chose 128 KB memory as it was sufficient for solving lattice dynamics and similar problems. Besides, memory was expensive. Thus, each CE in the concurrent computer used an Intel 8086 with 128K memory as its main processor, with an Intel 8087 as a floating-point coprocessor. Seitz decided to build a computer with 64 CEs and interconnect them as a hypercube—a set of cubes with corresponding nodes connected.

Seitz picked a hypercube topology to connect the CEs, as any CE can communicate with any other CE in the hypercube with not more than six links ($6 = \log_2 64$). As the number of links in a hypercube is the logarithm of the number N of CEs, Seitz figured that building a concurrent computer as a hypercube with a large N would not complicate its wiring.

Hypercubes can be elegantly defined mathematically. An isolated node is a 0-cube—two 0-cubes connected by a line form a 1-cube. Two

1-cubes connected by lines is a 2-cube. A 3-cube is formed by linking the corresponding nodes of two 2-cubes. A *n*-cube is the structure resulting from two (n – 1)-cubes after links connect the corresponding nodes of these two (n – 1)-cubes. (See Figure 50.1).

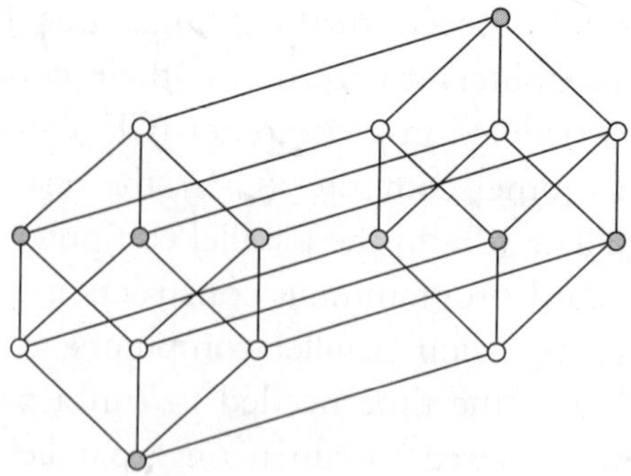

Figure 50.1 Two cubes connected as a hypercube
(Figure thanks to Wikipedia)

Seitz's group built a concurrent computer in 1981 with 4 CEs to test their ideas on programming the machine. They designed a small program to send data from a source computer to a destination computer. This message-passing program ran on all computers and was called the Crystalline operating system—even though it was not a conventional operating system. The lattice dynamics program was run successfully on this computer with good speedup. It gave them the confidence to build a concurrent computer with 64 CEs.

Charles Seitz
(Photo courtesy Caltech)

Geoffrey Fox
(Photo courtesy Wikipedia)

Seitz and his team built the 64 CE computer (Caltech Cosmic Cube – C_3) during the summer of 1983, and it was ready for use in October 1983. The peak speed of the message-passing link was 2 Mbits/second, and the sustained speed was 0.8 Mbits/second. C_3 was 5 feet long, 8 inches high, and 14 inches deep. It consumed 700 watts and was approximately ten times faster than VAX 11/780. It cost $ 80,000 to build the first C_3—10 times cheaper than VAX 11/780. The computer ran reliably, with only two failures during its first year of operation.

When the 64 CE computer was ready, many research groups with compute-intensive problems at Caltech were eager to use it. Caltech researchers solved ten problems, including lattice gauge theory, acoustic wave equations, Monte Carlo simulation, hydrodynamics, travelling salesman problem, chemical process dynamics, and sorting, encouraged by Fox and Seitz. Users wrote programs in a high-level language with Seitz's group's assistance in using message-passing instructions. The researchers found that the inter-CE communication was slow and reduced the overall computation speed.

Caltech's 64 CE hypercube
(Photo courtesy Charles Seitz)

JET PROPULSION LABORATORY (JPL) HYPERCUBES [2]

JPL and Caltech were neighbours and collaborated in solving many research problems. JPL was eager to cooperate with the Caltech group to build larger hypercubes. By June 1985, JPL had built a 128 CE hypercube with Intel 8086/8087 and a 256 KB memory in each CE. The next JPL model, Mark III, was ready in 1986 and used a Motorola 68020 chip with a 68881 floating point coprocessor. It also increased inter-processor message passing speed by dedicating a 68020 as a communication processor at each node. Research and building better hypercubes continued at JPL and culminated in 1989 with a 128 CE machine that used a high-performance Weitek XL floating-point chip. Its speed was 500 MFlops—similar to that of supercomputers of that era.

INTEL'S IPSC RANGE OF HYPERCUBES [3]

The success of Caltech's concurrent computer led to several companies building parallel computers using hypercube interconnection. Among them were Intel and nCUBE.

Intel set up a group led by Justin Rattner and Cleve Moler in Oregon to develop parallel computers using Intel's microprocessors. Intel called it the Intel Personal Supercomputer—iPSC. The first model, iPSC/1, built in 1985, used Intel's 80286 as the processor and 80287 as the floating point coprocessor and had 256 KB memory. It used Ethernet for message passing between CEs. Each CE had 8 Ethernet ports. The parallel computer used seven ports for inter-CE communication and the eighth port to connect to a host computer that managed the hypercube and performed I/O operations. Intel's engineers developed an inter-processor message-passing program. Intel built and sold various models, starting with 16 CEs up to 128 CEs. The 128 CE model cost half a million dollars. iPSC/1 was difficult to program to reach its maximum potential speed.

Intel followed up this mode with iPSC/2 in 1987. iPSC/2 used Intel's 80386 processor with a 16 Mhz clock with an 80387 floating point coprocessor. Each CE had a 4 MB memory. A specially designed communication processor that could transfer data between CEs at a 2.8 MB/second speed interconnected the CEs of the hypercube. An 80286-based host computer managed the hypercube. The largest model had 128 CEs. A 64 CE model with 8 MB per CE cost around $1.5 million, and its peak speed was about 300 Mflops.

Intel iPSC/1 parallel computer
(Photo thanks to Wikipedia)

The last in this line of Intel parallel machines was iPSC/860, which used Intel's fast i860 processor that ran at 40 Mhz. Each CE had an 8 MB memory. It also used a specially designed communication processor. The maximum configuration had 128 CEs, and its speed was 7 Gflops for 64-bit calculations and 10 Gflops for 32-bit calculations. It cost around $3 million.

nCUBE PARALLEL COMPUTERS [4]

In 1983, John Palmer and five more employees of Intel were unhappy that Intel was not interested in entering the emerging parallel computer market. They had seen Caltech's hypercube and were keen on building higher-speed parallel computers using a specially designed integrated circuit chip that would be tuned to be a CE of a hypercube. They founded nCUBE in Beaverton, Oregon. They decided to design a custom chip that would be the CE of the hypercube they named nCUBE/10. They planned a 10-dimensional hypercube (1024 CEs). The custom chip was a 32-bit processor with a built-in 64-bit floating point processor, 22 communication channels, and an 8 MHz clock. Ten pairs of channels were to be used to connect to a maximum of 10 CEs and one pair to connect to the front-end management computer. The custom chip used CMOS technology and had 160,000 transistors. The computer with 1024 CEs was ready in 1985 for Yale University, its first customer. It cost $1.5 million and ran at 500 Mflops. A 64 CE machine cost $200,000 and had a speed of 31 Mflops. It was more cost-effective than Cray 2, the fastest computer in 1985, which ran at 1.9 Gflops and cost around $30 million. Cray was much easier to program, had a vast library of standard programs, and a large 256 MB (64-bit) memory.

nCUBE/2 succeeded nCUBE/10 in 1989 with a new custom integrated circuit chip with 500,000 transistors that could support an 8192 CE hypercube. It ran at 30 MHz. Each processor had a 4 to 16 MB memory. A 1024 CE system ran at 1.9 Gflops and cost around $4 million.

The next model was nCUBE3, which was released in 1999. It used a new custom 64-bit chip running at 50 MHz. It increased the connectivity at each node to 16 other CEs and the link speed to 100 Mbits/second. The maximum hypercube with 65,536 CEs had an aggregate memory of 65 TB and ran at 6.5 Teraflops. This computer heralded the arrival of massively parallel computers. Larry Ellison of Oracle invested heavily in nCUBE in 1988. The systems were modified to support large databases. Subsequently, nCUBE shifted its focus from high-performance scientific computers to Video on Demand

(VoD) servers. A company named C-COR acquired nCUBE in 2005 for around $ 89.5 million.

EPILOGUE

1983 heralded the beginning of a decade of a quest for high-performance computers with numerous interconnected off-the-shelf microprocessor chips. Research also began to design and build specialised processors appropriate to build parallel computers, one of the earliest being the nCUBE processor. They were more cost-effective than supercomputers of that period, consumed very little power, and were not as fast and difficult to program. Research began on methods of parallel programming that led to many new techniques and programming standards to facilitate portability. In this Anecdote, I have described a class of parallel computers known as message-passing parallel computers. Nowadays, they are called Non-Uniform Memory Access (NUMA) parallel computers to emphasise that the time to access data in a remote computer's memory takes longer than in the local memory of the processor. The term NUMA distinguishes them from shared memory parallel computers such as Cray XMP4, in which the memory access time is the same for all processors in the parallel computer. By the end of 1994, there was a vast variety of parallel computers, some of which we will describe in later Anecdotes. Supercomputers built by Cray Research, such as Cray YMP and Cray 2, became cost-ineffective and vanished.

REFERENCES

[1] J.S. Dietrich, Cosmic Cubism, https://calteches.library.caltech.edu/3419/1/Cubism.pdf

[2] Birth of the hypercube, https://netlib.org/utk/lsi/pcwLSI/text/node13.html

[3] Intel iPSC computer, https://en.wikipedia.org/wiki/Intel_iPSC

[4] nCUBE and the Rise of the Hypercubes, https://www.cpushack.com/2013/11/01/ncube-and-the-rise-of-the-hypercubes/

51

Evolution of Domain Name System

PROLOGUE

The US government's Department of Defence (DoD) funded the development of ARPANET and the maintenance of other associated systems such as Request for Comments (RFCs) and addresses of host computers (See Anecdote 27). When ARPANET allowed CSNET to connect, other networks, such as the Department of Energy and the National Aeronautics and Space Administration (NASA), joined. The administration of the ARPANET was handed over to the National Science Foundation (NSF) by the DoD in 1990. ARPANET transformed to NSFNET. NSF permitted international networks to join NSFNET, and the Internet was born. Internet snowballed. Soon, many Internet Service Providers (ISPs) started commercial operations, providing mainly email service. NSF privatised NSFNET, and the US government agreed with this policy. As long as NSF was funding the Internet, it set all policies. When the Internet was privatised and internationalised, it was evident that another organization was required to devise policies on its governance. The most contentious problem was naming host computers connected to the Internet. In this Anecdote, I will describe how the naming problem evolved into the Domain Name System and its management.

DOMAIN NAME SYSTEM

In the early days of ARPANET, the designers gave each computer connected to it a numerical address and an easy-to-remember name. For example, SRI was the host's name at the Stanford Research Institute. The network managers kept a mapping of host names of computers connected to the ARPANET and their IP addresses in a file named HOSTS.TXT at the Network Information Centre (NIC) of the SRI. Elizabeth Fainler of SRI updated this file regularly based on information sent by members (i.e., host computers connected to ARPANET), and all the members copied it for their use. This informal manual process was cumbersome and error-prone. As the number of hosts in ARPANET increased, the file HOSTS.TXT became larger, unmanageable, and frequently outdated. The problem worsened when CSNET joined ARPANET. Jonathan Postel at the Information Sciences Institute of the University of Southern California (ISI-USC) was managing RFCs and IP addresses on behalf of ARPANET. He decided to automate registering host names and their addresses and requested his group members to propose solutions. His group members proposed five solutions. He asked Paul Mockapetris, a doctoral student in his group, to select one. Instead, Mockapetris came up with another solution called the Domain Name System (DNS). His idea was to map the IP address of a host that was a string of digits in a dotted decimal format, for example, 192.168.0.105 to an orderly meaningful string of characters using a directory service. Mockapetris, Postel, and Craig Partridge of BBN refined the initial version of DNS in November 1983. In October 1984, Postel and Joyce Reynolds of USC proposed the idea of thirteen generic Top-Level Domain Names (gTLD). Some of them are .com for commercial, .edu for education, .org for non-profit, .gov for government, .mil for military, etc. A typical domain name is cs.wisc.edu (Computer Science Department of the University of Wisconsin, Madison, WI, USA). When the Internet became international, one more component was added as the right-most part of the domain name to indicate the name of the country where the host computer is located. This part of the domain name is, for example, .in for India, .ca for Canada, and .uk for the United Kingdom. For example, the domain name of the Indian Institute of Science, Bengaluru, is iisc.ac.in.

Jon Postel
(Photo courtesy postel.org)

Paul Mockapetris
(Photo courtesy isi.edu)

ASSIGNING DOMAIN NAMES

The task of assigning domain names, maintaining RFCs, and help desk for user queries was the responsibility of Postel (ISI-USC), who used the services of SRI NIC until 1991. In 1991, as the system grew, DoD contracted these services to Government Systems Inc. The situation changed when the US government gave NSF the responsibility to manage the Internet based on an act passed by the US Congress in 1991 (commonly known as the Gore Act, as Senator and later Vice President of the USA, Al Gore steered it). In 1993, NSF decided to outsource these tasks (for five years) to three organizations based on competitive bids. The job of registering domain names was given to Network Solutions Inc. (NSI), maintaining the directory and databases to AT&T, and providing general information and help desk to General Atomics. Based on a review, NSF found that General Atomics performed poorly, and it gave AT&T the tasks performed by General Atomics. NSI registered domain names in the generic Top-Level Domains (gTLD) and maintained a directory of IP addresses of these names. NSI gave Domain names on a first-come, first-served basis. Domain name registration was free.

Meanwhile, Réseaux IP Européens Network Coordination Centre (RIPE NCC) was established in 1992 in Europe to manage IP addresses and domain names in European countries. In 1993, the Asia Pacific Network Information Centre (APNIC) was based in Japan to assign its region IP addresses and domain names.

With the emergence of the World Wide Web (WWW), organizations realised the commercial importance of domain names. The demand for domain names rapidly increased, with many commercial organizations wanting to register their names. Several speculators jumped in to register popular names or use the names of established companies as domain names to enable them to sell them to interested parties at a high price. Some registered thousands of domain names and kept them active by renewing them regularly. They were called *cyber squatters.* Confusion prevailed because there was no clear policy governing the assignment of domain names.

The work of NSI increased as the Internet grew, and in September 1995, NSF decided to allow NSI to charge US$100 for registration and US$50 as a yearly maintenance fee. NSF also decided to put 30% of this fee in a fund called Preservation Assessment to be managed by NSF for improving Internet facilities [1]. There was a furore against this high fee. A court in the US opined that the Preservation Assessment of 30% was a tax that only the US Congress had the authority to levy and collect. NSF had no power to collect it. Another contentious issue was the policy of NSI not to register domain names that it considered "indecent". NSI tried automating the process of filtering "indecent" domain names, which led to some bizarre decisions. To rectify this problem, NSI flagged some names for manual inspection and rejection if it found them "indecent".

Internet Assigned Number Authority (IANA) opined that the assignment of IP addresses must be decentralized and each region be allowed to manage it by separate entities. Following this opinion, the American Registry of Internet Numbers (ARIN) was established in 1997 for assigning IP addresses in the USA.

The controversy over the registration of domain names led to the formation of an International Ad Hoc Committee (IAHC) in September 1996 to find a solution. Besides NSF and NSI, this committee had the World Intellectual Property Organization (WIPO), the International Telecommunication Union (ITU), and the US Federal Networking Council as members. IAHC suggested streamlining the registry function and establishing a separate organization to manage it. It also proposed establishing several registrars to assign domain names [1]. IAHC's report was unacceptable to commercial organizations as they felt IAHC did not solicit their opinions. The US government feared ITU might take over as the domain name assignment authority and shift it to Switzerland. The US president, Bill Clinton, acted quickly and asked the Department of Commerce (DoC) to find a solution. The National Telecommunications and Information Administration (NTIA) of DoC published a draft paper on domain names in early 1998 and placed it for comments. Based on the comments it received, NTIA issued a "White Paper" titled "Management of Internet Names and Addresses," which it published in June 1998. This paper proposed privatisation of the domain name registry function and give it to several competing companies. It also suggested establishing a not-for-profit company to supervise the operation of these companies, provide technical assistance to them, and keep the Internet stable, secure, and interoperable. All stakeholders accepted this proposal of NTIA.

Consequently, in September 1998, IANA and NSI collaborated and released articles of incorporation and bylaws for a new not-for-profit company named the Internet Corporation for Assigned Names and Numbers (ICANN). NTIA approved the establishment of ICANN with the power to supervise its activities. ICANN was incorporated in California on September 30, 1998, on the premises of IANA. Jon Postel actively participated in the establishment of ICANN and was slated to become its founding Chief Technology Officer (CTO). Unfortunately, he suddenly died on October 16, 1998.

Following the establishment of ICANN, NSI lost its monopoly. ICANN separated the registry and registrar functions. It appointed five new registrars and asked NSI to allow these registrars to access the registry. Even then, the market considered NSI a valuable company with around 8 million customers. Verisign, a security company, acquired it for US$ 19.3 billion [2] in 2000! Slowly, ICANN added more registrars. Today, there are around 1000 registrars. The cost of registering domain names is a few dollars and sometimes free if a customer buys other services from the registrar.

EPILOGUE

One of ICANN's early decisions was the separation of the management of IP addresses and domain names. Apart from the American Registry of Internet Numbers (ARIN), RIPE NCC for Europe, Central and West Asia, and APNIC of Asia Pacific, two more registries–one for Africa (AFRINC), and the other for Latin America and the Caribbean islands (LATCNIC) were added and given a bunch of IP addresses and limited freedom to assign domain names. The status of ICANN has been shaky right from its inception. The US government incorporated ICANN as a not-for-profit corporation with a broad-based "multiple stakeholder" board of directors formulating policies. NTIA of the US government supervised ICANN's activities. There was an ongoing tussle between ICANN and international organizations such as ITU to gain control of DNS. In successive meetings of the World Summit on Information Society and the Internet Governance Forum, held between 2006 and 2011, the summit discussed the functioning of ICANN. Based on suggestions in these meetings, ICANN permitted the use of non-Roman scripts, such as Arabic, Chinese, Hindi, Tamil, etc., in domain names. Many more Top Level Domain (TLD) names such as .ai and .consultant, were added—some not very wise—for example, .sucks (American slang for highly unpleasant or disagreeable). There are around 1500 TLDs in 2021. ICANN charges huge fees (US$ 185,000) for TLDs. In 2014, NTIA formally relinquished control of ICANN. ICANN is now an autonomous not-for-profit corporation incorporated in California, USA, answerable to international stakeholders.

REFERENCES

[1] History of DNS, https://www.cybertelecom.org/dns/history.htm

[2] Oscar M. Bonastre and Andreu Vea, Origins of the Domain Name System, IEEE Annals of the History of Computing, April–June 2019, pp. 48–60.

52

Multimedia Digitisation and Compression

PROLOGUE

Digital computers store and process strings of bits. Decimal numbers are coded or converted to strings of bits for storage and processing by computers. Characters are coded using the American Standard Code for Information Interchange (ASCII) and, of late, an International standard known as Unicode for processing and storage. When integrated circuits arrived, digital processing and storage became inexpensive. Computer scientists began to explore digital processing and transmission of multimedia data, namely, pictures/images, sound/audio, and movies/video, because it is cheaper and more reliable to process and transmit digital data than analog data. By nature, images, audio, and video are analog. They must be converted to an equivalent digital form, namely, a sequence of 0 s and 1 s, for computer processing and reconverted to analog for human use. The number of bits required to represent multimedia data is enormous. For example, the number of bits/pixels needed to represent a 10 cm × 15 cm black and white image using 100 bits or pixels/cm is 1.5 Mbits ~ 0.2 MB. One hour of stereo music-quality audio requires around 600 MB of storage. One hour of low-quality (640 × 480 pixels per frame, 30 frames/sec) colour video requires 100 GB of storage. Therefore, users should compress multimedia data without losing quality for economical storage and transmission. The history of multimedia digitisation and compression is fascinating and took many years, beginning with the ideas of Nyquist, who invented a method of sampling and digitising audio without loss of quality in 1928, to the development of digitising and compression standards for video by the Motion Picture Experts Group (MPEG) in the 1990s.

DIGITISING AND COMPRESSING IMAGES

Photographs, paintings, printed/handwritten documents, and other media, such as palm leaves and similar materials, are called images. Russel Kirsch led a group that invented a device called a scanner at the National Bureau of Standards in the United States in 1957. The main components of the scanner were a drum, a light beam, and a light sensor. He mounted a black and white picture of his three-month-old son on the drum. The drum rotated slowly, and a light beam was focussed on the photograph.

Russel Kirsch's First scanned image
(Photo courtesy NBS/USA)

A photoelectric tube sensed a white spot reflected from the photo and stored it as a 1 on a magnetic tape and a black spot as 0. A mechanism moved the beam gradually, and the drum scanner scanned the photo on the drum and stored it as a 176-bit × 176-bit array.

Willard Boyle

George Smith

(Photos courtesy Wikipedia)

Willard Boyle and George Smith revolutionised scanners and digital photography when they invented a charge-coupled device (CCD) in 1969 at Bell Telephone Laboratories. They received the Nobel Prize in Physics for their invention in 2009.

A CCD is an integrated circuit etched on a substrate of light-sensitive elements. When light reflected from picture elements falls on it, the substrate converts the photons to electrons and stores them as charge. The amount of charge depends on the intensity of light and represents several shades of grey. Colour images are stored using red, blue, and green filters and combining their intensities. CCD arrays are used in scanners, barcode readers, telescopes, and digital cameras. Since 2004, image sensors based on CMOS technology, which consume less power and are cheaper, are replacing CCD arrays in many applications.

Working in Eastman Kodak, Steven Sasson invented a CCD-based digital camera in 1975. He used a 100 × 100 pixel Fairchild CCD array and a lens system to focus an image onto the array. The CCD array captured the image. The captured image was stored on a magnetic tape and projected on a TV screen. The camera was battery-operated and weighed 3.2 kilos. Kodak patented the invention but did not pursue it further because they were leaders in film manufacturing and feared an end to their core business if CCD cameras became popular.

Steven Sasson, with the first digital camera he invented
(Photo courtesy Inventor's Hall of Fame)

In 1988, Fuji Films of Japan released the first fully digital camera, Fujix DS-1P. It had a 2 MB memory card to store 10 monochrome photos. The first digital camera with an LCD viewfinder, the Casio QV-10, was released in 1995. By 1999, smartphones had digital cameras. The first camera phone was the Kyocera Visual Phone VP-210, which had a 110,000-pixel camera made in Japan in 1999.

By 1992, compression algorithms appeared, which reduced the storage required to store digital images. A standard called jpeg (joint photographic experts group) emerged that could trade the quality of the image against the amount of compression. The jpeg compression is called "lossy compression" as it eliminates many bits irrelevant to human perception in a picture. Compression by a factor of 144 using a jpeg algorithm gives a moderate-quality image, and compression by a factor of 15 gives an indistinguishable image from the original.

Smartphone cameras have enough computing power to use a JPEG compression program. The Kyocera VP-210 phone could store 20 jpeg compressed images. In 2003, a front-facing camera with a lens facing the owner appeared. This camera allowed owners to take their pictures called "selfies". By 2010, all smartphones had cameras as a standard feature, and by 2015, the word "selfie" entered the Oxford English dictionary. Nowadays, most high-end smartphones, such as Apple's iPhone, have 48-megapixel cameras and can store several thousand jpeg images depending on the phone's storage and the required image quality. These phones can also record videos.

DIGITISING AND COMPRESSING VIDEO

Video cameras capture motion by photographing images at least 30 times per second. Auguste and Louis Lumiere built the first 35-mm motion picture camera and projector as early as 1895. Philo Farnsworth built the first electronic video camera in 1927. His camera focussed an image on a caesium oxide-coated plate that emitted electrons. Electronic circuits gather these electrons and amplify them. Vladimir Zworykin invented a competing system for television cameras in 1930. Colour TV cameras emerged in 1950. Portable camcorders appeared in the 1970s. All these were analog devices. Digital video cameras emerged when CCDs came. In 1986, Sony released the first all-digital video camera that captured images 30 times per second and stored the bits in memory. The storage required to store videos is large. 100 GB is needed to store one hour of low-quality – (640 × 480) pixels, 30 frames/sec – colour video. Therefore, it is necessary to compress videos for economical storage and transmission. Image compression algorithms use the fact that most pixels in an image do not change between successive frames. Thus, only those that change are stored. International Standards Organization (ISO) and the International Telecommunication Union (ITU) developed standards for compressing videos in the 1990s. A series of standards evolved by the Motion Picture Experts Group and endorsed by ISO is called MPEG-1, MPEG-2, and MPEG-4. MPEG-1, developed in 1993, standardised digital video and audio storage in CDROM. MPEG-2 standardised videos for DVDs and HDTV in 1995. MPEG-4 was standardised in 1999 to support transmitting videos over the Internet and for use on mobile devices. The ITU standards corresponding to the MPEG standards are H.261, H.262, and H.264. Currently, the most commonly used standard is MPEG-4/H.264. It supports video streaming on the Internet and mobile devices with a compression ratio between 100 and 150. With this compression, a one-hour colour video requires only 1 GB of storage. Devices called Video Coders/ Decoders (CODECS) with standard compression software are now widely available.

The standardisation process is arduous, with pushes and pulls from vendors and academics. Professor Thomas Wiegand of the Technical University of Berlin and Gary Sullivan of Microsoft Corporation co-chaired the ITU/ISO standardisation committee that developed and adopted the video compression standards described above.

DIGITISING AND COMPRESSING AUDIO

Voice or audio signals vary continuously and are called analog signals. To use computers to store and process audio signals, they have to be converted to digital form. In 1928, Harry Nyquist explored digitising audio signals while working at the Bell Telephone Laboratories. His motivation was to improve voice communication over noisy telephone lines. He realised that digitising and transmitting analog signals over a telephone line improved their quality. The digital signals are converted back to analog signals at the receiving end. His method, called *pulse code modulation* of voice signals, was used in telephone systems. Nyquist proved that the information in an analog signal is preserved if it is sampled at a rate slightly higher than $2f_h$, where f_h is the highest frequency component in the signal. The highest frequency that an average human can hear is 22 kHz. Therefore, slightly more than 44,000 samples per second, say 44,100 samples, of an audio signal are sufficient to reproduce it faithfully. The amplitude of an audio signal sample can be represented as a binary number. The number of bits needed to represent this amplitude depends on how many sound levels a human ear can discriminate. Experimentally, it was found that a human ear cannot distinguish more than 64,000 levels. As $2^{16} = 65{,}536$, 16 bits are used to represent each sample of an audio signal.

An electronic circuit whose input is an analog signal and output is a sequence of bits is called an analog-to-digital (A/D) converter. A/D converters were fabricated as IC chips in the 1960s. A circuit whose input is a sequence of bits and outputs an analog signal that humans can hear is called a D/A converter, also an IC chip.

Harry Nyquist
(Photo courtesy Wikipedia)

In 1984, CD recorder manufacturers arrived at a standard for recording CDs that used 44100 samples of an audio signal per second and 16 bits to represent each sample. An audio signal is converted to its standard digital equivalent by an A/D converter and recorded on a CD. It is played back by converting the digital output to an analog signal using a D/A converter. One hour of stereo music requires $2 \times 44100 \times 60 \times 60 \times 16$ bits ~ 600 MB, which can be stored in one CD.

Audio signals can be compressed without loss of quality. The main principles used to compress audio are to take fewer samples when the frequency of audio is low, take no samples during silent intervals, use a smaller number of bits per sample when the volume is low, and adjust the number of bits per sample based on the physiology of the human hearing system. A compression algorithm known as mp3 was developed using these principles at the Fraunhofer Institute in Erlangen, Germany, in 1989 by a group under the leadership of Karlheinz Brandenburg. It is a lossy algorithm; in other words, it does not preserve all the information in the original signal. However, it reproduces music without any loss in quality for human hearing. It reduces the number of bits in a normal telephone conversation by 96. It compresses music by a factor between 10 and 14. Thus, a standard CD can store almost 10 to 14 hours of mp3 music. In 1993, mp3 compression became a standard.

By 1998, several audio system manufacturers started marketing portable mp3 players. Music sharing among owners of music CDs using the Internet became rampant in 1999 with the advent of a music distribution intermediary called Napster. Napster led to copyright litigation and it was shut down. In 2001, Apple introduced the iPod, a portable music player with a 5 GB hard disk that could store 1000 music tracks and cost $399. Apple continuously improved iPods using the latest memory technology, such as memory cards, and coupled it with iTunes, its music store. With the advent of smartphones, these devices have disappeared. Now (2024) smartphones have audio recording and playback features, can download oodles of music from the Internet and music stores, and compress audio.

EPILOGUE

Digitisation and compression of images, audio, and videos have led to the efficient usage of storage, ease of processing, and reduced the cost of transmitting them on communication systems, particularly the Internet. Digitisation has not only lowered costs but also improved the quality of multimedia. Video on Demand systems such as Netflix has emerged due to the digitisation and compression of video and audio. High Definition TV systems are based on digitisation and compression. Smartphones appeared in the late 1990s and have become all-purpose devices, replacing still and video cameras, video and audio recorders, players, and scanners. WhatsApp, a messaging system that emerged in 2009, has become indispensable for multimedia communication because of the symbiosis of digitisation, compression, and the Internet.

REFERENCES

[1] V. Rajaraman, Introduction to Information Technology, Third Edition, PHI Learning, 2018, pp. 41–88.

[2] Lawrence Harte, Introduction to IP Video: Digitization, Compression, and Transmission, Althos Publishing, USA, 2007.

[3] R. Steinmetz and K. Nehrstedt, Multimedia: Computing, Communication, and Applications, Pearson Education India, Delhi, 2002.

53

Transputer-based Parallel Computers

PROLOGUE

Inmos, an integrated circuit manufacturing company, was founded by Iann Barron, a British computer scientist, along with two semiconductor industry veterans, in 1978 in Bristol in the UK. The British government wanted to be self-reliant in the strategic area of integrated circuit manufacturing and gave a start-up grant of £50 million to Inmos. A factory to fabricate integrated circuits was ready in 1982. Inmos initially started manufacturing Static RAMs, and later Dynamic RAMs, and EEPROMs. Soon, Inmos captured 60% of the international SRAM market. Barron foresaw the emergence of parallel computers and was eager to design and fabricate a novel computer-on-a-chip that would become a component of a parallel computer by integrating communication capabilities besides a processor and memory. He envisioned a future where this computer would become a building block in systems with multiple computers, just like a transistor was a component of complex integrated circuits. Barron named such a computer "*Transputer,*" combining the terms <u>*Trans*</u>mitter and com<u>*puter*</u>.

Transputer
(Photo courtesy Wikipedia)

In 1983, he recruited David May of Bristol University and Robert Milne, a telecommunication consultant, to design Transputers [1].

David May
(Photo courtesy May's home page)

Iann Barron
(Photo courtesy archivesit.org.uk)

TRANSPUTER [2]

The Transputer designed by May consisted of a Central Processing Unit (CPU), a small, fast Static Random Access Memory (SRAM), and four serial communication links that could link it to four neighbouring Transputers (See Figure 53.1). It could concurrently process data and communicate. It had a minimal instruction set (32) and a micro-coded control unit. The CPU clock was 15 to 20 MHz, depending on the model. The Transputer could carry out one instruction in each clock cycle. The serial communication links had a speed varying between 5

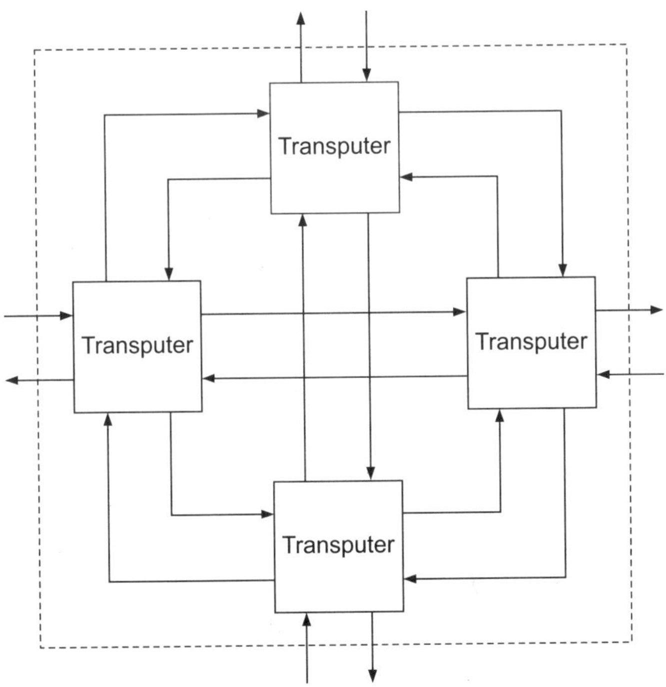

Figure 53.1 Four Transputers connected using bi-directional serial links

and 20 Mbps depending on the model. The links were full duplex; in other words, they could send or receive data simultaneously with a twisted pair of wires. Transputer hardware included a scheduler that controlled traffic over the communication links. While a process waited for input/output, another process was allocated to the processor by the hardware. The first Transputer with 16-bit words, the T2 series, was released in 1984. T212 was a processor without memory. It was followed by T 222 and 225, which had 2 KB and 4 KB Static Random Access Memory (SRAM), respectively. These Transputers had a 15 MHz clock.

The next series was 32-bit computers—the T4 series launched in October 1985. The first one, T414, in this series, had 2 KB SRAM (later enhanced to 4 KB) and had either a 15 MHz or a 20 MHz clock. This model did not have floating point arithmetic.

In 1987, Inmos released model T 800 with an extended instruction set. This 32-bit Transputer had a built-in 64-bit floating point processor. The floating point processor adhered strictly to the IEEE 754-1985 floating point standard. This unit was proven to work correctly using a formal proof of correctness. This effort was significant as Intel's 80287 floating point processor had a bug when it was released. The floating point speed was 2.25 Mflops. Two models, 801 and 805, were released. It had 4 KB SRAM with an access time of 40 ns per word. The processor had a 20 MHz clock. Inmos improved T 805 in 1988 to run at 30 MHz with a maximum floating-point speed of 3.6 Mflops. It could support a 4 GB addressable memory with an access time of 120 ns. It cost $400, which was high compared to other similar microprocessors.

Inmos also released a support chip to interface communication links of the T800 series with an 8-bit data bus. Another vital support chip was a 32-way programmable link switch model IMS C004 to interconnect 16 Transputers. This switch was handy for configuring parallel computers using Transputers as building blocks.

The next model was the series T 9000, designed to be much faster with a larger 16 KB cache. It was, however, abandoned in 1990 due to delays in fabrication and financial constraints.

David May designed the Transputer to be programmed using a programming language, *Occam*, which may be viewed as the assembly language of Transputers. The name Occam is derived from the writings of the thirteenth-century philosopher William of Ockham, who enunciated the principle of Occam's Razor—"entities are not to be multiplied without necessity" or, in other words, "keep things simple." David May developed Occam with the support of Tony Hoare of Oxford University. The development of Occam was a pioneering effort based on the idea of Communicating Sequential Processes (CSP), which Hoare proposed to simplify writing programs for message-passing parallel computers. Transputer hardware supported concurrency by scheduling several Occam processes in a round-robin fashion in a single Transputer. These processes may also be spread over several interconnected Transputers.

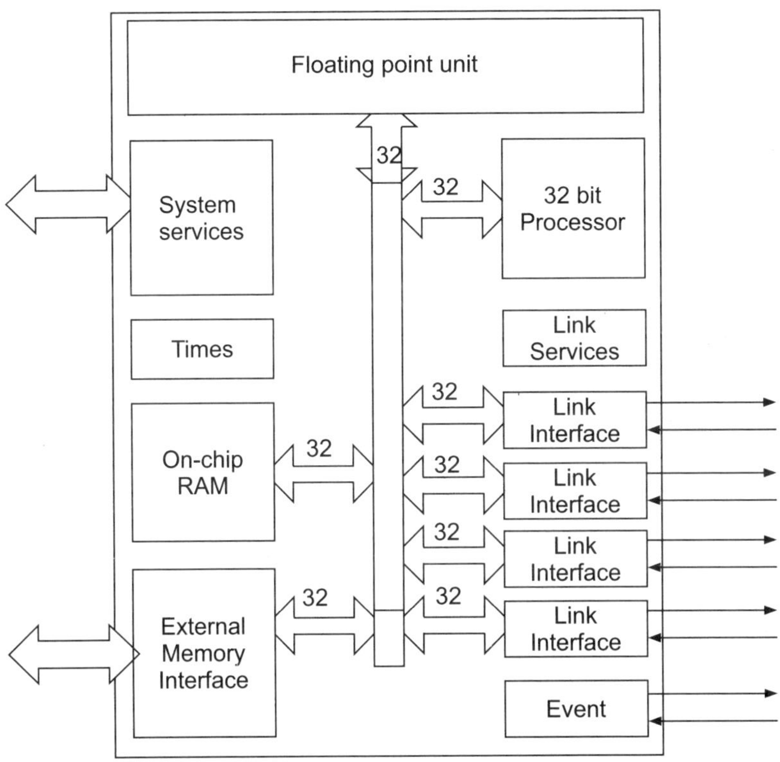

Figure 53.2 Transputer 800 series architecture
(Figure courtesy transputer.net)

Inmos marketed a Transputer Development System that comprised an integrated editor, file manager, compiler, and debugging system to support programming a network of Transputers using Occam.

Even though Occam was an excellent language for parallel programming, it did not become popular. Programmers preferred to stick to Fortran and C with added constructs for parallel programming.

Transputer users developed Fortran and C compilers for Transputers, later bowing down to market demand.

Inmos was not profitable despite the UK government pumping in £ 211,000. SGS-Thompson, another UK company (that was later renamed ST Microelectronics), took it over in April 1989.

PARALLEL COMPUTERS BUILT USING TRANSPUTERS

Several computer manufacturers found the Transputer an attractive device for quickly building parallel computers. Among them was Meiko Scientific Ltd., based in Bristol, Parsytec, based in Aachen, Germany; Floating Point Systems, based in Beaverton, Oregon, USA; and the Centre for Development of Advanced Computing (CDAC), based in Pune, India.

MEIKO SCIENTIFIC LTD. [3]

Meiko Scientific Ltd. was first off the block to build a parallel computer using Transputers. Meiko is a Japanese word meaning well engineered. It was founded in Bristol in March 1985 by six former Inmos employees eager to build parallel computers based on Transputers. In July 1985, Meiko Systems demonstrated a 16-bit Transputer-based parallel computer at the San Francisco SIGGRAPH (Special Interest Group On Graphics) conference, kindling interest in Transputers among engineers. The next model based on T414, a 32-bit Transputer, was called Meiko Computing Surface (CS1) and was launched in 1986. Meiko upgraded it with the T 800 when it became available in 1988. A customer could buy a set of boards, each board with one to four Transputers, mounted in a cabinet with a power supply, I/O ports, and a graphics board. Each Transputer had an external RAM ranging from 256 KB to 8 MB memory. Meiko designed a switch to interconnect Transputer boards to build a parallel computer. The interconnection topology could be software-controlled based on the application. CS1 was initially programmed using Occam. As Occam was not widely used, Meiko quickly provided Fortran, Pascal, and C compilers and designed message-passing primitives. Meiko provided a UNIX-like OS called Meiko OS. CS1 required a front-end computer that was usually a Sun Workstation. Meiko sold around 300 units of CS1 by 1990. Edinburgh Supercomputer Centre installed one of the largest CS1 with 450 Transputers in 1989.

Meiko also manufactured smaller T212 and T414 Transputer-based systems for applications using microcontrollers.

By 1990, new higher-speed microprocessors had arrived, and Meiko could not market Transputer-based CS1. The next model, CS2, released in 1993, switched to SUN SPARC as the main processor in each node, providing 40 Mflops. Another model added a Fujitsu vector microprocessor to the SPARC processor, giving 200 Mflops per node.

Meiko could not compete in the growing parallel computer market and merged with Quadrics Supercomputer World Ltd. in mid-1996.

PARSYTEC [4]

Parsytec (Parallel system technology) was founded in 1985 by three German engineers with a grant of DM 800,000 from the German government's Ministry of Research and Technology. Parsytec decided to build Transputer-based parallel computers. The range of products began with the brand Megaframe in 1987, which used one model T 414/800 Transputer per board. Parsytec marketed it as an add-on board to an IBM PC and 10 boards in one rack as a parallel computer. Parsytec followed this with Multicluster in 1988 with 64 T800 Transputers in a single rack inter-connected by Transputer's switch, and Supercluster with 16 to 1024 T800 Transputers in 1989. The last and the biggest parallel computer was the Gigacluter. Gigacluster was designed to use the T9000 Transputer but substituted T805 when Inmos did not manufacture the T9000. Parsytec built Gigacluster with 64 to 16384 Transputers (Model T805). Parsytec designed an operating system named PARIX (Parallel Unix extensions). It used a Sun SPARC workstation as the front end. Parsytec sold around 700 parallel computers in Europe, the UK, and the USA until it discontinued the Transputer-based computers in 1994.

FLOATING POINT SYSTEMS INC. [5]

Floating Point Systems (FPS) was established in Beaverton, Oregon, in 1970 by former Tektronix engineers. FPS started by designing and marketing floating-point co-processors to minicomputers and later array processors and was a profitable company. When parallel computers appeared in the market, FPS decided to enter it and built T-Series Hypercubes in 1986. The architecture was modular in that each module was a 3-D hypercube (8 CEs) with one external disk drive. Each CE had a T800 Transputer providing communications/control, a Weitek floating-point co-processor (16 Mflops), and 1 MB of external RAM. These modules could be inter-connected to make larger hypercubes. FPS used Occam with the Transputers. It could configure up to 14 modules. FPS delivered around a dozen parallel computers of various sizes. The I/O system was slow, and software tools for developing parallel programs were unavailable. This problem resulted in poor sales and massive losses as FPS did not recover the investment in developing T-Series machines. In 1991, Cray Research bought FPS for $3.25 million.

CENTRE FOR THE DEVELOPMENT OF ADVANCED COMPUTING (CDAC) [6]

In the late 1980s, India wanted to buy supercomputers such as Cray YMP for its research and weather prediction. The US government placed restrictions on their sale. To make India self-reliant in the area of high-performance computers, the government of India established CDAC in August 1988 with the mission to build high-performance parallel computers with a gigaflop speed and develop related software. Vijay Bhatkar was appointed CDAC's Executive Director, and the government allocated a budget of ₹375 million. After examining various alternatives, CDAC decided to build a parallel computer using Transputers primarily because Transputers had built-in communication that would simplify building message-passing parallel computers. Meiko and Parytec had already successfully built parallel computers using Transputers. In 1987, T 805 Transputer was available with a built-in 64-bit floating-point arithmetic unit whose speed was 3.6 Mflops. Support chips and boards were also available from Inmos. The IMS C 004 programmable link switch to interconnect transputers was particularly interesting. CDAC built a 64-transputer parallel computer and exhibited a prototype at CONPAR 90 in Europe. It was called PARAM 8000. PARAM stands for PARAllelMachine—meaning Supreme in Sanskrit. CDAC developed a software environment named PARAS to ease parallel programming. CDAC also developed many application programs in collaboration with academic institutions. CDAC's software team wrote a million and a half lines of code. A 256 Transputer model was ready in 1991 with a maximum nominal speed of around a Gigaflop. The actual speed was 100 to 200 Mflops on benchmark problems. PARAM

8000 with 256 Transputers had a total aggregate main memory of 1 GB (4 MB per Transputer), and distributed disk storage was 20 GB. The front end may be a high-end personal computer, Sun Workstation, or a DEC VAX computer. One could buy a 16, 32, 64, or 256-processor PARAM, depending on one's budget. CDAC sold around 20 computers in various configurations in India and exported around 4 machines to the erstwhile USSR, Germany, and the UK.

The next model was PARAM 8600, which used an Intel i860 as the main floating-point processor with four Transputers for communication with other i860s in the parallel computer. A 256-node computer was capable of delivering 5 Gflops. It had an aggregate main memory of 5 GB and a distributed 80 GB of disk storage. It was ready in 1993.

Later, computers in the PARAM series stopped using Transputers as better processors overtook them. One of the latest and fastest parallel machines built by CDAC is PARAM PRAVEGA, with a speed of 3.3 Teraflops, installed at the Indian Institute of Science, Bangalore, in February 2022.

EPILOGUE

The Transputer was the first microprocessor explicitly designed to build parallel computers. Parallel computer hardware was relatively easy to assemble using the Transputer as a building block. Occam, designed for Transputers, was a good language for writing parallel programs. However, languages such as Fortran and C had excellent compilers and a large population of users. Professionals were not keen on learning a new language. Companies had to invest considerable resources in creating software environments for Transputer-based parallel computers.

Meanwhile, giant manufacturers like Intel developed and marketed much faster microprocessors, and Inmos could not compete due to a lack of resources and marketing skills. Inmos designed a fast new-generation Transputer 9000 but abandoned it before production due to financial constraints and management doubt about its marketability. Transputer-based parallel computers could not keep pace with the large number of parallel computers that started to appear in the market in the late 1980s. After 1994, no company built Transputer-based parallel computers.

REFERENCES

[1] David May's Transputer Page, http://people.cs.bris.ac.uk/~dave/transputer.html

[2] D.A.P. Mitchell et al. Inside the Transputer, Blackwell Scientific Publications, Oxford, 1990.

[3] The Meiko Computing Surface: An example of a massively parallel system, https://dl.acm.org/doi/pdf/10.1145/62297.62418

[4] https://nytimes.com/1987/10/09/business/india-and-us-agree-on-supercomputer-sale.html

[5] John Gustafson, Programming the FPS T Series, http://www.johngustafson.net/pubs/pubt1986.2/FPS.pdf

[6] V.P. Bhatkar, PARAM Parallel Supercomputer: architecture, Proceedings IEEE 8th International Parallel Processing Symposium, 1994.

54

Cray–1's Successors

PROLOGUE

The cold war between the West and the USSR was at its height in the mid-1970s. Many government laboratories in the USA were designing nuclear bombs. The nuclear test ban treaty of 1963 stopped real-life testing in the atmosphere or underwater. Laboratories used computer simulation extensively to design and "test" atomic bombs. The US government's National Security Agency was a significant user of supercomputers in cryptography and code-breaking. Private companies such as General Electric were designing nuclear reactors, and their design required supercomputers. Aircraft companies were using supercomputers extensively to design jumbo jets. The National Science Foundation was also setting up supercomputing centres for use by universities conducting cutting-edge research in many areas of science and engineering. Computer simulation was coming of age, and the demand for high-speed computing was insatiable. Cray Research was the leader in supercomputing, and the demand for Cray-1 was high despite its cost. It was prestigious to own a Cray supercomputer, and many countries bought them. Cray Research saw the growing demand for faster supercomputers and started designing a successor to Cray-1.

THE CRAY-2 SUPERCOMPUTER [1]

Los Alamos Laboratory bought the first Cray-1 in 1976, and soon after, Seymour Cray started designing its successor, Cray-2. His goal was to make it at least ten times faster than Cray-1. Cray did not change the vector architecture of Cray-1. Cray felt that he could achieve the high speed aimed for Cray-2 using a three-pronged approach: increasing parallelism in processing, increasing clock speed by minimising signal delays using closer packaging and reducing wire lengths, and using faster integrated circuits; Cray did not believe in massive parallelism. He was conservative in selecting component technology.

Cray started his design at Chippewa Falls but was disturbed by constant interruptions as Cray Research had become a large organization. He requested a move to another location with a small team to start the project. Cray established a new laboratory in Boulder, Colorado, and moved there in 1980. The first problem he had to tackle was packaging the printed circuit boards to reduce the length of wires connecting them. After several attempts, he found an innovative idea of arranging the printed circuit boards in a three-dimensional structure. This arrangement immediately caused a cooling problem as the method used in Cray-1 was unsuitable. Cray decided to cool the entire processor and memory by immersing them in an enclosure containing a fluid that was a good thermal conductor but an electrical insulator. 3M, a company based in St. Paul, Minnesota, manufactured such a fluid called Flourinert. The designers of Cray-2 pumped Flourinert into the Cray-2 enclosure and pumped out the heated fluid into another chamber, spurting like a fountain and cooled by a refrigerating system (See Photo below). Cray-2 used four vector processors working in parallel that shared a 256 megaword (64 bits per word) memory. The clock speed was 4.1 nanoseconds. The processor architecture was the same as Cray-1, with each processor having a local memory for storing vectors, scalars, and instructions. Cray-2 could use the processors to execute four independent programs or a single program cooperatively. The operating system was Unix. It had an assembler, vectorising Fortran, C language, and application libraries. It needed a front-end computer for attaching peripherals, hosting the operating system, and compilers.

Cray-2 with a cooling fountain at the back
(Photo courtesy of Cray Research Inc.)

Cray-2 took nine years from conception to completion. The speed of Cray-2 was 1.9 Gigaflops. Cray Research shipped the first unit in

1985 to the US National Fusion Energy Laboratory. It was the fastest supercomputer in the world from 1985 to 1990. The average cost of Cray-2 was $ 15 million. Cray Research sold 27 Cray2s.

THE CRAY XMP [2]

While Cray was developing Cray-2, Lester Davies, the general manager of Cray Research, was more conservative and hired Steve Chen to design a successor to Cray-1. It was called Cray XMP. The architecture of the Cray XMP processor was similar to that of Cray-1. It used faster integrated circuit components and a faster 9.5 nanosecond clock. The computer had 2 to 4 processors working in parallel with shared memory. It used improved memory technology. The maximum main memory size was 16 megawords. The speed was 200 Megaflops per processor. It had the same cylindrical shape as Cray-1. It ran a version of Unix called UNICOS. It had improved vectorising Fortran and application libraries. Chen started the design in 1977 and delivered the first computer in 1982. The four-processor Cray XMP's speed was 800 Megaflops, and it was the fastest computer in the world from 1982 to 1985 when Cray-2 overtook it. The price of Cray XMP 24 (2 processors, 4 megaword memory) was $10 million. The largest was Cray XMP 48 (4 processors, 8 megawords), costing $ 15 million.

One of the customers of Cray XMP 48 was Apple Computers [3]. Apple used the Cray computer to design the aerodynamic floating head of its disk drives and the moulds of its casing. Interestingly, Cray used Apple Computer to design circuit boards and custom integrated circuits.

After protracted negotiations that lasted for over three years, the smallest model of Cray XMP, Cray XMP 14, was installed at India's National Centre for Medium-Range Weather Forecasting, New Delhi, in 1988 [4]. The US government was reluctant to sell a Cray Computer to India as it thought that India could use it for developing nuclear weapons and missiles. Cray sold Cray XMP 14 with numerous conditions, including maintenance only by Cray engineers, inspection of software that would run on the computer, etc.

THE CRAY YMP [5]

Cray YMP followed Cray XMP with the same vector architecture and similar shape. With the progress in integrated circuit technology, it used the latest and fastest integrated circuits for the CPU and memory. It used a 6 nanosecond clock. The smallest version was a single processor with 16 megaword memory; the largest had 8 processors and 64 megaword memory. The speed of a single-processor model was 333 Megaflops. Cray delivered the first Cray YMP in 1988.

The Indian Institute of Science, Bangalore, ordered Cray YMP 132 in November 1988 for $ 9.625 million. Cray Research was confident it would get an export clearance from the US government to sell it. Cray Research could not obtain an export clearance within the stipulated period of 1 year, so the Institute cancelled the order.

THE CRAY 90 SERIES [6]

Cray C90 succeeded Cray YMP in 1991. It had double the number of vector registers in the processor compared to Cray YMP. It used a 4.1 nanosecond clock, and its speed was 1 Gigaflop per processor. The maximum number of processors was 16, and the maximum shared memory was 128 megawords (64-bits per word). Cray also marketed a cheaper air-cooled model at a lower speed.

The last of the Cray XMP's successors was Cray T90, released in 1995 and marketed until 2000. It had a clock speed of 2.2 nanoseconds and a peak speed per processor of 1.8 Gigaflops. T90 models were Cray T94 (4 processors) to Cray T932 (32 processors). The maximum memory size was one gigaword (64-bits per word). The peak speed of T932 was 57.6 Gigaflops, costing $35 million. Cray sold around a dozen T90 series computers.

All the Cray series machines ran the UNICOS operating system and continued to use improved versions of Cray's vectorising Fortran and C.

THE CRAY-3 SYSTEM [7]

Seymore Cray started designing Cray-3 as soon as Cray-2 was in production in 1985. He aimed to develop a computer that would be 12 times faster than Cray-2 and ready in 1991. As Cray-2 sales were poor, the management of Cray Research was not very keen on starting another expensive project. Cray Research had expanded with Cray XMP and YMP sales, and Cray Research was no longer a small group. Cray Research managers decided to spin off a new entity called Cray Computer Corporation (CCC) to design Cray-3. Cray Research provided

CCC with $ 85 million to develop Cray-3. Seymour Cray explored new locations for the CCC laboratory to design Cray 3 and zeroed in on Colorado Springs. Cray was a consultant to CCC.

The high speed aimed for Cray-3 required multiple processors to work cooperatively, tighter packaging to reduce signal delays, and faster circuit components. Cray did not believe in massive parallelism and was conservative in selecting component technology. He found that silicon devices were not keeping pace with the increased speed he sought. He decided to use faster gallium arsenide (GAs) semiconductors that dissipated less heat. GAs technology, however, was not mainstream. CCC had to set up its own GAs integrated circuit fabrication unit. With innovative packaging, the computer was accommodated in an enclosure that was 1.1 m wide, 0.71 m deep, and 1.3 m high (See Photo aside). Cray-3 was immersed in a Flourinert bath just as Cray-2. The first and only Cray-3 built was a 4-processor model with 128 megawords (64-bit per word) memory. Lawrence Livermore Laboratory (LLL) ordered Cray-3. However, due to the long delay in the production of Cray-3, LLL cancelled the order and ordered a Cray 90 instead. Cray-3 was installed as a free demonstration system at the National Centre for Atmospheric Research in Boulder, Colorado, in May 1993. Cray-3 had a 2.11 nanosecond clock and a speed of around 4 Gigaflops. CCC produced only one Cray-3.

Cray posing with Cray-3 System
(Photo courtesy of Wikipedia.org)

Cray started designing Cray-4 as soon as Cray-3's production began in 1992. CCC went bankrupt in 1995. Cray died in an automobile accident on 5 October 1996.

SUMMARY OF CRAY COMPUTERS

Below is a summary of the Cray computer model, year released, lead designer, speed of single processor, and the maximum number of processors. The maximum speed of a system is the product of the number of processors and the speed of one processor. Seymour Cray designed Cray-1, Cray-2, and Cray-3. Cray XMP's lead designer was

Steve Chen, who worked in Chippewa Falls, Wisconsin, while Seymour Cray was designing Cray-2 in Boulder, Colorado. Teams designed Cray YMP, Cray C90, and Cray T90 in Chippewa Falls, while Seymour Cray designed Cray-3 in Colorado Springs.

SUMMARY OF CRAY VECTOR COMPUTERS

Cray Model	Year	Designer	Speed of 1 Processor	Max. Processors
Cray-1	1976	Cray	160 Megaflops	1
Cray XMP	1982	Chen	200 Megaflops	4
Cray-2	1985	Cray	1.9 Gigaflops	Built-in 4
Cray YMP	1988	Team	333 Megaflops	8
Cray C90	1991	Team	1 Gigaflop	16
Cray-3	1993	Cray	4 Gigaflops	Built-in 4
Cray T90	1995	Team	1.8 Gigaflops	32

EPILOGUE

The Cold War between the West, led by the USA, and the Eastern Bloc, led by the USSR, ended in late 1990. The USSR split, and all its satellite countries became free. The US and the USSR signed START (Strategic Arms Reduction Treaty) that limited the deployment of nuclear weapons and missiles in July 1991. Consequently, the US government cut the budget of laboratories developing nuclear weapons and other arms. These laboratories, major customers of Cray's supercomputers, reduced their purchases. The annual revenue of Cray started dwindling. The 1990s also saw two other developments. Microprocessors were becoming very fast, and their word size increased to 64 bits. For instance, MIPS Computer Systems released R4000, a 64-bit microprocessor with a clock speed of 100 MHz, and cost around $1000 in 1991. Digital Equipment Corporation released Alpha 21064, a 64-bit processor with clock speeds between 100 and 200 MHz in 1993 that cost around $3500. The availability of fast, moderately priced microprocessors led many companies to design parallel computers using these processors that achieved one Gigaflop speed and were ten times cheaper than Cray's computers as they did not require expensive cooling systems. Programming these computers was also becoming simpler. Cray Research jumped on the bandwagon and built model T3D in 1993, a parallel computer that used 32 DEC 21064 (150

MHz) microprocessors connected like a torus with a peak speed of 4.8 Gigaflops and cost $2.2 million. Cray Research sold it attached to Cray vector computers [8].

In 1995, Cray Research lost $ 226 million on revenue of $ 676 million. In February 1996, Silicon Graphics (SGI), a manufacturer of high-end graphics workstations, acquired Cray Research for $ 740 million. SGI tried merging its high-end workstations with Cray's proprietary technology to interconnect these and design parallel supercomputers. This attempt was unsuccessful. Cray was sold to the Tera Computer Company in March 2000 for $100 million. Tera changed its name to Cray Inc. as the name Cray had an excellent brand value. Tera Computers, a pioneer in parallel computer design, developed Cray Inc. into a high-end massively parallel supercomputer company with many successful products. Hewlett-Packard Enterprises acquired Cray Inc. for $ 1.3 billion in September 2019. The Cray brand name survived, and HP called the new company HPE Cray.

REFERENCES

[1] Cray-2 Supercomputer, Cray Research Inc. http://s3data.computerhistory.org/brochures/cray.cray2.1985.102646185.pdf

[2] Cray XMP, https://en.wikipedia.org/wiki/Cray_X-MP

[3] What are the Cray Research Connections with Apple Computers? https://cray-history.net/2021/07/16/apple-computer-and-cray-research-some-notes/

[4] https://nytimes.com/1987/10/09/business/india-and-us-agree-on-supercomputer-sale.html

[5] https://en.wikipedia.org/wiki/Cray_Y-MP#:~:text=The%20Cray%20Y%2DMP%20was,liquid%20cooling%20system%20was%20devised.

[6] https://en.wikipedia.org/wiki/Cray_C90

[7] https://en.wikipedia.org/wiki/Cray-3#:~:text=The%20Cray-3%20was%20a,(0.028%20m3)%20CPU

[8] R.E. Kessler and J.L. Schwarzmeier, Cray T3D: A New Dimension for Cray Research, COMPCON Spring Conference, San Francisco, February 1993.

55

Connection Machine—The First Massively Parallel Computer

PROLOGUE

In the early 1980s, Daniel Hillis was a doctoral student at the Massachusetts Institute of Technology in Cambridge, Massachusetts, working under Professor Marvin Minsky, an Artificial Intelligence (AI) pioneer. He was designing a computer system appropriate to solve common sense reasoning problems in AI. It culminated in a massively parallel computer design with 64 K (where K = 1024) tiny processors, called a Connection Machine. It was an innovative design, and Hillis's Ph.D. thesis won the ACM Doctoral Dissertation Award in 1985. The Connection Machine was a paper-pencil design, and Minsky felt it would be worth building. Building such a massively parallel computer in a university environment would have been difficult, so he suggested that Hillis start a company to build and market it while pursuing his doctoral program. Minsky knew Sheryl Handler, who had an eclectic background with a Master's degree in landscape architecture from Harvard University, where she had helped start the Genetics Institute, a genetic engineering company, and was pursuing a doctoral programme in town planning at MIT. Minsky and Hillis talked to Handler to assist them in starting a company to build and market Connection Machines, and Handler agreed. Handler was a persuasive conversationalist, and she, along with Minsky and Hillis, convinced the head of CBS, a media company, to invest with some others $16 million to start a company to build the Connection Machine. Hillis named the company Thinking

Machine Corporation (TMC) because, as he stated, "we wanted a dream we weren't going to outgrow" [1]. Hillis and Handler incorporated TMC in Cambridge, Massachusetts, in May 1983. Handler became the chief executive officer of TMC, and Hillis became the chief technical officer.

In 1982, the Japanese Ministry of International Trade and Industry initiated a ten-year-long "Fifth Generation Computer Systems (FGCS)" project to build massively parallel computers with supercomputer-like power to solve AI problems. It was a good time for TMC to pitch the Connection Machine to the US Defence Advanced Research Project Agency (DARPA) to respond to the Japanese challenge. DARPA gave a multi-year contract of $4.5 million a year to TMC starting in 1984 to build the Connection Machine.

Soon, TMC attracted several gifted engineers and scientists to work for it. The most famous was Richard Feynman, a Nobel Laureate physicist, who worked at TMC during the summer of 1984 and acted as a sounding board for ideas on the Connection Machine's design and designed the first model's routing system.

Daniel Hillis
(Photo courtesy Wikipedia)

Sheryl Handler
(Photo courtesy zoominfo.com)

CONNECTION MACHINE [2]

The Connection Machine -1 (CM-1) was the first model that TMC built. It had 64 K (K=1024) Computing Nodes (CN). Each CN had a single-bit processor and 4 K bits of memory. TMC designed a single custom integrated circuit chip with 16CNs. Each CN in this set of 16 CNs was inter-connected as a grid with four nearest neighbours. Besides the 16 CNs, each chip had a serial router to send data to a CN in another chip. CM-1 thus had 4 K chips with 16 CNs per chip. The 4 K chips were inter-connected as a 12-dimensional hypercube using the router in each chip. CM-1 used a hypercube topology to connect the chips, as any chip could communicate with any other chip in the hypercube using not more than 12 links ($12 = \log_2 4096$). (For a definition of a hypercube, see Anecdote 50).

Physically, TMC mounted 32 chips on a printed circuit board and housed 16 boards in a cube with a 1.5 m side. A Light Emitting Diode (LED) displayed each CN's status on the cube's front panel. If all the lights are on, it implies that all CNs are busy. CM-1 consisted of 8 cubes, each accommodating 16 boards (8K processors). Tamiko Thiel, an MIT-trained designer, headed the industrial design team. Her design gave an impressive look to CM-1 with eight inter-connected cubes of cubes. CM-1 supported an array of disks as secondary memory via a high-speed bus. The computer was ready for marketing in 1985.

Connection Machine–I (See eight cubes and display)
(Photo courtesy Wikipedia)

CM-1 used either a VAX mainframe of the Digital Equipment Corporation or a Symbolics-3600 made by Symbolics, an AI computer manufacturer, as its front-end machine to compile programs and for I/O. Initially, CM-1 was built to address the AI market and supported its version of Lisp called *Lisp—an AI programming language.

CM-1 was what is known as a Single Instruction Multiple Data Machine (SIMD). If one wants to count the occurrence of the word "pure" in a book with 64 K pages using a sequential computer such as a PC, the computer would read one page after another and count the number of occurrences of "pure" on each page and add them. If it takes 1 second to read and count the number of "pure" in one page, the total time taken to read and count the number of occurrences of "pure" in 64 K pages would be 64 K seconds, around 18.2 hours. CM-1 stores 64 K pages by distributing one page per computer. Instructions are broadcast to all the computers to count the number of occurrences of "pure" on its page. All computers count simultaneously, store their result in 1 second, and add the results. CM-1 is almost 64 K times faster than a single computer as it requires some time to distribute the pages to processors and add the counts per page. CM-1 is an excellent computer for solving problems that allow the input data to be stored in all the computers and execute the same set of instructions on all the 64 K computers simultaneously. Using this style of computing, professionals can solve many problems in database search, image processing, AI, and fluid dynamics. CM-1 did not have a time-sharing operating system. However, up to 4 users could use it from the front end by partitioning 64 K computers into four sets of 16 K computers.

CM-1 had several shortcomings. The one-bit serial processor was slow. The memory of 4 K bits in each computer was too small to store the data to be processed in many real-world problems to use the data parallel programming model effectively. The absence of a floating-point processor made the CM-1 virtually useless to solve problems in science and engineering. CM-1 was an excellent machine for solving AI problems, but the AI market was limited to mainly academic institutions, which could not afford its $5 million price tag. Deep discounting was required to sell CM-1 to universities, which made sales unprofitable. Soon, Hillis and other researchers realised that advancement in AI needed new ideas and algorithms rather than hardware. To make CM-1 attractive to the non-AI market, TMC developed parallel versions of Fortran and C named Fortran* and C*. Despite these attempts by TMC to make CM-1 attractive, it sold only 7 CM-1s, several with the help of DARPA. The Infusion of funds by DARPA kept TMC alive.

To make massively parallel machines attractive to solve business data processing problems and problems in science and engineering, TMC built the next improved version named CM-2, which was ready in 1987 [3]. It increased the storage in each CN of CM-2 to 64 Kbits. Each chip integrated 16 processors, as in CM-1. TMC chose Weitek 3132, a floating-point coprocessor (25 MFLOPS speed for 32-bit floating-point numbers) to enhance CM-1. Thirty-two CNs shared one floating point coprocessor. CM-2 thus had 2048 floating-point processors, giving it a peak speed of 50 GFLOPS. It used VAX or Symbolics-3600 as a front-end. Besides these, it had a disk secondary storage of up to 25 GB (called a DataVault) connected by a high-speed data bus. Besides *Lisp, it supported parallel versions of C language named C* and Fortran named Fortran*. The price of a CM-2 was around $10 million, and only a few could afford it. TMC marketed two cheaper versions, CM-2a (approximate cost $1.2 million) with 8 K processors and CM-200 with 16 K processors with smaller disk storage. CM-2a series machines were more attractive to customers, and TMC sold several machines in the late 1980s. Professionals used CM-2a extensively to solve many real-world problems such as data mining, financial modelling, chip design, computational chemistry, computational fluid dynamics, and climate modelling. In 1989, TMC made a profit of $700,000 on sales of $ 45 million for the first time.

CM-5 COMPUTER [4]

The market for SIMD machines, such as the CM-2 series, was limited and shrinking. Many new companies, such as nCUBE, entered the market and sold cheaper parallel computers using off-the-shelf commodity microprocessors that were becoming very powerful. After an 18-month-long debate, Hillis and his group decided to scrap the single-bit processors used in Connection Machines and start building more conventional message-passing Multiple Instruction Multiple Data (MIMD) parallel computers using commodity microprocessors which would also support the SIMD style of programming. TMC built the new computer called Model CM-5 using SUN SPARC processors. The SPARC processor chosen was a 64-bit RISC processor with a 40 MHz clock. It had 32 MB external RAM and an attached floating-point coprocessor with a peak speed of 128 MFLOPS. Each computing node (CN) was thus very powerful, unlike CM-2's one-bit processor. A novel interconnection network called a *fat tree* [5] was used to interconnect the CNs. The fat tree was invented by Charles Leiserson in 1985 when he was a doctoral student at MIT. He joined TMC and implemented it with a group of engineers in CM-5. The fat tree network is more flexible and expands gracefully compared with the hypercube as the computer adds more nodes. The architecture of CM-5 was called CHARM (Coordinated Homogeneous Array of RISC Microprocessors). The interconnection network's unique features were high bandwidth between CNs and low latency to access any CN's memory from any other CN. A fast global synchronization mechanism allowed the entire machine to a defined state at a specified point during computation. CM-5 could broadcast and synchronize instructions that permitted SIMD style of programming.

TMC could configure CM-5 starting with 32 CNs and going up to 1024 CNs. Theoretically, however, the design could accommodate up to 16K CNs. The peak speed of a 32 CN CM-5 was 4 GFLOPS, and the average speed was 2.5 GFLOPS. The speed increased linearly when the designers added more CNs. The peak speed of the largest 1024 CN model was 128 GFLOPS, and the average speed was 80 GFLOPS. The machine also supported a large array of disks as secondary memory.

CM-5 used a version of Unix as its operating system. Several users could time-share CM-5. The software also permitted the partitioning of the machine into sub-sets of processors and allocating these sub-sets to groups of users. It supported several programming languages, including *Lisp, C*, and Fortran 77, 90.

CM-5 was ready in October 1991. The price of a 32 CN machine was around $1.5 million. In 1993, the total sales of TMC were $82 million, much below expectations.

EPILOGUE

CM-5 was not a successful supercomputer, and its sales were much below expectations. The CM-1 and CM-2 series machines had survived primarily due to subsidies amounting to $55 million doled out by DARPA [1]. DARPA's funding was drying up. In 1992, TMC reported a loss of $17 million. Despite the loss, Handler was splurging money on face-lifting its leased building and extending the lease. In the middle of 1993, Richard Fishman, a lawyer, replaced Handler as the CEO. He started looking for partners and approached IBM and SUN Microsystems, which were interested. They were unwilling to take on TMC's massive debt, and Fishman could not strike a deal. In August 1994, TMC went bankrupt. Fishman and Hillis left the company. Subsequently, TMC re-emerged as a software company selling application programs for Connection Machines and other supercomputers.

REFERENCES

[1] Gary A. Tubes, The Rise and Fall of Thinking Machines, Inc. Magazine, 1995. http://www.bitsavers.org/pdf/thinkingMachines/The_Rise_and_Fall_of_Thinking_Machines_1995.pdf

[2] W. Daniel Hillis, The Connection Machine, Scientific American, Vol. 256, No. 6, pp. 108–115.

[3] Connection Machine-2, Technical Summary, Thinking Machine Corporation, http://bitsavers.org/pdf/thinkingMachines/CM2/HA87-4_Connection_Machine_Model_CM-2_Technical_Summary_Apr1987.pdf

[4] W. Daniel Hillis, and Lewis W. Tucker, The CM-5 Connection Machine: A Scalable Supercomputer, Communications of ACM, Vol. 36, No. 11, November 1993, pp. 31–42. https://course.ece.cmu.edu/~ece740/f13/lib/exe/fetch.php?media=hillis_cm5.pdf

[5] For fat tree definition and properties, see:
https://en.wikipedia.org/wiki/Fat_tree

56

Free Open Source Software Movement

PROLOGUE

Users of computers freely shared software in the early days of computing. One of the first formal groups was SHARE, a group of users of the IBM 704 computer set up in Los Angeles in 1956. This group was dissatisfied with the assembly language provided by IBM for the 704 mainframe computer and cooperatively wrote an assembler called SAP (SHARE Assembly Program), which IBM distributed to its users (The first computer program I wrote was in SAP). IBM encouraged user groups, financed some meetings, and distributed user-developed application software during the 1950s and 60s. IBM's business model was to lease computers along with the services of customer engineers who maintained the computers and systems engineers who assisted the users with their application programs and, in some cases, even wrote programs for customers. By the mid-1960s, IBM dominated the computer market and became a near monopoly with the release of the IBM 360 series of computers. Control Data Corporation (CDC), which had entered the mainframe computer market in 1960, filed a case against IBM in 1968, charging it with monopolistic practices, including giving its customers free application software and services. The US government's Department of Justice was also mulling over initiating an anti-trust case against IBM. To pre-empt this case, IBM set up a group in December 1968 to examine "unbundling" their services. Unbundling meant pricing hardware, applications software, maintenance, education, and system engineer services separately. Based on its recommendations, IBM unbundled hardware from software and services in June 1969. Hardware and systems software (operating system and utilities) were bundled and priced separately from customer engineering services, application software, and education (This was in the US market. IBM World Trade Corporation, which sold IBM computers in India, carried on business as usual). IBM reduced the hardware price by 3%, which many felt was a minuscule reduction, but IBM justified it. Meanwhile, IBM settled with CDC out of court by giving CDC its service bureau business and $100 million. In return, IBM took from CDC all the legal papers that CDC had gathered to fight its case and destroyed them to prevent the Department of Justice from using them (Apparently, this act was legal) [1].

In the mainframe era, all vendors sold hardware and systems software (OS and utilities) as a single entity. The situation changed with the advent of Personal Computers (PC). Independent vendors sold Operating Systems (OS) separately. CP/M in the early days (1974 to 1983) was the de facto standard PC OS, superseded by Microsoft's PC-DOS and MS-DOS in 1981. Apple was an exception; it bundled its OS with the hardware and continues this practice.

The PC software business expanded rapidly in the early 1980s. OS and application software, such as word processors, spreadsheets, database management, presentation software, etc., were separately sold as object codes (binaries) in media such as floppy disks. Users had no freedom to modify or improve them to suit their requirements as they were binaries. Most device drivers were also binaries. The first significant change occurred in 1971 with the release of the Unix source code by Bell Labs. The source code of Unix was in C, and this code was initially widely available (See Anecdote 25). The US government split AT&T, which owned Bell Labs, as a follow-up of an anti-trust suit. Soon after, AT&T clamped down Unix distribution. It was no longer freely available. Software became a very profitable business in the early 1980s, and the market capitalisation of companies such as Microsoft overtook those of many hardware companies. Software companies began protecting their programs by copyright and later by patents. Users lost the freedom to modify programs as vendors distributed only object code. Even when vendors gave source code, they protected them by non-disclosure agreements and an agreement not to alter or share them with other users.

THE GNU PROJECT [2]

Richard Mathew Stallman (RMS to his friends) was born in 1953 in New York. He obtained a BS in physics from Harvard University in 1974 and joined MIT as a doctoral student in physics. Stallman was, however, more interested in programming. He dropped out of the doctoral programme and became a research assistant at MIT's Artificial Intelligence (AI) Laboratory. Stallman started working on several programs, including programs for the Lisp machine the AI laboratory was building. He and a group of hackers (ardent programming experts) promoted a culture of freely sharing ideas and programs. While working in the AI group, the laboratory bought a laser printer that was frequently jamming due to a bug in the software. Stallman wanted to fix it but could not, as the software was a binary object code. He asked a friend at Carnegie Mellon University (CMU) who had the source code to send it. The friend declined, as CMU had signed a non-disclosure agreement. This incident disturbed Stallman as he felt that when a customer buys a machine with software, the vendor should enable buyers to repair/improve it and not prevent it by not giving the source code. He made it his life's mission to free software from the shackles of copyright, non-disclosure agreements, and the non-availability of source code. In 1985, he resigned from his position at MIT to avoid legal problems that may arise in freely distributing software he developed as an MIT employee. The head of the AI laboratory allowed him to use the laboratory facilities and his office, which doubled as his home for many months.

Stallman began developing an OS modelled after Unix by writing an Emacs editor. He placed it in an anonymous FTP site on the Internet for anyone to copy. The Internet was not universally available in the mid-1980s, so Stallman distributed the editor on a tape for $150. He got an average of three or four requests weekly, and the money collected helped him defray his living expenses.

Gradually, he and volunteer hackers developed compilers and most Unix utility programs. He named it GNU (GNU is Not Unix). However, it lacked a Kernel (Kernel is a crucial portion of an OS resident in the main memory and performs tasks such as process and memory management, file systems, device control, and networking).

To freely distribute GNU, Stallman started a charitable foundation named "The Free Software Foundation" (FSF) in 1985 with the primary goal of promoting the development and distribution of source code of programs. The Foundation enunciated fundamental freedoms for the users of the programs. They were:

1. The freedom to run programs as they wish, for any purpose.
2. The freedom to study how the program works and change it to suit their need.
3. The freedom to redistribute original or modified copies of the original program.

These freedoms imply that a developer distributes a program's source code with appropriate documentation.

Stallman consulted legal experts and developed the format of an agreement to be signed by recipients of "free software". He called it a "copyleft" agreement (More technically, it is called GNU General Public licence). He also made it amply clear that free meant freedom/ liberty rather than no cost. A developer can sell a Copyleft software provided it adheres to the licence terms.

Richard Stallman **GNU Logo**

(Photos courtesy Wikipedia)

Meanwhile, he started lecturing about the merits of Free Software with missionary zeal, travelling worldwide. He was a persuasive talker, and computer scientists welcomed his ideas. Several countries established replicas of the Free Software Foundation. Richard Stallman inaugurated the Free Software Foundation of India at Thiruvananthapuram in 2001.

THE LINUX PROJECT

Linus Torvalds was a computer science student at the University of Helsinki in Finland from 1988 to 1996. He obtained a Bachelor's and a Master's degree from there. Operating Systems (OS) was a course of study, and he used a popular textbook on OS written by Andrew Tannenbaum. Tannenbaum illustrated the design of an OS by using a tiny version of Unix named Minix in his book. Meanwhile, Torvalds bought an IBM PC clone in 1991 with an Intel 80386 processor. He decided to write a Unix OS for this computer using the ideas gleaned from Minix. It was not a copy of Minix, as some alleged. He heard a talk by Stallman in Helsinki in 1991 and got a copy of GNU developed by Stallman. He found it did not have a kernel and decided to write one. He initially released a version of a kernel in late 1991. He named it Freax and sent it to Ari Lemmke, one of his friends, who was a volunteer administrator of the university's FTP server, to upload it. Lemmke did not like the name Freax and named it Linux (pronounced Leenux) without consulting Torvalds. Torvalds thought the name was too egoistic but consented.

The Linux source code was released as an open source licence-free software as it was mainly in C. Some device drivers, however, used assembly code. In mid-December 1992, he published version 0.99, integrating the Linux kernel with GNU components to create a fully functional free OS. It was freely accessible on the Internet, and many users found and fixed bugs. Over a period, the software evolved, improved, and became excellent. When Stallman saw a copy, he was unhappy as Torvalds had developed only the kernel and named the OS Linux. He suggested instead GNU-Linux as an appropriate name. The GNU group independently developed a kernel called Hurd, but it was less popular than the Linux kernel, which was considered better by most professional programmers. In 1996, Torvalds announced a penguin as the mascot for Linux. He chose a penguin as he was bitten by one in the Canberra Zoo while thinking about what to choose as the mascot. His friend Larry Ewing drew the first draft of a penguin, and another friend, James Hughes, named it Tux (Torvalds' Unix).

Linus Torvalds **Linux Logo Tux**

(Pictures courtesy Wikipedia)

Linux became very popular, and programmers developed and distributed many improved versions over the years. Debian Linux, Ubuntu, Fedora Linux, Linux Mint, and Open SUSE are among them. A company named Red Hat pioneered in distributing a cleaned-up and priced version of Linux with excellent documentation, educational material, and user support. IBM acquired Red Hat for $ 34 billion in July 2019. Versions of Linux are used today in various computers, from the tiny Raspberry Pi to the behemoth Frontier, the fastest supercomputer in the world. Professionals estimate that it has around 3 to 3.5 billion users worldwide.

THE OPEN SOURCE MOVEMENT

In 1997, a software developer, Eric Raymond, gave a talk at the Linux Kongress in Würzburg, Germany, titled "The Cathedral and the Bazaar: Musings on Linux and Open Source by an Accidental Revolutionary". In this talk, later written as a widely read essay [3] and subsequently expanded as a book, he expounded on the software development methodology based on his observations of the Linux kernel development and his experiences managing *fetchmail*, an open-source software. In his essay, he contrasted two styles of software development: The "Cathedral Model," in which an exclusive group of professionals develop complex software, and the "Bazaar Model," in which software developers publish a source code on the Internet and several users gradually improve it over time. Raymond credited the Bazaar Model to Linus Torvalds, whose Linux software was available widely for improvement. He also wrote about his experience in developing *fetchmail* using the Bazaar model. His central thesis is that if a source code is widely available for public use, testing, experimentation, and scrutiny, as in the Bazaar model, the faster bugs, design faults, security holes, and missing use cases are discovered and corrected by users, leading to better quality software. He succinctly stated his proposition: "*Given enough eyeballs, all bugs are shallow*". In contrast, in the Cathedral Model, only a few people develop software in a closed shop, and consequently, bug fixes will be slow, and there could be poor security.

Raymond's espousal of the Bazaar software development model had a broad impact. Collaborative software development using the Internet became popular. A new mantra, "release early, release often," was adopted by many groups. The Free Open Source Software (FOSS) movement with similar (but not identical) licencing terms to GNU took root. A slew of open-source software was released starting in 1998. Among them are Apache Web Server, Open Office, Firefox browser by Mozilla, GIMP photo editor, MySQL Relational Database Management System, Word Press content management system for web design and blogging, VLC media player, Blender 3D modelling software, GNU Compiler Collection (GCC), Python computer language, Ruby on Rails for developing Web applications, and Moodle Course management system. A notable free software is Android OS, produced by Google and used almost universally by smartphones. Android is free as it is based on Linux 2.6.

Eric Raymond **Logo of FOSS**

(Photos courtesy of Wikipedia)

Free software has permeated academic research. Many academic groups have released software tools to write compilers, optimisers for parallel programs, tools to benchmark computer architectures, and similar tasks to assist researchers.

EPILOGUE

The open source movement has changed the attitude on copyright and fostered collaboration and transparency in many fields besides computer software. A prime example is Wikipedia, written by volunteers and freely available and frequently updated by several authorised experts. Other movements are open hardware, in which design data, circuit diagrams, integrated circuit layouts, etc., are made public. Examples are Raspberry Pi and Arduino microcontrollers. Open Educational Resources (OER) are released under an open license and contain learning, teaching, and research material that permit no-cost access, re-use, re-purpose, adaptation, and redistribution. Examples include MIT

Open Course Ware, NPTEL, promoted by the Ministry of Human Resource Development in India, and Khan Academy. Other examples of open source movement are Open Data, which fosters publishing freely available data in several fields to be used and distributed, Open Journals, and Open Science.

REFERENCES

[1] Burton Grad, A Personal Recollection: IBM's Unbundling of Software and Services, IEEE Annals of the History of Computing, Vol. 24, January–March 2002, pp. 63–71.

[2] David Bretthauer, Open Source Software: A History, University of Connecticut. https://opencommons.uconn.edu/cgi/viewcontent.cgi?article=1009&context=libr_pubs

[3] Eric S. Raymond, The Cathedral and the Bazaar. https://firstmonday.org/ojs/index.php/fm/article/download/578/499?inline=1 https://pld.cs.luc.edu/courses/412/spr21/mnotes/cathedral-bazaar.pdf

57

ETA 10 Supercomputer—Genesis and Demise

PROLOGUE

Control Data Corporation (CDC) was a mainframe computer manufacturer established in 1957 in Minneapolis, Minnesota. It started manufacturing computers intended for intensive scientific computation as a competitor of IBM, which was dominant then. The central team of designers in CDC included the legendary Seymour Cray and William Norris. The first large computer it designed and marketed was CDC 1604, followed by CDC 3600, installed by many universities in the USA and at TIFR in Mumbai. CDC went on to manufacture faster computers, including CDC 6600 in 1964 and CDC STAR-100 in 1974, the first CDC supercomputer that used vector processing, and its speed was 100 Megaflops (Million floating point operations per second) (See Anecdote 18). Seymour Cray, one of the leading designers of CDC computers, decided to leave CDC in 1972 to form his own company devoted exclusively to design, develop, and market supercomputers (See Anecdote 40). The first supercomputer he designed was Cray-1, which used a pipelined vector processor achieving a speed of 160 Megaflops, making it the fastest supercomputer in 1975. It cost $8 million, and Cray Research sold around 80 systems. CDC, in competition, designed the CDC Cyber 203, 205 series of supercomputers. They were also vector-processing computers but were slower as the vectors were stored in the main memory rather than in vector registers in the CPU. In some problems that required long vectors, CDC supercomputers outperformed Cray. However, Cray dominated the supercomputer market.

In 1983, CDC decided to design the next generation of supercomputers to succeed the CDC Cyber 20x series. A group of Lloyd Thorndyke, head of the CDC advanced design laboratory, Neil Lincoln, the chief engineer of the CDC 205 project, and several other engineers convinced the CDC top management headed by William Norris that a separate corporation should be spun off from CDC to design it. The reasons given were:

- A new company devoted primarily to manufacturing supercomputers can generate capital by selling public and private investors shares.
- A small, specialised new company can be nimbler and make quick decisions to meet the challenging deadline of designing and marketing a new architecture supercomputer in three years.
- A specialist company set up to design state-of-the-art supercomputers can get government funding as an R&D project.

CDC established a new company named ETA Systems in 1983, a few kilometres from CDC headquarters, to design, build, and market a 10 Gigaflop supercomputer ETA 10 in three years.

HARDWARE DESIGN OF ETA 10

One of the first decisions taken by the designers of ETA 10 was to select the integrated circuit chip technology for the Central Processing Unit (CPU). Most supercomputers in the 1980s used Emitter Coupled Logic (ECL) as the fastest technology. However, ECL circuits consumed more power, and the packing density of ECL transistors was lower than the Complementary Metal Oxide Semiconductor (CMOS) logic. CMOS was an emerging technology, and the semiconductor industry put much effort into increasing the number of transistors packed in a chip. However, CMOS's switching speed was slower than that of ECL. The ETA design team decided to use CMOS technology in its CPU. To increase CMOS's switching speed, the team conceived an innovative idea of immersing the CPU in a liquid nitrogen bath at –196.5°C (Nitrogen is an electrical insulator). Studies showed that cooling CMOS circuits increased their switching speed by a factor of two, a speed similar to ECL circuits. The packing density of transistors in a chip increased dramatically by choosing CMOS.

The CPU consisting of 250 integrated circuit chips could be packaged in a single printed circuit board, eliminating error-prone back panel interconnection circuits. ETA engineers designed a printed circuit board with space to place 260 one sq. cm IC chips, each with 20,000 gates. Each IC had 284 pins, including 40 power and ground connections. The printed circuit board was a marvel of technology in the 1980s. It was a 41.9 cm × 57.2 cm × 0.64 cm 44 layers board on which the designers mounted logic chips and interconnected them using 75000 plated through holes. Each IC chip had innovative self-checking logic circuits to ensure reliability. At the board's end was a 3864-pin connector to connect the CPU to the memory system and I/O. ETA engineers designed an enclosure to store liquid nitrogen; up to 2 CPU boards could be immersed in it [1]. The system was a shared memory parallel computer with up to 8 CPUs. The memory system was mounted on the CPU enclosures and connected to the CPUs. Each CPU had 32 MB SRAM. It was a shared memory parallel computer with 2GB DRAM shared by all CPUs. Besides these, there was a fast communication system buffer memory to speed up communication between CPUs in the parallel configuration.

ETA 10 CPU Board being shown to me (third from left) and my team at the ETA factory

ETA 10 system had 10 I/O processors and used fibre optics to connect them to the memory—an innovation then. The CPU clock speed was 7 nsec. The largest 8 CPU liquid nitrogen-cooled system, ETA 10 G, had a speed of 10 GFlops, a very high speed in 1986. ETA systems also marketed an air-cooled version, ETA 10P, whose clock was 19 nsec and speed was 370 Mflops. To sum up, the hardware design was highly innovative and met the design goal of 10 Gflops computers.

SOFTWARE OF ETA 10

While hardware design was a triumph of technology, software design was an enormous failure. ETA software group decided to design an entirely new Operating System (OS) named EOS that was to be upward compatible with VSOS, the OS of the CDC 20x series of supercomputers. They also made a wrong decision to use Cybil, CDC's proprietary language (a derivative of Pascal), instead of C to write the OS programs. The non-availability of ETA prototype hardware compounded the software developers' problem in testing the OS. Cray supercomputer was shifting to Unix-based OS away from proprietary OS. Customers were also becoming more comfortable using Unix and were demanding it. The development effort of EOS was so slow that when ETA delivered the first ETA 10 to Florida State University, it was not ready, and the University had to run one program after the other manually. Towards late 1985, ETA bowed down to market demand and started developing Unix with the assistance of an outside contractor, and it was ready by 1987. Most users preferred Unix OS as EOS had many bugs. ETA could not run many important application programs as it had not developed the necessary software, including an optimizing Fortran compiler. Indian Institute of Science was evaluating ETA along with Cray and other supercomputers in the market in 1987. The institute sent 15 application programs to all the vendors that included ETA. ETA could not run some critical applications, such as NASTRAN, due to the non-availability of appropriate software. In contrast, Cray could run all the programs in record time.

EPILOGUE

ETA Systems sold seven liquid nitrogen-cooled and 27 air-cooled systems and had the best price/performance ratio of any supercomputer in the market in 1989. Despite this, CDC decided to close down ETA Systems in April 1989. The HRD manager asked around 800 employees of ETA Systems to assemble in an auditorium in Minneapolis and announced that all employees would be given one month's salary and terminated.

The three reasons for starting ETA Systems, namely obtaining capital from the market, making it independent of CDC's management, and getting R&D funding from the government, were not seriously followed up. CDC treated ETA System as a fully funded and controlled subsidiary, interfering even in its day-to-day functioning. The government gave no R&D funding. CDC's mainframe business was becoming unprofitable, and it was difficult for CDC to support ETA Systems. CDC tried to sell ETA Systems but found no buyers [2]. The software of ETA was poor. Liquid nitrogen cooling of the CPU board put off customers as the board cannot be removed abruptly from liquid nitrogen to repair as it would crumble. Each CPU repair required the CPU board to be slowly heated, brought to room temperature, repaired, immersed, and then cooled slowly to liquid nitrogen temperature. This repair problem was one of the most intimidating features of the computer, as the time to repair each fault would be a few hours. Besides this problem, liquid nitrogen needs replenishment as it would evaporate as the CPU board gets heated during its operation. To replenish liquid nitrogen ETA systems designed a compressor to take nitrogen vapour, liquify it, and pump it back to the liquid nitrogen tank. Customers wondered if they bought an ETA system, whether they would run a computer or a liquid nitrogen plant!

REFERENCES

[1] D.M. Carlson et al., The ETA10 Liquid-Nitrogen-Cooled Supercomputer System, IEEE Transactions on Electron Devices, Vol. 36, No. 8, August 1989, pp. 1404–1413.

[2] Rob Peglar, The ETA Saga, https://yarchive.net/comp/eta_peglar.html

58

Internet Goes Public

PROLOGUE

The United States government's National Science Foundation (NSF) funded CSNET in 1981 with some trepidation (See Anecdote 48). NSF soon found out that networking improved the productivity of researchers, justifying its investment. Meanwhile, researchers in the US were upset that they did not have access to supercomputers made in the USA, whereas their European colleagues had easy access to these supercomputers. NSF set up a panel in 1982 to find a solution. In 1984, NSF decided to fund the creation of 5 supercomputing centres with a budget of US$200 million and network them. The NSFNET network was a backbone net connecting the supercomputers and several regional networks. Any researcher who required access to a supercomputer could log on to one via NSFNET. The NSFNET was gradually upgraded and ultimately privatized, evolving into the Internet. I will trace this evolution in what follows.

ARPANET EVOLUTION

The US government's Defense Communications Agency managed ARPANET; by 1981, it shifted to TCP/IP protocol from the Network Control Program. In 1981, NSF funded CSNET and used TCP/IP protocol to connect to ARPANET, as we saw in Anecdote 48. In 1983, ARPANET was split into a civilian ARPANET and a defence network MILNET. The civilian net had 45 hosts, primarily universities and government research laboratories. On 1 January 1983 (called the "flag day"), ARPANET discontinued using NCP permanently and shifted to TCP/IP protocol. The US Department of Defence (DoD) made TCP/IP the standard communication protocol and encouraged all computer vendors to implement TCP/IP in their operating systems. Bill Joy, a University of California, Berkeley graduate student, incorporated TCP/IP in the Unix operating system. By 1983, TCP/IP had become the standard for interconnecting diverse computer networks.

THE EVOLUTION OF NSFNET

In 1982, NSF, DoD, NASA, and the Department of Energy of the US government set up a panel of 15 members that included representatives of academia and government research laboratories under the chairmanship of Professor Peter Lax of the New York University to advise the government on providing access to supercomputers to researchers in science and engineering in the USA. The panel submitted a report [1] in December 1982 and recommended that all researchers in science and engineering should have easy access to supercomputers through high bandwidth connections. The panel also recommended increased research in computational mathematics, algorithms, and software necessary to use supercomputers effectively and efficiently. Based on these recommendations, NSF allocated US$ 200 million in 1984 to set up supercomputer centres and invited proposals from universities. This initiative by NSF resulted in the establishment of five supercomputer centres beginning in 1985. They were the Cornell Theory Centre at Cornell University, the John Von Neumann Centre at Princeton University, the National Centre for Supercomputer Applications (NCSA) at the University of Illinois at Urbana-Champaign, the San Diego Supercomputer Centre at the University of California, San Diego and the Pittsburgh Supercomputing Centre as a joint project of Carnegie Mellon University, the University of Pittsburgh and Westinghouse. Immediately, NSF appointed Dennis Jenkins to establish NSFNET to connect these centres and the National Centre for Atmospheric Research (NCAR) at Boulder, Colorado, funded by NSF. These six centers were linked by a 56 kbps leased line using TCP/IP protocol in 1986, with technical consultation provided by NCSA, the University of Delaware, and Merit Networks. These computers were linked using DEC LSI-11/73 minicomputers, with TCP/IP software called Fuzzball (written by David Mills of Delaware University) as routers. NSF Network Services Centre (NNSC) was managed by BBN technologies and assisted end users of NSFNET. Figure 58.1 shows the NSFNET backbone.

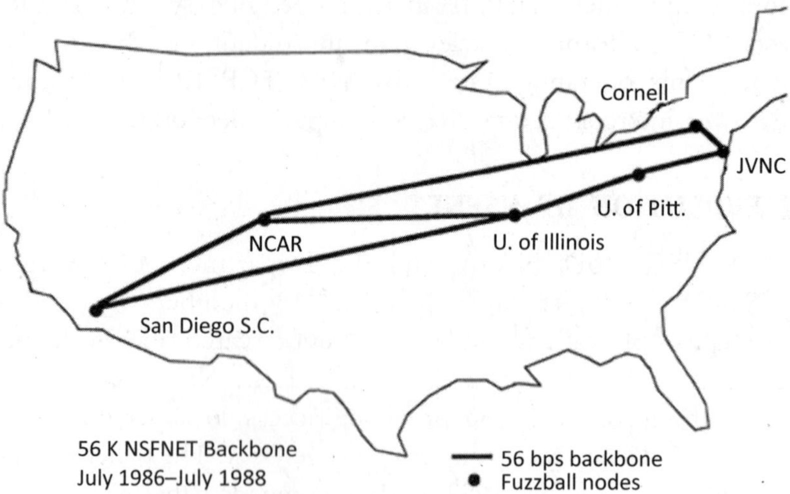

Figure 58.1 NSFNET with 6 nodes (Figure courtesy NSF)

Starting in 1985 and up to 1987, NSF assisted in creating several Regional Computer Networks connecting universities in various geographical areas in the USA. These included BARRNET in the San Francisco Bay Area, MIDnet in the US Midwest states, Northwest Net, NYSER net in New York State, Sequinet in Texas, WESTnet in Rocky Mountain states, SURAnet in the southeast US, and Merit Net of Michigan. NSFNET's 56 kbps backbone connected these regional networks. By 1985, PCs and Workstations with TCP/IP software were available at a reasonable cost, and they were connected to campus-wide Local Area Networks (LAN) using the Ethernet protocol. These campus networks were connected to the Regional Networks near them. Most university researchers were using PCs and Workstations for their work and could access supercomputers of their choice connected to NSFNET via LAN and the regional network. This three-level network configuration (See Figure 58.2) allowed easy communication and collaboration among researchers in almost all the universities in the USA. By the end of 1986, NSFNET connected over 10000 computers, and the backbone speed of 54 kbps was too low, leading to network congestion and user frustration due to long waiting time to get a response from the computers.

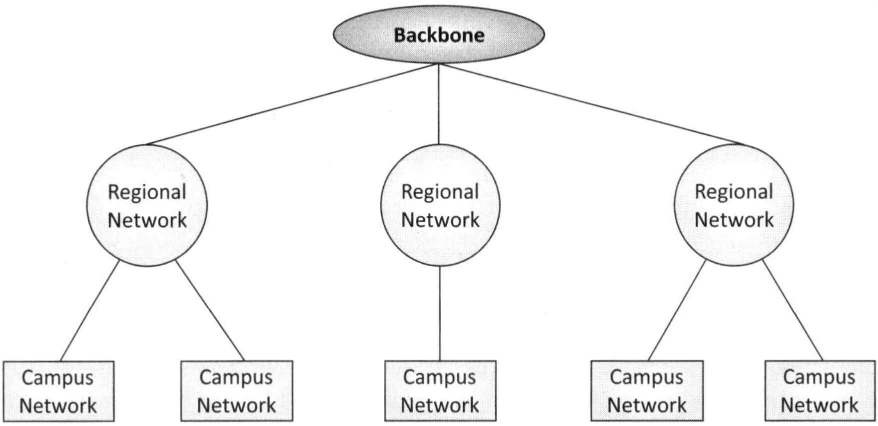

Figure 58.2 NSFNET backbone connected to Regional Nets and to member university networks (Figure courtesy NSF)

NSF decided in early 1987 to increase the speed of the backbone to 1.54 Mbps, a massive increase. Experience in installing such a high-speed network called the T1 network was scarce. Six vendors responded in response to the request for proposals to build the network; the best was from a consortium led by Merit Networks with IBM and MCI as partners. Merit provided research input and acted as the operations manager and user support. IBM supplied the routers and software. MCI provided the communication system. The consortium's bid to NSF was $14 million, $10 million less than the next lowest bid. This low bid was due to a grant of $5 million to Merit by Michigan state to get this prestigious project and provide employment in Michigan. MCI also reduced their cost by $6 million and IBM by $10 million. IBM's motivation was to participate with universities and learn in-depth the use of TCP/IP protocol in inter-networking. For MCI, it was a pioneering project as such a high-speed network did not exist, and there were promising future opportunities. The consortium did a commendable job, and the new T1 backbone was ready by July 1988 [2]. When the T1 backbone was ready for operation, the regional networks had increased to 13, connecting 170 campuses in the US and carrying 152 million packets per month. Usage was growing at the rate of 10% each month. As the T1 backbone speed was high, NSF decided to permit universities in several overseas countries (connected to their respective countries' education and research networks) to connect to

NSFNET. This NSF decision allowed US researchers to collaborate internationally. NSFNET became a global Internet.

PRIVATISATION OF THE NSFNET

In parallel with the growth of NSFNET, several private Internet Service Providers (ISPs) started email services, and the proliferation of PCs increased demand for their service. NSF enunciated an elaborate Acceptable Use Policy (AUP) of NSFNET and communicated it to all its users. As the US government funded NSFNET, no private or commercial use was permitted. This policy of NSF prevented industries from sending even emails to entities connected to NSFNET. Many grey areas emerged. Some regional networks allowed commercial use without using the NSFNET backbone. The ISPs improved their backbones and cooperated to share traffic with appropriate settlement policies. By 1990, the T1 backbone of NSFNET was operating successfully, and NSF allowed most universities to connect to it. ARPA decided to close its network in mid-1990. It was also clear that the T1 network would be congested soon as traffic was doubling every seven months. Foreseeing this, the Merit consortium decided in June 1990 to build a 45 Mbps T3 network to replace the T1 backbone. As this transition was expensive and the consortium saw future commercial traffic on this network, it decided to form a new not-for-profit company, Advanced Network and Services (ANS), with the same partners. IBM and MCI pledged to invest several million dollars in ANS. Merit informed NSF that it would subcontract all services to ANS and take overall responsibility for the operation of the network. NSF accepted this arrangement in September 1990 as it felt it could not invest as much as the consortium would. It allowed ANS to charge for commercial use of the net and reinvest the money collected in improving the network infrastructure. This decision was the beginning of NSF's privatizing its network. Meanwhile, the number of regional networks increased to 16.

In May 1991, ANS started a for-profit subsidiary named ANS CO + RE (Commercial + Research and Education) to provide a purely commercial service using the T3 backbone. This decision surprised other ISPs as they felt it was unfair competition. Universities were also unhappy as they thought the cost of using NSFNET would increase. An enquiry ordered by the US government cleared NSF of any blame as the long-range goal of NSF was to privatize the Internet [3]. Subsequently, ISPs and ANS compromised, allowing ISPs to use the T3 backbone. The transition to semi-commercial operation diluted the AUP of NSF, and commercial use of NSFNET started.

Meanwhile, the US Congress passed the High-Performance Computing Act in 1991, steered by Congressman and later Vice-President Al Gore. This act envisaged building a National Research and Education Network (NREN) connecting all libraries, high schools, and colleges. NSFNET became "interim NREN" [2] and asked to upgrade its backbone and regional networks to allow new members to connect to it. As NREN was to be funded by the government, NSF was in a dilemma as it was gradually privatizing the Internet. There was debate about upgrading the backbone net to a higher speed of 44 Mbps to accommodate the impending extra traffic.

After extensive consultation and public debate, the NSF decided in May 1993 not to have a new NSF-funded backbone. Instead, NSF asked the Regional and local networks to buy backbone services from commercial ISPs. NSF decided to fund building of four routers called Network Access Points (NAP) to connect the ISPs to exchange traffic among them and a separate very high-speed Backbone Network Service (vBNS with a speed of 155 Mbps) primarily to connect the supercomputer centres.

NSF awarded contracts in early 1994 (based on competitive bidding) to four companies for NAPs, MCI to build vBNS, Merit, and the University of Southern California's Information Systems Institute to manage routing in the entire network. The new network (Figure 58.3) started working in early 1995, and the T3 backbone was closed in April 1995. The US government diverted the budget allocated for NREN to developing Internet applications for education.

EPILOGUE

The number of ISPs grew with the privatisation of the Internet in the USA. The bigger operators did have an advantage, but there was no monopoly. The US government decided not to appoint a regulatory body to oversee the Internet. The policy of NSF to allow other countries to join the Internet led to its rapid worldwide growth. The invention of the World Wide Web in 1989 and search engines in 1990 led to a massive increase in Internet use, which became an

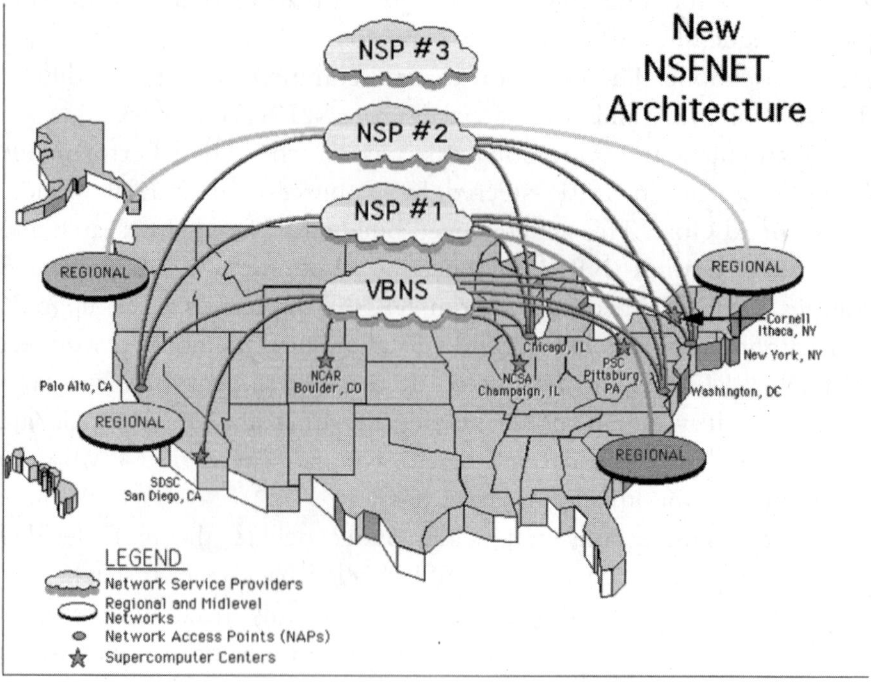

Figure 58.3 NSF Network in April 1995 (Figure courtesy NSF)

essential infrastructure in the World. Numerous problems arose with the rapid growth of computers connected to the Internet. The first was assigning addresses to computers connected to the Internet to ease communication. Postel and his team invented the Domain Name System to solve this problem (See Anecdote 51). The second was managing the backbone and solving technical issues, including security. This task was assigned to the Internet Engineering Task Force (IETF). The third was ensuring international cooperation and standards. Currently, the Internet Society is responsible for this activity.

REFERENCES

[1] Peter Lax, Report of the Panel on Large Scale Computing in Sciencc and Engineering, December 28, 1982. https://www.nsf.gov/news/special_reports/nsf-net/images/lax_report_1982.pdf

[2] Janet Abbate, Privatizing the Internet: Competing Visions and Chaotic Events, !987–1995, IEEE Annals of the History of Computing, January–March 2010, pp. 10–22.

[3] Report of Inspector General, National Science Foundation, USA, https://www.nsf.gov/pubs/stis1993/oig9301/oig9301.txt

59

Beowulf Cluster—A Poor Man's Supercomputer

PROLOGUE

The early 1980s were exciting times for researchers in parallel computers. The Cosmic Cube built at Caltech in 1983 showed that scientists could use a parallel computer built using off-the-shelf microprocessors to solve compute-intensive problems (See Anecdote 50). Several companies, including Intel, nCUBE, Thinking Machines Corporation, Meiko, Parsytech, and CDAC built parallel computers and successfully marketed them in the early and mid-eighties. In parallel with these developments, Cray also built the XMP and YMP series of expensive parallel supercomputers, which had the advantage of numerous well-tested application programs. However, users of parallel computers confronted significant problems in the late 1980s. One was vendor instability. Many parallel computer manufacturers had a short life span. In addition, these parallel computers were incompatible. Even programs written in a high-level language such as Fortran on one machine could not be run on another vendor's machine because the primitives developed by vendors to communicate among processes were proprietary.

Meanwhile, in 1991, the US Congress passed the High-Performance Computing Act, which led to the creation of the High-Performance Computing and Communication Program (HPCC) in early 1992. One of the significant successes of HPCC was the creation of the

Internet (See Anedote 58). Besides, HPCC also funded many academic institutes government research laboratories to buy supercomputers and provided research funding to develop parallel computers. The National Aeronautics and Space Administration's (NASA) laboratories were among the laboratories that received funding from HPCC to design and develop parallel computers.

THE GENESIS OF THE BEOWULF CLUSTER

A Center of Excellence in Space Data and Information Sciences (CESDIS) was established at the Goddard Flight Center of NASA at Greenbelt, Maryland, as one of the HPCC-funded projects. One of its goals was to build a supercomputer with a teraflop speed by 1997. James Fischer, who headed the supercomputer project, started a project to build one and invited Thomas Sterling, a scientist at NASA, to join the effort. Coincidentally, Donald Becker, a friend and a previous colleague of Sterling's, was his house guest waiting to join another government laboratory. Becker was an expert in Linux, an open-source operating system. Sterling and Becker informally discussed issues related to the networking of computers and the role of Linux in such networks. Becker's prospective employer did not issue the appointment letter due to some bureaucratic problems. Sterling, who had been grappling with the problem of building a parallel computer, had a flash of intuition and thought it would be possible to construct a parallel computer using the processors of PCs and networking them using Linux as the operating system. He felt that Becker's expertise in Linux would be invaluable in this effort.

Sterling requested Fischer to recruit Becker to work with him on the supercomputer project. Fischer agreed and formed a team of half a dozen scientists with Sterling and Becker in the lead. When the administrator of the NASA laboratory asked Sterling for the name of the project, he had not thought of one. In the spur of the moment, he remembered that he had an old English epic belonging to his mother (a scholar in English), which had Beowulf as its hero and named the project Beowulf [1]. In the epic, the warrior Unferth doubted Beowulf's ability to slay the monster Grendel, who had been tormenting the Danes for twelve years. To everyone's surprise, Beowulf slayed it. However, when colleagues and others asked, "Why Beowulf?" his standard reply was "an underdog challenging a formidable opponent," meaning the established parallel computer vendors.

Thomas Sterling standing in front of a Naegling 10 GFLOPS Beowulf cluster at Caltech (Photo courtesy https://spinoff.nasa.gov/Spinoff2020/it_1.html)

THE FIRST BEOWULF CLUSTER [2]

The team led by Sterling decided to use motherboards with an Intel 40486 (model DX4) with a clock speed of 100 MHz and 16 MB RAM as the primary computing engine. The model DX4 was one of the fastest in the x486 family, with 16KB primary cache and 256 KB secondary cache memory. It had a built-in math co-processor. A 500 MB disk drive was attached to each board. Sixteen of these computers (without keyboard and display) were networked using two Ethernet cables, each with a peak speed of 10 Megabits per second. The team used two Ethernets to increase the speed of communication between processors to around 20 Megabits per second. This decision enabled faster message-passing between processes running on remote computers. Higher-speed Ethernets were not available when the team built this cluster in 1993. The group wrote a special device driver to manage the communication of packets in the network with a dual Ethernet connection. Writing a special device driver was possible as the system used a Linux operating system whose source code was available. A PC with a display and a keyboard managed the networked computers, called a *cluster.*

This cluster was named Beowulf and was used to solve benchmark problems, such as a 2-dimensional fluid dynamics code and a gravitational n-body simulation. Parallel programs were written for these problems using standard message-passing primitives. A 16-computer cluster was able to attain a speed of 60 MFLOPS. A Cray CRI T3D parallel computer with 16 processors ran the same program 2.5 times faster. Experiments showed that problems requiring many inter-computer communication did not perform very well.

The beauty of the system was that Sterling's group built it using Commodity Off-The-Shelf (COTS) components with not a single custom-made component. It also used an open-source operating system. This method made it a "make-it-yourself" parallel supercomputer.

PROGRAMMING BEOWULF CLUSTER

In the early 1990s, programming distributed memory parallel computers was not standardized. Each vendor added a set of primitives to Fortran or C to enable communication among processes running on remote processors. An effort was initiated under the leadership of Jack Dongarra in 1992 and resulted in a draft Message Passing Interface (MPI) Standard. He presented it at the Supercomputing '93 conference in 1993 and invited comments (Supercomputing is a conference on Supercomputers organized by the Association for Computing Machinery (ACM) and the Institute of Electrical and Electronics Engineers (IEEE) annually in the US). Based on the feedback, the first version of the MPI standard was released in June 1994 by a body of professionals known as the *MPI Forum* (www.mpi-forum.org). MPI specifies a public-domain, platform-independent, message-passing library of routines for several languages, including Fortran and C that a programmer can use to write programs for distributed memory parallel computers. Programs for Beowulf clusters are written in popular high-level programming languages such as Fortran, C, or C++ using the MPI library of routines for inter-process communication. This method makes the programs portable.

TWO INTERESTING BEOWULF CLUSTERS

A significant development was the demonstration of a Beowulf Cluster designed by the Centre for Advanced Computer Research of the

California Institute of Technology (Caltech) at the Supercomputing '97. Caltech's cluster consisted of 138 PCs using a Pentium Pro processor (100 MHz clock with a built-in floating-point processor) and 16 PCs with dual Pentium Pro processors. A gigabit Ethernet switch interconnected the PCs, providing fast communication between them. The front-end computer was a quad Pentium Pro with a keyboard and display. The cluster ran a benchmark program called the n-body problem to predict the individual movements of a group of objects attracted by gravitational forces. It attained a speed of 10.9 GFLOPS [3] and won the Gordon Bell Prize for the best performance at the lowest price at Supercomputing '97 [4].

Engineers at the Australian National University designed another interesting Beowulf Cluster called Bunyip. The computing node was a dual Pentium III with a 550 MHz clock, built-in floating-point processor, 384 MB RAM, and 13 GB disk [5]. Each node had three Ethernet Interface Cards running at 100 Mbps. There were two front-end computers Pentium IIIs each with a keyboard, display, hard disk, and CDROM. They also had two spare nodes to substitute for the failed nodes. It ran Linux operating system. The entire system including labour cost around $151,000. The system ran at 163 GFLOPS speed for an ultra-large-scale neural network training problem that was demonstrated at Supercomputing 2000 and won the Gordon Bell Prize for the best performance of a high-performance computer at the lowest price at this conference.

EPILOGUE

The building and demonstration of the Beowulf Cluster was a landmark in parallel computing. It heralded a flurry of activity by several universities which started building PC-based clusters in their laboratories. This gave experience to students in building and programming parallel computers. Researchers without access to expensive supercomputers could use clusters that ran at almost a GFLOP speed in the mid-1990s. Such a cluster gave users full control of the computer, unlike a time-shared centrally administrated supercomputer.

With the performance of PCs and networking speed increasing steadily and the cost per GFLOP of processors going down continually, Beowulf clusters are becoming very fast and cost-effective. Many companies are now custom-building clusters for universities based on the specifications given by them. The Beowulf community is active with a mailing list at Beowulf.org.

It is interesting to note that, in the last twenty years, more than 80% of systems in the Top 500 supercomputers list are clusters many of them using commodity off-the-shelf components.

Top 500 is a list published every 6 months of the fastest 500 supercomputers in the world [6].

REFERENCES

[1] Beowulf clusters make supercomputers accessible, NASA publication, 2020 https://spinoff.nasa.gov/Spinoff2020/it_1.html

[2] Donald J. Becker, Thomas Sterling, Daniel Savarese, John E. Dorband, Udaya A. Ranawake, and Charles V. Packer, Beowulf: A Parallel Workstation for Scientific Computation, Proceedings, International Conference on Parallel Processing, 1995.

[3] Supercomputing gets a new hero, "The Free Library", 1998 Nelson Publishing https://www.thefreelibrary.com/Supercomputing+gets+a+new+hero-a021071072

[4] What is Beowulf? http://yclept.ucdavis.edu/Beowulf/aboutbeowulf.html

[5] Douglas Aberdeen, Jonathan Baxter, and Robert Edwards, 92¢/MFlop/s, Ultra Large-Scale Neural-Network Training on a P III cluster. https://arxiv.org/pdf/1911.05181.pdf

[6] See https://www.tops50.org

60

World Wide Web is Born

PROLOGUE

With the opening up of the Internet for public use in 1988, Internet Service Providers started operations. Email became a killer application of the Internet. File transfer protocol (FTP) was invented by Abhay Bhushan at MIT in 1971, which facilitated the exchange of files between computers connected to the Internet. Scientists and engineers started storing files in their Internet-accessible computers and letting others share them. Various newsgroups began functioning. The Internet became a vast international network of information resources. However, accessing information was difficult as there was no universally accessible directory. The situation was similar to a vast library without index cards. Alan Emtage at McGill University developed a program called *Archie* to search for files on the Internet in 1990. *Archie* systematically visited anonymous file server sites and created a searchable database of files. Mark McCahill wrote *Gopher*, an application layer protocol over TCP/IP that navigated the Internet and created a menu-based catalogue of available files. It was a free service, but there was a move by the University of Minnesota to start charging for the service. There was a need for a better method of linking files stored in the computers on the Internet to enable search.

Meanwhile, in 1984, the Domain Name System was invented for naming computers connected to the Internet. By 1988, ICANN formulated procedures to allot names to computer servers of organizations. The time was ripe to create a system to systematically locate and retrieve files stored on computers connected to the Internet.

XANADU PROJECT

Ted Nelson was a visionary publisher and a computer enthusiast. In 1960, after completing graduate studies at Harvard University, he envisioned electronic publishing replacing paper publishing. Reading an article printed on paper is linear, and jumping to a related document and back is difficult. His vision of an electronic document was one in which a reader could navigate to related documents using embedded links and return. The links were two-way links that were unbreakable and called hyperlinks. Nelson started a project named Xanadu, whose aim was to create a digital repository scheme for worldwide electronic publishing. The system would allow authors to create, edit, and share interlinked documents, allowing the author to navigate to related documents and return. He was the originator of the idea of hypertext and hyperlinks. The project was named Xanadu after the fictional city in Samuel Coleridge's famous poem *Kubla Khan*. In Nelson's mind, Xanadu was to be a place where authors gathered and shared ideas to create new knowledge.

In 1970, he gathered a team of talented software professionals and started developing a novel electronic publishing platform with facilities to create hyperlinked documents. The project's primary objectives were non-linear linking of documents, version control, and micro-payments to authors whose documents are visited.

Ted Nelson
(Photo courtesy Wikipedia)

The project was too ambitious for its time. PCs had not appeared, and computer networking was just a dream. The project floundered. Nelson periodically resurrected it, but it is still a dream.

ENQUIRE SOFTWARE

Tim Berners-Lee was born in London in 1955, the same year Bill Gates and Steve Jobs were born. Both his parents were programmers. He tinkered with electronic components and built a small computer while he was a student at Oxford University, where he graduated in 1976. He worked in the software industry in the UK for four years. He was looking for a more challenging environment and joined CERN, an international particle physics laboratory near Geneva in Switzerland, in 1980 as a short-term contract employee for six months. CERN was a large laboratory with over 17,000 employees from over a hundred countries. It was building huge particle accelerators, besides research on particle physics. During his stay, he saw that scientists were writing research reports and storing them in their computers, and only a few close colleagues knew about them. There was no centrally accessible directory that scientists could use to know and, if relevant, retrieve the research reports. Computers were from various vendors and used different operating systems. He decided to write a program he named ENQUIRE that used hyperlinks within files and interconnected files. According to Berners-Lee, an old Victorian-era household compendium, *Enquire Within Upon Everything,* which he used to refer to as a boy in his home, inspired him to name the software ENQUIRE. He was primarily experimenting with hyperlinking within and across documents and experimenting with methods of accessing files on remote computers. When he left CERN, the program was orphaned and forgotten.

EVOLUTION OF THE WORLD WIDE WEB

Berners-Lee returned to England and started working for companies developing software for computer networks. He was unhappy with the routine work and applied for a fellowship at CERN. He re-joined CERN as a permanent employee in 1984. By 1988, CERN networked computers and connected them to the Internet. The old problem of scattered research reports in numerous computers and accessing them remained. The significant difference now was that CERN had networked its computers. Berners-Lee wrote a report, "Information Management—A Proposal", and gave it to his manager, Mike Sendall, in March 1989. In this proposal, he described his idea of structuring documents using markups and linking documents stored in diverse computers with hyperlinks to enable searching for and accessing research reports. Sendall did not fully comprehend the proposal's implications and was initially not enthusiastic. However, after discussions with Berners-Lee and Robert Cailliau, a Belgian computer systems manager at CERN, he was convinced and let Berners-Lee proceed with the project.

Tim Berners-Lee (Photo courtesy CERN)

Sendall gave Berners-Lee a newly acquired NeXT workstation (designed by Steve Jobs after he had quit Apple in 1984) to develop the software. NeXT had an excellent Unix-based operating system. However, it was not a popular machine. Berners-Lee proposed three crucial ideas. The first was to mark up each document using a notation called Hypertext Markup Language (HTML) that combined the ideas of Ted Nelson (hypertext) and of Charles Goldfarb, Edward Moshe, and Raymond Lorie of IBM, who had proposed Generalised Markup Language (GML) in 1969 and standardised it as Standard Generalised Markup Language (SGML) in 1986. HTML proposed a notation to mark documents with pre-defined tags and links to connect them with other documents. Unlike earlier hypertexts confined to linking textual documents located on a single host computer, HTML allowed linking multimedia documents stored in several inter-connected computers. HTML was a significant innovation of Berners-Lee. Berners-Lee documented HTML specifications in 1990. Berners-Lee's second idea was to use Hypertext Transfer Protocol (HTTP) to retrieve documents stored on interconnected computers. By 1988, the Domain Name System (DNS) had been standardised. Domain names came in handy, and Berners-Lee's third idea was to give a unique name to each document stored in computers connected to the Internet. He originally called it Universal Document Identifier (UDI). Later, he changed the name to Uniform Resource Locator (URL).

In late 1990, Berners-Lee proposed to build a system that described what a document contained (HTML), how it is related to other documents (hyperlinks), where a document is stored (URL), and how to access them (HTTP). After numerous discussions, Berners-Lee's system was named World Wide Web (WWW) by his collaborator Robert

Cailliau. While Berners-Lee was the innovator, Cailliau was a manager who was able to assist him in overcoming bureaucratic hurdles and devote his time in developing code. The first website of the World Wide Web containing information about the project was http://info.cern.ch.

It was not sufficient to have websites with documents stored in them. A means of finding and retrieving data from websites was necessary. Berners-Lee wrote software for this: a browser, but it could run only on a NeXT computer. He assigned writing a textual browser that could run on any computer to Nicola Pellow, an intern working with Berners-Lee at CERN. It was ready in December 1990 but was not easy to use.

In mid-August 1991, Berners-Lee published a project summary on the newsgroup *alt.hypertext.* This summary was the first announcement of the birth of a software application that was to revolutionise the usage of the Internet. Berners-Lee and Cailliau submitted a paper describing the World Wide Web to the *Hypertext'91* conference held in San Antonio, Texas, in December 1991. It was rejected. They, however, attended the conference and demonstrated the software.

Berners-Lee demonstrating World Wide Web at Hypertext'91
(Photo courtesy CERN)

In December 1991, Paul Kuntz, a particle physicist at the Stanford Linear Accelerator Center, was visiting CERN. Berners-Lee demonstrated the World Wide Web to him and retrieved information from a remote computer with his browser. Kunz was impressed, took the software, and created the first website in the USA, http://slacvm.slac.stanford.edu.

When CERN was informed about the World Wide Web, the administration initially wanted to copyright it. Berners-Lee persuaded CERN to place the entire software in the public domain. He argued that the purpose of the World Wide Web was to share information across national boundaries and that restricting the distribution would be counterproductive. In 1993, CERN placed the entire World Wide Web software in the public domain.

DEVELOPMENT OF BROWSERS

Nicola Pellow's browser was simple and handled only text. Soon, other institutions started developing better browsers that could work with multimedia. The University of Helsinki created a browser named *Erwise*, and the University of California, Berkeley developed *Viola*. These were not feature-rich, buggy, and were not supported.

Marc Andreesen was an undergraduate computer science student at the University of Illinois at Urbana-Champaign and was working part-time at the National Center for Supercomputer Applications (NCSA) there. In November 1992, he saw a demonstration of the World Wide Web and was impressed by its features. He was, however, disappointed with the browser he was using and decided to develop one. He persuaded Eric Bina, a full-time programmer at NCSA, to partner with him in designing a feature-rich browser that could support multimedia. They worked feverishly on the project and released, without much fanfare, a browser named *Mosaic* in January 1993. *Mosaic* became popular quickly as it could be installed easily on any computer, supported multimedia, and was relatively bug-free. Besides these, Andreesen reacted quickly to any suggestions for improvement and fixed bugs as soon as users reported them. Mosaic was available on PCs, Apple's iOS, and Unix. It made the World Wide Web well-known, and soon thousands of websites appeared. Mosaic became the standard browser as it was free and readily available.

After graduation, Andreessen moved to Silicon Valley, and venture capitalist Jim Clark funded him to start Netscape Communications. The company released in 1995 a commercial version of Mosaic called Netscape Navigator. It was very popular and one of the earliest user-friendly browsers with integrated graphics. Many browsers such as Internet Explorer, Mozilla, Firefox, Opera, Safari, and Chrome developed by many software companies followed.

EPILOGUE

Mosaic Browser made the World Wide Web famous by easing access to websites and navigating the Web. The World Wide Web grew from 130 websites in 1993 to around 2700 in 1994, 23,000 in 1995, 250,000 in 1996, a million in 1997, 2.4 million in 1998, a billion in 2007, and 1.5 billion in 2022. The main reason for this geometric growth of websites was because the World Wide Web software was free, non-exclusive, non-discriminatory, and required no permission to download and use. The Web became the most popular application on the Internet. In popular perception, the Internet and the World Wide Web became synonymous! Today, a Web presence is essential for every organization, big or small. Many individuals have personal websites. Many companies design and maintain websites for customers. Web page designing is an occupation!

The Web revolutionised publishing by allowing writers, musicians, and artists to self-publish quickly and inexpensively. Their works reached millions without their depending on intermediaries. It led to e-commerce, social media, and online education. Computing using remote computers was one of the goals of the Internet. Remote computing became easy with the availability of HTTP. The demand for information in many languages and the availability of articles on the Web gave an impetus to machine translation. The extensive corpus of easily accessible material on the Web enabled the creation of the now famous generative large language model-based AI systems such as ChatGPT. The Internet is an essential infrastructure, but it came alive due to the World Wide Web.

As I mentioned earlier, Berners-Lee persuaded CERN to place the World Wide Web software in the open domain. He moved to the Laboratory for Computer Science, MIT, in October 1994 and founded the World Wide Web Consortium (W3C) with financial assistance from the European Commission and the US Defence Research Projects Agency (DARPA). It evolved into an International standards organization for the World Wide Web and has branches worldwide. It conducts educational programs, develops software, and serves as an open forum for discussions about the Web.

REFERENCES

[1] Lenny Zelster, Early History of the World Wide Web: Origin and Beyond, 2015.
https://zeltser.com/web-history/

[2] History of the World Wide Web, World Wide Web Foundation.
https://webfoundation.org/about/vision/history-of-the-web/

[3] Walter Isaacson, The Innovators, Simon and Schuster, 2014, pp. 405–422.

61

Search Engines

PROLOGUE

When the Internet spread worldwide in 1988, several organizations, specifically universities, started storing research papers and reports in files on their server. Many were publicly accessible, called anonymous FTP sites, from where interested users could download the desired files. However, there was no catalogue of these files and no easy method to search and retrieve desired files. The World Wide Web was yet to be there. Alan Emtage, a computer science postgraduate student at McGill University in Montreal, created a searchable database of files available on anonymous FTP servers. He developed the software *Archie* in 1990 to search this database and retrieve a desired file. As the number of files was small, this simple system was adequate. The subsequent pioneering work was by Mark McCahill at the University of Minnesota. He, along with his colleague Farhad Anklesaria developed in 1991 an application layer protocol over TCP/IP he named *Gopher* (Gopher is a burrowing rodent and also the mascot of the University of Minnesota) that navigated the Internet and created a menu-based catalogue of a variety of files available on the Internet. Steve Foster and Fred Barrie at the University of Nevada, Reno, designed a search software *Veronica* in 1992 to search Gopher servers. Rhett Jones at the University of Utah developed in 1993 another search software to search Gopher named *Jughead* (Veronica and Jughead were named after the characters in the Archie comic). Jughead was faster and searched only a specified Gopher server, whereas Veronica was slower and searched all Gopher servers. Archie, Veronica, and Jughead were used extensively before the advent of the World Wide Web.

EARLY SEARCH ENGINES

Before the World Wide Web appeared, files on various servers connected to the Internet were isolated. The Web used hyperlinks to interconnect related files and the hypertext transfer protocol to navigate the Web. Web pages were scattered on the Web, and it was necessary to have software to retrieve the desired web page from this vast repository. Such software is called a *search engine.* Martijn Kester, an employee of Nextor, an ISP in the Netherlands, was perhaps the first to develop a search engine in November 1993. He named it *AliWeb* (Archie-like indexing of the Web). His method was to follow the links of a web page to other pages and create a searchable index. Most search engines have since used this technique known as *crawling the Web.* He also requested web administrators to send information about web pages in their websites and included them in the searchable database. AliWeb was not widely used.

Jonathan Fletcher, a postgraduate student at Stirling University in Scotland, designed a search engine called *JumpStation* in December 1993. It systematically crawled the Web and created an index of web pages using the document headings. Given a query, JumpStation searched the index and listed the URLs of web pages with the terms in the query. Fletcher announced the JumpStation search engine on Mosaic's "What is new" web page. The university was short of money, so Fletcher did not develop the search engine further or commercially exploit it.

At the University of Washington, Seattle, Brian Pinkerton developed the first search engine to be used widely. Called *WebCrawler,* it fully indexed the contents of all 4000 web pages in the World Wide Web in 1994. America On Line acquired it in 1995 and made it a commercial service.

Lycos, another search engine, was also based on web crawling and was developed at Carnegie Mellon University in 1994. Lycos was commercialised and was a successful search engine in the early 90s. It is still active.

Jerry Yang and David Filo, two Stanford University graduates, designed a search engine named *Yahoo!* in 1994. This engine used a manually created subject index of web pages. This method worked fine as long as the Web was small. Their engine had an excellent user interface and was popular. Indexing manually became impractical when the Web grew explosively. Yahoo acquired *Inktomi*, a search engine company, and expanded.

In the early 1990s, many search engine companies named *Excite*, *AltaVista*, and *Infoseek* appeared. Fierce competition developed among these companies. Danny Sullivan, a journalist, started *Search Engine Watch* in 1997, and it compares and describes search engines' features. It is still active.

RANKDEX AND BAIDU

Robin Li Yanhong was born in Beijing in 1968. After graduating in information management from Peking University, he joined the State University of New York at Buffalo in 1991 in the doctoral programme in Computer Science. He left in 1994 after obtaining an MS degree and joined IDD Information Services, a division of Dow Jones, soon after graduation. Besides his other duties, he started exploring search engines. In 1996, he invented an algorithm called RankDex, which ranked the importance of websites by examining the number of links pointing to them. Pages from higher-ranked sites are listed first when giving the search results. He patented his invention in 1996. Dow Jones was not interested in search engines, and Robin Li bought the patent. Li worked as an engineer at Infoseek, a search engine company, from 1997 to 1999.

Robin Li Yanhong
(Photo courtesy Wikipedia)

He returned to China in 2000 and started a search engine company named *Baidu* along with Eric Xu. It is now the foremost search engine company in China using the Chinese language. It filters search results and websites adhering to the rules laid down by the Chinese government.

THE BIRTH OF GOOGLE

Larry Page graduated from Michigan State University in 1995 and joined Stanford University's doctoral programme in computer science the same year. His doctoral adviser, Terry Winograd, a well-known AI researcher, suggested to Page, as a topic of doctoral research, modelling and analysing the World Wide Web theoretically as a giant graph. Sergey Brin graduated from the University of Maryland and joined Stanford University in 1993 as a doctoral student. His doctoral adviser was Rajiv Motwani (Incidentally, Motwani was a student of the first batch of BTech computer science at IIT, Kanpur). Motwani suggested the theoretical exploration of random walks on large graphs as a doctoral research topic to Brin. Brin and Page became friends and, while exploring their respective research topics, got interested in searching the World Wide Web for information.

Larry Page

Sergey Brin

(Photos courtesy Wikipedia)

Existing search engines crawled the Web, found web pages that had the search terms, and returned all these pages. As the Web grew, the number of results listed increased rapidly, and finding relevant pages from the list was slow. Page and Brin wanted to create a better search engine to retrieve the most relevant pages while searching and list them in descending order of relevance. In 1998, they invented an algorithm they named *PageRank*. PageRank determined the importance of a web page by the *number* and the *quality* of links to it. Larry Page acknowledged Robin Li's patent RankDex in his patent application for PageRank. RankDex ranked web pages by the number of links to them, whereas PageRank ranked pages based not only on the number of links to them but also on the *quality* of the pages linking to them. For instance, PageRank gives a web page from the Times of India site a higher weightage than a little-known newspaper. They named the search engine based on the PageRank algorithm *BackRub*. Scott Hassan, a colleague, wrote a program to test the idea.

Page and Brin had worked part-time on a library project as graduate assistants. Eugene Garfield, a library scientist, had suggested using citations of research papers to gauge their importance. A research paper with many citations is considered more important than one with a few citations. A citation by a Nobel Laureate is considered of higher value than that by an unknown researcher. Knowledge of citation index helped Page and Brin develop the PageRank algorithm.

Their research and algorithm implementation were promising, and they wanted to convert it into a product. Their research supervisors were keen to publish their work. In April 1998, they presented their results in a paper titled "The Anatomy of a Large-scale Hypertextual Web Search Engine" at a conference in Australia. The paper gave the basic ideas about PageRank but no details to enable them to patent it.

Page and Brin wanted to commercially exploit their search engine BackRub and find a more attractive name. A fellow student suggested googol (which is 10^{100}). They misspelled it as *Google* and gave it as the name of their search engine.

Page and Brin were academically inclined and wanted to complete their doctoral work. Instead of starting their own company to develop the software, they tried to sell Google to Yahoo, Excite, and AltaVista, among other companies, for a million dollars, including their consultancy. None of them was interested. Subsequently, Page and Brin started a company and began looking for venture capital. On the advice of David Cheriton, a professor at Stanford University, they approached, in August 1998, Andy Bechtolsheim, who had founded Sun Microsystems and was a venture capitalist. They demonstrated a working model of Google, which impressed Bechtolsheim, and he immediately gave them a cheque for $100,000 as seed capital. They rented a house with an oversized garage in Menlo Park and established Google Inc. in September 1998. Soon, other investors, including Ram Shriram, an angel investor, David Cheriton, and Jeff Bezos of Amazon, gave $250,000 each. With a seed capital of $1 million, Google grew rapidly.

The unique feature of the Google search engine was its acceptance of a natural language sentence as a query from which it picked the essential keywords. The user interface was clean. Like all search engines, it also listed numerous results to ensure all relevant answers are included. However, it listed the search results in order of their importance. Users found the most relevant search results within the first dozen or so. To do this, Google used the results of extensive research on information retrieval carried out over three decades from the 1960s by Gerald Salton and his team of researchers and numerous other groups. These information scientists had conducted theoretical and experimental research to refine the results of searching textual databases to obtain the most relevant answers to queries.

All search engines are free to users. They have to earn to survive. The Web is live; it has hundreds of millions of sites, users add thousands daily, and thousands become inactive. Search engines have to continuously improve to stay competitive. Their primary source of revenue is advertisements. Google did not spend money advertising its search engine. However, its reputation as a search engine that gives the most relevant answers to searches spread rapidly by word of mouth. Its clientele quickly increased. Google linked advertisements with search results and charged advertisers, earning a steady revenue. In August 2004, Google made an initial public offering of shares at $85 per share and earned $ 1.67 billion. Page and Brin had assigned the PageRank patent to Stanford University. Google bought it for 1.8 million shares from Stanford University. Stanford sold these shares in 2005 for $336 million.

OTHER SEARCH ENGINES

The success of Google spawned many competitors. Microsoft dominated operating systems and made Internet Explorer the default browser. It entered the search engine business with MSN search by using Inktomi and AltaVista at the beginning of 1998. It was not popular. It decided to design a search engine and make it the default engine in Internet Explorer in 2005. This engine was called *Bing*. Microsoft, with its vast resources, promoted Bing aggressively. Despite this, Bing has not been able to capture more than 5% of the searches.

Another notable search engine is *DuckDuckGo*, founded in 2008 with user privacy as its unique selling point. Several users allege that Google and other search engines "sell" the data on users and what they searched to third parties and government intelligence agencies. DuckDuckGo guarantees not storing user search data and respecting the privacy of customers.

At the last count, there are over a dozen search engines in the market, but Google is dominant with over 90% of the market share, with Bing being closest with around 5%. Russian language search engine Yandex is third, followed by Yahoo and DuckDuckGo. Baidu has captured the Chinese market. Google became so popular that it was added to the Oxford English Dictionary in 2006 as a verb!

Two graduates of IIT, Delhi, Anurag Dod and Gaurav Mishra, started a search engine called Guruji in 2006, catering to the specific requirements of Indian clientele. It became popular by retrieving music from music sites (allegedly hosting pirated music) and playing it at users' request. It folded up in 2010, accused of copyright infringement by music companies.

Establishing and running a search engine is expensive. There are over a billion websites, and they are dynamic. There are hundreds of millions of search requests every day. To cater to them satisfactorily, a search company must establish and maintain many data centres, each costing a billion dollars. Only very few giant companies can afford this capital investment.

EPILOGUE

Nowadays, smartphones are in almost everyone's pocket. It has become the most common device used to search the Web. To capture this market, Google wrote an operating system named *Android* in 2008 and gave it free to mobile phone manufacturers. Google also designed the Chrome browser, and it has become the default browser in Android phones and Google, the default search engine. The next most popular smartphone is Apple, with Safari as the default browser. Google paid Apple $ 9 billion a year to make Google its default search engine. Google thus captured the smartphone search market.

With smartphones, voice-based search would be more convenient than typing search terms using the device's small touchscreen keyboard. Speech recognition software is not yet mature enough to understand varying accents, and consequently, voice-based search on smartphones is not yet widespread.

Google is now part of Alphabet, its parent company, which has gone on an acquisition spree, acquiring Deepmind, an AI company, and many other start-ups. It is also a significant player in the emerging area of quantum computers.

There is an impending revolution in search engines with the advent of generative Large Language Models and Artificial Intelligence (See Anecdote 72). Bing search engine now uses ChatGPT to give search results in natural language. Google's answer is Gemini, which provides natural language answers to queries. The competition between Microsoft and Google is fierce (2023), and in due course, we will find out who wins.

REFERENCES

[1] Tom Seymour, Dean Frantsvog, and Satheesh Kumar, History of Search Engines, *International Journal of Management and Information Systems*, Vol. 15, No. 4, October 2011. https://clutejournals.com/index.php/IJMIS/article/view/5799

[2] The History of Search Engines. https://carlhendy.com/history-of-search-engines/#top

[3] Walter Isaacson, The Innovators, Simon and Schuster, New York, 2014, pp. 446–465.

[4] Gerald Salton and Michael J. McGill, Introduction to Modern Information Retrieval, McGraw Hill, NY, 1983.

62

History of Mobile Computers

PROLOGUE

As early as 1972, Alan Kay dreamt of a portable personal computer named *Dynabook*. Technology was not available in the 1970s to realise his dream. Xerox PARC researchers led by Charles Thacker built the first Personal Computer, Alto, in 1973, based on discussions Kay had with his colleagues (See Anecdote 34). Alto was a desktop computer. When microprocessors arrived, another team of researchers at Xerox PARC, Adele Goldberg, Douglas Fairbairn, and Larry Tesler, built a portable computer named NoteTaker weighing 22 kg in 1978. It was not marketed (See Anecdote 47). Osborne 1, the first commercially available portable computer, followed. It weighed 12 kg and was sold in 1981 (See Anecdote 47). When PCs arrived in 1975, they were soon interconnected using Ethernet to form Local Area Networks (LAN). These LANs and computers worldwide were interconnected to create the Internet in 1983. When the Internet was available for public use in 1986, followed by the World Wide Web in 1989, a computer not connected to the Internet was considered an orphan. Applications such as email and searching the Web for information require access to the Internet. Portable computers were linked to the Internet when Wi-Fi emerged in 1998 using Wi-Fi routers in a restricted area such as a home or an office. Natural mobility requires portable computers to be connected to the Internet while their owners are on the move, for example, while commuting to work on a bus. Such mobility requires a wide-area wireless mobile communication system to which portable computers are connected. A portable computer with a wireless connection to the Internet is called a *mobile computer.*

I trace the history of Wi-Fi in Anecdote 64. In this Anecdote, I will trace the history of cellular mobile communication systems and their use in connecting portable computers and smartphones to the Internet from anywhere at any time while one is on the move.

PORTABLE COMPUTERS AFTER OSBORNE 1

Osborne 1 sold in 1981 was very heavy, had a small screen, and was powered from the mains power supply. A genuinely portable computer would weigh less than 2 kg and would have a built-in battery power supply. Over fifty models of light-weight portable computers from different manufacturers appeared and disappeared during the years 1982–99. I describe notable portable computers in what follows.

Grid Compass 1100 was the first portable computer with a foldable screen (clamshell design). It was specially designed for NASA's space shuttle in 1982. It had 340 KB bubble memory, weighed around 4 kg, and cost over $8000. The first IBM PC-compatible portable was Compaq, which weighed 13 kg, had a 9" display, cost $2995, and was released in 1983. The first portable computer with a tiny LCD screen

Compaq Portable 1983

Epson HX-20 Portable

Apple PowerBook 500

Apple iBook 3G

(All pictures courtesy Wikipedia)

(4 lines with 20 characters per line) and a rechargeable nickel-cadmium battery weighing 1.6 kg was the Epson HX-20 manufactured by Seiko Epson, a Japanese company. It was released in July 1982 and cost $ 795. The first modern laptop computer with a trackpad, 10.4" LCD, Motorola 68040 processor, NiMH battery, and built-in Ethernet was Apple PowerBook 500, released in 1994 and weighed 3.5 kg. The first laptop computer with built-in Wi-Fi, Apple iBook 3G, was released in July 1999 and cost $1600. The antenna was at the back of the screen. Table 62.1 summarises this section.

TABLE 62.1 Summary of early portable computers

Portable Computer	*Year*	*Weight*	*Unique feature*	*Price*
Grid Compass 1100	1982	4 kg	Clamshell design	$8000
Compaq Portable	1983	13 kg	IBM PC Compatible	$2995
Epson HX-20	1982	1.6 kg	LCD 4 line display	$1600
Apple PowerBook	1994	3.5 kg	First modern laptop	$2200
Apple iBook 3G	1999	3 kg	First laptop—Wi-Fi	$1600

HANDHELD COMPUTERS

Handheld systems called Personal Digital Assistants (PDA) that had a diary, searchable address book, notepad, and calculator appeared in the mid-1980s. The first popular PDA was Psion Organizer I, manufactured by Psion, a British Company, in 1984. A popular PDA in the USA was the Palm Pilot 1000, released in 1996, which had an OS and graphics and was programmable. It used a touchscreen with a virtual keyboard. HP released a series of PDAs starting with Jaguar, marketed as Pocket PC. Even Microsoft entered the market in 1996 with a Microsoft pocket PC (Pegasus). Apple reciprocated with the eMate 300 pocket PC in 1997. Many PDAs/ pocket PCs appeared in the late 1990s and early 2000s, including a series from HTC and Compaq. Most later, PDAs/ pocket PCs could access the Internet using Wi-Fi.

Encore Software Ltd. and Picopeta designed a handheld low-cost computer called Simputer in Bangalore in 2002. It had Linux OS. The companies estimated it would cost less than $100, but it cost over $200 when they sold it. The vast market predicted at the estimated low price evaporated when the price increased. Another tablet, Akash, was designed and marketed in India in 2011 by an Indo-Canadian company named Datawind. Datawind priced it at $35 and could not sustain it due to the unrealistic price and poor quality control. The company ceased operation in 2016. With the advent of smartphones in the mid-2000s, handheld PCs disappeared.

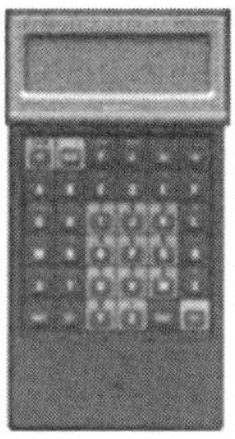

Psion Organizer

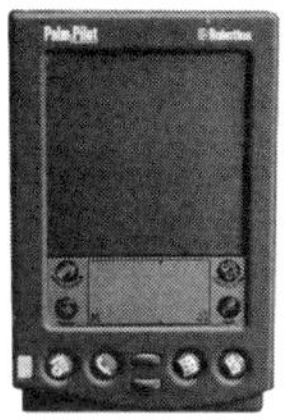

Palm Pilot

HTC Apache Pocket PC

Simputer

(Photos courtesy Wikipedia)

CELLULAR COMMUNICATIONS

Martin Cooper, an electronics and communication engineer, started his career at AT&T in 1953. He disliked the big company environment of AT&T and moved to Motorola in 1954. Concurrently, he earned a Master's degree in 1957, attending evening classes at the Illinois Institute of Technology in Chicago. He foresaw the need for wireless phones even though no wireless communication system for mobile phones existed in the USA in the early 1970s. In 1970, he convinced Motorola management to allow him and a team to develop a mobile phone. It eventually resulted in designing and developing a wireless phone in April 1973. Cooper called the wireless phone Motorola DynaTAC (Dynamic Adaptive Total Area Coverage) 8000X (nicknamed Brick). The first phone was 23 cm long, 4.5 cm wide, 13 cm deep, and weighed 1.1 kg. It had a 10 cm long rubber-coated antenna. A customer could use the mobile phone only for 30 minutes after fully charging its batteries for 10 hours! It had only three primary functions: dial, talk, and listen. Motorola applied for approval from the Federal Communication Commission (FCC) of the US government to deploy it in 1973, and the FCC took ten years to approve its use in 1983. Motorola released the first version of the DynaTAC mobile phone with an LCD screen and storage for 30 phone numbers in 1984 for $3995. Motorola reportedly spent $ 100 million to develop it, get approvals, and release it in the market.

Martin Cooper with his Mobile Phone (Photo courtesy Wikipedia)

MOBILE COMMUNICATION SYSTEM

A communication system for mobile phones was ready for use in 1982. This cellular mobile communication system consisted of several low-powered broadcast towers, each in the middle of a hexagonal cell. Each cell covered an area of a few km, forming a honeycomb. A mobile phone communicated with a broadcast station in its cell. When a phone moved from one cell to another, the cellular system handed over the signal to that station's broadcast tower. Thus, a person could converse using a mobile phone without a break as she moved around. AT&T and Bell laboratories developed an analog cellular mobile communication system in the USA during 1977–78. AT&T applied for permission to start a cellular mobile communication service soon after to FCC, the approval authority in the USA. FCC, however, was reluctant to issue a permit as it felt numerous mobile towers would spoil the looks of cities. After lobbying by AT&T, the FCC eventually permitted AT&T to start a mobile telephone system in 1983.

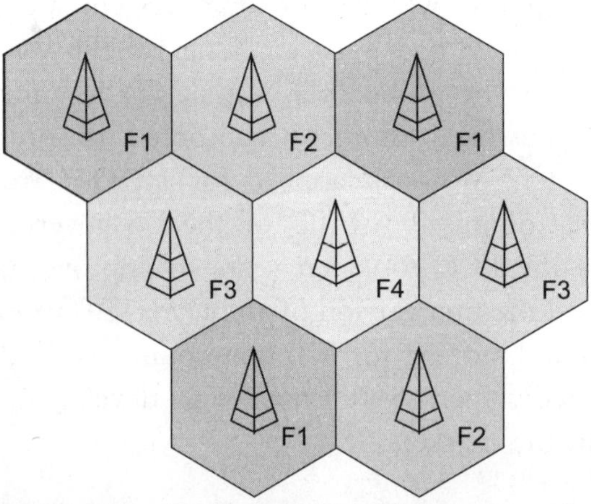

Meshed hexagonal cells used in mobile communication
(Picture courtesy Wikipedia)

Remember that Cooper invented the mobile phone in 1973! Telecommunication company NTT started a mobile phone system in Japan much before the USA in 1979.

The first mobile system in the world was called Advanced Mobile Phone Service (AMPS), an analog system. It is now named the 1G (First generation) system. The changeover from analog to digital systems occurred in the early 1990s. It was called the Global System for Mobile Communications (GSM) or 2 G. The European Telecommunication Standards Institute standardized it in 1991. GSM allowed SMS (Simple Messaging System) besides voice. It was a circuit-switched system. The next evolution, 2.5 G, allowed low-speed data communication (56 kbps to 115 kbps) and was followed by 2.75 G, Enhanced Data Rates for GSM Evolution (EDGE), which allowed data speeds up to 382 kbps.

An all-digital, packet-switched, Internet-compatible system called 3 G appeared in 1998. The 3 G system lasted for a decade. Staring with 200 kbps data download speed, it gradually increased the speed to 20 Mbps. The 4 G system appeared in 2008. It was an IP-based system using Voice over IP (VoIP) for conversations and IP for data. VoIP made conversations almost free, and mobile operators started giving unlimited free voice calls to subscribers. Mobile companies earn revenue from data usage. The primary use had changed to the Internet with the advent of smartphones in 2007. In India, Reliance Jio was a late entrant to mobile communication and started with a 4 G system, soon dominating the market by giving unlimited free voice calls and low-cost digital data downloads. The maximum data download speed of 4 G is 1 Gbps. The current mobile system is 5 G, introduced in 2019 in South Korea and 2022 in India. Data download speed in 5 G is 20 Gbps, upload speed is 10 Gbps, 1 msec end-to-end round-trip delay, and 99.999% availability. 5 G supports the Internet of Things (IoT), which professionals expect will increase. The next generation, 6 G, is expected to be launched commercially in 2030. Its minimum speed will exceed that of 5 G by an order of magnitude and will have enhanced security.

MOBILE HANDHELD DEVICES

IBM designed and marketed the world's first smartphone, called a personal communicator, in 1994. It was named Simon and manufactured by Mitsubishi Electric. It was a mobile phone, and users could also send/receive emails and faxes. It had PDA features such as an address book, calendar, calculator, appointment scheduler, notepad, and stylus to write on the screen. Users charged PDAs on a charging base. It weighed 510 gm, cost $899 (later reduced to $ 599), and sold 50,000 units.

The Nokia 9110 communicator, released in 1996, was also a combination of a PDA and a mobile phone. It could be used for email communication, sending/receiving faxes, browsing the Web, calculator, calendar, clock, etc. It ran a proprietary OS. It had a full QWERTY keyboard and LCD. It weighed 253 g and cost around $2500.

A very popular mobile phone cum PDA with a physical QWERTY keyboard, which could be used to send and receive email, and browse the Web, besides voice calls, named BlackBerry, appeared in 1999 and was popular with executives as it assured secure email. It had a proprietary OS. Research in Motion (RIM), a Canadian company, manufactured it. It was pocket-sized, weighing 140 g. It dominated the mobile phone market, and RIM sold over 100 million BlackBerrys between 2000 and 2010.

IBM Simon

Nokia 9110 Communicator

BlackBerry 7230

(Photos courtesy Wikipedia)

Steve Jobs of Apple computers revolutionized the mobile phone industry with the iPhone, which Apple released in June 2007. iPhone was the earliest smartphone with a large 9 cm (diagonal) glass touchscreen and a built-in powerful 32-bit ARM (412 MHz) processor with 128 MB main memory and 8/16 GB flash memory. It had a 2-megapixel camera, the first smartphone to incorporate a camera. It was small (11.5 cm H, 6.1 cm W, 1.16 cm D) and weighed 135 g.

Apple connected the iPhone to AT&T's 2G mobile communication system. iPhone had Internet access and could browse the Web and send/receive email. It could perform almost all the functions of a small computer. Apple also encouraged independent developers to write application programs (called apps) such as calculators, games, and spreadsheets for the iPhone and marketed them from Apple's App Store. Many apps appeared soon, making iPhones versatile and many app developers millionaires.

Steve Jobs with iPhone and iPad
(Photos courtesy Wikipedia)

Meanwhile, Google developed an operating system for smartphones named Android and distributed it free to smartphone manufacturers. The availability of Android encouraged several companies to manufacture and market smartphones with Android as the OS. Google started an App store named Google Play that allowed many independent software developers to develop apps for Android smartphones. Many inexpensive smartphones manufactured by companies such as Samsung, Motorola, and Chinese companies have appeared. Soon after 3G and 4G mobile communication systems appeared, smartphones proliferated, and currently, the number of smartphones worldwide exceeds 6.5 billion.

Another innovative handheld device was the iPad, introduced by Apple in 2010. It is called a tablet computer and has all the features of a full-fledged computer, including Wi-Fi. It has a large screen (26.6 cm). A mini model has a smaller screen (21 cm). Some recent models also have a SIM card and connect to mobile networks. Ten generations have appeared since 2010, and Apple has sold over 677 million iPads.

EPILOGUE

The advent of the Internet, mobile communication systems, and smartphones has changed how we live. Starting with reading the latest news, calling taxis to travel to work, making payments for the ride, sending and receiving emails, browsing the Web, searching for information, listening to music or radio, taking pictures and videos, making video calls, sending and receiving WhatsApp messages, video conferencing on-the-go and a plethora of daily activities now depend on smartphones and mobile computers. Wearable digital devices (often called smartwatches) have appeared that track our health parameters besides allowing phone calls and being wristwatches. The Internet of Things (IoT) also depends on mobile communication and is becoming ubiquitous. Environmentalists are concerned about how the massive amount of electromagnetic waves of various frequencies spewed would affect life forms. Only time will tell. We hope that we have not irreversibly changed the environment for future generations.

REFERENCES

[1] History and evolution of mobile computing, https://www.javatpoint.com/history-and-evolution-of-mobile-computing

[2] Lincoln Spector, A History of Portable Computing, PC World, May 2010. https://www.pcworld.com/article/506838/history_of_portable_computing.html

[3] Richard Frenkiel, A Brief History of Mobile Communication. https://www.winlab.rutgers.edu/~narayan/Course/Wireless_Revolution/vts%20article.pdf

63

ASCI Red—The First Teraflop Supercomputer

PROLOGUE

The United States of America signed the Comprehensive Test Ban Treaty (CTBT) in 1996 along with the USSR and most other nuclear-armed states. This treaty banned atmospheric, underground, and underwater tests of nuclear weapons. The US armed forces had an arsenal of nuclear bombs. The US government continued developing more powerful nuclear arms over the decades since Hiroshima. With a test ban, the US needed to develop advanced computer simulation models to design better nuclear bombs, test them, and assess the safety and reliability of the existing arsenal. These simulation models were validated using the data collected from earlier bomb tests and those from ongoing laboratory experiments. Scientists who wrote simulators estimated they needed advanced supercomputers with hundreds of Gigabytes of primary memory, Petabytes of secondary memory, and a CPU speed of around 100 Teraflops. Designing such high-speed computers with the state-of-the-art semiconductor chips available in the mid-1990s was not feasible. Researchers predicted that computers will meet these specifications only by 2000 or beyond, provided the government allocates adequate research and development funds.

The US Department of Energy (DOE) (which oversaw the development of nuclear weapons) initiated "The Accelerated Strategic Computing Initiative (ASCI)" in 1995 with a funding of $900 million, whose aim was to develop supercomputers with a speed of around

100 Teraflop by the year 2000. The DOE asked the three weapons development laboratories of the US government, namely, the Sandia National Laboratories at Albuquerque, New Mexico, the Los Alamos National Laboratory at Santa Fe, New Mexico, and the Lawrence Livermore Laboratory at Livermore, California, to acquire appropriate supercomputers for modelling and simulation of the design of advanced nuclear weapons using ASCI funds. These laboratories gave contracts to build supercomputers to Intel (Sandia), SGI-Cray (Los Alamos), and IBM (Lawrence Livermore). First, off-the-block was Intel's laboratory in Beaverton, Oregon, which built the first supercomputer to exceed 1 Teraflops speed, ASCI Red, by December 1996.

INTEL PARAGON [1]

Intel got an order in early 1996 from the Sandia National Laboratory to design, manufacture, and install a supercomputer before the end of 1996 with a speed exceeding a Teraflop. Intel had installed a parallel computer called Paragon XP/S 140 at the Sandia Laboratories in 1993. Paragon used 3680 Intel i860 chips, each with 16 MB RAM, as computing nodes interconnected as a two-dimensional mesh using custom-made chips. Most computing nodes did not have a disk and were compute nodes. A set of service nodes provided user interaction. Input/Output was via disks connected to some of the nodes. The operating system (OSF/1AD) supplied by Intel slowed down Paragon. Sandia Laboratories jettisoned Intel's OS and collaborated with the University of New Mexico to develop a lightweight kernel software called SUNMOS, speeding up the system. In June 1994, the Paragon XP/S 140 system ran at a speed of 143.4 GFLOPS and was ranked number 1 in the Top 500 list. (Top 500 is a list published every six months of the fastest 500 supercomputers in the world).

ASCI RED [2]

The design of ASCI Red began at the Beaverton, Oregon, Laboratories of Intel in early 1996. Intel decided to design ASCI Red based on the Paragon. Instead of the i860 used in Paragon, it chose a Pentium Pro 64-bit processor with a 200 MHz clock, 8 KB L1, 256 KB L2 cache, and a built-in math co-processor. Each computing node had two Pentium Pros with 64 MB RAM per processor. The computing nodes were inter-connected as a mesh. Intel designed two custom chips, a Network Interface Chip (NIC) and a Mesh Router Chip (MRC), to connect the computing nodes to form a mesh network. The bi-directional bandwidth for communication between computing nodes in the mesh was 800 Mbytes/second. Intel partitioned the computer into five parts: 4536 computational nodes that ran the programs, 32 service nodes that allowed user interaction with the programs, 32 disk I/O nodes, 2 system nodes for booting the computer, and 10 networking nodes to connect to Ethernet and the Internet. The total number of Pentium Pros in ASCI Red was 9216. The total memory of the computational nodes was 594 GB. The system had 2 TB of disk storage. The configuration above was realised in several steps, starting with the first with around 3632 computing nodes in December 1996 at Intel's factory. This computer broke the teraflop barrier and ran at 1.06 Teraflops.

The DOE security requirement stipulated the separation of the disk I/O into two sections. One section was to store the data relevant to all classified computations. This section was to be permanently and physically disconnected from any network outside the laboratory. The other section was for unclassified work. The disk I/O design adhered to this stipulation.

ASCI Red designer Stephen Wheat showing Intel Vice President Rick Stulen the innards of an ASCI Red rack (Photo courtesy of Sandia.gov)

The speed of the complete configuration, which was ready in mid-1997, was 1.6 Teraflops. It occupied a 1600 sq. ft. area and consumed 850 kW of power. Sandia paid $46 million for this parallel computer.

Intel paid particular attention to the system's Reliability, Availability, and Serviceability (RAS). Intel provided sixteen hot-swappable compute nodes. If an application encountered a hardware problem, only this application stopped while all other applications ran.

ASCI Red had two operating systems; one was for user interaction with applications, and the other was for the interaction among the computing nodes. The OS designed by Intel for users to interactively develop and execute programs was a version of UNIX called TFLOP OS. It ran in the service part of the computer. The compute nodes' primary purpose was to execute compiled machine code and interact with other compute nodes. Users did not interact with them. Thus, they needed the support of a tiny OS that could fit into around 500 KB of memory. Intel PARAGON successfully used this idea in SUNMOS. Intel improved SUNMOS later to an OS called Puma. Intel developed Cougar for ASCI Red as a successor of Puma. It was lightweight, used around 500 KB, and ran on all compute nodes.

ASCI Red installation
(Photo courtesy of Wikipedia)

ASCI Red provided Fortran 77, Fortran 90, High-Performance Fortran, C, and C++ compilers. It used Message Passing Interface (MPI) standard libraries to develop parallel programs (Anecdote 59 describes MPI).

EPILOGUE [3]

The complete configuration of ASCI Red was operational in mid-1997 and ran at 1.34 Teraflops. Intel upgraded ASCI Red when it manufactured faster processors. The successor of Pentium Pro was Pentium II overdrive, which had a clock of 333 MHz, 32 KB of L1 cache, and 512 KB L2 cache. ASCI Red was upgraded using this processor in 1999 and ran at 3.1 Teraflops. ASCI Red was the fastest supercomputer in the Top 500 list seven successive times from June 1997 to June 2000—a record. It found a place in the Tops 500 list up to 2005, nine years after launch! Despite having numerous processors, the system was highly reliable. When Sandia Laboratory finally decommissioned ASCI Red in 2006, Sandia Director Bill Camp said, "*ASCI Red had the best reliability of any supercomputer built and was supercomputing's high-water mark in longevity, price, and performance.*" It was retired not because of reliability problems but due to the need to accommodate a faster computer. ASCI Red was the last supercomputer designed and manufactured by Intel. Intel focused its future efforts on designing faster processors rather than building systems.

IBM Blue Gene/L supercomputer, which ran at 136 Teraflops at the Lawrence Livermore Laboratory in California, achieved the goal of 100 TeraFLOPs computer set by the US Department of Energy in June 2005.

REFERENCES

[1] Intel Paragon, https://www.top500.org/resources/top-systems/intel-xps-140-paragon-sandia-national-labs/

[2] Timothy G. Mattson and Greg Henry, An Overview of the Intel TFLOPS Supercomputer, *Intel Technology Journal*, Q1, 1998. http://www.ai.mit.edu/projects/aries/course/notes/ascii_red.pdf

[3] Sandia's ASCI Red, world's first teraflop supercomputer, is decommissioned, Sandia News release, June 29, 2006. https://newsreleases.sandia.gov/releases/2006/asci-red-decom.html

64

Who Invented Wi-Fi?

PROLOGUE

Wi-Fi is now the most commonly used technology to access the Internet. At home, several devices such as smartphones, tablet computers, and laptops wirelessly access the Internet via a router connected to an Internet Service Provider (ISP) such as ACT or BSNL. Wireless access points to the Internet (called hotspots) are available at airports, railway stations, hotels, etc. In remote villages, Wi-Fi access is a boon. We cannot imagine a world without Wi-Fi.

A Wi-Fi hotspot connecting many devices.
(Photo thanks to techviral.net)

International Telecommunication Union (ITU) reserved several radio frequency bands called Industrial, Scientific, and Medical (ISM) bands in the ranges 902 to 928 MHz, 2.4 to 2.48 GHz, and 5.725 to 5.875 GHz for gadgets that used radio frequencies such as microwave ovens and MRI scanners. ITU did not permit their use for data communication.

Wi-Fi research began when the Federal Communications Commission (FCC), the telecom regulator of the USA, decided in 1985 to allow the ISM bands to be used for wireless data communication over short distances (less than 50 metres) in addition to their use in gadgets. Anyone could avail these bands without a licence or payment to the government in a restricted range with the transmitted power of wireless signal below 1 watt. Soon, the International Telecommunication Union (ITU) followed suit (ITU has now opened many more radio frequency bands for data communication in a restricted range without a licence or a fee).

WAVELAN

As soon as the ISM band was made licence-free by ITU, NCR corporation's Wireless and Communication Networks Division at Utrecht in the Netherlands started a research project to wirelessly send and receive data between their computer and cash registers using the 915 MHz and the 2.4 GHz bands. The research began in 1986–87 with Bruce Tuch as the Chief Technology Officer. NCR aimed to develop a system to connect devices wirelessly to a LAN (WLAN). It involved the development of both methods of modulating digital data to be carried by carriers in the ISM band and designing a protocol for orderly communication among devices in the WLAN [1].

Bruce Tuch
(Photo thanks to wifinowglobal.com)

There are three major problems in wireless communication using the open ISM band. One is interference from other nearby devices, such as microwave ovens that use the band. The second is security, as unauthorised parties may easily tap wireless signals. The third is that a wireless signal a transmitter sends to a receiver passes through thick walls, and the walls on the route reflect the signal. Thus, the signal arrives at the receiver along multiple paths with varying delays. This fact leads to interference and fading and, consequently, errors in received data.

NCR engineers designed a wireless transceiver system with the brand name WaveLAN that alleviated these problems. It used Direct Sequence Spread Spectrum (DSSS) modulation of the carrier of digital data that increased the bandwidth of the transmitted signal, thereby reducing interference from other devices. In addition, it used error-correcting codes. It encrypted the data sent for security. It solved multipath interference using a complex design of wireless receivers and having multiple antennas in routers. Data to be sent by WaveLAN was broken into frames (or packets) and sent one after another. As many devices transmit data using the shared wireless medium, a protocol is required for orderly communication. The protocol was Carrier Sense, Multiple Access with Collision Avoidance (CSMA/CA). WaveLAN Network Interface Cards (NIC) for devices were ready for marketing in 1990. WaveLAN used 912 MHz and 2.4 GHz bands and operated at a speed of 2 Mbps [1].

WI-FI EVOLUTION

When WaveLAN was successful, NCR offered its design for standardisation by IEEE LAN/MAN standards committee in 1990. IEEE agreed to standardise wireless LANs and formed a committee named IEEE 802.11. Victor (Vic) Hayes, a group member who designed WaveLAN and was a Senior Consultant on standards and Regulation at NCR, was appointed its chairman. He diplomatically steered the committee's deliberations between 1990 and 2000 as the committee agreed on many standards, such as 802.11b, 802.11a, 802.11g, 802.11n, etc., for WLAN. He is generally known as the "Father of Wi-Fi" because he successfully persuaded a group of industry participants, academia, and government representatives with diverse interests to agree on WLAN standards.

Vic Hayes
(Photo thanks ethw.org)

WI-FI ALLIANCE

IEEE published the 802.11 standard in 1997 with a 2 Mbps speed. This standard had two variants: IEEE 802.11b and IEEE 802.11a. IEEE 802.11b operated in the 2.4 GHz band and used DSSS modulation with a maximum speed of 11Mbps. It was published in 1999 and ratified in 2000. IEEE 802.11a, operated in the 5.8 GHz band with a speed of 54 Mbps, was published in 1999 and approved in 2002.

It used a modulation method called Orthogonal Frequency Division Multiplex (OFDM), which can pack more bits in a given bandwidth, thereby delivering higher data rates. A consortium of half a dozen companies decided to cooperate and built a transceiver in the 2.4 GHz band conforming to the IEEE 802.11b standard. The transceiver power was around 100 milliwatts, and the range was around 50 to 100 metres, depending on obstructions such as thick walls. The consortium employed a branding company, Interbrand, that coined the term Wi-Fi to rhyme with hi-fi, which was a popular term and created a logo. Using this logo and the name Wi-Fi indicates that a company using it conforms to the IEEE 802.11 standards and ensures the interoperability of devices manufactured by its members. By the end of 1998, Wi-Fi devices were available on the market (Wi-Fi has no expansion; it is a brand name). The Wi-Fi Alliance group initially had around six members and now has 550 members.

Following the IEEE 802.11b standard, IEEE 802.11a, g, n, ac, and ax standards appeared. All standards after IEEE 802.11b use OFDM modulation with forward error correction. IEEE 802.11ax standard released in 2020 works in either 2.4 or 5.8 GHz band at a maximum speed of around 10 Gbps.

WLAN PATENT OF CSIRO

A team led by John O'Sullivan with his colleagues Terence Percival, Graham Daniels, Diet Ostry, and John Deane started designing a WLAN at the Commonwealth Scientific and Industrial Research Organization (CSIRO) in Australia in 1990 using the ISM band to achieve a speed of 100 Mbps [2, 3]. John O'Sullivan was an engineer working on a Radio Telescope built by the laboratory that used radio frequency transceivers. His team independently found that OFDM with forward error correction would be appropriate in the design of WLAN. They also built novel transceivers that sent/received data at 100 Mbps. CSIRO filed a US patent for its invention of transceiver hardware design for WLAN in November 1993 and was granted a patent in January 1996. CSIRO scientists worked independently and were not part of the IEEE WLAN standards committee.

The WLAN Project Team (L–R) Graham Daniels, John O'Sullivan, Terry Percival, Diet Ostry, John Deane (Photo thanks to CSIRO Australia]

When Wi-Fi became popular, and many companies sold products conforming to IEEE 802.11a and subsequent standards, CSIRO filed a patent infringement case in a patentee-friendly court in East Texas in the USA in 2003 against a small company, Buffalo Technologies, of Japan for using WLAN technology without paying royalty. CSIRO won the case. Subsequently, it filed lawsuits in 2005 in the same court for patent infringement against a group of nine big companies, including Broadcom, Lenovo, and AT&T, selling Wi-Fi products. The companies argued vehemently that all the components of CSIRO technology, such as OFDM and forward error correction, were well known and were part of the IEEE 802.11a standard. The companies had, however, not patented their products. A trial took place in 2009, and before the court passed a judgment, the companies decided to settle the case out of court on their lawyers' advice. CSIRO won a settlement of US$ 430 million from these companies [4].

EPILOGUE

A patent case settlement does not automatically imply that the patentees were the inventors of Wi-Fi. The primary technologies used in the IEEE 802.11a and subsequent WLAN standards were OFDM and methods to correct errors that invariably occur due to environmental noise and radio signals' multipath interference due to reflections from walls indoors. These technologies were well-known and used in other earlier wireless systems. The CSIRO team had done several experiments and independently found how to combine the existing technologies to design a high-speed WLAN optimally. NCR had developed and marketed WLANs using DSSS modulation as early as 1990. The IEEE

802.11a standard that used OFDM and forward error correction to achieve high speed arrived at the standard after extensive debates that naturally took a long time. CSIRO, however, obtained a patent in 1996, whereas several companies marketed the first products conforming to IEEE 802.11a standard only in 1998.

REFERENCES

[1] W.Lemstra and V. Hayes, Unexpected Innovation: The Case of Wi-Fi, http://www.eurocpr.org/data/2008/Paper4-Lemstra.pdf

[2] Colin Ward, Wireless LAN, CSIROpedia, https://csiropedia.csiro.au/wireless-lans/

[3] John O'Sullivans talk, https://www.youtube.com/watch?v=tKQVocx33dA&feature=youtu.be

[4] https://arstechnica.com/tech-policy/2012/04/how-the-aussie-government-invented-wifi-and-sued-its-way-to-430-million/

65

Evolution of Graphics Processing Hardware

PROLOGUE

From the early days of computing, engineers were interested in processing and displaying pictures. Users wrote programs to transform the results of computation, which were tables of numbers, into graphs, bar charts, and pie charts and print them. Ivan Sutherland wrote the first program to draw, process, and display images on a Cathode Ray Tube (CRT) display in 1963 using an interactive TX-2 computer. (See Anecdote 37). An interactive computer with a CRT screen is essential for a meaningful graphics display. A group of computer science students at the University of Utah led by David Evans and Ivan Sutherland were pioneers in graphics processing. They wrote programs to process and display realistic 3D images and animation using powerful time-shared computers such as DEC 10 (See Anecdote 37). The Central Processing Unit (CPU) performed all graphics-related calculations. As the CPUs of computers were not designed for processing graphics, the display of results was slow.

A significant development in graphics was the release of the IBM 2250 graphics processing and display unit in the mid-1960s, which was used up to the late 1970s as an add-on unit to IBM's 360 and 370 series mainframe computers. It relieved the CPU from performing graphics operations. It had a dedicated graphics processor and memory and could display images on a specially designed CRT display with a 1024 × 780 pixels resolution. It was expensive, costing around $30,000, and only big-budget organizations used it for computer-aided design and complex simulations in science and engineering. IBM 2250 displayed the results as graphs.

Evans and Sutherland established a company to develop graphics-oriented computers and display devices in 1968. Only medium-scale integrated circuits were available in the late 1960s and early 1970s. Evans and Sutherland's graphics-oriented computers used these; consequently, they were good during this period but expensive. Graphics processing hardware came of age only when large-scale integrated circuits emerged in the late 1970s.

GRAPHICS PIPELINE

In essence, graphics processing involves displaying three-dimensional (3D) objects on a two-dimensional (2D) display. The appearance and colour of a 3D object (such as a teapot) and the shadow it casts depend on the light source that illuminates it and the point from where one views it. These are mathematically modelled and processed to display them realistically. The model usually consists of a set of triangles of various sizes with their vertices represented by (x, y, z) coordinates with added data related to colour, shininess, transparency, and transformation matrices used to position, rotate, and scale objects in 3D space, lighting information, camera position, texture, etc. This set, called graphics primitives, is quite large, with tens of thousands of elements. Graphics programmers mathematically model the object. The transformation of this model into pixels to be displayed on a 2D display with appropriate colours, shading, culling (removing objects that do not contribute to the final image), and texture requires a series of mathematical calculations using matrices performed one after the other in stages such as in an assembly line. These stages constitute what is known as a *graphics pipeline*. Graphics processing streams the graphics primitives modelling 3D objects through the graphics pipeline one after another. As the calculations carried out at successive stages overlap in time (as it is an assembly line), the graphics pipe vastly increases the number of frames displayed per second. Graphic pipeline simultaneously processes (in parallel) thousands of graphics primitives representing a scene and pixels, as they are independent. Thus, graphics processing uses several graphics pipelines that work in parallel. The history of graphics processing hardware is how the computations performed by these graphics pipeline stages evolved from being programmed on a CPU to being carried out entirely by hardware. The pipeline stages were gradually integrated into chips over two decades (1980 to 2000) with the increase in transistors in a chip. Graphics chip designers added pipeline stages to a graphics chip starting from the rendering stage, with some programmable. In the final avatar, thousands of graphic pipelines working in parallel were all integrated into a single graphics processing unit.

GRAPHICS CARDS

When Personal Computers (PC) appeared in the late 1970s, with a CRT display as an output unit and interactive capability, graphics hardware got a push. IBM released in 1981 a graphics card for PCs called the Monochrome Display Adapter, which supported text and simple graphics on monochrome screens. IBM's next card was Colour Graphics Adapter (CGA), supporting 16 colours at a low resolution in 1982, a Professional Graphics Adapter (PGA) card with its own Intel 8088 processor for the computer-aided design market in 1984, and Video Graphics Array (VGA) with high resolution and 256 colours in 1985. These were primarily 2D graphics.

IBM assigned the task of designing the development of the next-generation graphics card to Mark Dean, who had an innovative idea of developing a dedicated processor for graphics rendering. In 1987, he and his team released the IBM 8514/A graphics accelerator card for PCs and workstations. It supported a high resolution (1024 × 768) display, 256 colours, animation, and scrolling. One of its features was programmability. It could accommodate different resolutions and colour depths. It was compatible with both OS/2 and MS Windows.

Meanwhile, Intel released its new generation of 32-bit processors, which led to a demand for sophisticated PC games and drove many companies to start manufacturing 3D graphics cards for this new generation of processors.

In the early 1980s, workstations from Sun, Apollo, Silicon Graphics, and other companies appeared. They mostly used Motorola 32-bit chips, had 21-inch displays, and targeted the computer-aided design, engineering, and science simulation markets. These workstation manufacturers designed sophisticated 3D graphics cards using integrated circuits. Silicon Graphics was a leader in graphics-oriented workstations with excellent 3D graphics. Silicon Graphics designed an application programming interface called Open GL (Open Graphics Library) in 1992 which was used extensively in graphics-oriented programming in areas such as computer-aided design, scientific visualisation, and video games. Silicon Graphics also developed graphics accelerators for its workstations: Reality Engine and Infinite Reality. It became a premier graphics workstation vendor in the mid-1990s. The rapid growth of PCs with excellent graphics at lower cost ate into its market. It went bankrupt, and Rackable Systems acquired it in 2009.

Graphics chips started appearing as the demand for sophisticated 3D graphics increased, particularly from PC gamers. 3D Labs introduced one of the first 3D graphics accelerator chips called GLINT in 1994. It gave almost workstation-style graphics to PCs. Another manufacturer, Diamond, released the Stealth video card in 1994, which had fast 2D performance and excellent 3D capabilities and was popular among computer gamers. A significant milestone was the release of the Voodoo 3D graphics accelerator card by a company named 3Dfx in 1996, which was a top-rated add-on card to PCs.

Another notable development was a project initiated by Sony to design a graphics processor for the Sony Play Station 3 gaming console. Sony, Toshiba, and IBM developed the Cell Broadband Engine for high-speed graphics processing in 2005.

GRAPHICS PROCESSING UNITS [1,2]

As I mentioned earlier, the history of graphics processing hardware began from the rendering stage of the graphics pipeline made into an integrated circuit chip. This chip was used in add-on cards to computers to relieve the CPU of this task. As the number of transistors that IC designers could integrate into an integrated circuit chip increased, IC designers integrated the entire graphics pipeline in chips in stages. It finally became a single chip called a graphics processing unit (GPU). GPU worked as coprocessors of the CPUs of computers, relieving them from all graphics-related tasks.

NVIDIA was the first to design and market a GPU named GeForce 256 in 1999. It defined a GPU as *"a single chip processor with integrated transform, lighting, triangle setup/clipping, and rendering engines that is capable of processing a minimum of 10 million polygons per second."* (NVIDIA was struggling to name the chip when one of its engineers suggested

GeForce based on "G-Force" which describes the physical sensation of very high acceleration, and the name stuck. It is now one of the most recognized brand names).

NVIDIA GeForce 256 chip
(Photo courtesy of Wikipedia)

GeForce 256 was an integrated circuit with 23 million transistors. It had hardware transform and lighting, multiple textures, and programmable shading and could process 15 million triangles per second. NVIDIA steadily improved the GeForce series until the next big breakthrough happened in 2007. It was the transformation of a GPU into a General Purpose GPU (GPGPU). The adjective "General Purpose" implied that the chip was programmable and could be used not only for graphics processing but for many other applications for which the GPU architecture was suitable. The internal memory of GPUs had increased to hundreds of MB, and it had numerous parallel pipelines with fast mathematical computation capability using matrices. NVIDIA realised that scientists could use the chip to solve several parallelizable matrix-based numeric-intensive computation problems provided it was programmable. In 2007, it released CUDA, a language extension to C, C++, and Fortran. CUDA allows programming the GPU for many applications besides graphics. NVIDIA developed several Software Development Kits (SDK) using CUDA. NVIDIA implemented it first in a GeForce 8800 GT, with 512 MB memory, a 700 MHz clock, and a floating-point processor speed of 36 GFLOPS (32-bit). With the release of CUDA, the market for GPGPUs rapidly increased. High-performance Computers (HPC) started using GPGPUs as floating-point coprocessors. Its use in HPC demanded 64-bit floating-point computation capability and matrix multiply operations. GPGPUs improved, and by September 2022, NVIDIA released GPGPU GeForce

RTX 4090. This GPGPU has 24 GB memory, a processor clock speed of 2235 MHz, renders pixels at the rate of 443.5 GPixels/sec, and has 64-bit, 32-bit, and 16-bit floating-point arithmetic units. The floating-point speeds of this chip are 1.29 TFLOPS for 64-bit floating-point and 82.58 TFLOPS for 16 and 32-bit floating-point calculations. It has an additional execution unit called Tensor-core for matrix multiply operations in its pipeline. It has 76,300 million transistors, 16,384 CUDA cores, and 512 Matrix cores, dissipating 450 watts. It cost $1600—a reasonable price.

MAJOR MANUFACTURERS OF GRAPHICS PROCESSORS

Many companies started manufacturing graphics processors beginning in the mid-1980s. However, since the mid-1990s, two companies have dominated this field. They are ATI Incorporated (which was acquired by AMD in 2006) and NVIDIA. Besides these, Intel also manufactures graphics processors, but it has paid more attention to integrating graphics with general-purpose microprocessors. Recently, it has started designing graphics processors for mobile computers.

Jensen Huang
(Photo courtesy Wikipedia)

Kwak Yuen Ho
(Photo courtesy itbusiness.ca)

Three engineers, Kwok Yuen Ho, Lee Ka Lau, and Benny Lau, founded ATI in Markham, Ontario, Canada in 1985. ATI's first product was a 2D graphics accelerator card for PCs in 1991, followed by a 3D accelerator in 1996. A landmark was the release of a series of sophisticated graphics processors named Radeon 256 in 2000 with programmable shaders. It was a direct competitor of GeForce 256 of NVIDIA but did not have good programming support. AMD, a microprocessor manufacturer, acquired it in 2006. AMD continued with the Radeon line of graphics processors, steadily improving it. One of its most recent graphics processors is the Radeon Instinct Mi250X chip, used as the floating-point accelerator in the Frontier ExaFLOPS computer. It has 128 GB memory, 14,080 stream processors, a 1700 MHz clock, and 95.7 TFLOPS (64-bit) speed.

NVIDIA was founded in 1993 by three engineers, Jensen Huang, Chris Malachowski, and Curtis Priem, in Santa Clara, California. Starting with its first product, NV1, in late 1995, the company pioneered many graphics processing advancements, which I described in the previous section.

Intel is a dominant player in the manufacture of general-purpose microprocessors. It has also incorporated graphics processors as add-on chips with its CPUs. NEC designed the first high-performance graphics display controller chip μPD 7220 in 1982. Intel licenced it in 1983, called it 8720, and used it in an add-on graphics board. In 1986, Intel designed a graphics coprocessor (82786) for its 80386 processor. When it designed the i860, it incorporated graphics in it. It was, however, unsuccessful. In 1999, it designed the i810, a chipset integrated with Intel CPUs. This chipset provided an inexpensive graphics capability to processors in desktops and laptops. Intel continued to produce better graphics chipsets until 2018 when Intel embedded an AMD GPU - Radeon RX Vega M graphics to its 8th generation processor in a surprise move. All these graphics add-ons had reasonably good graphics performance for gaming, animations, and scientific visualisation but were no match to the GPUs of NVIDIA and AMD in graphics performance. However, in sales volume, Intel's graphics chips far out-paced NVIDIA and AMD [3] in 2020.

Intel, however, had ambitions to become a significant player in GPUs and consequently hired AMD's graphics architecture group leader, Raja Koduri, in late 2017 and several other AMD graphics group members and others in 2018. It started building a GPU for use in laptops for high-performance graphics. It was also to be used as a floating-point coprocessor for its HPCs. In October 2020, it announced a GPU named Intel IRIS Xe Max. It is paired with Intel's 11th-generation mobile processors, has good graphics performance, and consumes relatively low power (25 watts).

EPILOGUE

Graphics processing units have evolved over the last three decades from simple graphics renderers to programmable ones and perform arithmetic with matrices. Their arithmetic speed is in the TeraFLOPS range, and they are used as coprocessors in high-performance computers. Designers of GPGPUs have added Deep-learning-specific data types (8, and 16-bit floating-point) and instructions. The floating-point arithmetic speed of the lower-precision data types is double/quadruple 32-bit speed, which has spurred the use of GPGPUs in training deep neural networks. They provide intelligence to robots, self-driving cars, and many novel smart devices. They also generate high-resolution photo-realistic images in real time for gaming and entertainment.

The architecture of GPGPUs, with many programmable pipeline processors working in parallel, has made them the preferred processor in many applications. Two recent deep learning applications designed by OpenAI, ChatGPT, and DALL-E2, use high-performance GPGPUs such as A100 of NVIDIA. ChatGPT gives natural language answers to natural language queries. DALL-E2 draws pictures given a word description. For example, if you ask it to " Draw a picture of a man with a large hat riding a horse", it gives four different pictures, all with a man with a large hat riding a horse.

REFERENCES

[1] William J. Daly, Stephen W. Keckler, and David B. Kirk, Evolution of the Graphics Processing Unit, IEEE Micro, November/December 2021. https://ieeexplore.ieee.org/document/9623445

[2] Thomas S. Crow, Evolution of the Graphics Processing Unit, https://www.cse.unr.edu/~fredh/papers/thesis/023-crow/GPUFinal.pdf

[3] Jon Peddie, Famous Graphics Chips: Intel's GPU History https://www.computer.org/publications/tech-news/chasing-pixels/intels-gpu-history

66

IBM Blue Gene Series of Supercomputers—First to Breach 100 TeraFLOPS Speed

PROLOGUE

In 1999, researchers at IBM's Rochester, Minnesota, laboratories started designing a family of supercomputers for solving problems in cutting-edge biology research. The primary goal of the computer was to assist in the simulation of protein folding and gene mapping. IBM allocated a budget of US $100 million to develop this computer. It was named Blue Gene, Blue as IBM was known as "the Big Blue" (IBM painted its early computers blue), and Gene as IBM intended to use it to solve complex simulation problems in biology. Among the primary goals of the design of Blue Gene were speed of the order of 100 TeraFLOPS (Tera = 10^{12}), low power consumption (minimum watts/FLOPS), small size, ability to handle vast data of the order of Tera bytes, and modular design to enable the computer to be expanded in stages. IBM formed a small team led by Alan Gara, the chief architect, to design the computer. The team decided to use many custom-designed microprocessor chips that attained a speed of order of GigaFLOPS and consumed very little power. As the design progressed, Lawrence Livermore Laboratory, with a contract from the National Nuclear Safety Administration (NNSA) of the US government, decided to finance the development of the computer and install the largest computer of the series named IBM Blue Gene/L in its laboratory.

Blue Gene/P followed Blue Gene/L in 2007. Blue Gene/Q came in 2012. This supercomputer series was famous for its low power consumption, low floor area requirement, and high speed. These supercomputers found a place in the Top 500 list almost every year from 2004 to 2015 when IBM discontinued the Blue Gene series.

IBM BLUE GENE/L SYSTEM HARDWARE [1]

The building block of the Blue Gene computer was an Application Specific Integrated Circuit (ASIC) Chip. This chip consisted of two IBM Power PC 440 processors, each with two 64-bit floating-point arithmetic units, 64 KB L1 cache, 256 KB L2 cache, and 4MB L3 cache. The processor clock was kept low at 700 MHz to minimise power dissipation. The chip had built-in support to network it with other chips, support for a global broadcast of instructions, global interrupts, testing processors, and gigabit Ethernet for Input/Output. Each chip had an external 512 MB main memory. The dual processor chip was a computing node whose peak speed was 5.6 GFLOPS for single precision (32-bit operands) and 2.8 GFLOPS for double precision (64-bit operands) and power dissipation of 17 watts. The computer could operate the chip in two modes. The first mode used one chip for computation and the other for sending/receiving data to/from other nodes. In the second mode, both processors could compute and communicate.

The computing nodes were interconnected as a torus [2] (See Figure 66.1). The designers chose a torus because each node had only six links, provided high-bandwidth connectivity to its nearest neighbours, and allowed any node to connect to any other node with simple routing. The bi-directional communication speed between the nearest neighbours was 1.4 Gbps, and the latency was 3 μs.

Figure 66.2 shows the packaging of the chips to construct IBM Blue Gene/L. It was designed modularly as a set of racks (or cabinets). A rack of the computer had 1024 computing nodes arranged as an 8 × 8 × 16 torus (8 computing nodes along the X-direction (horizontal), 8 computing nodes along the Y-direction (vertical), and 16 computing nodes along the Z-direction (depth)). The largest configuration had 64 racks with 65,536 computing nodes configured as a 64 × 32 × 32 toroid. The 3D toroid was connected to 1024 I/O nodes. Each I/O node handled the communication to groups of 64 computing nodes.

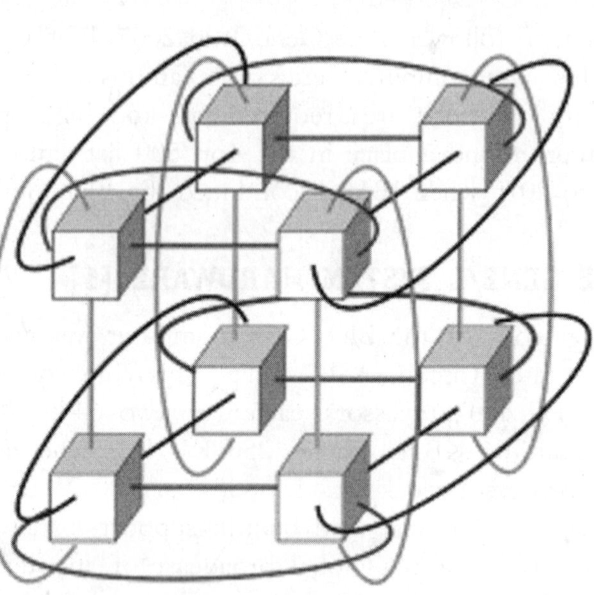

Figure 66.1 A 2 × 2 × 2 Toroid interconnection
(Figure courtesy of Wikipedia)

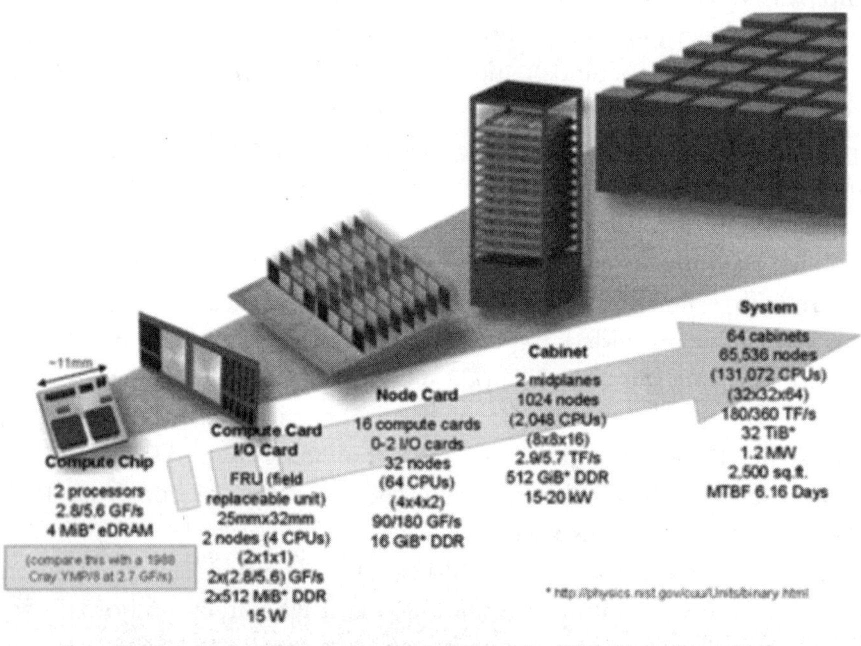

Figure 66.2 The packaging of chips in IBM Blue Gene/L
(Picture courtesy Wikipedia)

The I/O nodes were connected to a Gigabit Ethernet. This Ethernet was also connected to a huge disk system, front-end computers for program development by users and their interaction with the computing nodes, a service computer for maintenance, and a wide area network.

An individual rack with 1024 computing nodes could function as an independent parallel computer with front-end computers, a system supervisor computer, gigabit Ethernet connections to the I/O system, a disk system, and a wide area network. The peak speed of a single rack Blue Gene/L was 2.9 TeraFLOPS for 64-bit computation. A single rack dissipated 27.5 kW and was air-cooled. It cost between $1.5 million and $2 million. IBM sold Blue Gene systems in integral multiples of racks. The system used an innovative cooling method to uniformly cool the computer when multiple racks were interlocked and stacked side by side.

The designers paid particular attention to the computer's Reliability, Availability, and Serviceability (RAS). A supervisory computer was attached to the parallel computer to oversee the operation of the computing nodes to ensure RAS. The designers provided redundant computing nodes that could replace faulty ones while the computer ran.

Alan Gara
(Photo courtesy ibm.com)

The peak speed of the largest (65,536 computing nodes) system was 185.6 TeraFLOPS (64-bit operands), and the speed of running the Linpack double-precision (64-bit) benchmark was 140 TeraFLOPS. It was ranked number 1 in the Top 500 list in November 2004. It remained at the top of the list until November 2007. The power dissipation of the 64 rack system was 1760 kW. LLNL paid $133 million for the Blue Gene/L computer.

IBM BLUE GENE/L SOFTWARE

The individual computing nodes of Blue Gene had a lightweight operating system to control a single process and essential communications. The primary operating system users used to interact with Blue Gene was based on Linux, and it ran on front-end computers. The parallel computer could be partitioned into chunks of multiples of 32 computing nodes, and these chunks could be allocated to different users who could simultaneously and independently use these chunks. The computer provided compilers for Fortran, C, and C++. MPI standard library was also available for parallel programming for all these languages.

MARKETING OF IBM BLUE GENE [3]

IBM was known as an excellent marketing company. The marketing group knew that a computer costing over $100 million would have few takers. Lawrence Livermore National Laboratories (LLNL) required top-of-the-line supercomputers for weapons research, and cost was not a significant concern. Partnering with LLNL was valuable to IBM as the researchers there were experienced users and had programmed various supercomputers. Their feedback was invaluable during the development of Blue Gene. LLNL underwrote a significant part of the development cost of Blue Gene by buying the first IBM Blue Gene/L. As I mentioned earlier, a single rack of Blue Gene ran at 2.9 TeraFLOPS and cost between $ 1.5 and $2 million (depending on front-end, peripherals, etc.), which was affordable to many organizations. IBM sold around 17 IBM Blue Gene/L, mostly one or two rack systems. Customers were in the US, the UK, the Netherlands, Germany, Switzerland, India, and Japan. The Indian Institute of Science, Bangalore, bought a four-rack Blue Gene/L in 2007.

In another innovative marketing initiative, IBM announced the on-demand availability of Blue Gene/L to institutions in the US from their Deep Computing Capacity on Demand Centre in Rochester, Minn., in March 2005. Customers who could not afford to buy or rent the computer could get computing power remotely when they needed it by paying for the number of processors used by the hour. IBM provided a secure remote connection to customers and assured the security of customers' data and programs. This facility was used by many pharmaceutical companies for drug design, financial analysis, electronic design automation, computational fluid dynamics, and airframe design, to mention a few.

SUCCESSORS OF BLUE GENE/L [4]

Blue Gene/P (P stands for PetaScale) followed Blue Gene/L and had an architecture similar to Blue Gene/L. IBM announced it in June 2007. The processor of the Blue Gene/P model was an ASIC that had four Power PC 450 cores operating at 850 MHz. It also had built-in 64-bit floating-point units. The speed of a single computing node was 13.6 GFLOPS. The processor's main memory, external to the ASIC, was 2 to 4 GB. The computing nodes were connected as a toroid similar to Blue Gene/L. The communication speed between computing nodes was double that of the Blue Gene/L. A rack with 1024 computing nodes had a peak speed of 13.9 TeraFLOPS (64-bit operands) and a Linpack speed of 11.9 TeraFLOPS. The power dissipation was 370 MFLOPS/Watt, making it one of the most power-efficient computers. The computer was air-cooled.

IBM sold Blue Gene/P as one or more racks to around 16 customers worldwide, including the Tata Institute of Fundamental Research, Mumbai. Argonne National Laboratories bought the largest Blue Gene/P with 40,960 computing nodes, funded by the US government. This computer's theoretical peak speed was 139 TeraFLOPS, and its Linpack speed was 119 TeraFLOPS. It consumed 315 kW. It ranked number 10 in the Top 500 list of June 2008.

In 2007, the Top 500 organization introduced a new measure of ranking supercomputers called the Green 500. The top rank in the Green 500 was for the most energy-efficient supercomputer. The Top 500 measured energy efficiency of supercomputers as the ones with the maximum MFLOPS (64-bit operands) per watt. This measure came out of the concern about global warming as supercomputers were becoming power guzzlers. At 370 MFLOPS/watt, Blue Gene/P was near the top of the Green 500 list in 2008.

The Blue Gene/Q system followed the Blue Gene/P system in November 2011. The computing node of this computer was an ASIC chip that integrated 18 cores [5]. Each core was a 64-bit Power PC A2 processor with a built-in high-performance 64-bit floating-point unit. The cores shared a 32 MB memory. Of the 18 cores, 16 were used for computation, one for the operating system, and one was a spare. The processor used a 1.6 GHz clock. The computing node speed was 204.8 GFLOPS. Each computing node had an external 16 GB memory. Computing nodes were inter-connected as a 5D torus using fibre optic links. The link speed was 16 Gbps. A computer rack had 1024 computing nodes and a separate I/O system.

The largest Blue Gene/Q system was installed at the LLNL in June 2012, primarily for nuclear weapons research and development. It was a 96-rack system with 98,304 compute nodes and 1.6 PB memory. Its peak speed was 20.1 PetaFLOPS, and the Linpack speed was 16.32 PetaFLOPS. It occupied first place in the Top 500 list in June 2012 for speed and was first in the Green 500 list with a power consumption of 2 GFLOPS/watt.

EPILOGUE

IBM Blue Gene series of supercomputers were unique in using low-power dissipation ASICs as their building block. They were compact and used minimum floor space. Interestingly, a single dual-processor node of Blue Gene/L ran at 2.8 GFLOPS in 2004 and consumed 17 watts. In comparison, an 8-processor Cray YMP ran at 2.7 GFLOPS and dissipated 120 kW in 1989—a considerable improvement in 15 years! When parallel computers with a thousand microprocessors emerged as competitors to Cray computers in the early 1990s, Seymour Cray famously quipped, " *If you are ploughing a field would you rather use two strong oxen or 1024 chicken.*" By 2004, chickens turned into oxen!

The Blue Gene series of computers received many awards. In 2005, scientists of the Lawrence Livermore National Laboratories (LLNL) and those of IBM received the Gordon Bell award for peak performance for the first scientific application to exceed 100 TeraFLOPS of sustained performance using Blue Gene/L. In 2009, the Blue Gene family of supercomputers received the National Medal for Technology and Innovation from President Barack Obama. At the Supercomputer Conference of 2020, scientists of LLNL and IBM received the "Test of Time Award" for a paper outlining the features of LLNL's Blue Gene/L supercomputer. The award committee chair stated while giving the award, "*For nearly a decade, the Blue Gene/L series won multiple Top 500 awards and Gordon Bell Prizes, including finalists, and served as a vehicle for many research publications.*"

REFERENCES

[1] A. Gara et al., Overview of the Blue Gene/L System Architecture, *IBM Journal of Research and Development*, Vol. 40, No. 2/3, March/May 2005, pp. 196–212. http://rsim.cs.illinois.edu/arch/qual_papers/systems/19.pdf

[2] Torus Interconnect, Wikipedia

[3] Josè E. Morieva, The Evolution of the Blue Gene/L Supercomputer, (PPTs). https://dcc.ufrj.br/~gabriel/arqcomp2/BlueGeneL.pdf

[4] G. Almasi et al., Overview of the Blue Gene/P project, *IBM Journal of Research and Development*, Vol. 52, No. 1, January 2008, pp. 199–220. https://www.researchgate.net/publication/298154650_Overview_of_the_IBM_Blue_GeneP_project

[5] IBM Blue Gene team, "Design of the IBM Blue Gene/Q Compute Chip," *IBM Journal of Research and Development*, Issue 1/2, January–March 2013.

67

The Facebook Story

PROLOGUE

Soon after the advent of the Internet, people realised its power as a communication medium. Bulletin board systems came in 1978. They were primitive because bandwidth was at a premium, and the number of people with access to the Internet was small. Berners-Lee released the World Wide Web to the public in 1993, allowing people to create websites and interact. Many new computer languages, such as Java, PHP, and ColdFusion, tailored to use the web effectively appeared. The web became widely available with the emergence of ISPs in the mid-1990s and a concurrent increase in communication bandwidth. These developments enabled web users to interact, collaborate, and create thematic communities, leading to *social networks.* Oxford Dictionary defines a social network as *"a dedicated website or other application which enables users to communicate with each other by posting information, comments, messages, images, etc."*

One of the earliest social networks was *Bolt,* launched in 1996 for teenagers to create content, meet friends, and play games. It was active for about a decade. Another pioneer was *SixDegrees,* founded in 1997, which allowed users to list family members, friends, and acquaintances and communicate with them. It closed down in 2001. *Open Diary* started in 1998 as a "*website that brought online diary writers together into a community.*" It is still alive. *LiveJournal* began in 1999 to share ideas and create a community of bloggers. A Russian company acquired it in 2007, and it is still active.

In November 2001, Orkut Büyükköten, a doctoral student of Turkish origin in computer science at Stanford University, designed the first social network explicitly intended for college students and named it *Club Nexus*. Only students with the stanford.edu email ID could join it. It had features to enter one's profile, send email, invite friends to join, chat, post items in a classified column, write blogs, search for students with similar interests, and many more. It enrolled 1500 members within the first six weeks of its launch. It did not grow beyond 2500 members as it was difficult to use. Büyükköten followed it up with another social network called *inCircle* for Stanford alums. He and an undergraduate student, Tyler Ziemann, started *Affinity Engines* in 2002 to commercialise *Club Nexus* and *inCircle*, but it failed. Büyükköten joined Google in 2004 and convinced Google management to use his technology to start a social network. Google agreed and launched a social network named *Orkut* on 22 January 2004. It was available for all and named *Orkut* as Büyükköten had registered the website orkut.com, and he designed it. *Orkut* was popular in Brazil and India in 2008 but did not take off in the US. It gradually lost its members as it was slow, its user interface was poor, and it had limited features. Google closed it in 2014.

Friendster was a successful social network that started in 2002 as an online community connecting people to find dates and make new friends. It was initially successful, with a membership of over 100 million. However, its popularity declined, and it closed in 2018.

In 2003, two successful social networks started. *LinkedIn* was for professionals to network and strengthen contacts for better career opportunities. It is active with over 900 million members in 200 countries. The other was *MySpace* which allowed members to create customised profiles, highlight close friends, publish blogs, share photos, join groups, discover music, and play games. It grew and, between 2005 and 2009, became the largest social networking site in the world. It did not thrive because of poor management and the emergence of better-managed social networking sites, particularly Facebook, and rapidly lost its members. MySpace changed its name to *Myspace*, which is active with a focus on music.

BIRTH OF FACEBOOK

Mark Zuckerberg, a restless, computer programming savvy (in popular parlance, a *hacker*), brilliant 19-year-old, second-year undergraduate student (sophomore in American vocabulary) at Harvard University, saw the Internet and the World Wide Web as technologies that would disrupt society. As a prank, he designed a website named *FaceMash* in late 2003. He downloaded pictures of students from the Harvard University website, placed two images side by side on *FaceMash,* and asked students to vote for the more attractive. The website attracted the attention of numerous undergraduates who logged on to the site overnight. The traffic was heavy and crashed Harvard's computer network. The Harvard student newspaper, the *Crimson,* criticised the website as being in poor taste. The university disciplinary committee hauled up Zuckerberg for copyright and privacy infringement and asked him to close the website. They placed him on academic probation for six months.

FaceMash's notoriety spread rapidly among Harvard students. Three final-year Harvard undergraduate students, Cameron Winklevoss, his twin brother Tyler Winklevoss, and Divya Narendra, were planning to start a social network *HarvardConnections*, exclusively for Harvard students and alums. They were not computer savvy and, having seen *FaceMash,* requested Zuckerberg to design a website for *HarvardConnections* in late 2003. Zuckerberg agreed but did not design the site, giving various excuses. Instead, he created another website, *thefacebook.com,* as a social network to connect Harvard students. His dormmates Eduardo Saverin, Andrew McCollum, Dustin Moskovitz, and Chris Hughes assisted him in creating the website. They were sceptical about the success of *thefacebook* as *Friendster* and *MySpace* were already popular social networking sites. However, Zuckerberg argued that his website was exclusive for Harvard students and that he would include features of interest to them. He launched the website on 4 February 2004. He invited Harvard students to become members, and each member's account had their name with @harvard.edu email id, profiles with a photo, gender, birthday, dorm, phone number, courses already taken and current courses, favourite books and music, friends and friend requests, invitations with email ids, search by name, class, year, course, etc. Some privacy restrictions allowed a user to specify who could see the profile. Within the first 24 hours of launch, 1200 students joined as members of *thefacebook*. When the Winklevoss brothers and Narendra saw the website, they were incensed because it was similar to what they had planned for *HarvardConnect*. They complained to the Harvard administration that Zuckerberg had stolen what they termed as "*their idea and intellectual property*". The administration advised them to take legal action. After prolonged litigation, they settled the case out of court, and the Winklevoss brothers and Narendra were paid $65 million in settlement in 2008. By that time, *Facebook* had become a successful company.

Mark Zuckerberg
(Photo courtesy Wikipedia)

GROWTH OF FACEBOOK

The first version of *thefacebook* was exclusively for Harvard students. Half of Harvard's students joined during the launch's first month. Soon, there were requests from other university students. *thefacebook* added Columbia, Stanford, New York University, Cornell, Dartmouth, Pennsylvania, Brown, and Yale. Membership increased rapidly. To pay more attention to the site, Zuckerberg and Moskovitz dropped out of Harvard and moved to Palo Alto, California, a fertile start-up area, in June 2004. Soon, Sean Parker, a young hacker and entrepreneur (famous for starting the peer-to-peer music file-sharing platform called *Napster* along with Shawn Fanning), joined as the company's president. He persuaded Zuckerberg to rename *thefacebook* to *Facebook*. He knew his ropes around Silicon Valley and persuaded Peter Thiel, a venture capitalist, to invest $500,000 in Facebook for 10.2% of the company in August 2004. In December 2004, the number of users increased to 1 million. In May 2005, Facebook expanded to more than 800 colleges in the US and soon allowed high school students to become members. Facebook introduced a "wall" feature, which allowed users to post and receive messages on it. In October 2005, Facebook became international. By December 2005, there were more than 12 million users. It admitted anyone with a legitimate name (no pseudonym allowed) in 2006 and businesses in 2007. Zuckerberg paid considerable attention to product development and ensured a good user experience.

Facebook upgraded the servers before admitting new member groups and enhanced features to ensure users' response time was excellent. Facebook became multilingual in 2007 and gradually increased the number of languages, and currently supports 112 languages, including Hindi, Kannada, and Tamil. By July 2010, there were 500 million users. The networking effect took over, and the user base increased geometrically, reaching 2.85 billion by 2021.

Gradually, Facebook added features such as messaging, exchanging gifts, news feeds, creating groups, posting videos, posting comments, posting likes, dating, forming groups, creating a marketplace to sell and buy items, and gathering memories from earlier posts. It became a one-stop site absorbing the facilities provided by many social networks. When the mobile phone revolution occurred in the late 2000, Facebook was ready to embrace this new platform by making appropriate design changes.

The primary source of revenue for Facebook is advertising. Facebook cleverly used members' profiles to precisely target advertisements of interest to them. Advertisers found that targeted advertisements were cost-effective compared to media such as newspapers and Television. The advertisement revenue of Facebook multiplied. It was $764 million in 2009 and increased to $113,642 million in 2022 (www.statistica.com).

FACEBOOK BUSINESS

Zuckerberg and Saverin invested $1000 each to register the website and buy computers when *thefacebook.com* started at Harvard in 2004. Saverin invested $15,000 for 37% of the company when the number of *thefacebook.com* users increased, and the server capacity was insufficient. Zuckerberg diluted Saverin's shares when the two friends fell apart. They settled their dispute out of court for an undisclosed number of Facebook shares rumoured to be worth approximately $5 billion. Saverin renounced US citizenship and settled down in Singapore to avoid paying the capital gains tax due in the USA. He became a venture capitalist.

As mentioned earlier, Thiel invested $500,000 in August 2004. As Facebook's user base grew, more investment was needed. In April 2005, Accel, a venture capital company, invested $12.7 million, followed by others who chipped in $ 27.5 million in 2006. Meanwhile, there were many offers to acquire Facebook for amounts ranging from $1 billion to $5 billion that Zuckerberg rejected as he wanted to control Facebook. Microsoft invested $240 million in October 2007, followed by a Chinese investor who invested $ 60 million. A Russian company made another significant investment of $ 200 million in 2009. In 2011, Facebook made a profit of $1 billion.

FACEBOOK CONTROVERSIES

Facebook has proliferated and is currently (2024) the dominant social network company in the world. It has 3 billion registered users spread worldwide, of which around 2 billion use it daily. It is also estimated that there are approximately 450 million registered users in India. This large size and high traffic require Facebook to maintain a humongous computing infrastructure that consumes enormous power, estimated at 28 MW. Facebook faces many problems due to its large user base, specifically handling content posted by users, which is a challenge. Users have criticised Facebook for not caring enough about user data privacy. A notorious case was that of a British company, Cambridge Analytica, that collected the personal data of 87 million Facebook users without their consent and used it to provide analytical assistance to the 2016 US presidential campaign of Ted Cruz and Donald Trump. Facebook was fined $5 billion by the US Federal Trade Commission and £500,000 by the UK Information Commissioner's Office for inappropriate use of its members' data. Besides privacy and data leak concerns, Facebook has also been criticised for poor content management, such as allowing its users to post fake news, violent content, and copyrighted material.

EPILOGUE

On February 1, 2012, Facebook announced its first Initial Public Offer (IPO) of shares at $38 per share for $16 billion. The IPO was fully subscribed. Its market capitalisation in December 2023 is $562 billion. Its revenue in 2022 was $116.8 billion, and its profit was $23.1 billion (www.businessofapps/facebook).

Facebook went on an acquisition spree, acquiring 13 companies during the next decade. Notable acquisitions were Instagram, a photo and video sharing site for $1 billion in 2012, and WhatsApp, an instant messaging and voice-over-IP site on mobile phones, for a staggering price of $19 billion in 2014.

Zuckerberg stated in 2021, "*Right now, our brand is so tightly linked to one product that it can't possibly represent everything we are doing today, let alone the future. To reflect on who we are and the future we hope to build, I am proud to share that our company is now Meta*". He also stated that Meta planned to build a "*metaverse. In this online world, people can game, work, and communicate in a virtual environment, often using VR headsets.*"

REFERENCES

[1] Ben Mezrich, The Accidental Billionaires—The Founding of Facebook, Doubleday, 2009. (Adapted as the movie "The Social Network" in 2010).

[2] Kristi Haines, The History of Social Media, https://www.searchenginejournal.com/social-media-history/462643/#close

[3] Nicholas Carlson, At last—the full story of how Facebook was started, https://www.businessinsider.com/how-facebook-was-founded-2010-3?IR=T

[4] Niels Brüger, A Brief History of Facebook as a media text: The development of an empty structure. https://firstmonday.org/ojs/index.php/fm/article/download/5423/4466

[5] David Kirkpatrick, The Facebook Effect, Simon & Schuster, New York, 2010.

68

Cloud Computing Arrives

PROLOGUE

John McCarthy joined the faculty of the Massachusetts Institute of Technology (MIT) in 1959 and started research in Artificial Intelligence (AI). Soon, he began using IBM 704, a mainframe computer at MIT. Users of IBM704 submitted programs punched on cards as program decks to a computer operator in the centre. The operator collected a batch of programs, fed them to IBM704 which executed them, and the printed results were given to users after a few hours. Often, the results were just error messages as, initially, programs had errors and had to be corrected. Programmers often required three or four attempts to correct the mistakes and get useful results. McCarthy was frustrated with these delays and wrote to Philip Morse, the director of the computer centre, suggesting that the center provide users with teletypewriters on which they typed their programs, submitted to the computer, and the results printed on the teletype. He suggested several users can simultaneously use the computer in a time-shared mode. Morse requested Fernando Corbató, the computer centre's associate director, to follow up on McCarthy's suggestion. Corbató and his colleagues designed the world's first time-shared operating system for IBM 709, called CTSS, in 1961 (See Anecdote 15). When time-shared computers became a reality, McCarthy, in a speech at the centenary celebration of MIT in 1961, wondered why time-shared computers could not be made available as a public utility similar to a telephone system. In such a system, several users could use a giant computer system from wherever they were and pay for the computer time they used. He opined that such a system could be the basis of a new and important industry.

Project MAC at MIT, funded by the Advanced Research Project Agency (ARPA) of the US Department of Defence(DoD), followed up on this idea. One of the goals of project MAC (See Anecdote 26) was to provide an advanced time-shared computing utility. By 1969, a time-shared computer using the Multics operating system could support 300 simultaneous users. In 1966, Douglas Parkhill, a Canadian engineer, wrote a book titled "Challenges of the Computing Utility" in which he foresaw the emergence of a computer utility similar to today's cloud computing. Technology was not ripe to implement his vision. Some commercial time-shared data centres were set up in the 1970s to mimic a computing utility. However, due to high communication costs and expensive storage systems, the idea of several users sharing a giant computer from remote locations did not succeed.

Meanwhile, PCs appeared, and computing became personal. The client-server model of computing became popular in the 90s. The idea of utility computing became dormant.

EVOLUTION OF TECHNOLOGY

Between 1970 and 2000, computer and communication technologies grew rapidly. The speed of CPUs doubled every 24 months at a constant cost. The disk storage capacity doubled every 15 months with no increase in price. The reliability of disk systems also increased. Most significantly, communication bandwidth has doubled every year in recent years with no increase in cost. This development has allowed customers to use computers at remote locations as if they were in the next room. Bandwidth increase enables users to send gigabytes of data almost instantly to remote computers. The Internet came of age. Computers could be remotely accessed from anywhere at any time, permitting interactive use of computers regardless of their location. The emergence of the World Wide Web in 1993 facilitated accessing websites from anywhere at any time to retrieve information and compute.

Software innovations took place in addition to the improvement of CPU power, storage, and communication systems. Time-shared operating systems matured, allowing hundreds of users to access a computer simultaneously. IBM developed the Virtual Machine (VM) operating system for the IBM 370 series of mainframes in the late 1960s by placing a software layer on the operating system. This layer allowed the software environment of computer "A" *to look and feel* like that of another computer "B", called *Virtualization.* Virtualization allows multiple users with diverse application requirements to use the same hardware infrastructure transparently. Several companies developed complex virtualization software to manage multiple virtual machines, called a *hypervisor*, in early 2000.

Management philosophy also evolved during the early 2000s. Organizations started outsourcing functions they considered not their primary or core to service providers. Instead of maintaining in-house computing infrastructure, organizations prefer to outsource it to reliable computing service providers. This decision created a group of service providers who serviced requests for the software and hardware of those who requested them.

All these developments rekindled the dormant idea of utility computing and saw the emergence of *cloud computing.*

WHAT IS CLOUD COMPUTING?

Cloud computing is accessing computing resources such as CPU power, storage, or application software on demand from anywhere at any time, using a terminal connected to a service provider via a communication network. The network is usually the Internet. Computing resources requested may grow or shrink. A customer may assume that unlimited resources are available. A provider charges a customer only for the resources used. The provider assures the security and privacy of users' data and programs and guarantees a specified quality of service.

It is somewhat like a power utility in which users assume power is available 24 hours a day, 7 days a week, and is "unlimited" within reasonable bounds. The customer pays only for the energy used. The power utility has to adhere to specific regulations on the quality of service.

The origin of the term "Cloud", a metaphor that evolved in the 1990s, for computing services available on the Internet is unclear. Sean O'Sullivan and George Favaloro, working for Compaq, a computer company, in a brainstorming session in 1996, used the term cloud for computing services on the Internet. O'Sullivan started a company named NetCentic, now defunct, to provide computing, storage, and entertainment services over the Internet and tried unsuccessfully to obtain a trademark for the term cloud. Wikipedia attributes the term cloud to a distributed computing platform designed by General Logic and AT&T in 1993. Ramesh Chellappa, a professor of management at Emory University, reportedly used the term cloud computing in an academic publication in 1997. The term "Cloud" became popular after Eric Schmidt, CEO of Google, used it in 2006 at an industry conference.

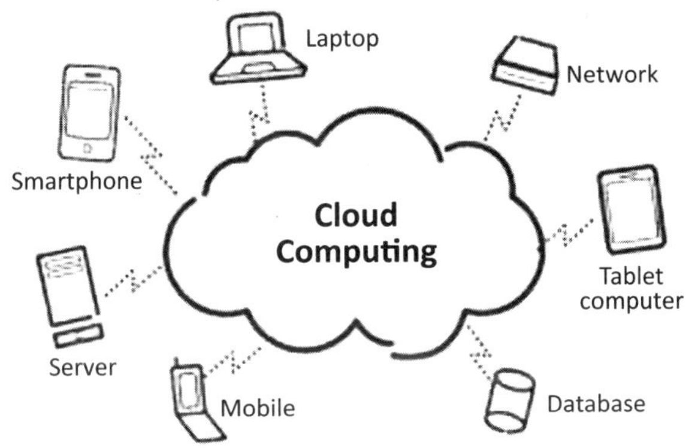

Cloud Computer
(Picture courtesy Visual Edge)

Various cloud computing services are available. They are *IaaS* (Infrastructure as a Service), in which a provider provides CPU power and storage on demand. *PaaS* (Platform as a Service) is a system in which a provider offers, besides hardware, an operating system and a program development environment. *SaaS* (Software as a Service), in which a provider provides application programs such as accounting software.

Three types of clouds are available: private cloud, public cloud, and hybrid cloud. A *private cloud* is a computing infrastructure maintained by a provider for the exclusive use of a customer. A *public cloud* is an infrastructure shared by several customers. A *hybrid cloud* is a combination of a private and public cloud. An organization usually uses a private cloud for its proprietary software applications and storing confidential data. In contrast, a public cloud hosts publicly accessible services like its website. An organization may use a combination of private and public cloud, namely a hybrid cloud, when there is seasonal high demand for computing and shift some non-critical applications to a public cloud.

Another recent cloud type is the *personal cloud.* The term is used for a system in which laptops and other computers in a home or a small office are connected to a Wi-Fi network and to a large storage system where shared programs and archival files are stored.

EVOLUTION OF CLOUD COMPUTING

Salesforce, a software company, began operations in 1999. Its main business was developing Customer Relationship Management (CRM) software. The World Wide Web had matured by 1999, and the company hosted CRM software on its website and allowed users to use it for payment. Salesforce was the first company to provide SaaS on the cloud.

Jeff Bezos, a software engineer working for D. E. Shaw & Co., a hedge fund, got in 1994 a brilliant idea of selling books using the World Wide Web. He wanted to pick an appropriate name for his novel enterprise. Looking through a dictionary, he stumbled on Amazon, the biggest river in the world, exotic and different, which was his vision for the new enterprise. Bezos soon expanded Amazon and started selling other items to customers worldwide. Customers found it convenient to shop from the comfort of their homes and to have the items delivered to them on their doorstep. Amazon was the beginning of what is now known as *e-commerce*. Amazon grew rapidly and had to establish massive and reliable hardware and communication infrastructure to cater to the maximum demand from customers, which was seasonal, for example, during Christmas. Very often, Amazon used only 10% of the installed computer capacity. Bezos saw a business opportunity to sell the excess computing and communication capacity Amazon had built. In 2006, Bezos started Amazon Web Services (AWS) and sold computer time to customers "on-demand" using the Internet for communication. AWS was the first cloud service.

Jeff Bezos
(Photo courtesy Wikipedia)

Google provided customers with a free search engine to retrieve information from the World Wide Web (Anecdote 61). The search engine required a vast computing infrastructure, which Google financed from the revenue it earned from advertisements. Google started a free email service in 2004 using this infrastructure. It gave its customers in 2006 free office productivity software and 2GB disk storage. It saw a business opportunity to sell its excess computing capacity and started Google Cloud as a publicly available service in 2011. Google provides IaaS, PaaS, and SaaS.

Many other companies followed. Rackspace started a cloud service in 2006, Microsoft began a cloud computing service called Azure in 2008, followed by IBM's SmartCloud in 2011. Several cloud computing service companies started over the past decade, and hundreds of companies exist worldwide. The major providers of cloud computing services in India are TCS, Infosys, Wipro, Cloudthat, and Zenith, besides multinationals AWS, Azure, IBM, and Google Cloud.

INFRASTRUCTURE FOR CLOUD COMPUTING

The hardware infrastructure for cloud computing consists of large clusters of tens of thousands of computing blades (See Anecdote 69) mounted on standard 19" racks. Each rack typically accommodates around 48 blades, and a fast Ethernet switch interconnects them. A hierarchy of switches interconnects several racks. Banks of disk drives are connected to the blades by a fast network. Plenty of redundancy is there to ensure very high availability, which should exceed 99.99%, as users do not tolerate even a few seconds of outage. Such a computer system is known as a *Warehouse-scale Computer* (WSC). As thousands of users would be requesting cloud services simultaneously, the system caters to what is known as *request-level parallelism.*

The power dissipated by WSC is high, and an excellent cooling system is required. The total power consumption would be in the hundreds of megawatts range. The cost of power usage of a typical WSC is estimated at around \$ 400,000 per month. To reduce the cost of running WSC, Cloud providers locate them in cool locations and places where the power cost is low. In an experiment, Microsoft immersed an entire WSC in a seabed to reduce the cooling cost! WSCs used by companies such as Microsoft and Google are expensive, costing around \$150 million.

The software environment of WSC should accommodate several customers simultaneously with their applications running on their operating systems, which is called *multi-tenancy*. Cloud vendors allocate sets of blades to a customer. Allocation of blades would be dynamic. The WSC software supports Virtualization and incorporates a hypervisor. Parallelization software called *MapReduce* and its open-source version *Hadoop* are used to distribute and efficiently run several users' programs on banks of servers in WSC.

EPILOGUE

Cloud computing is the new normal. It is one of the landmark developments in computing in the first decade of this century.

Organizations have four apprehensions about using cloud computing. They are:

1. The security of their data and programs when hosted on a cloud used by several users simultaneously.
2. Difficulty in shifting applications from one provider to another if the quality of the service of the provider deteriorates or the provider ceases operation.
3. The failure of communications with a cloud.
4. Difficulty in resolving disputes between a provider and a customer as cloud computers may span national boundaries and countries' legal systems differ.

Some of these anxieties have solutions. It is advisable to encrypt data and programs before they are sent to cloud computers to ensure security. Organizations may use a private cloud for highly secure applications.

The second concern is genuine. A move toward a federated cloud has begun with several providers cooperating and using common standards to shift applications from one provider to another. Brokers who would negotiate with several providers and give assured service to customers may emerge.

Users should have backup communication systems to alleviate the third problem.

Organizations may solve the last concern by using a cloud provider in their own country until an international treaty is signed to create an International Cloud Union similar to the International Telecommunication Union.

REFERENCES

[1] V. Rajaraman, Cloud Computing, *Resonance*, Vol. 19, No. 3, March 3014, pp. 242–258.
https://www.ias.ac.in/public/Volumes/reso/019/03/0242-0258.pdf

[2] A.P. Shanthi, Warehouse-scale Computers, https://www.cs.umd.edu/~meesh/411/CA-online/chapter/warehouse-scale-computers/index.html

[3] John Roach, Microsoft finds underwater datacentres are reliable, practicable, and use energy sustainably, September 2020.
https://news.microsoft.com/source/features/sustainability/project-natick-underwater-datacenter/

[4] https://www.technologyreview.com/2011/10/31/257406/who-coined-cloud-computing/

69

IBM Roadrunner—The First Supercomputer to Breach the PetaFLOPS Barrier

PROLOGUE

In a press release on 6 September 2006, the US government's National Nuclear Security Administration stated that it had selected IBM to build a supercomputer with an estimated speed of 1 PetaFLOPS that would be installed at the Los Alamos National Laboratory (LANL), Albuquerque, New Mexico. (PetaFLOPS is 10^{15} Floating Point Operations per Second). The supercomputer was named "Roadrunner". Roadrunner is the state bird of New Mexico, which, although it can fly, typically runs away from predators at a high speed of 32 km/h. The supercomputer was to be used to ensure that the US nuclear weapons stockpile was safe and reliable despite ageing by using modelling and simulation on the computer without conducting underground nuclear tests. The supercomputer would simulate the behaviour of a hydrogen bomb in the first fraction of a second during an explosion. IBM took up the challenge of designing and building a computer to break the PetaFLOPS barrier. IBM formed a group at their laboratory in Poughkeepsie, NY, led by Don Grice as the chief engineer. It started the design of the computer

Roadrunner
(Photo courtesy Wikipedia)

as soon as the contract was awarded, with a deadline for delivery to LANL by 2008.

IBM CELL BROADBAND ENGINE [1]

It was clear to the engineering team at IBM that it would be difficult to breach the PetaFLOPS barrier with existing microprocessors. The team got the brilliant idea of using an improved version of a special high-speed microprocessor called Cell Broadband Engine (CBE) as one of the microprocessors in Roadrunner. CBE was designed in 2005 by IBM, Sony, and Toshiba for Play Station 3 gaming console use. Gaming consoles require very high-speed processors to play video games in real-time with computers (See Anecdote 33). Sony was one of the leaders in building gaming consoles. Sony released the highly successful PlayStation 2 gaming console in 2000. PlayStation 2 used IBM's Power microprocessor as the computing engine. As soon as the PlayStation 2 was released, Ken Kutaragi, the President and CEO of Sony, challenged IBM to design a much faster processor for Sony's next-generation gaming console, PlayStation 3. Sony, Toshiba, and IBM set up a group of around 400 engineers in Austin, Texas, in March 2001 to design and fabricate a new-generation microprocessor for PlayStation 3. This group built the CBE architecture microprocessor in 2005, reportedly costing $400 million to develop. This microprocessor consisted of nine cores. One core was a Power PC Processing Element (PPE), and the other eight were Synergistic Processing Elements (SPE). A very high-speed bus connected the PPE and the SPEs. The PPE was a 64-bit RISC processor with a 64 KB L1 cache, 512 KB L2 cache, and a clock of 3.2 GHz. It was the primary control processing core of the microprocessor and hosted a Linux-based Operating System. Each SPE had a 256 KB local storage and was a Single Instruction Multiple Data (SIMD) processor specialised in fast arithmetic operations.

QS 22 BLADE

IBM gradually improved the CBE architecture to broaden its use in many applications. In May 2008, IBM announced a chip called PowerXCell 8i with the same overall architecture of CBE with SPEs having enhanced floating-point double precision calculation ability. The speed of each SPE was 12.8 GFLOPS for 64-bit operands. The speed of the microprocessor was 108.8 GFLOPS for 64-bit operands and 230.8 GFLOPS for 32-bit operands.

PowerXCell 8i was highly power-efficient at 1.05 GFLOPS/watt. IBM used this microprocessor in Blade Server QS22 (A Blade Server typically has a microprocessor, support chips, external memory, and communication interfaces and does not have a power supply. It is usually air-cooled). IBM configured a QS22 blade with 2 PowerXCell 8i microprocessors, each with 4 GB of external memory—an InfiniBand switch interconnected QS22 blades.

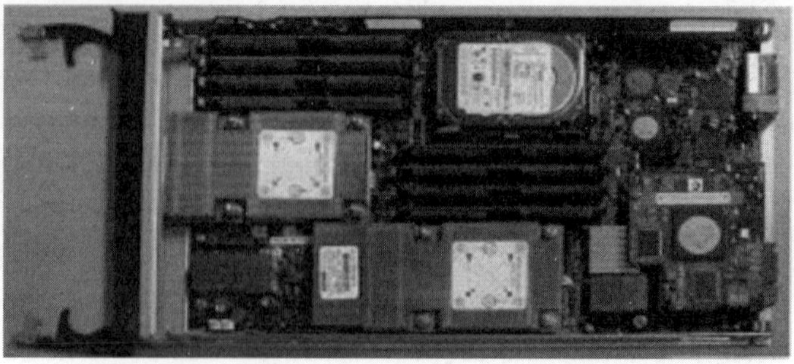

IBM QS22 blade server (Photo courtesy Wikiwand)

IBM LS21 BLADE

The PPE processor in PowerCell 8Xi was too slow to design a PetaFLOPS computer. It also could not support more than 32 GB of external memory. IBM, therefore, decided to use, in addition to PowerCell 8Xi, an AMD dual-core Opteron microprocessor to design the Roadrunner. IBM selected an AMD Opteron 2210 dual-core processor with a 1.8 MHz clock, 128 KB L1 cache, and 2MB L2 Cache. A blade (LS21) was configured with two Opteron processors with 8 GB external RAM each and had a peak performance of 14.4 GFLOPS for 64-bit operands and 28.8 GFLOPS for 32-bit operands. It dissipated 86 watts.

TRIBLADE

A building block of the Roadrunner was what was known as a Triblade. A Triblade (See Figure) consisted of two QS 22 blades and one LS21 blade interconnected by an expansion blade. Each QS 22 blade was connected to one Opteron 2210 processor in the LS21 blade. Each

Triblade had a peak speed of 1.769 GFLOPS for 64-bit operands and a total memory of 32 GB.

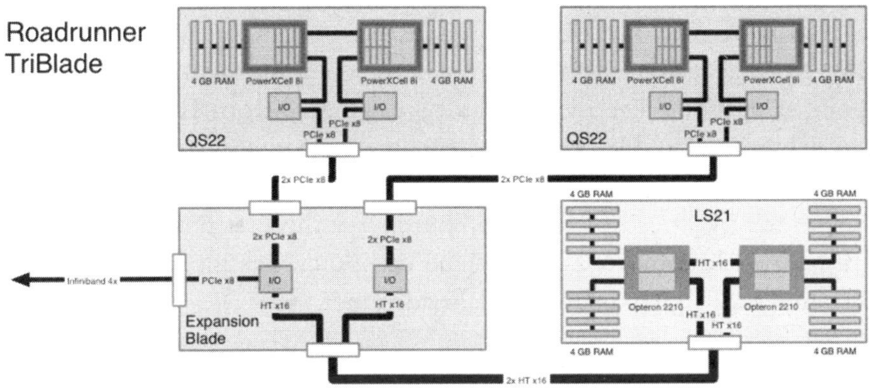

A Triblade—building block of Roadrunner (Diagram courtesy Wikipedia)

A CONNECTED UNIT (CU)

A Connected Unit is a powerful cluster of 180 Triblades and 12 I/O nodes. The I/O nodes use AMD Opteron 2210 processors and connect disk files to the system. A high-speed (768 GB/s) switch interconnected the Triblades and the I/O blades. The CU has an aggregate 5.78 TB memory and a peak speed of 76.3 TeraFLOPS for 64-bit operands.

THE ROADRUNNER SYSTEM [2]

The Roadrunner is a cluster of clusters. Eighteen CUs are interconnected as a fat tree by InfiniBand switches to make up the final Roadrunner. The Roadrunner has 12960 IBM PowerCell 8Xi processors used as accelerators to 6480 AMD Opteron 2210 dual-core processors. In addition, it has 216 AMD Opteron 2210 processors for I/O, front end, and supervisory functions. The blades used in the Roadrunner were fabricated at the Rochester, Minnesota facility and shipped to IBM's laboratory at Poughkeepsie, NY, for assembly.

Triblade	Connected Unit	Roadrunner
2 QS 22 + →	(180 Triblades cluster) →	(18 Connected units cluster)
1 LS 21	360 QS 22 + 180 LS 21+ 12 I/O	6480 QS 22 + 3240 LS 21+216 I/O

The architecture of the Roadrunner

The computer was assembled and tested in phases. In the first phase, only 3240 Opteron blades (LS21) were clustered with 12 Opteron I/O, supervisory, and front-end computers and tested. This system ran at 71 TeraFLOPS. When this test succeeded, IBM added the QS 22 accelerators and assembled the computer with 17 Connected Units at its Poughkeepsie laboratory. Engineers from IBM and LANL ran a Linpack double-precision benchmark program on 25 May 2008, attaining a speed of 1.026 PetaFLOPS and breaking the PetaFLOPS barrier for the speed of supercomputers for the first time in the world. IBM added one more CU when the computer was installed in LANL, resulting in 18 CUs in the final Roadrunner.

Other data about the Roadrunner with 18 Connected Units are:

Peak speed (64-bit operands)	:	1.456 PetaFLOPS (As stated in Tops 500 list November 2008)
Sustained speed (Linpack 64-bit operands)	:	1.105 PetaFLOPS (Tops 500 list November 2008)
Total Processor Cores	:	130464
Interconnection of processors	:	26, 288 port InfiniBand switches
Total memory size	:	103.68 TB
Total Disk store	:	1000 PB
Total Power dissipation	:	2,345 kW
The floor area occupied	:	296 Racks, 560 sq.m.
Cooling	:	Air
MFLOPS/Watt	:	444.94 (Fourth coolest supercomputer in November 2008)
Price	:	$ 110 million

The Roadrunner was first on the Tops 500 list in June 2008—more than double the speed of IBM Blue Gene/L, which occupied second place. It remained first in the following two lists (November 2008 and June 2009) until Cray's Jaguar supercomputer overtook it in November 2009. The Roadrunner, however, was twice as power efficient as the Jaguar.

SOFTWARE FOR ROADRUNNER

The operating system that ran on both QS 22 and LS 21 was a version of Linux known as Fedora Linux. Programming languages available for Roadrunner included High-performance Fortran, C, and C++. Besides this, it used the MPI library extensively. Programming was complex on the system, which had three types of processing cores. Programming the QS 22 blade was challenging. IBM provided tools and trained programmers extensively to use the system effectively. Besides the top-secret weapons-oriented applications, LANL allowed scientists to use the Roadrunner to solve compute-intensive problems. Among them was the Monte Carlo calculation of Supernova light curves, instabilities in compressible turbulence, mechanical properties of nanowires, and scattering in laser beam collisions, to mention a few.

MARKETING ROADRUNNER COMPONENTS

We saw that IBM assembled the Roadrunner using IBM's blades QS 22 and LS 21. These blades required only power supplies to function independently. QS 22, a derivative of the processor used by the PlayStation 3 console, could be used in applications such as video processing, signal processing, and graphics rendering. Its high speed at a reasonable cost allowed IBM to market it for medical imaging, financial analytics, petroleum exploration, and electronic design automation. IBM successfully marketed both individual blades and clusters of QS 22. IBM sold clusters of QS 22 as lower-performance supercomputers. Many of them found a place in the Top 500 list.

IBM marketed LS 21 as a general-purpose computer and clusters of LS 21 as low-cost high-performance computers.

EPILOGUE

LLNL shut down the Roadrunner on 31 March 2013, a mere five years after installation. All Roadrunner components were shredded for security reasons as they were used in top-secret weapons research [3]. You may wonder why LLNL shut down a $110 million computer so early.

LLNL shut it down as faster computers, which consumed less power, emerged in 2013. The Roadrunner consumed 2345 kW of power, had to be kept in an airconditioned room, and cost $300 per hour to run. If LLNL used Roadrunner 24 hours, 7 days a week, its running cost would be around $1.8 million annually. Meanwhile, supercomputers such as Titan at the Oakridge National Laboratory ran at 17.6 PetaFLOPS, consumed 8209 kW, and cost around $ 97 million for 17 times the speed of Roadrunner. It was five times cheaper to run. The US government's Department of Energy saved money by shutting down Roadrunner and buying the latest supercomputer.

REFERENCES

[1] M.W. Riley et al., Cell Broadband Engine Processor: Design and Implementation, *IBM Journal of Research and Development*, Vol. 51, No. 5, pp. 545–57, September 2007.
https://ieeexplore.ieee.org/document/5388682

[2] Ken Koch, Roadrunner: What Makes it Tick, LANL Computer Science Symposium, 14 Oct 2008. https://www.lanl.gov/conferences/lacss/2008/slides/Roadrunner_LACSS.pdf

[3] Sebastian Anthony, World's first petaflop computer is obsolete after just five years, will be shut down, April 1, 2013.
https://www.extremetech.com/computing/152191-worlds-first-petaflop-supercomputer-is-obsolete-after-just-five-years-will-be-shut-down

70

Raspberry Pi—The Story of a $35 Computer

PROLOGUE

Eben Upton was the director of undergraduate admissions at St. John's College of Cambridge University in 2005. He was shocked to observe that the number of students applying to study computer science at the college had dropped precipitously to around 250 for 90 to 100 seats from around 600 to 700 when he joined the college as an undergraduate in 1995. In addition, most applicants had not programmed computers. He remembered that his interest in computers was kindled by the availability of low-cost BBC computers in the late 1980s when he was a high school student in Wales. He had programmed it and spent many hours playing around with it.

In the early 1980s, the British Broadcasting Corporation (BBC) started broadcasting a Computer Literacy Project on TV. It followed a TV documentary series, "The Mighty Micro", broadcast in 1979, which predicted the microcomputer revolution and its effect on the economy and lifestyle in the UK. BBC wanted a computer to demonstrate various applications of computers, including programming, graphics, playing games, and even AI during the TV programme. BBC's idea was to spread computer literacy to the public and young students who wanted a moderate-cost computer available in the market. BBC floated a tender for a personal computer with basic features. Acorn Computers won the tender and released the first version of its Proton computer (later renamed BBC Micro) in December 1981 for £ 335. It used a MOS

Technology 6502 microprocessor, 32KB memory, a floppy disk, and a display. It had an excellent BASIC language interpreter, a word processor, and a simple proprietary OS. On turning the computer on, a cursor appeared, allowing students to enter BASIC programs. About 80% of British high schools bought BBC Micros, which was instrumental in kindling students' interest in computers and programming. British schools used BBC Micros for more than a decade. Upton had used a BBC Micro when he was a high school student, which kindled his interest in computers, and consequently, he applied to Cambridge University to study computer science. (Incidentally, BBC Micro was distributed in India to some schools by the erstwhile Department of Electronics of the Government of India and used in the Computer Literacy and Studies in Schools (CLASS) Programme during 1984–89).

By 1995, micros disappeared from schools. With the advent of mobile phones and gaming consoles, computers became a "black box" appliance. Students were no longer interested in programming and knew nothing about computers' innards. Upton was convinced that there was a need for an inexpensive computer that cost the same as a book (around $35) that students could buy without worrying about losing or breaking. Students could carry such a computer in their backpack, program it, and play around with it, adding hardware and software. Upton felt that if such a computer were readily available to high school students, it would arouse their interest in studying computer science.

BEGINNING OF RASPBERRY Pi

Upton left Cambridge after obtaining a doctorate and started working at Broadcom (a microprocessor design and manufacturing company). He was still interested in pursuing his passion to design a low-cost computer for use by high school students. In 2006, Upton designed a single-board computer using an Atmel microcontroller of Broadcom, which was not very powerful—it was as fast as a BBC micro of the 1980s. As he could not identify an appropriate processor for an inexpensive computer and was busy in his new job, he suspended his efforts to build a low-cost computer. In 2008, he met Professor Alan Mycroft and engineer Pete Lomas at Cambridge and discussed his idea of a low-cost computer for use by school students. They were excited about this and joined him in the design effort.

Meanwhile, Broadcom had released a more powerful chip suitable for building a low-cost computer. Upton and Lomas built a prototype using this processor on a credit card-sized printed circuit board. It could run a Python program on booting (By 2008, Python had replaced BASIC as a simple programming language for beginners). They also wanted to find an appropriate name for the computer. Many computer companies named themselves after fruits: Apple, Tangerine, Apricot, Acorn, etc. This observation made them call the computer *Raspberry Pi.* Pi was in the name as it was programmed using Python.

Eben Upton **Raspberry Pi Logo**
(Photo courtesy Wikipedia)

Upton and Lomas made a better prototype of Raspberry Pi, and they approached Mycroft to take the idea further. He suggested formalising the effort by creating a charitable foundation by inducting more persons interested in carrying forward the vision and mobilising initial funding.

RASPBERRY Pi CHARITABLE FOUNDATION

Upton, Lomas, Mycroft, Jack Lang, Rob Mullins (all of Cambridge), and computer games creator and entrepreneur David Braben formed the Raspberry Pi Charitable Foundation in 2009. The foundation aimed "to promote the study of computer science and related topics, especially at the school level, and put the fun back into learning computing". The foundation mobilised funding to carry the idea of building Raspberry Pi further. Meanwhile, Broadcom released a low-cost System-on-a-Chip (SoC) 2835 with an Arm 11 core and an in-built graphics processing unit. The chip could run an entire Linux-based OS. Upton and Lomas built a pen drive-sized board with this chip, which cost less than $35, and ran Python on bootup. Upton showed it to the BBC technology correspondent Rory Cellan-Jones in May 2011, who promptly created a YouTube presentation of Raspberry Pi.

To Upton's surprise, 600,000 persons viewed this presentation within the first two days of its uploading. He was delighted, but his wife Liz brought him to the ground by warning him that he had no choice but to build and market Raspberry Pi (knowing that he had been toying with the idea of a low-cost computer since 2006). Upton had joined the MBA programme at Cambridge part-time and was working at Broadcom. Juggling these roles, he, Lomas, and Cambridge colleagues started designing Raspberry Pi. There were plenty of challenges: lack of funding, the realisation that the cost of the board was not entirely determined by the price of the microprocessor but by the additional small components needed to make it a working computer, and the need to build a minimum of 10,000 boards to reduce the cost of the components. The group held numerous discussions to make a usable computer, keeping the price down to $35. They built several prototypes on printed circuit boards throughout 2011. Many were auctioned on eBay to mobilise resources. The final system was a credit-card-sized system named Raspberry Pi 1 Model B, released on 29 February 2012. This model had a Broadcom BCM2835 SoC, which had an ARM 11 processor and Video Core IV Graphics running at 700 MHz, 256 MB RAM (later upgraded to 512 MB), two 2.0 USB ports, one HDMI port, an SD card slot for a memory card, a 100 Mbps Ethernet port, General Purpose IO slots, and a micro USB port to attach an external power supply (5 Volts, 700 mA). It ran a version of Linux (Debian) with several programming languages including Python and many open-source applications. They built 10,000 units initially, as Upton and his colleagues expected sales to be in the thousands. The idea was to use the revenue from selling the first batch of 10,000 to produce the next set. They were startled as orders started pouring in, reaching 100,000 by March 2012.

The high demand forced the Raspberry Pi Foundation to change its business model. The foundation decided to outsource production and sales to two electronics manufacturers, RS Components and Premier Farnell, in the UK and collect royalty. Initially, the companies manufactured the boards in China, but from late 2012 they are being manufactured in a Sony plant in the UK. In 2012, the companies sold 700,000 Raspberry Pis. The sales grew at an astronomical rate to 4 million in 2014 and steadily grew as the Raspberry Foundation introduced newer models. The cumulative sales of Raspberry Pi reached 46 million on its 10th anniversary (28 February 2022) and generated sales revenue of over a billion dollars. The scarcity of semiconductor components in 2021–22 restricted its availability.

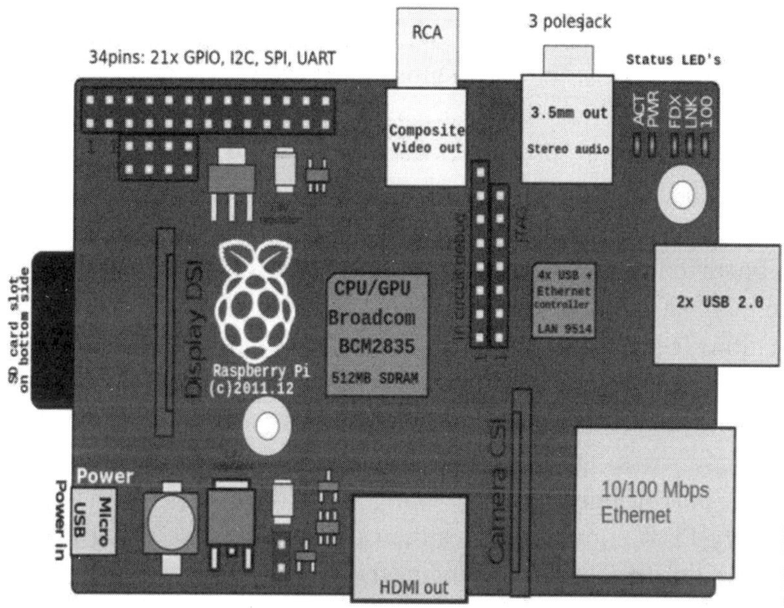

Raspberry Pi I Model B (Picture courtesy Wikipedia)

EPILOGUE

Raspberry Pi is the highest-selling British computer in its history. Two years after its unprecedented reception, the Raspberry Pi Foundation decided to split into two parts: a part called Raspberry Pi Trading to look after all commercial operations of Raspberry Pi, and the other the charitable foundation that would receive the profits from the trading company and use it for computer education. Upton became the CEO of the Raspberry Pi Trading Company. He and his team started designing numerous Raspberry Pi models. By 2022, they released four models and 14 versions of these models.

The last significant high-end model released in 2019 was Raspberry Pi 4 Model B with 1.5 GHz 64-bit quad-core ARM Cortex-A72, onboard Gigabit Ethernet, 8 GB memory, 4 USB ports, and HDMI port priced at $150. Raspberry Pi Trading released Raspberry Pi Pico in January 2021 at the other end of the spectrum. It uses a microcontroller chip RP2040 designed in-house, Dual-core Arm Cortex M0+ processor running at 133 MHz, 264 KB memory, 2 MB flash memory, USB 1.1, and 26 multi-function IO pins and priced at $ 4.

Professionals have used Raspberry Pis for various applications besides its primary goal of enabling students to learn to program. They are widely used to control robots and as the Internet of Things (IoT) brain. They have been used in weather balloons, International Space Stations, hospital ventilators, and even to build inexpensive supercomputers. Over 40% of the sales are for industrial uses. In 2019, Oracle built a 1060 Raspberry Pi 3 B+ ($35 per board) cluster with 22 Ethernet switches running Oracle Linux. Its 64-bit Linpack benchmark speed was around 2 TeraFLOPS.

Concurrently, the Raspberry Pi Foundation and two partners have trained 26,000 teachers through the National Centre for Computer Education. It has created online courses in computing using Raspberry Pi. It has made online resources that give project ideas, programming puzzles, etc., to school students, which have reached millions of students in 100 countries, igniting their interest in computer hardware and software. Surprisingly, many students seemed more interested in using Raspberry Pi to control gadgets than programming them. It is creating more budding mechatronics engineers rather than software engineers.

A large number of vendors sell Raspberry Pi in India. Models cost ₹5000 to ₹500. It is a favourite system students use in many school and college projects.

REFERENCES

[1] Nick Heath, Inside the Raspberry Pi: The Story of the $35 computer that changed the world, Tech Republic, December 19, 2018 https://www.techrepublic.com/article/inside-the-raspberry-pi-the-story-of-the-35-computer-that-changed-the-world/

[2] Nilay Pillai, The future of computers is only $4 away with Raspberry Pi CEO Eben Upton, The Verge, March 8, 2022. (A conversation with Eben Upton) https://www.theverge.com/22966155/raspberry-pi-ceo-interview-eben-upton-computer-chip-shortage-diy

[3] Liam Tung, Oracle: This 1060 Raspberry Pi is world's largest Raspberry Pi cluster, ZDNET, September 18, 2019. https://www.zdnet.com/article/oracle-this-1060-raspberry-pi-supercomputer-is-worlds-largest-pi-cluster/

[4] Raspberry Foundation, Annual Review, 2020. https://www.raspberrypi.org/annual-review-2020

[5] Raspberry Pi, Wikipedia. https://en.wikipedia.org/wiki/Raspberry_Pi

71

Cray HPE Frontier—The First Supercomputer to Breach the ExaFLOPS Barrier

PROLOGUE

When IBM's Roadrunner breached the PetaFLOPS barrier in 2008, computer engineers set their sights on breaching the next barrier—ExaFLOPS—a thousand times PetaFLOPS, that is 10^{18} (One followed by 18 zeros—billion billion or a quintillion) Floating Point Operations per Second. Many countries joined the race to build an ExaFLOPS computer. Among them were the US, Europe, Japan, and China. Building an ExaFLOPS computer was considered necessary as such machines would be able to solve many problems, such as short-term weather prediction, aid research in materials science at the molecular level, predict earthquakes, design personalised drugs, design new drugs for treating cancer, study stellar explosions, find effective vaccines for new viruses, and a myriad of other hitherto intractable problems. An ExaFLOPS computer would be able to reduce the time to obtain solutions to such problems from weeks to hours. Computer Scientists also wanted to combine modelling and simulation with big data analytics and machine learning, which, they felt, would lead to new insights and inventions.

Building the first ExaFLOPS computer would demonstrate a country's technological leadership, so the US government allocated resources to ensure it was the first to achieve this goal.

On 29 July 2015, US President Barack Obama issued an executive order titled "National Strategic Computing Initiative" [1], which had among its objectives: accelerating the delivery of an ExaFLOPS computer, unifying technologies used in modelling and simulation, and data analytics, forging a path to continue increasing the speed of High-Performance Computers (HPC) even after the current semiconductor technology reaches its performance limit, continue research and development in HPC by supporting work on relevant areas such as networking technology, workflow, algorithms, and software. Ensure accessibility to HPCs for researchers, develop human resources in HPC and related areas, and ensure public-private collaboration to share research and development results with industries and academia.

THE EXASCALE COMPUTER PROJECT

As a follow-up, President Obama assigned the primary task of fulfilling the strategic objectives to the US government's Department of Energy (DOE). In 2016 DOE started a programme called Exascale Computing Project (ECP) [2] and gave the National Nuclear Safety Administration (NNSA) and the Office of Science (OS) the responsibility of carrying out the project. NNSA was primarily responsible for nuclear weapons development and maintenance, and the Office of Science was responsible for funding basic science and engineering research in HPC development and applications. DOE planned ECP as a seven-year project to advance not only the hardware art to build an exascale computer but also to develop system and applications software that would enable the optimal use of exascale computers. The plan started with a large number of workshops to educate scientists on the benefits of exascale computers, their potential applications, and the challenges of building the complete ecosystem (high-speed compute nodes, interconnection network to connect them, system software stack, and applications) for the exascale era. ECP is a collaboration of the six premier US government laboratories: Argonne National Laboratory (ANL), Los Alamos National Laboratory (LANL), Lawrence Berkeley National Laboratory (LBNL), Lawrence Livermore National Laboratory (LLNL), Oak Ridge National Laboratory (ORNL), and Sandia National Laboratory (SNL). Initially, DOE planned three exascale computers. The first, called "Aurora," was to be designed by Intel and ANL and located at Argonne; the second, called "Frontier," to be developed by Cray-HPE and ORNL and located at Oakridge; and the third, called "El Capitan," designed by Cray-HPE and LLNL and located at Livermore. Aurora and Frontier were to be used primarily for research in the frontier areas of science and technology and El Capitan for weapons research and scientific uses. Intel encountered difficulties in designing the multi-core microprocessor to be used by Aurora, which delayed it. Cray-HPE built the computer system at ORNL first and broke the exascale barrier in May 2022, achieving a speed of 1.102 ExaFLOPS executing a double-precision (64-bits) Linpack benchmark program and a peak speed of 1.68 ExaFLOPS using double-precision operands. It topped the June 2022 TOPS 500 [3] list, and its speed of 1.102 ExaFLOPS was more than double that of the next computer in the list, Fugaku of Japan, whose speed was 442 PetaFLOPS. On the HPL-Mx benchmark that uses mixed precision programs (32-bits, 24-bits, and 16-bits) appropriate for machine learning programs, Frontier's speed was 7.94 ExaFLOPS. Besides this, it was also the second most power-efficient computer in the world in the June 2022 Green 500 list, with a power efficiency score of 52.23 GFLOPS per watt.

THE ARCHITECTURE OF THE FRONTIER COMPUTER [4]

Each computing node of the Frontier computer consists of an AMD EPYC "Trento" 64-core processor with a 2 GHz clock to perform general computation (CPU) with four AMD Radeon Instinct Mi250X General Purpose Graphics Processing Units (GPGPU) to perform high-speed floating-point operations. The GPGPU chip uses 6 nm technology, allowing it to perform double-precision floating-point calculations as fast as single-precision. Each GPGPU has 220 processing cores. AMD designed a custom-interconnect fabric to interconnect the CPU with the GPGPU, boosting the coherency between them and providing a unified view of shared data. The GPGPUs have 128 GB memory. Each computer node has a 5 TB non-volatile flash memory. A blade has two computing nodes. The blades are water-cooled. A rack has 64 blades. The Frontier computer has 74 racks. Multiple 64-port switched Ethernet connections called HPE Slingshot provide an aggregate bandwidth of 12.8 Tbits/sec to interconnect the blades. The Slingshot Network Interconnection system maximises throughput and minimises latency. It has adaptive routing, congestion control, and excellent Quality of Service (QoS). A "Dragonfly" topology system interconnects groups of blades, ensuring that there are no more than three hops to communicate between any two nodes of the Frontier [5].

The Frontier computer has 74 × 128 = 9472 AMD EPYC processors, which comprise 606,208 processing cores. There are 4 × 9472 = 37888 GPGPUs, each with 220 cores, giving 8,335,360 cores. The primary memory size is 47.360 PetaBytes. One hundred forty-five kilometres of networking cables interconnect the computing nodes. The computer consumes 21 megawatts of power. It cost approximately $600 million to build.

The Frontier computer also supports the world's largest and fastest parallel file system as its secondary storage. The system provides around 700 Petabytes of storage with a peak write speed of 5 Terabytes per second.

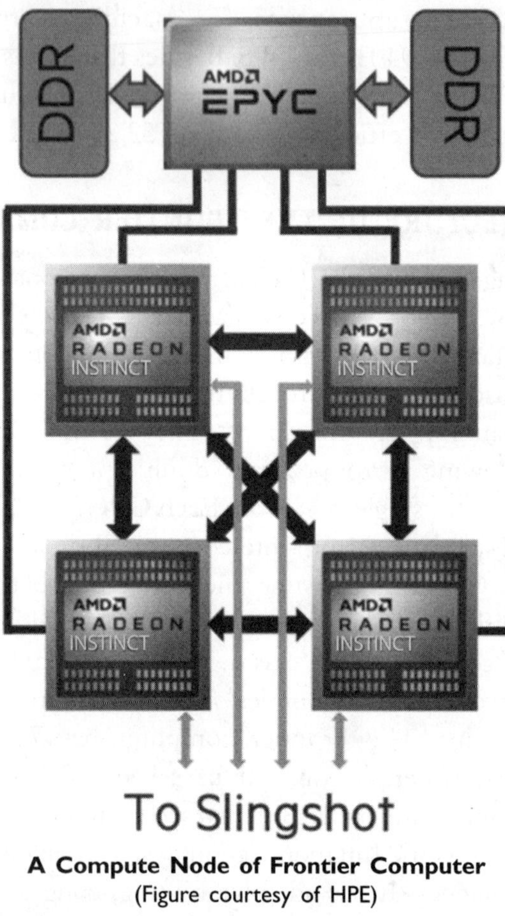

A Compute Node of Frontier Computer
(Figure courtesy of HPE)

Frontier Exascale High-Performance Computer
(Photo courtesy of Wikipedia)

SOFTWARE SYSTEM OF THE FRONTIER COMPUTER

The operating system of the Frontier computer is Linux, modified to suit Frontier's architecture. Frontier uses the AMD RoCM open-source software for graphics. It has numerous compilers that include C, C++, and Fortran. It provides a Cray Message Passing Interface (MPI) and Open MPI for parallel programming. A mathematics library is available that includes BLAS (Basic Linear Algebra Subprograms), LAPACK (Linear Algebra Package) to solve Linear Systems of Algebraic Equations, an Interactive Refinement tool kit, etc. A list of software available for Frontier is at https://www.olcf.ornl.gov/frontier/.

EPILOGUE

Oak Ridge National Laboratory set up the Oak Ridge Leadership Computing Facility (ORLF) under the direction of the US DOE Office of Science. ORLF aims to offer exascale computing resources to researchers from the government, academia, and industry who can convince a group of peers of the importance of the problem they want to solve and why they need high-performance computers to solve it. In preparation for the Frontier computer's release for general use in early 2023, ORNL selected various projects to participate in the Frontier Centre for Accelerated Applications Readiness (CAAR) programme [6]. These projects combine simulation and data-intensive machine learning and require exascale performance. Initially, work will start using the existing IBM Summit supercomputer and will be scaled up to the Frontier computer when it is released for general use. Some of the selected projects are: processing massive amounts of astrophysical data collected from the milky way to predict the behaviour of galaxies, human genome studies to explore genetic predisposition to Alzheimer's disease, addiction to opioids, autism, etc., numerical simulation of turbulent fluid flows in many fields, the behaviour of physical processes within rock structures that have embedded fluids, simulate at the atomic level various electronic and magnetic properties of materials, nano-scale simulation to predict the behaviour of viruses to invent drugs and vaccines to fight them, study time-dependent nuclear reactions such as fusion and fission, and design plasma accelerators that would have several applications including in medical devices.

REFERENCES

[1] National Strategic Computing Initiative, Issued by Barack Obama on July 29, 2015.
https://obamawhitehouse.archives.gov/the-press-office/2015/07/29/executive-order-creating-national-strategic-computing-initiative

[2] Exascale Computing Project, https://www.exascaleproject.org/about/

[3] Tops 500, June 2022. https://www.top500.org/lists/top500/2022/06/

[4] Charles Q. Choi, Beneath the Hood of the First Exascale Computer, IEEE Spectrum, Volume 69, Issue 8, August 2022. https://spectrum.ieee.org/frontier-exascale-supercomputer.

[5] Reference for Dragonfly Topology. https://www.hpcwire.com/2019/07/15/super-connecting-the-supercomputers-innovations-through-network-topologies/
See also https://www.olcf.ornl.gov/frontier/

[6] Frontier Center for Accelerated Applications Readiness. https://www.olcf.ornl.gov/caar/frontier-caar/

72

ChatGPT and AI Assistants

"Vast words they hold, these minds of machine, Can mimic thought, but feeling's unseen"
—Gemini

PROLOGUE

Research on human-computer conversation systems began with ELIZA in 1966, a simple system that mimicked a conversation between a psychiatrist and her patient (See Anecdote 22). Many such systems followed and became better with the improvements in computer technology. Michael Mauldin named them chatterbots in 1994, later abbreviated as chatbots. Chatbot entered Dictionaries around 2000. Oxford Dictionary defines a chatbot as "*A computer program designed to simulate conversation with human users, especially over the Internet.*" When chips to synthesise speech from text appeared in early 2000, chatbots started speaking in natural language. Chatbots also started using neural networks to learn and improve their performance. A significant event was the release of Alexa, a neural network-based natural language chatbot by Amazon in 2014.

The availability of almost inexhaustible computing power from clouds such as Microsoft's Azure and vast amounts of multimedia data from the Internet rekindled research in multi-layer neural networks and large language models (LLM) in the first decade of this century. Scientists rapidly advanced natural language recognition and learning systems training large multi-layer neural networks with huge amounts of publicly available data. It culminated with the release of *ChatGPT*, a chatbot with the astonishing capability to synthesise a natural language answer to any random natural language question in November 2022. It was followed by a competing chatbot, *Bard* designed by Google researchers in late 2023 which was improved and renamed *Gemini.* Another landmark was the release of *Copilot* by Microsoft in late 2023. It is touted as an AI assistant to the users of the Microsoft 365 suite of software and has been integrated into the Windows 11 Operating System.

CHATGPT [1]

OpenAI, a private research laboratory, was founded by Sam Altman and Elon Musk in late 2015 in San Francisco as a "not for profit" organization to develop "safe artificial general intelligence products" to benefit humanity. An endowment capital of $1 billion was raised by the group. In February 2018, Musk left due to a possible conflict of interest. Altman gathered a group of gifted AI researchers and OpenAI was on the verge of creating a breakthrough product in 2019 and became a for-profit company losing its altruism. OpenAI's first product was DALL-E, released in January 2021 which drew pictures from a word description. OpenAI released a revolutionary text-based chatbot named ChatGPT 3.5 to the public in November 2022. It caused a furore in the world of AI and astonished its users with its prowess. The term GPT stands for Generative Pre-trained Transformer. The term Transformer stands for a type of multi-layered neural network that has special features to analyse relationships between words far apart in a long sentence and is amenable to parallel processing. Transformer was invented by a group of Google researchers led by Ashish Vaswani and described in a paper titled "Attention is All You Need" in 2017 and used for language translation.

GPT 3.5 pre-trained a transformer network with 96 layers of transformer blocks, each with many layers of neurons, and 175 billion parameters on diverse textual data of size between 570 GB and a few TB including web pages and books (data available until 2021). It is estimated that the training process took several months and cost several million dollars. OpenAI has not disclosed these data. The term "Generative" indicates that the system generates a coherent, human-like natural language answers to any question one may ask (I got most of the data about ChatGPT by asking it). After its pre-training, it has features to refine its learning based on feedback from users. To illustrate its power, I reproduce below my conversation with ChatGPT 3.5 on April 26, 2024.

You

How many languages can be used with ChatGPT?

ChatGPT

ChatGPT can comprehend and respond in multiple languages, including but not limited to English, Spanish, French, German, Italian, Chinese, Japanese, Korean, Dutch, Portuguese, Russian, Arabic, and more. The availability of languages may vary depending on the model and the platform where ChatGPT is deployed.

You

What are the shortcomings of ChatGPT?

ChatGPT

While ChatGPT can generate human-like responses across a wide range of topics, it also has some limitations:

1. ***Lack of contextual understanding:*** *ChatGPT may struggle to maintain context over long conversations, leading to responses that are off-topic or nonsensical.*
2. ***Inability to generate original ideas:*** *While ChatGPT can provide information and opinions based on its training data, it may struggle to generate truly novel or creative ideas.*
3. ***Limited world knowledge:*** *ChatGPT's responses are based on the information it was trained on, which means it may not always have the most up-to-date or accurate knowledge about current events or specific topics.*
4. ***Potential for biased or inappropriate responses:*** *ChatGPT may inadvertently generate biased or inappropriate responses based on the biases present in its training data or the prompts it receives.*
5. ***Difficulty with nuanced language:*** *ChatGPT may have difficulty understanding and responding to nuanced language, humor, sarcasm, or cultural references.*
6. ***Lack of emotional intelligence:*** *While ChatGPT can simulate empathy to some extent, it lacks true emotional intelligence and may struggle to provide appropriate emotional support or understanding in sensitive situations.*

7. ***Vulnerability to adversarial attacks:*** *ChatGPT can be manipulated by malicious users to generate harmful or misleading content through carefully crafted prompts or inputs.*

These shortcomings highlight areas where ChatGPT's capabilities are still evolving, and ongoing research is being conducted to address them.

You

Is it correct to say that ChatGPT has passed the Turing Test?

ChatGPT

The Turing Test is a benchmark for evaluating a machine's ability to exhibit intelligent behavior indistinguishable from that of a human. While ChatGPT can produce human-like responses in many situations, it has not definitively passed the Turing Test.

Passing the Turing Test would require ChatGPT to consistently fool human judges into believing they are conversing with another human during unrestricted conversations over an extended period. While ChatGPT can simulate human-like conversation to some extent, it still exhibits limitations and shortcomings that make it distinguishable from human intelligence in many cases.

Therefore, it would be premature to claim that ChatGPT has definitively passed the Turing Test. However, it's continually improving, and future iterations may come closer to achieving this milestone.

ChatGPT can make mistakes. Consider checking important information.

I earlier asked the same questions to ChatGPT 3.5 in April 2023 and its answers were different and more verbose [2].

In addition to answering questions, ChatGPT can perform numerous language-related tasks such as summarising, translating, and completing a text. It can also write articles, stories, poems, and small programs requested by users.

ChatGPT has been a runaway success since its launch. It had 100 million users by January 2023 and 1.6 billion visits by March 2023. It is reported that it had 1.8 million users in April 2024. OpenAI upgraded it to ChatGPT-4, which uses a more extensive database for training. It is a paid service. OpenAI reported that ChatGPT-4 placed in the top 90th percentile in the International Math and Biology Olympiads and the US Bar examination.

DALL-E

OpenAI released in January 2021 a natural language system called DALL-E, which generates pictures from a natural language description. Given a text such as "a girl standing in a desert wearing a Texas hat," it generates four images that match the description. A request to "paint a man in a boat in the style of Cezanne" generates four pictures matching the request. An improved version DALL-E 3 was released in October 2023 which was integrated with paid versions of ChatGPT.

A girl standing in a desert wearing a Texas hat. Painting of a man in a boat style of Cezanne. Samples of pictures generated by DALL-E
(Pictures courtesy of OpenAI)

GOOGLE'S GEMINI [3]

Many chatbots appeared soon after the success of ChatGPT [4, 5]. Google had been working on neural networks for language analysis and the Transformer model was created by Vaswani's group at Google as I stated earlier. In March 2023 Google released its version of a Chatbot Bard. Bard is based on a large language model PaLM (Pathway Language Model) which also uses transformer neural net architecture. Its main feature is its massive multi-layered neural net with 540 billion parameters. Its large size allows it to learn from massive data and its performance is superior. Bard's release was probably premature as in a public demonstration in February 2023 it gave incorrect answers. Another LLM named Gemini using a successor to PaLM 2 was developed by DeepMind, a Google subsidiary, which used multimedia training data and was released by Google in December 2023. In addition to its preliminary training, it uses the latest data from Google's search engine and provides up-to-date answers to queries. Besides this, it can also write poetry, simple computer programs, and musical compositions.

It has additional features to analyse data fed to it and provide insight from raw data. It is trained in several languages. Gemini claims that it is trained with a focus on safety and avoids giving inappropriate responses. Bard was discontinued and Gemini replaced it in February 2024. Whereas ChatGPT3.5's training data is up to 2021, Gemini's is up-to-date. Gemini is also superior as it gives fewer inappropriate answers compared to ChatGPT. Its data analysis feature is an added feature. Several paid models of Gemini have been released by Google. Some Gemini models can generate video, besides images given natural language requests.

The couplet below the heading of this Anecdote was generated by Gemini responding to my request "Write a couplet on Large language models in AI".

MICROSOFT'S COPILOT

Microsoft invested over 10 billion dollars in OpenAI and had access to its technology in return. Initially, some of the ChatGPT's features were integrated with Microsoft's Bing. It was not very popular. Microsoft had its own large AI group. Its goal was to design an AI assistant to assist programmers. It acquired a company called GitHub in June 2018 for $ 7.5 billion. GitHub had a huge repository of computer programs in several languages and was used as an assistant by programmers. In addition, Microsoft developed an AI assistant named Copilot using ChatGPT technology and released it in mid-2023 for limited enterprise users. It integrated Copilot with Github to assist programmers write programs from unambiguous specifications.

Copilot's primary goal is to enhance the productivity of the users of Microsoft's apps such as Word, Excel, and PowerPoint. It can summarise documents, answer questions on their contents, and suggest improvements. It can review an email chain and draft a reply. It can aid users of Excel to use appropriate formulae and generate PowerPoint presentations from documents. It is integrated with Microsoft 365 and has become part of the Windows 11 OS.

COPYRIGHT AND CHATGPT

The New York Times sued OpenAI and Microsoft, which funded OpenAI, for copyright infringement on 24 December 2023 in a US court for the unauthorised use of millions of articles published by it for training the ChatGPT's neural network. ChatGPT and similar chatbots have extensively used published material from books, newspapers, magazines, and the Internet without explicit permission from their authors. New York Times sought monetary compensation from OpenAI and Microsoft for using its intellectual property. These companies declined, citing a clause in the copyright law on "fair use" for public good. It is a complex case. Judges have to rule on this.

In a pre-emptive move, OpenAI has negotiated with Axel Springer, a media company, to use their data on payment.

Essays, poetry, etc. generated by ChatGPT and Gemini are not copyrightable.

DALL-E also uses a corpus of paintings by artists and photos stored by many companies, such as Getty, and other images from the Internet and books for training and OpenAI may be sued. The legal issues are unresolved and may ultimately reach the US Supreme Court for a ruling that will have profound implications for the future development of generative AI that uses publicly available textual and artistic material.

EPILOGUE

Human-computer interaction in natural language has come a long way from 1965 to 2024. After the release of chatbots like ChatGPT, many competitors have emerged [4, 5]. Among them is *Claude* released by Anthropic, a company founded by several ex-OpenAI employees and funded partially by Amazon. It claims to use "Constitutional AI", a framework developed to align AI systems with human values and ensure during training that they are helpful, harmless, and honest. Another system is *Perplexity AI* founded in August 2022 and funded by several venture capitalists. It is an AI-based search engine that gives natural language answers to natural language questions with citations.

The advent of advanced chatbots and large language-based AI tools has made many groups and governments anxious. Teachers worry that students may use these AI tools to write essays, poetry, and minor programs and do homework. New-generation chatbots may affect many professions that depend on routine writing skills. Lawyer's assistants and advertisement copywriters feel threatened. These AI tools will assist many in improving their productivity and will not make them redundant. All companies need to develop strategies to train their staff to effectively use these new AI assistants The nature of work would change, and quality would improve.

There are also concerns about the accuracy and bias in the responses by some current chatbots. The technology is very young—less than two-year-old. I expect that chatbots will improve over time.

REFERENCES

[1] Partha Prathim Roy, ChatGPT: A comprehensive review on background, applications, bias, ethics, limitations, and future scope, Internet of Things and Cyber-Physical Systems, Elsevier, Vol. 3, pp. 121–154, 2023.

[2] V. Rajaraman, From ELIZA to ChatGPT, Resonance, Indian Academy of Sciences, Vol. 28. No. 6, June 2023, pp. 889–905.

[3] blog. google bard to gemini

[4] Caroline M. Nyce, Nine Chatbots you can play with right now, The Atlantic, March 28, 2023. https://www.theatlantic.com/technology/archive/2023/03/chatgpt-generative-ai-chatbots-bing-google-bard/673533/

[5] Sabrina Oritz, The best AI Chatbots, ZD NET, April, 2024, https://www.zdnet.com/article/best-ai-chatbot/

Index